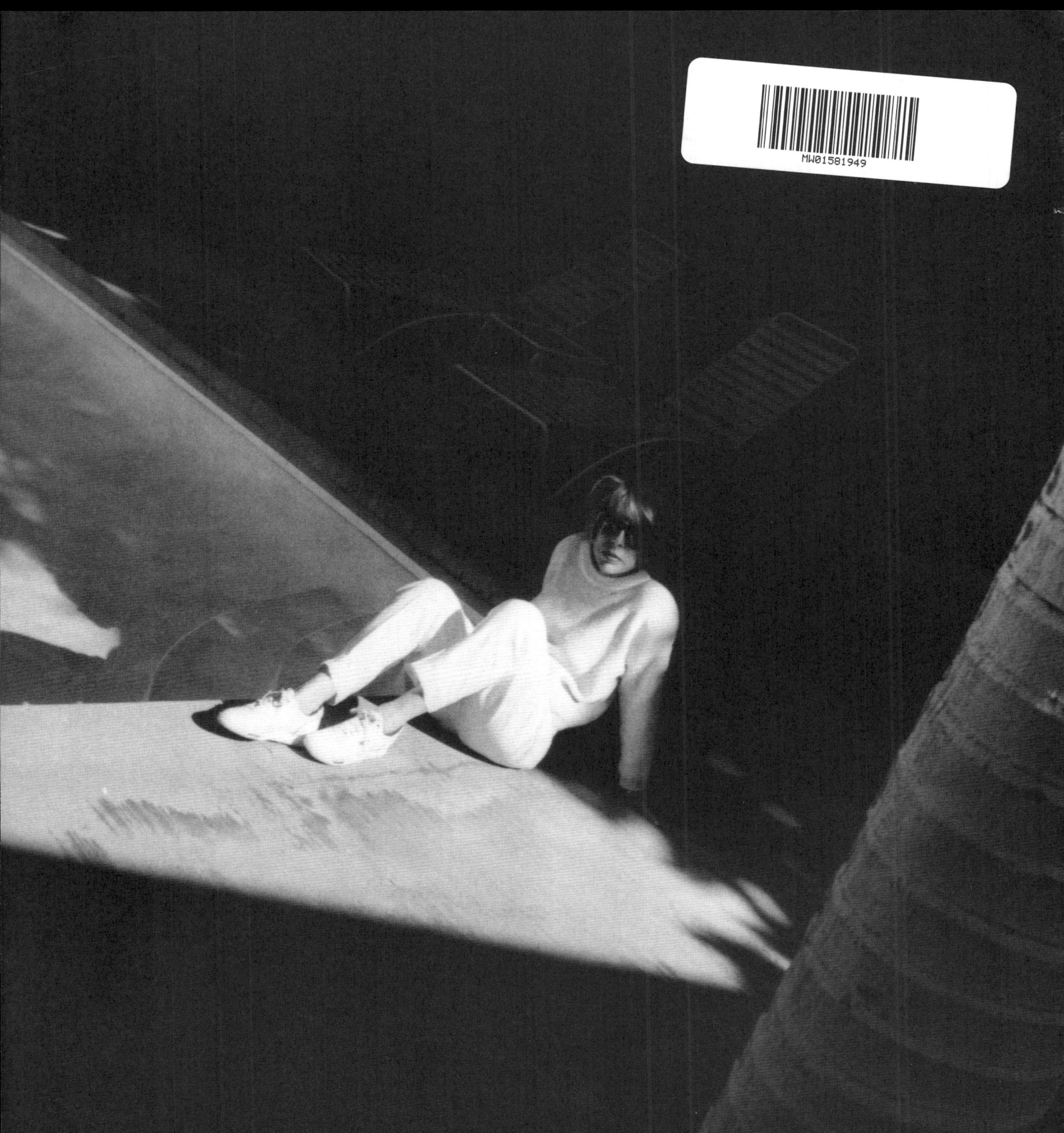

THE BAD & THE BEAUTIFUL

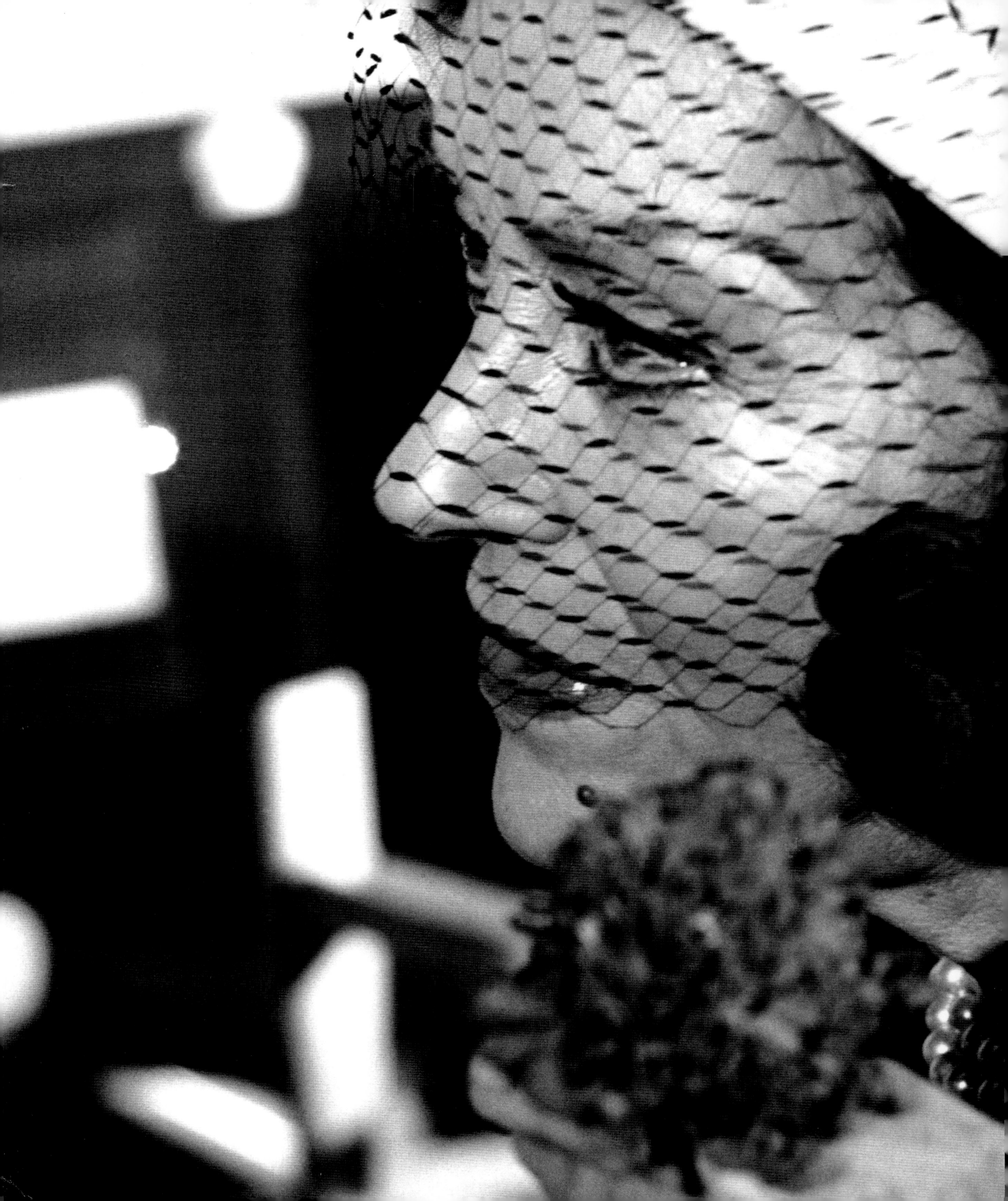

PHOTOGRAPHS BY **ELLEN GRAHAM**

THE BAD & THE BEAUTIFUL

INTRODUCTION BY JOHN LORING

HARRY N. ABRAMS, INC., PUBLISHERS

For Ian Graham, without whom this book could never have happened,
and for John Loring, who made it happen.

The Metropolitan Museum of Art

SPECIAL CONSULTANT   February 13, 1975

Dear Ellen:

I simply adore these pictures and think you're a terrific photographer. Please get yourself known in San Francisco and up and down the West Coast. I have given your name and address to the San Francisco Fashion Group.

I think all your photographs are excellent and I am terribly touched by the ~~three~~ you sent me. The ones by the elephant are for my children in Paris and London. For once I like a picture of myself and am "willing" to give some away to a friend or two.

Diana Vreeland

Miss Ellen Graham
9915 Robbins Drive
Beverly Hills, California 90212

My best to you
Diane.

ENDPAPERS: ELLEN GRAHAM, SELF-PORTRAIT

FRONTISPIECE: GLORIA SWANSON, *AIRPORT '75* SET, UNIVERSAL STUDIOS, HOLLYWOOD, 1974

RIGHT: DIANA VREELAND AND GLORIA SWANSON, THE COSTUME INSTITUTE, THE METROPOLITAN MUSEUM OF ART, NEW YORK CITY, 1975

PROJECT MANAGER: Eric Himmel
EDITOR: Samantha Topol
DESIGNER: Laura Lindgren
PRODUCTION MANAGER: Maria Pia Gramaglia

Library of Congress Cataloging-in-Publication Data
Graham, Ellen.
  The bad and the beautiful : photographs / by
  Ellen Graham ; introduction by John Loring.
    p.   cm.
  ISBN: 0-8109-6750-2
  1. Celebrities—Portraits. 2. Portrait photography.
  3. Graham, Ellen. I. Title.
TR681.F3G73 2004
779'.2'092—dc22   2004008970

Copyright © 2004 Ellen Graham

Published in 2004 by Harry N. Abrams, Incorporated, New York
All rights reserved. No part of the contents of this book may be reproduced without the written permission of the publisher.

Printed and bound in Singapore
10 9 8 7 6 5 4 3 2 1

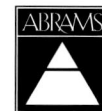 Harry N. Abrams, Inc.
100 Fifth Avenue
New York, N.Y. 10011
www.abramsbooks.com

Abrams is a subsidiary of
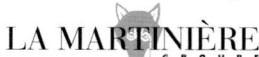

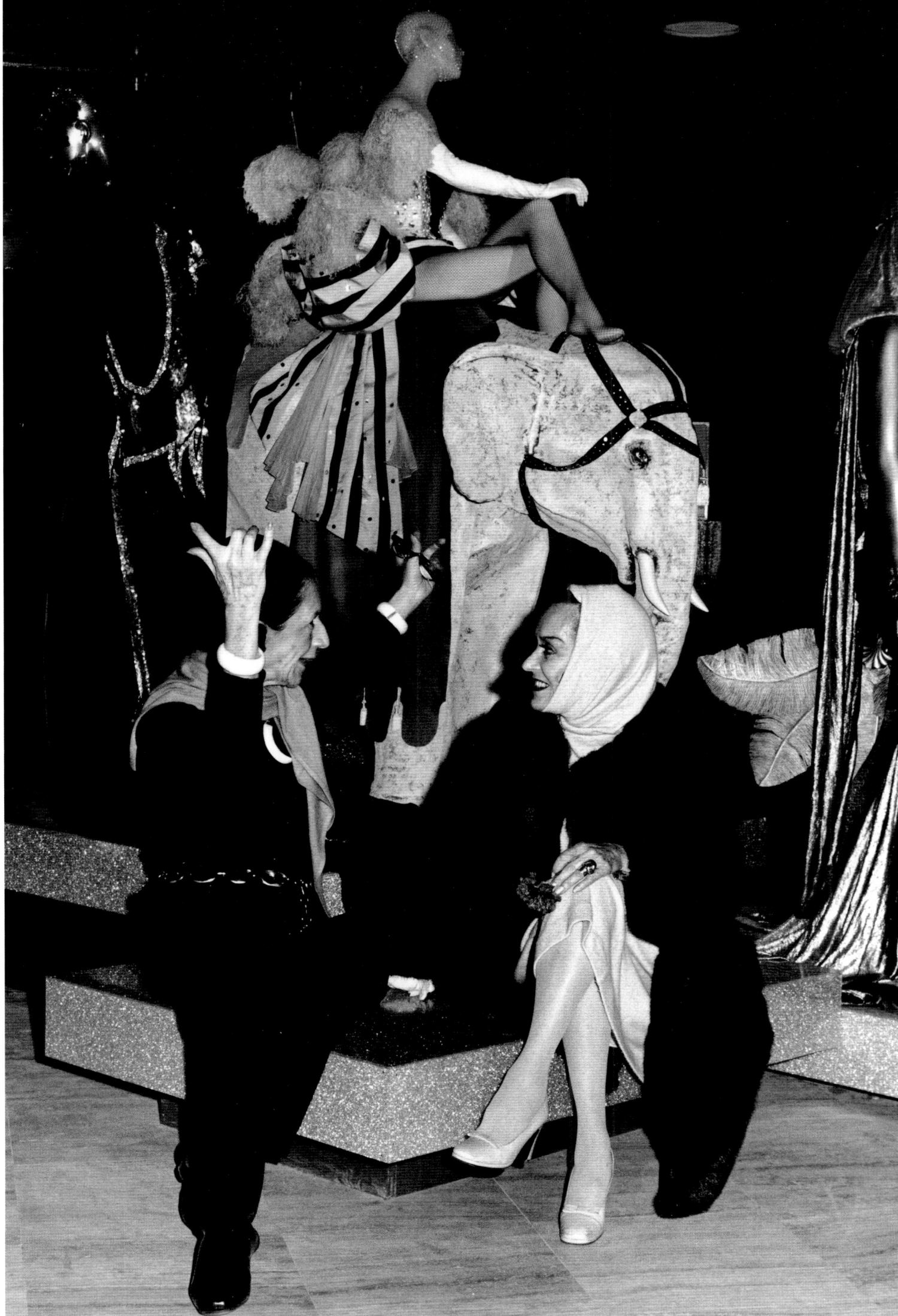

SHOOTING STARS AND IDENTITY PHOTOS

"The portrait, that genre so modest in appearance, demands immense intelligence. Without doubt, the obedience of the [portraitist] must be great, but his perception must be just as great.

. . . The artist must first see what is apparent, but must also guess at what's hidden.

I would compare the [portraitist] to an actor, who out of necessity adapts to all characters and all costumes.

Nothing, if you want to examine it, is indifferent in a portrait."

CHARLES BAUDELAIRE, "Le Portrait," *Salon de 1859. Lettres à M. le Directeur de la revue française*

If Baudelaire is correct, by nature of being a portraitist Ellen Graham is as much an actor as the stars she photographs—obliged to adapt to the personalities and to the roles her subjects play as they reveal or hide themselves in front of the lens.

Her subjects are actors of one sort or another. Most are "stars"—movie stars, singing and dancing stars, social stars, star artists, star athletes, imaginary stars (there are a fair number of drag queens) and the occasional lost star, or survivor putting on a brave face despite the overwhelming odds. They play their games; she plays hers. Both clearly have their bags of tricks as they shift identities, each trying to catch the other off guard—or off script.

While vacationing with her mother on the Lido in Venice almost fifty years ago, Ellen Graham photographed the legendary Russian-born pioneer of American fashion Valentina. Valentina was fifty. Graham was only seventeen, but the aloof beauty that could almost rival Valentina's one-time companion Greta Garbo was all there in her first photo, as glamorous—as a Hollywood studio star portrait—but far more revealing. The photo jump-started a career.

Twenty-five years later, Garbo came to Ellen Graham's Beverly Hills house for dinner and saw the extraordinary image of her old friend Valentina hanging on a bedroom wall surrounded by portraits of Andy Warhol, Fred Astaire, David Bowie, Gloria Swanson, and so on.

"Who are these people?" Garbo demanded, "Are they your friends? Who took the pictures?" After confessing to having done the work herself, Graham was sure that the lens-allergic megastar was about to walk. Instead, she gave her a judgment: "Well," she said, "they *are* first class!" She stayed for dinner and returned many times. Graham never asked to photograph her. "That would have ended our friendship."

Staged Hollywood portraits of the type made of Garbo at MGM in the late 1920s by Ruth Harriet Louise or in the early 1930s by Clarence Sinclair Bull have only a distant relationship to Graham's work, which relentlessly breaks down the barriers of aesthetic distance between performer and the observing camera, so strong in Hollywood studio shots. The glamour and the sense of theater are there, but so too is the reality and idiosyncrasy of the subject, stripped bare and fixed in an absolutely personal moment of revelation before the photographer, egomaniacal and vulnerable, human, caught in the act.

Over the years, Graham's photos of icons of both the performing and the fine arts have continued to be, to quote Garbo, "first class." There is an acute eye for physical beauty that never idealizes. If there are flaws, they are all there. The imperfections add to the sensuality, and often to the irony or wit, of the situation; they sidestep sentiment. The nude and the outrageous and even the freaky are included in her work much in the same way as they are in Fellini films, with an arresting mix of bluntness and compassion. Beauty has a thousand faces and as many disguises. Appearances both lead and mislead. Surface is seldom superficial.

Graham's first major assignment took her to Hollywood forty years ago to photograph "The World's One Hundred Most Attractive Men" for *Men's Bazaar*. The list included Fred Astaire, Warren Beatty, Kirk Douglas, Clint Eastwood, Rock Hudson, Steve McQueen, and Robert Wagner. They liked the results. They came back for more, and she continued to rephotograph many of her original subjects for years . . .

Hollywood became aware of Ellen Graham's genius for shooting stars the way they see themselves. She directs, to be sure, but it never shows. After all, she is only telling them where they want to go anyway, even if they don't openly admit it. Without realizing it, they reveal themselves the way they are in their own imaginations, not as film directors (and therefore audiences) see them "on script."

She was, for example, asked to photograph that redoubtable and most enduring of stars, Gloria Swanson, during the filming of *Airport '75*. "How am I going to make a seventy-four-year-old woman look good? Well, she made *me* look good," she recalls. "She never lost it, she was incredibly beautiful at seventy-four. She had pale blue eyes that didn't look at you—they looked through you. Those eyes had seen it all, everything. And I could never get over how beautiful she was."

"I suggested shooting Gloria on a bare stage surrounded by the empty chairs of the other stars of the film. Two hundred people watched at Universal Studios as Miss Swanson walked out and sat down in her chair. She was magnificent. She was the only real star and she knew it. *Of course* the other chairs were empty, just names, only circumstantially famous.

"She wore a veil that reminded me of the great 1924 Edward Steichen photo of Gloria Swanson looking through lace. I asked her if we could match the photo fifty years later. *Time* magazine ran the two photos side by side on a double-page spread—'Gloria at 24' and 'Gloria at 74.'

"We became friends. My husband, Ian, and I celebrated her eightieth birthday at Le Club in New York with a hot fudge sundae and one candle instead of a cake. She tangoed all night with Ian.

"I photographed her in denim and sables for *Vogue* and for the cover of her autobiography, *Swanson*. I photographed her everywhere, that beautiful, unrivaled, incisive, charming and ironclad woman who had been—and still was—Gloria Swanson."

Graham often employs the double sense of "shooting stars." Stars of film, high society, and the arts are marketed to the public via photographs like her own. Shooting stars blaze across the night sky on their relatively short trajectory and forever disappear. There is in every Ellen Graham image the haunting sense of seeing a person who is, was, or will be also a star for whatever time is allotted to them to blaze on their trajectory through the media firmament, before they too disappear, their fleeting images made more poignant over time as their destinies—tragic, comic, or heroic—have been fulfilled. There are those like Swanson, who were and remain legends: Groucho Marx, Alfred Hitchcock, Anthony Quinn, George C. Scott, Jack Lemmon, Sammy Davis Jr., Marlene Dietrich, Joe Louis, Rudolph Nureyev, Diana Vreeland, Fred Astaire. There are those whose fame has skyrocketed since Graham first photographed them: Candice Bergen, Christopher Walken, Anthony Hopkins, Viggo Mortensen, Kevin Kline, Lorenzo Lamas, Melanie Griffith. There are those who survive everything and continue: Prince Philip, Valentina Cortese, Arlene Dahl, Kirk Douglas, Roman Polanski, Jack Nicholson, Olivia de Haviland, Joan Fontaine, Paul Newman, Warren Beatty, Dominick Dunne.

There is always a darker side, if a story is complete. Along with spectacular success in real life, there is always failure and tragedy. There are sad little make-believe stars: the inevitable travesties of Marilyn Monroe and the transsexual prostitutes in the Bois de Boulogne. Lives senselessly cut short like Natalie Wood's. And more tragic still are the four celebrated American beauties spectacularly and brutally murdered: Sharon Tate, Vicki Morgan, Dominique Dunne, and so recently, one of the two magnificent granddaughters of fashion great Elsa Schiaparelli, Berry Berensen, whose star abruptly crashed into the North Tower of the World Trade Center on September 11, 2001.

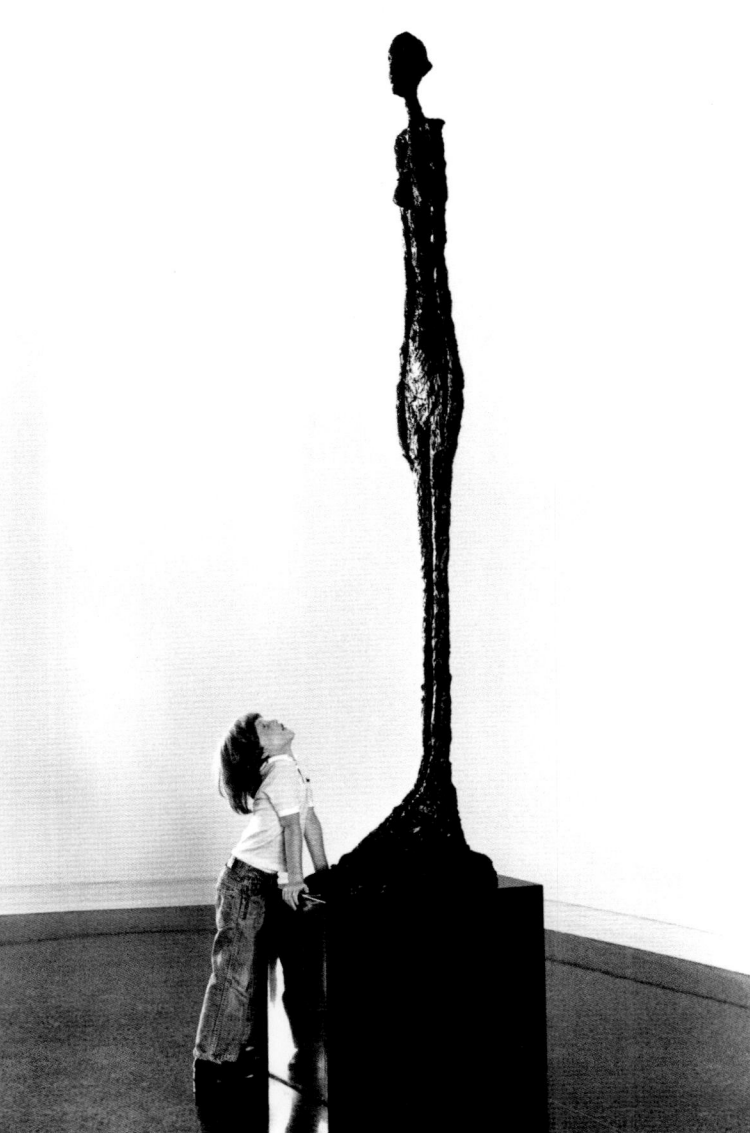

ALEXIS GRAHAM, PASADENA, CALIFORNIA, 1977

Finally there are everyday people photographed on the everyday stages of racetracks, parks, or in the time warp of Havana "whose charm," Graham explains, "transcends physical beauty. They have an intensity about them. They refuse to be sad and picturesque, even when their surroundings give them every reason to be sad and picturesque. A poor teenager with the nerve to publicly wear American flag bathing trunks in Castro's Havana can have all the panache of a young Hollywood movie actor. Or a street photographer hustling with an antiquated bellows camera can be as intriguing as Helmut Newton inspecting film in a Paris café."

The theme of identity in flux rampages throughout Graham's work—intriguing, inviting speculation. As with all successful portraits, Graham's are not overly concerned with documenting the face of a bigger-than-life spirit, but with stealing a bit of the spirit itself in a moment of joy, frivolity, defiance, pride, bravado, chagrin, distraction...

Like all photographs, they show us a moment snatched from the past. Something we weren't there to see and that we can only know from a black-and-white shadow. But nothing in these shadows (photographs) is irrelevant, and to the astute observer there is so much to recognize, to identify—to reflect whatever one's own hidden or revealed identities might be.

Ellen Graham's camera is a mirror where we, like her "stars," can speculate on our own reflections, and that is its power.

John Loring
New York, January 2004

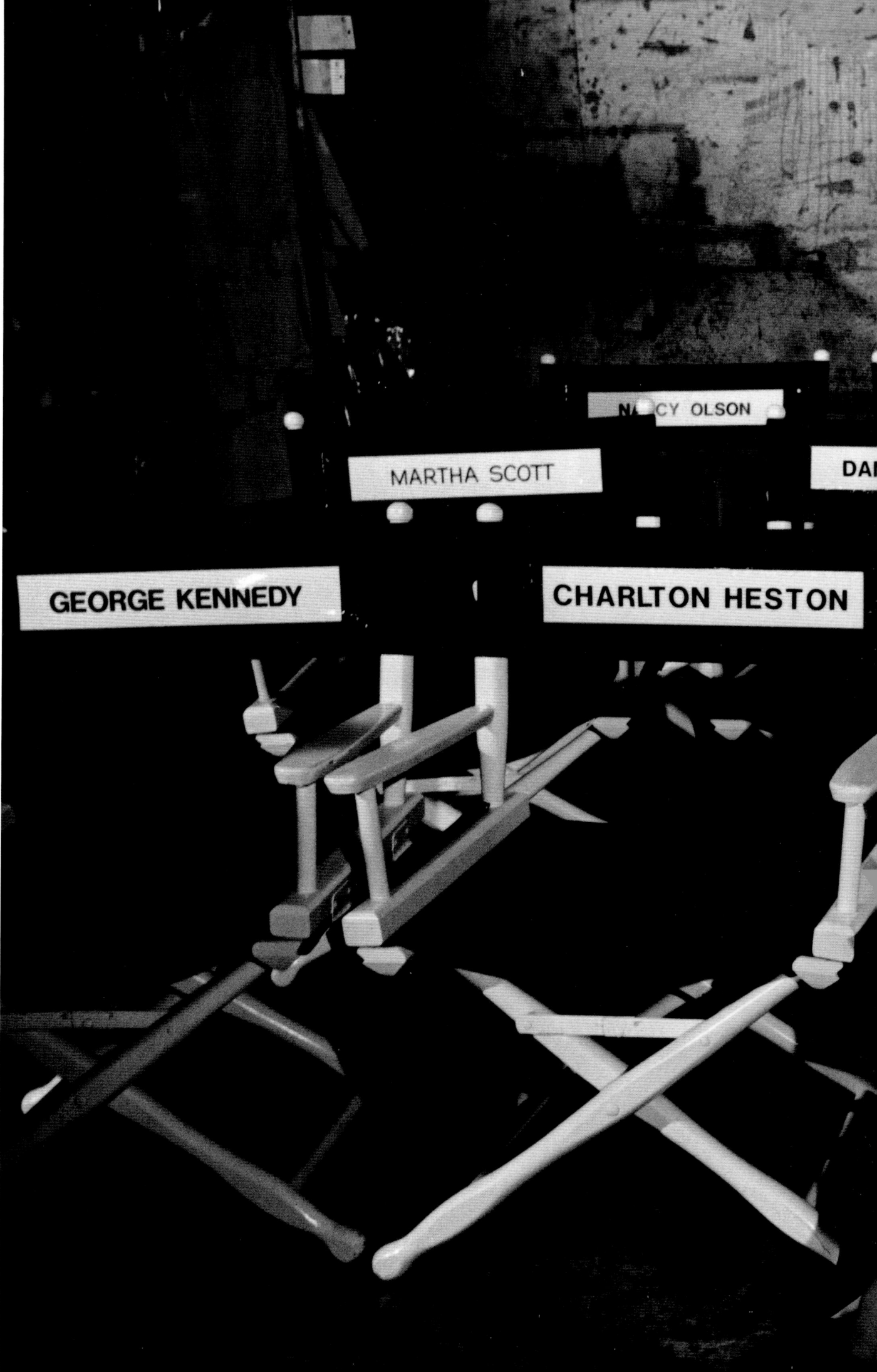

GLORIA SWANSON,
AIRPORT '75 SET,
UNIVERSAL STUDIOS,
HOLLYWOOD, 1974

OVERLEAF: HUBERT
DE GIVENCHY,
CAP FERRAT,
FRANCE, 1981

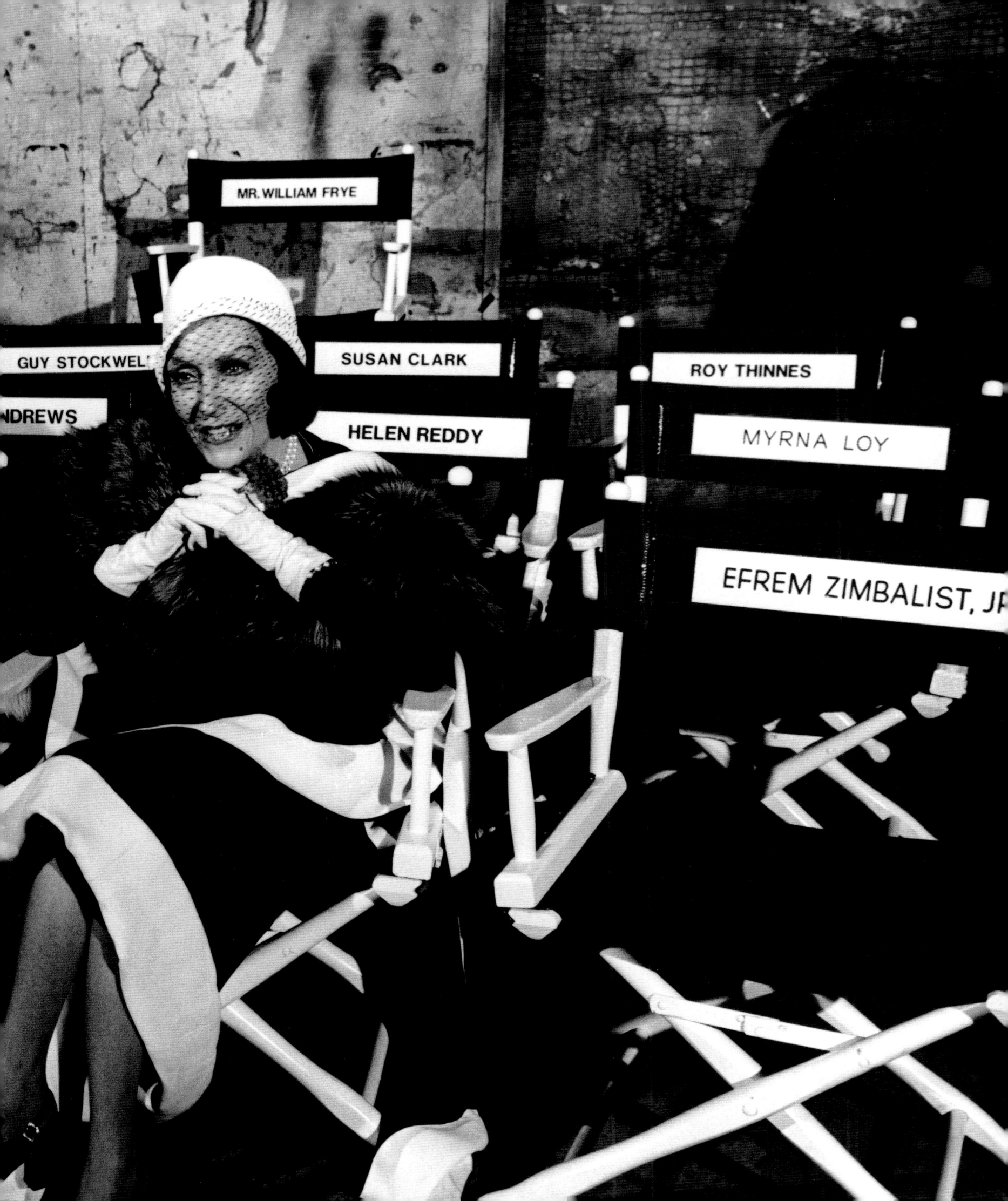

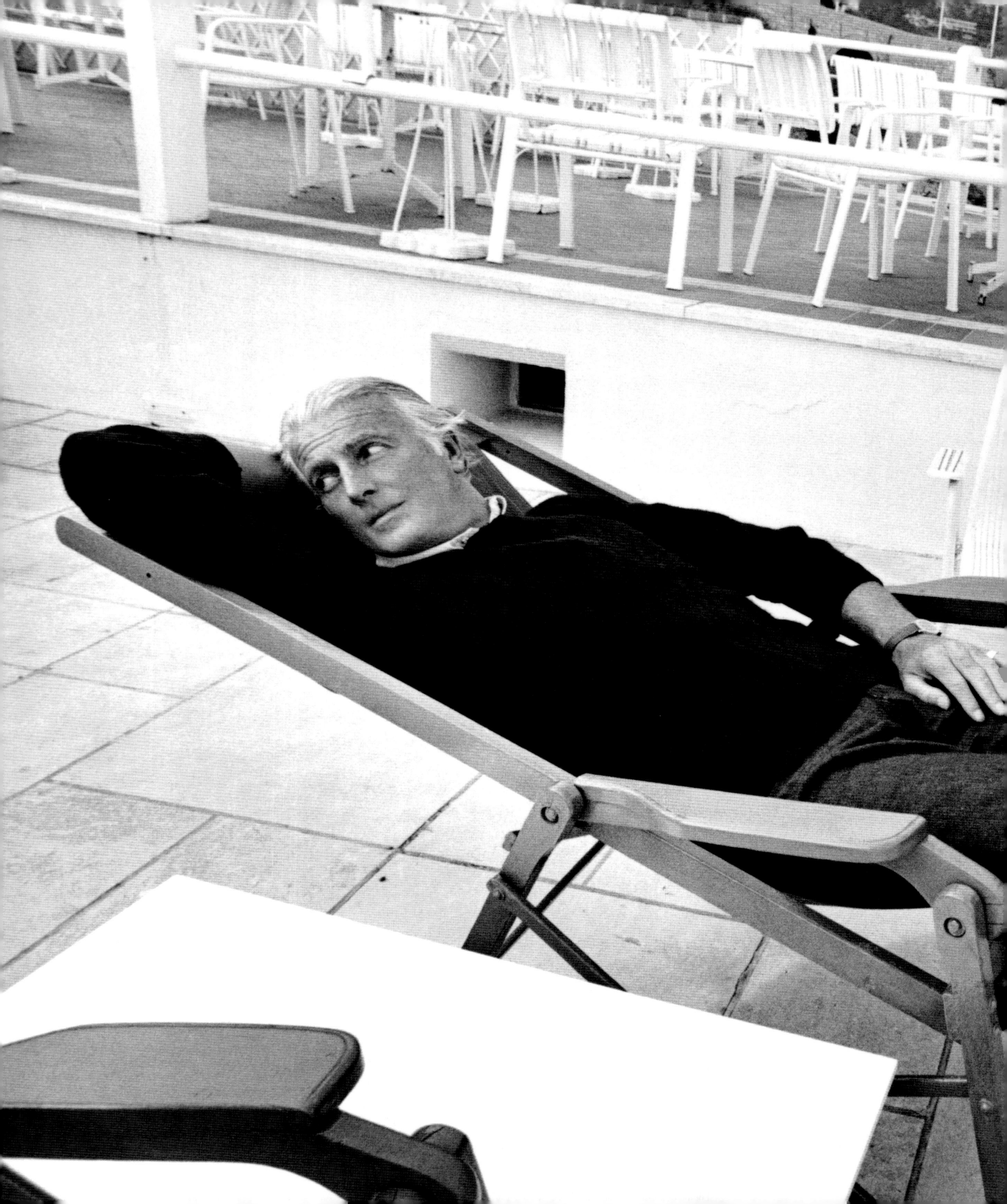

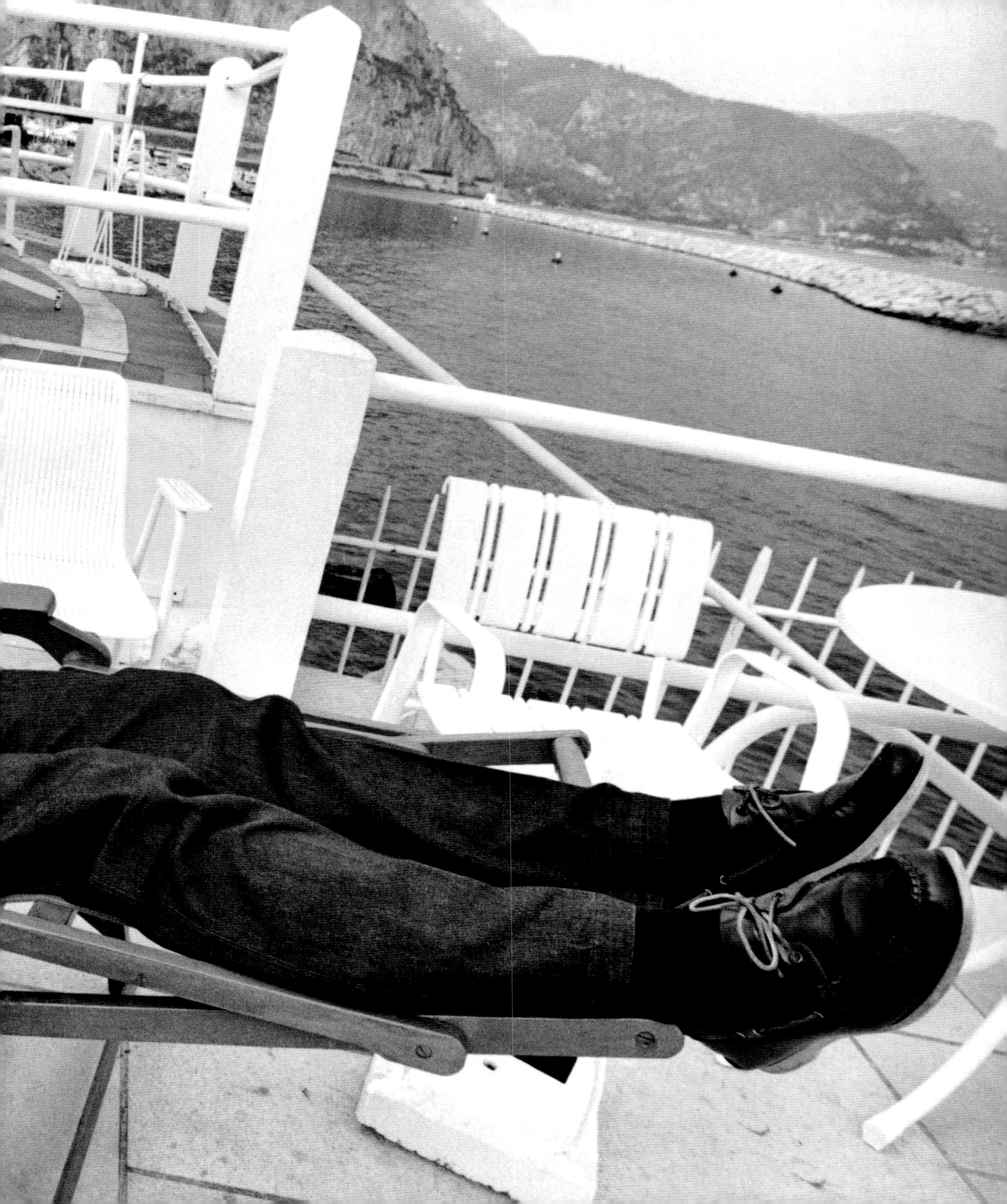

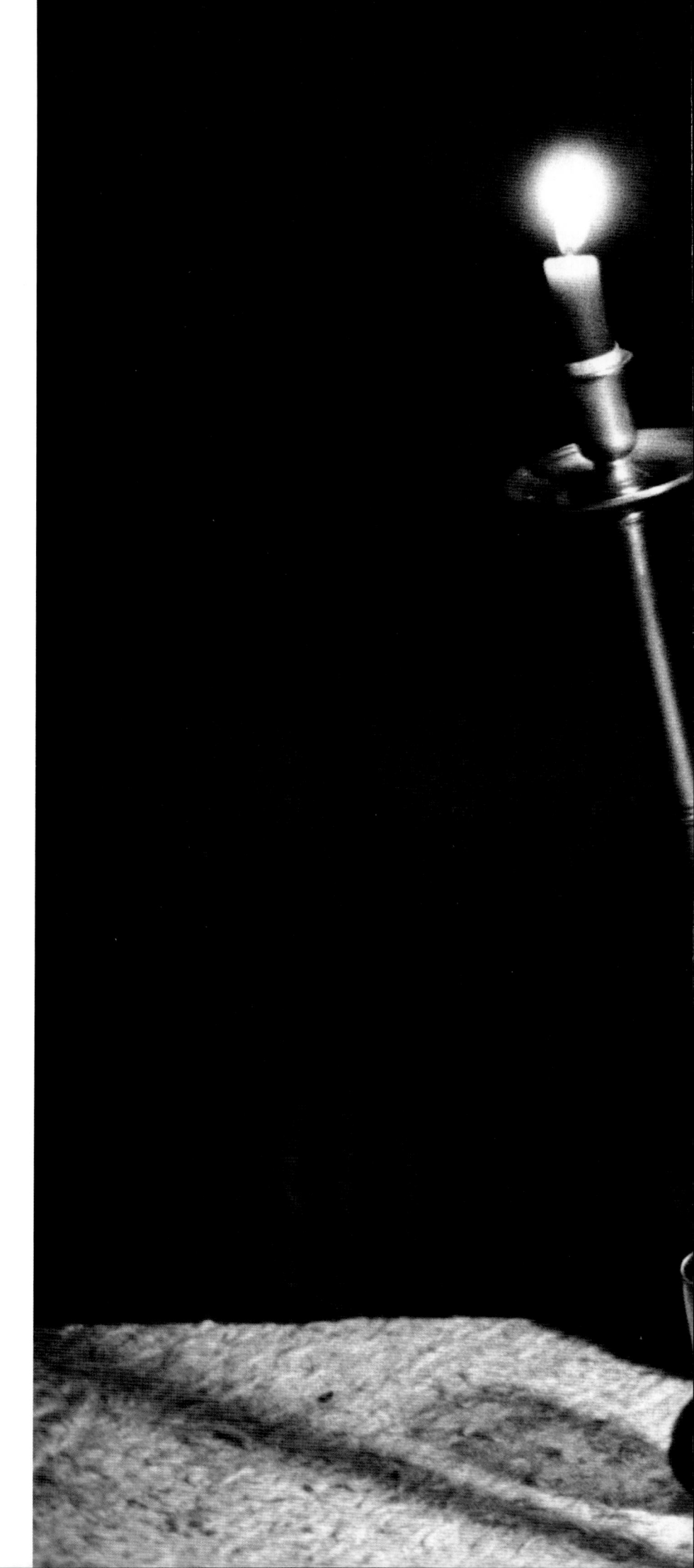

OMAR SHARIF, MALIBU, 1967

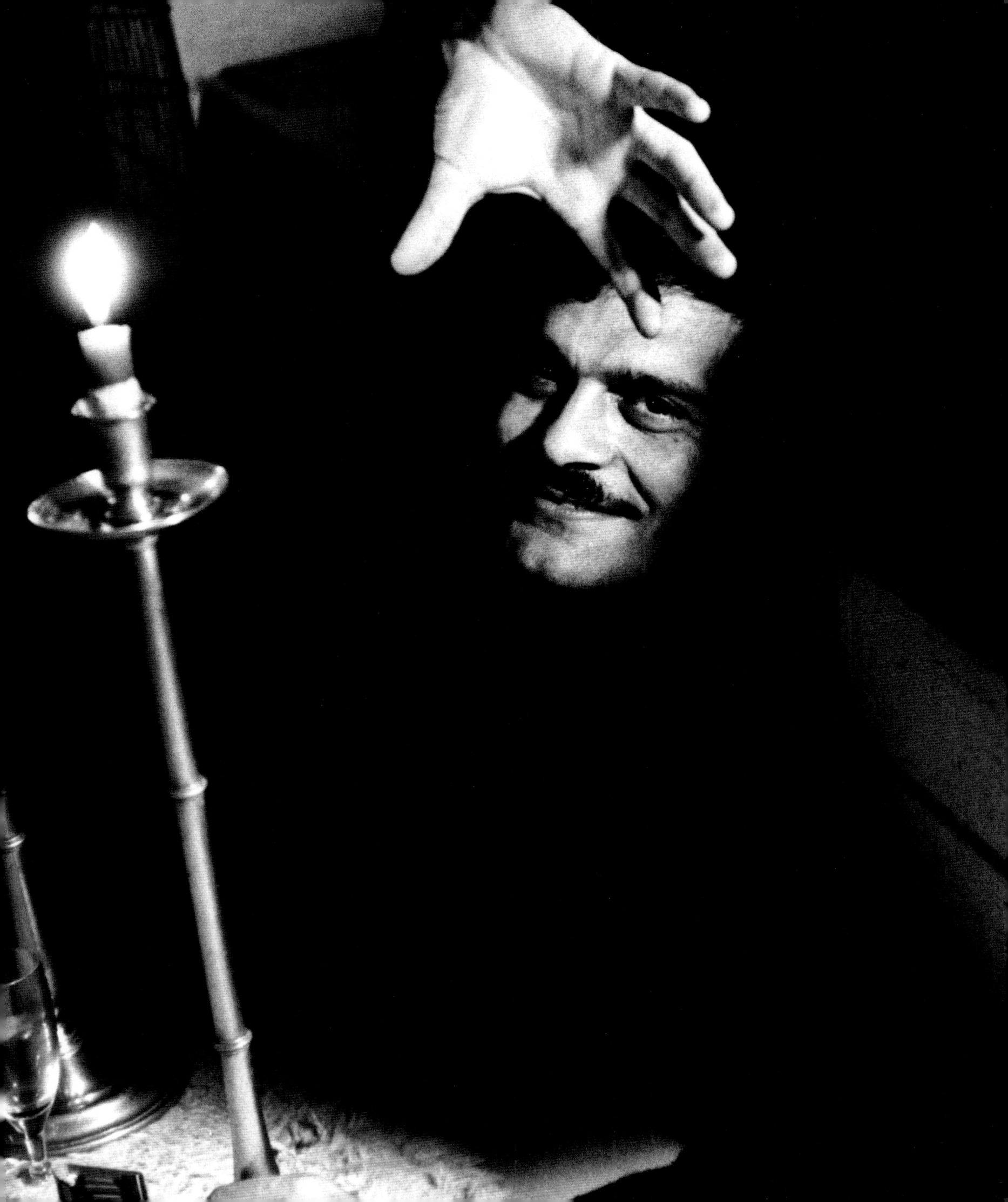

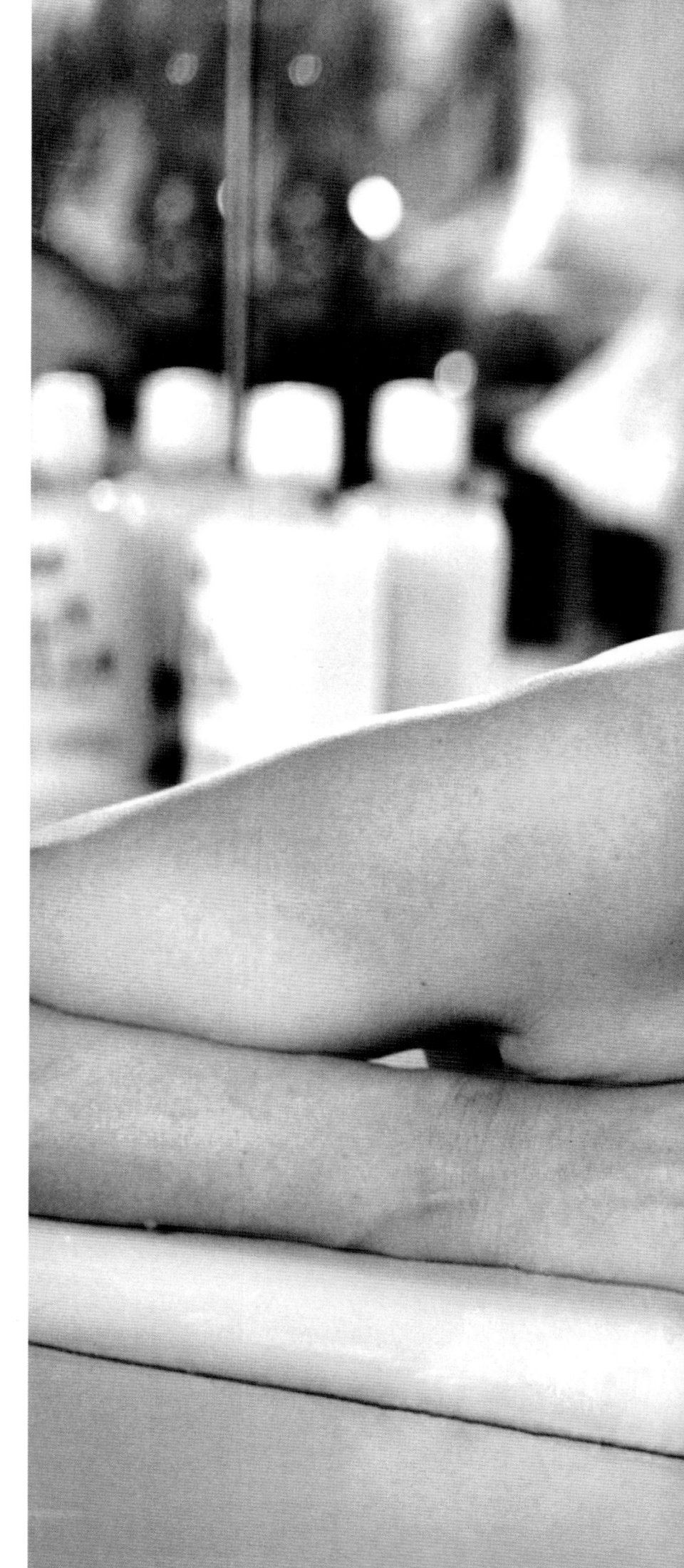

NADIA GARDINER, BEVERLY HILLS, 1962

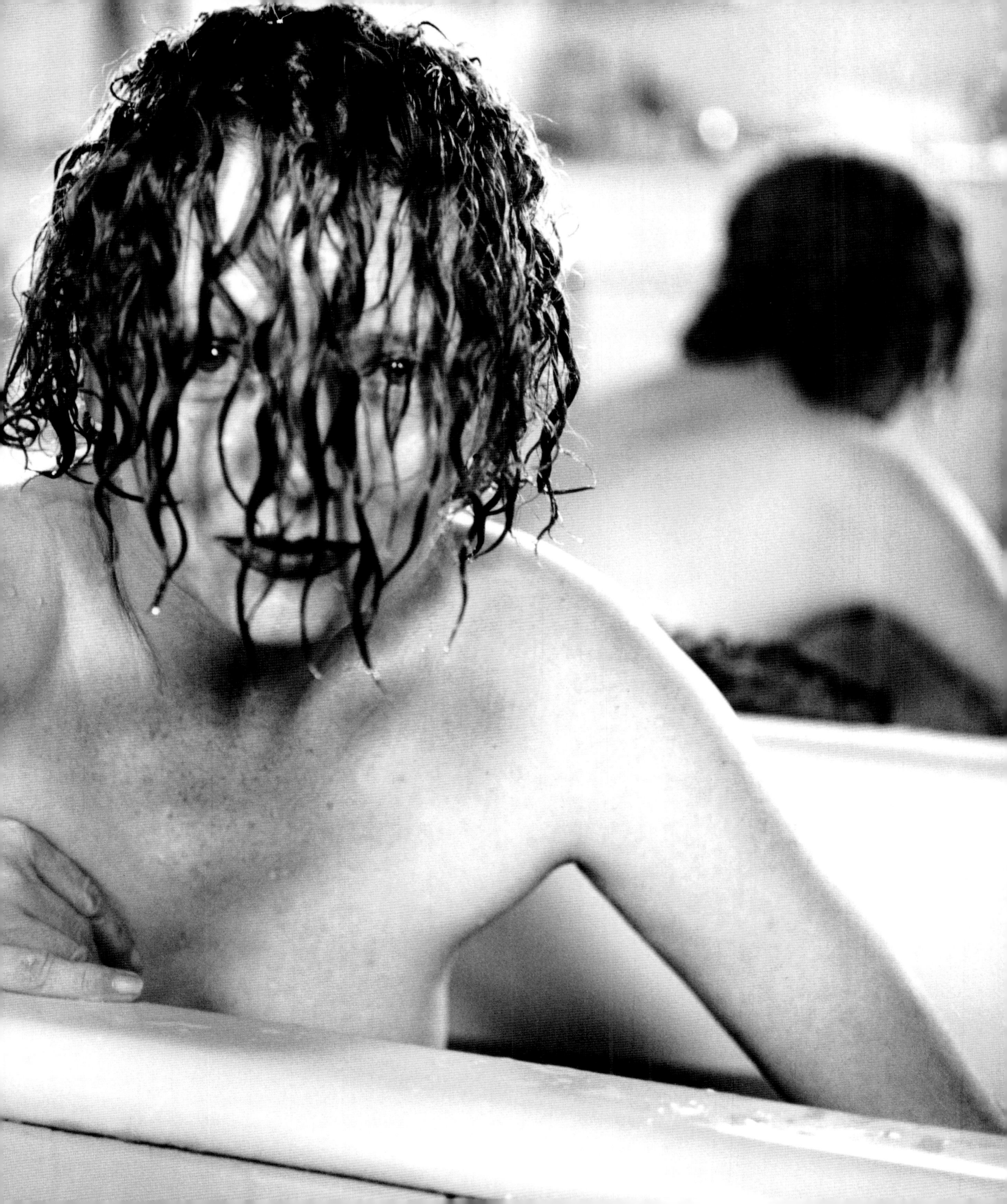

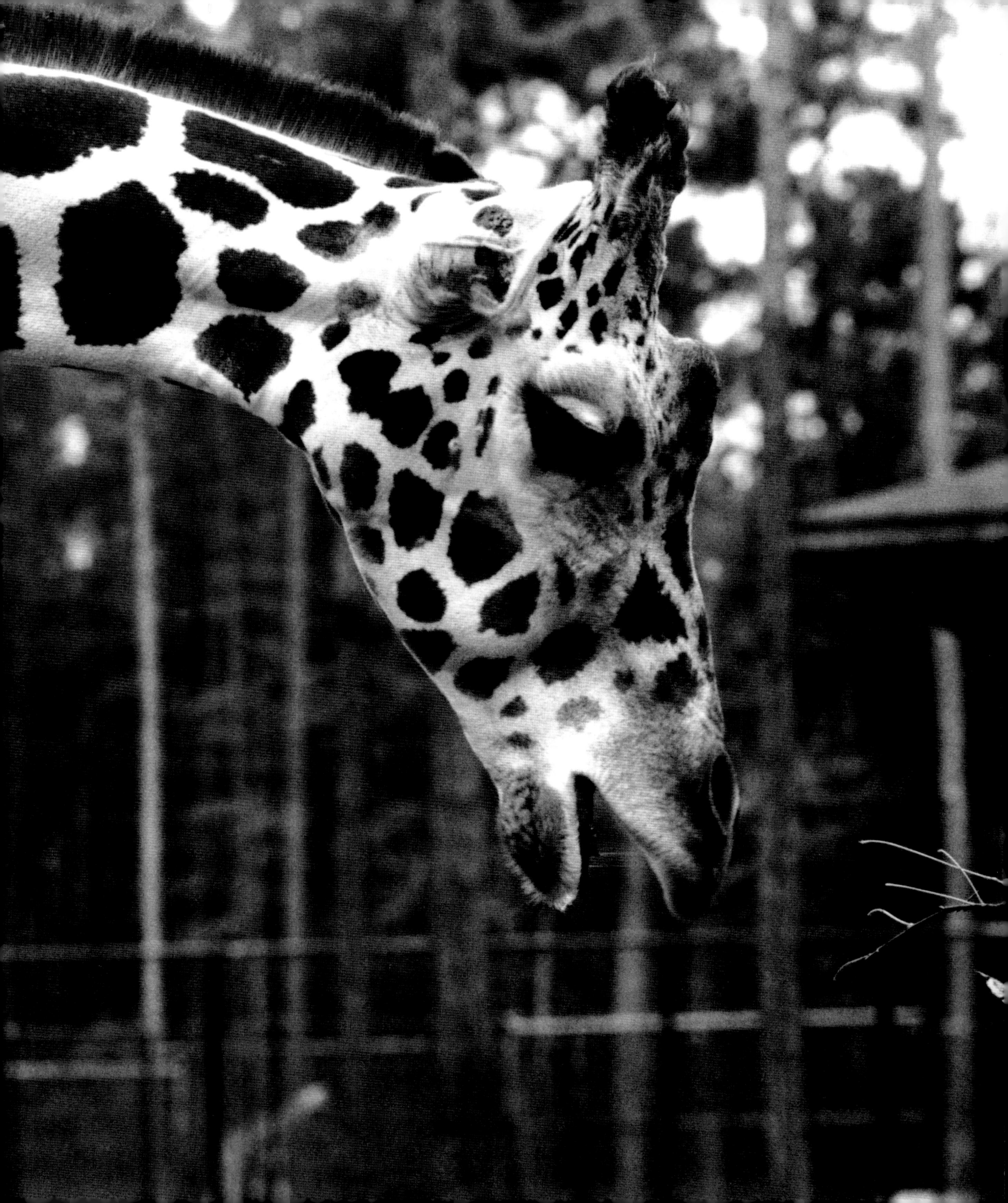

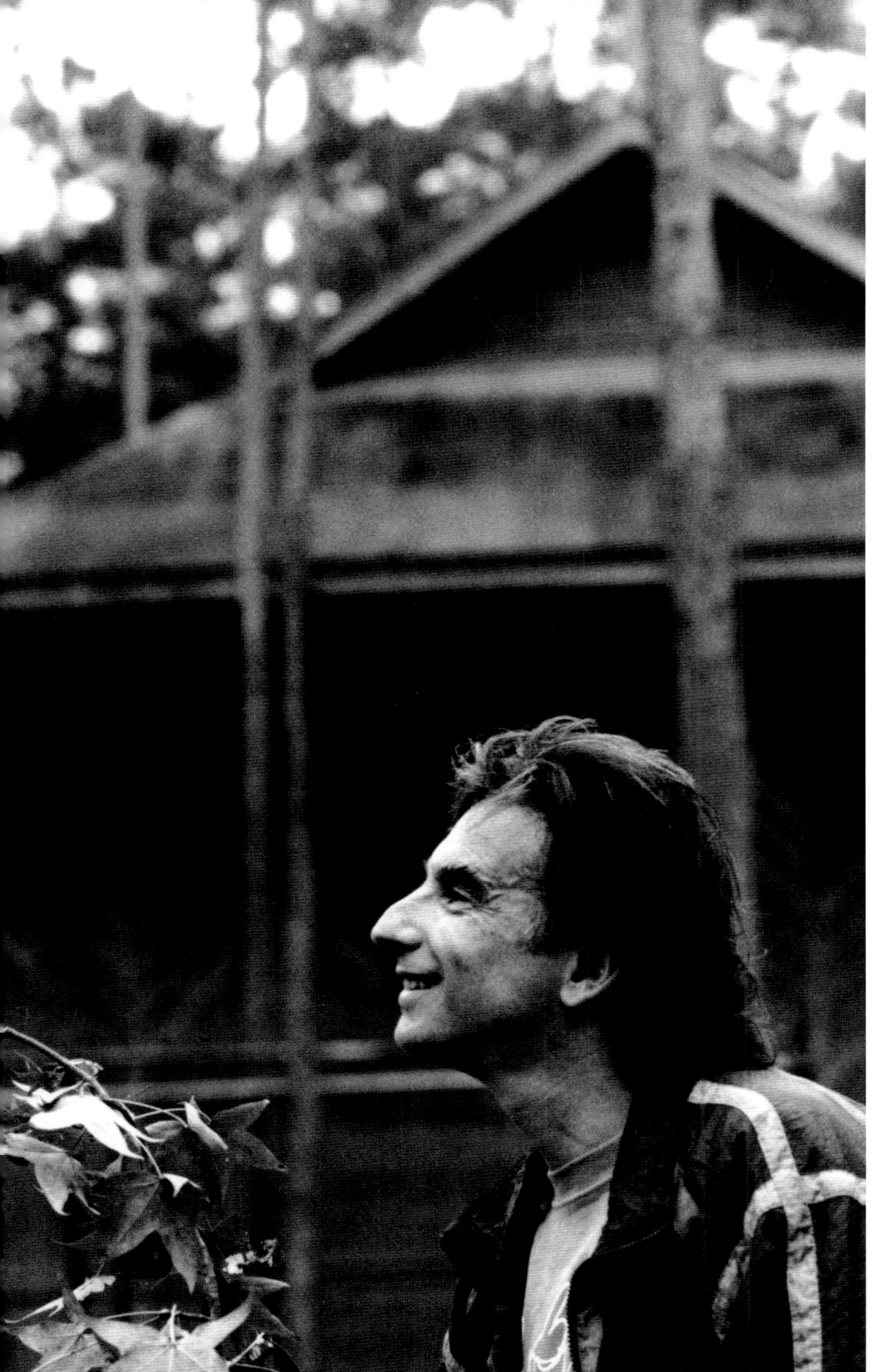

MICHAEL TILSON THOMAS, WHITE OAK PLANTATION, ST. MARY'S, GEORGIA, 1993

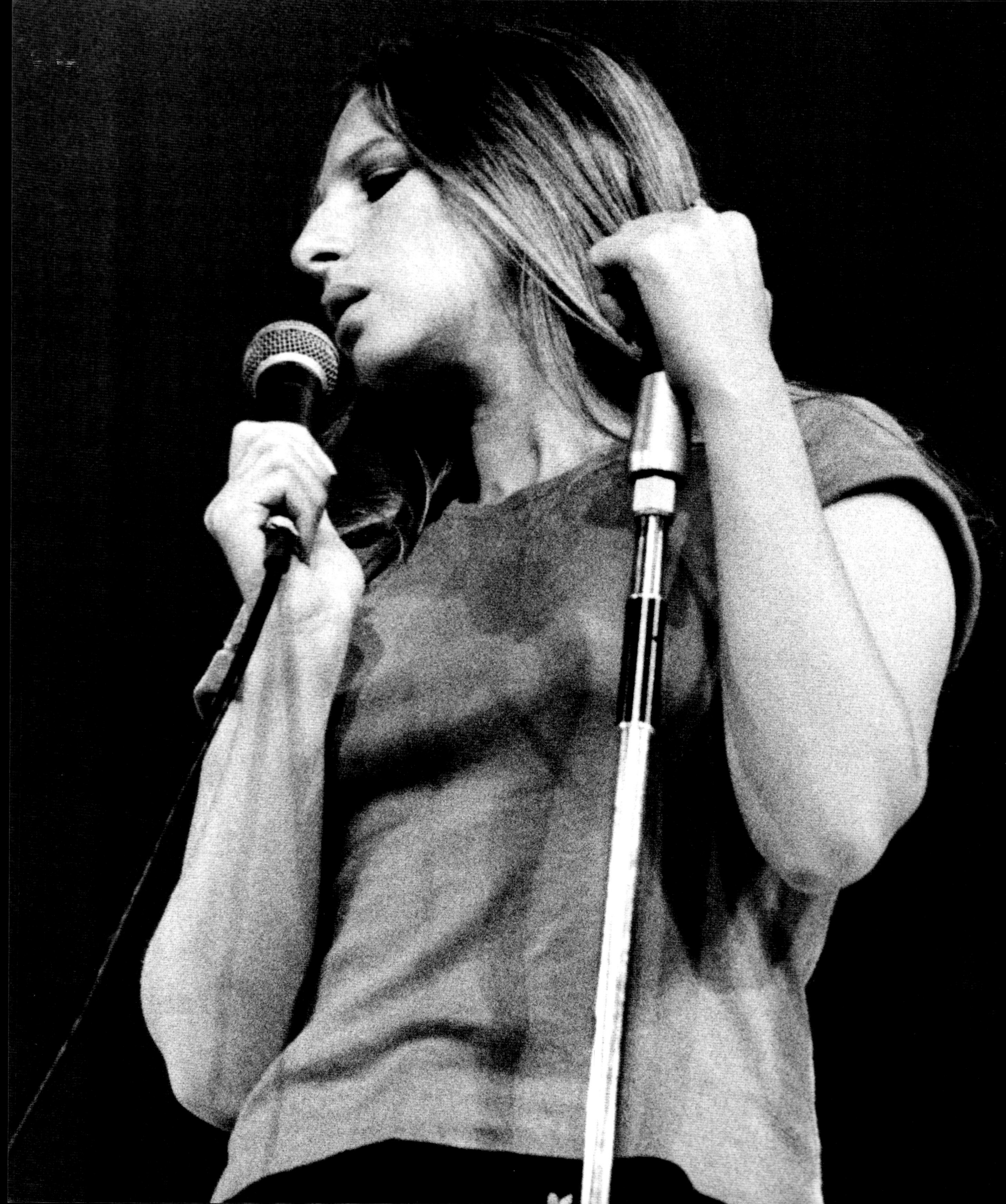

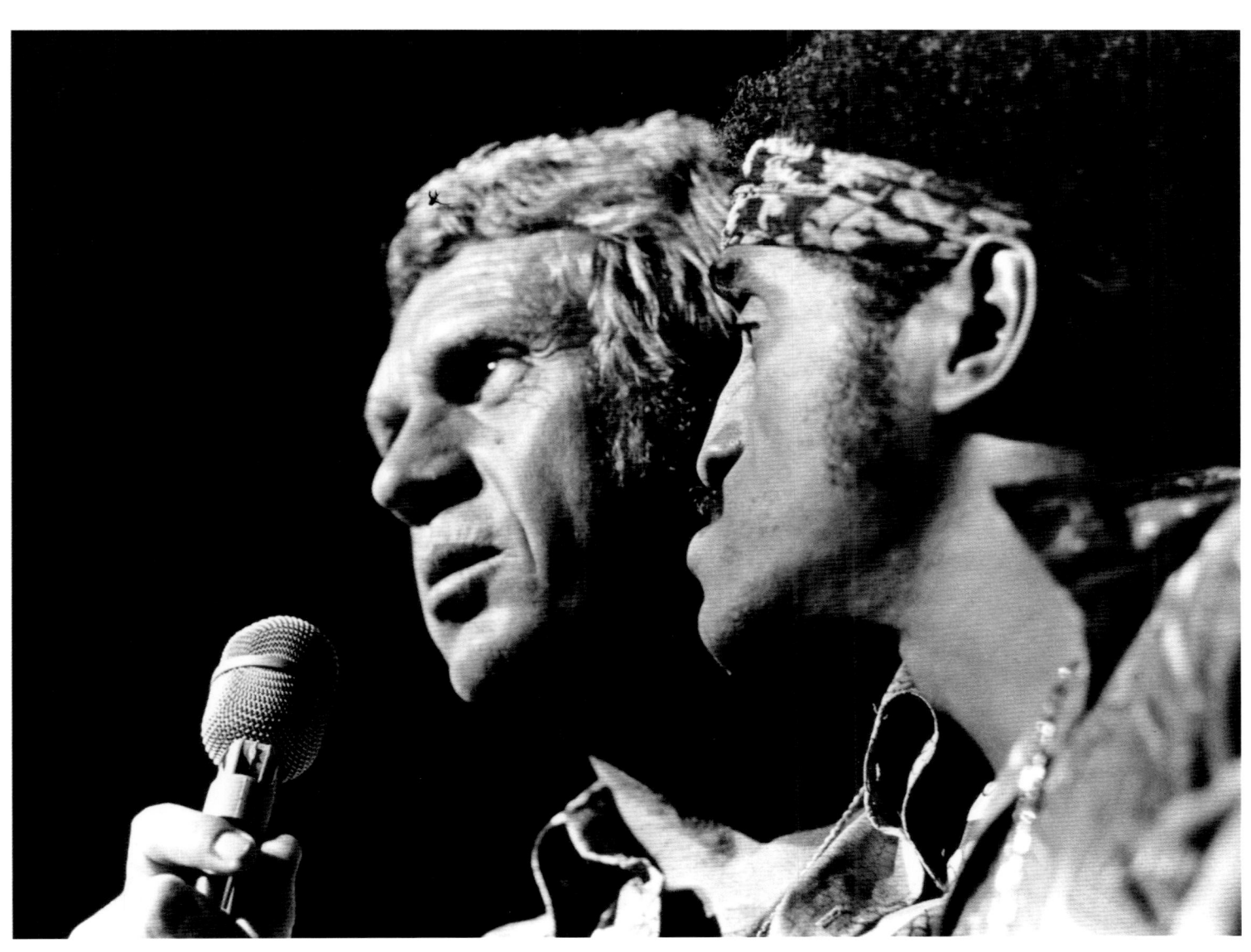

STEVE McQUEEN AND SAMMY DAVIS JR., LOS ANGELES, 1970

OPPOSITE: BARBRA STREISAND, LOS ANGELES, 1971

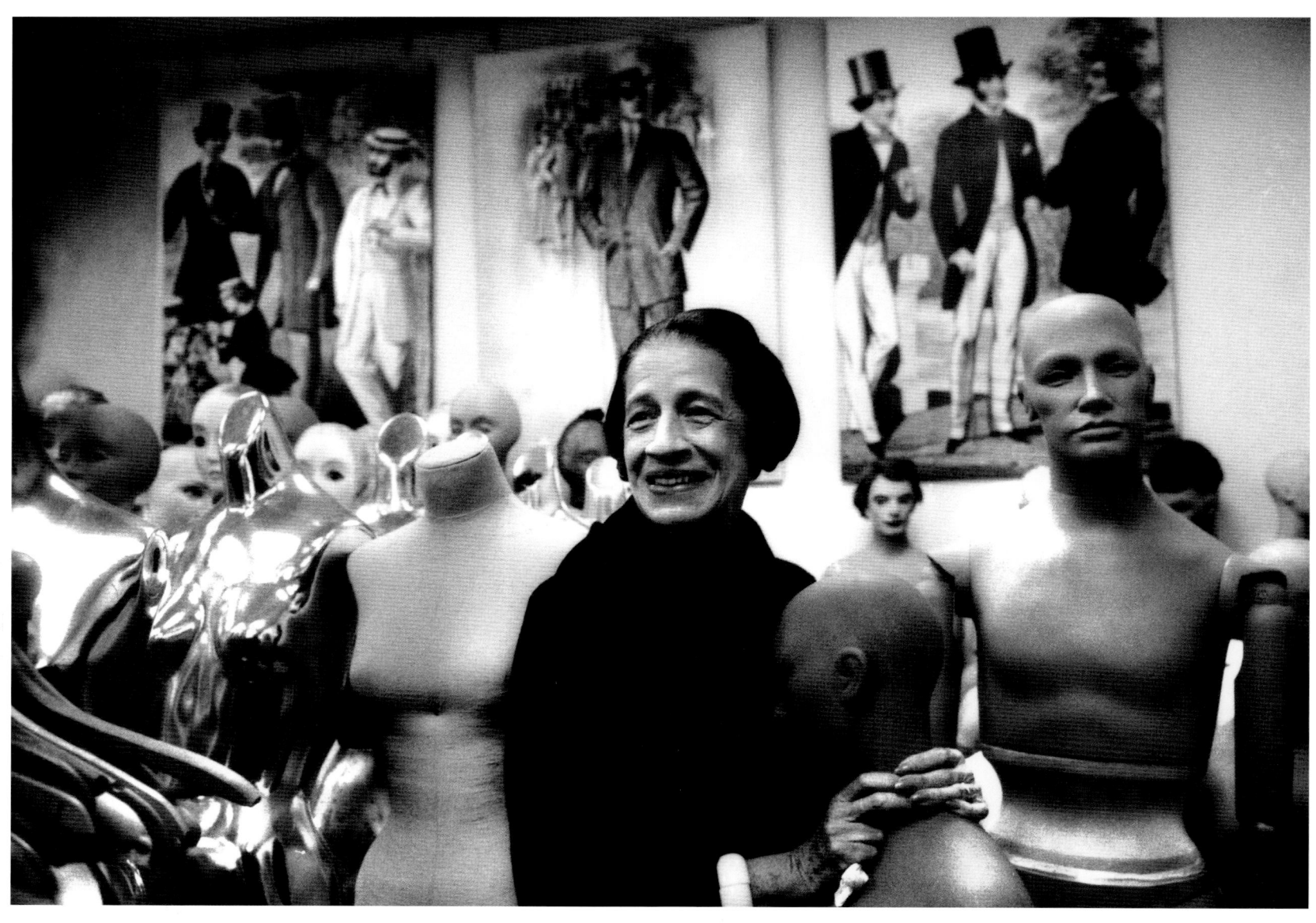

DIANA VREELAND, THE COSTUME INSTITUTE, THE METROPOLITAN MUSEUM OF ART, NEW YORK CITY, 1975

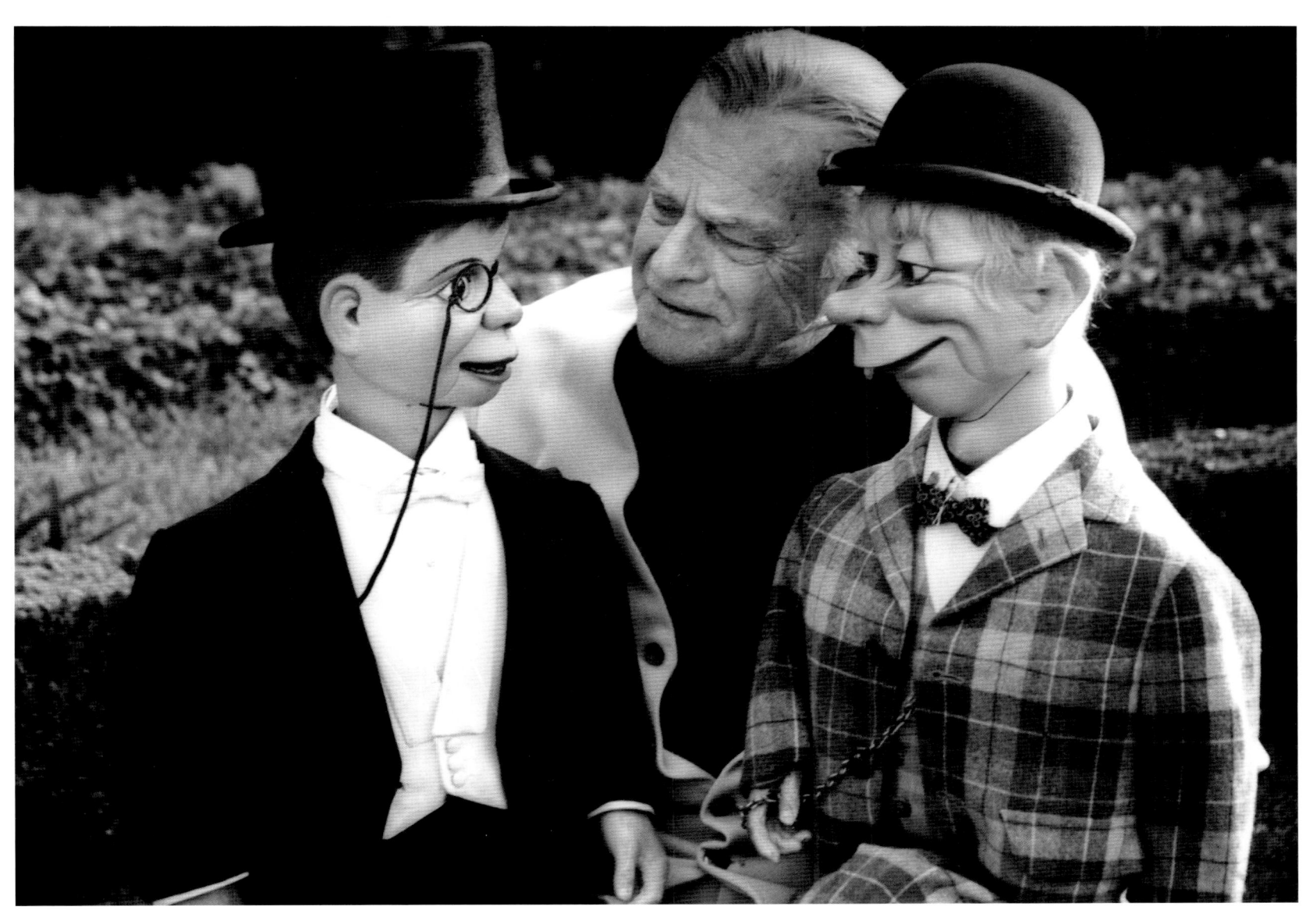

CHARLIE MCCARTHY, EDGAR BERGEN, MORTIMER SNERD, BEVERLY HILLS, 1974

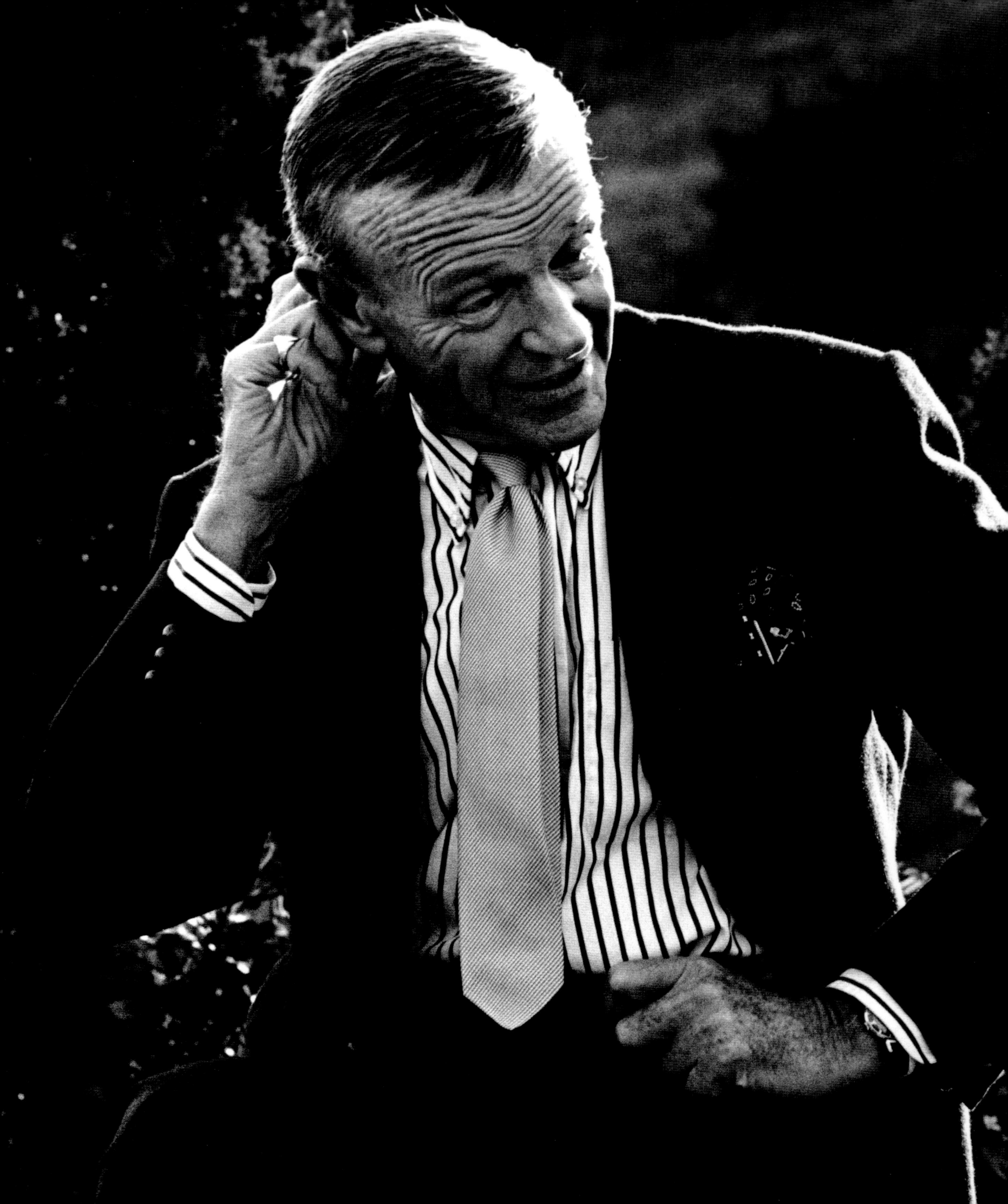

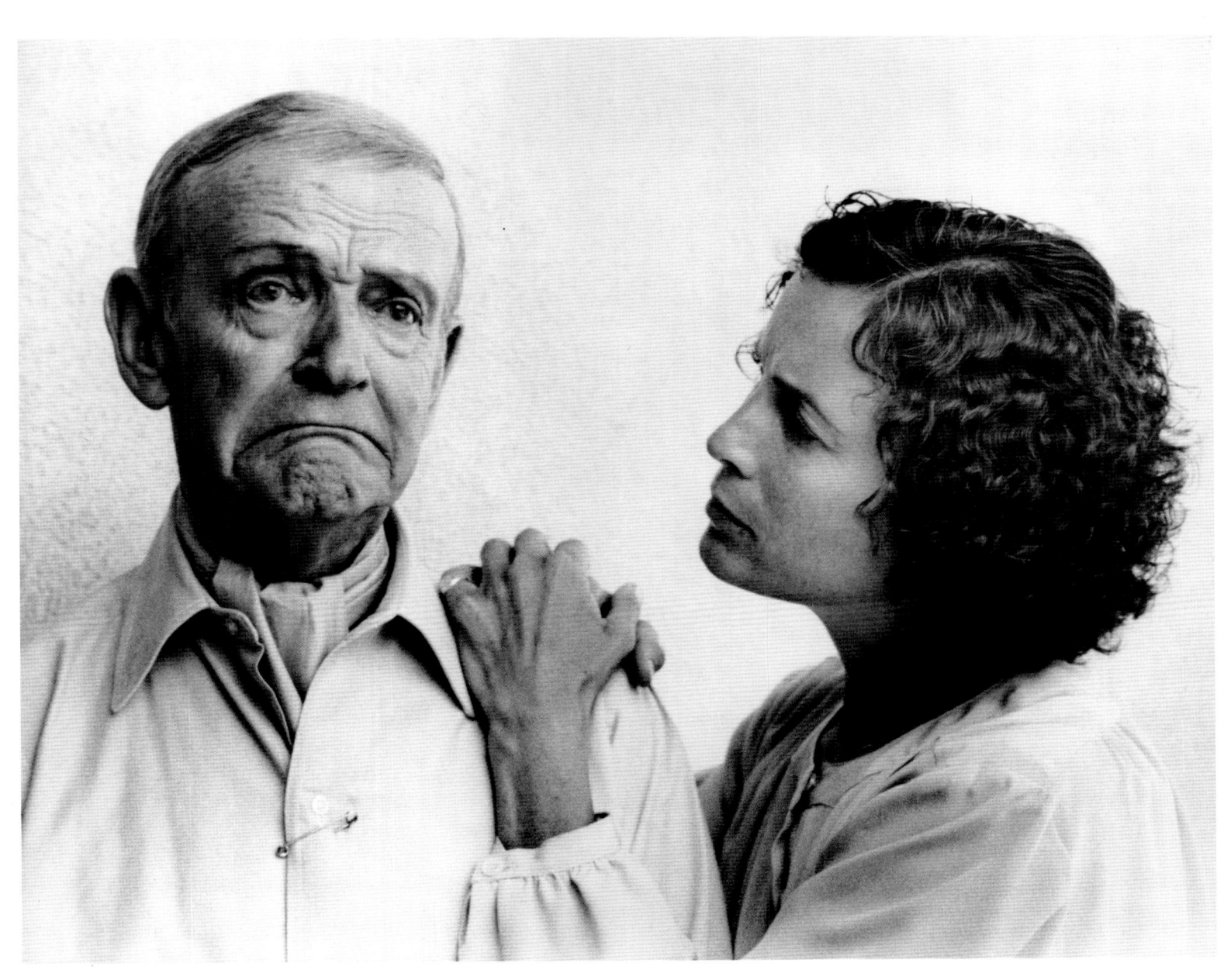

FRED AND ROBYN ASTAIRE, BEVERLY HILLS, 1984

OPPOSITE: FRED ASTAIRE, BEVERLY HILLS, 1966

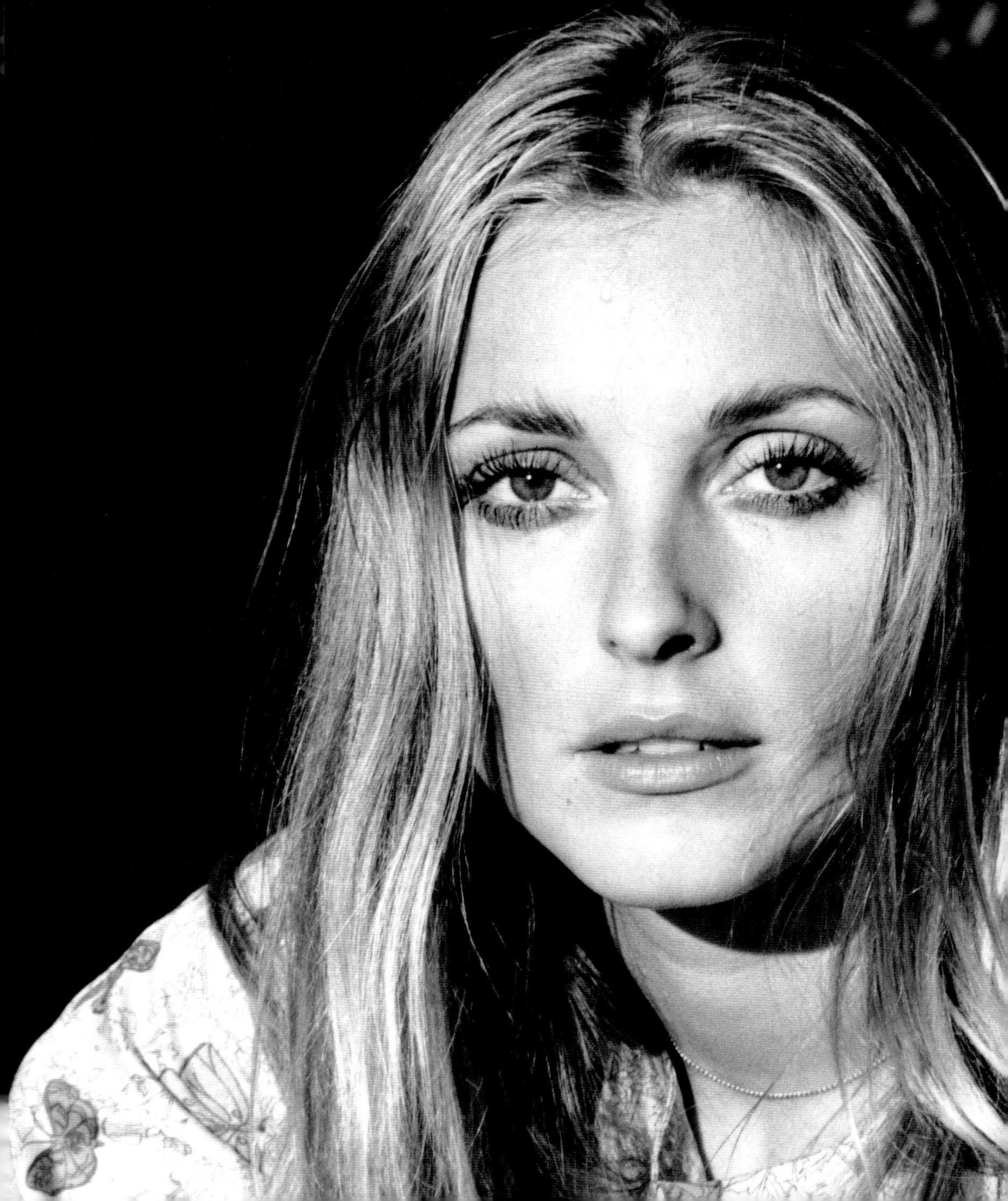

SHARON TATE, CIELO DRIVE, BEVERLY HILLS, 1969

OVERLEAF: SHARON TATE'S HUSBAND, ROMAN POLANSKI, AND JACK NICHOLSON, PARIS, 1990

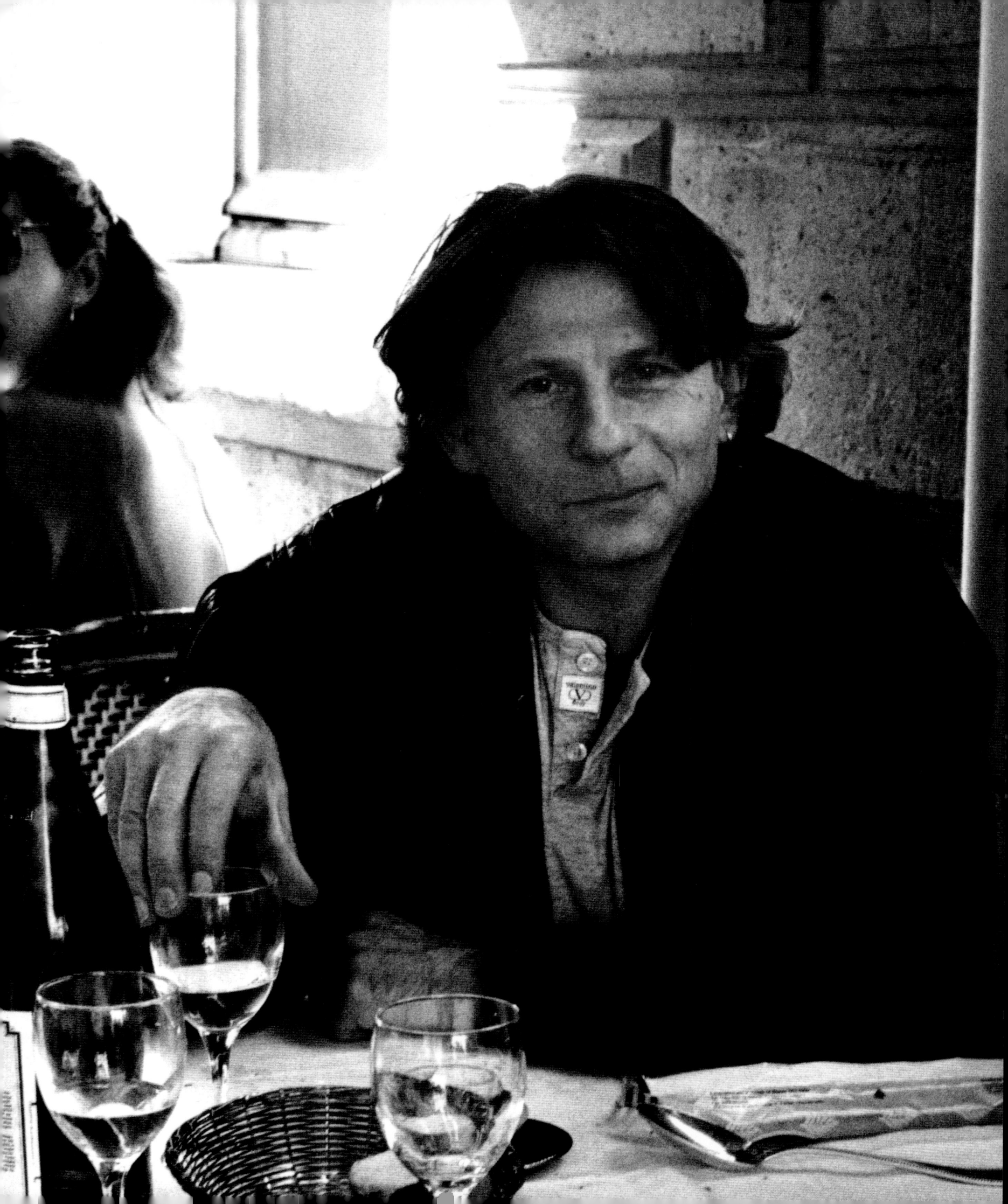

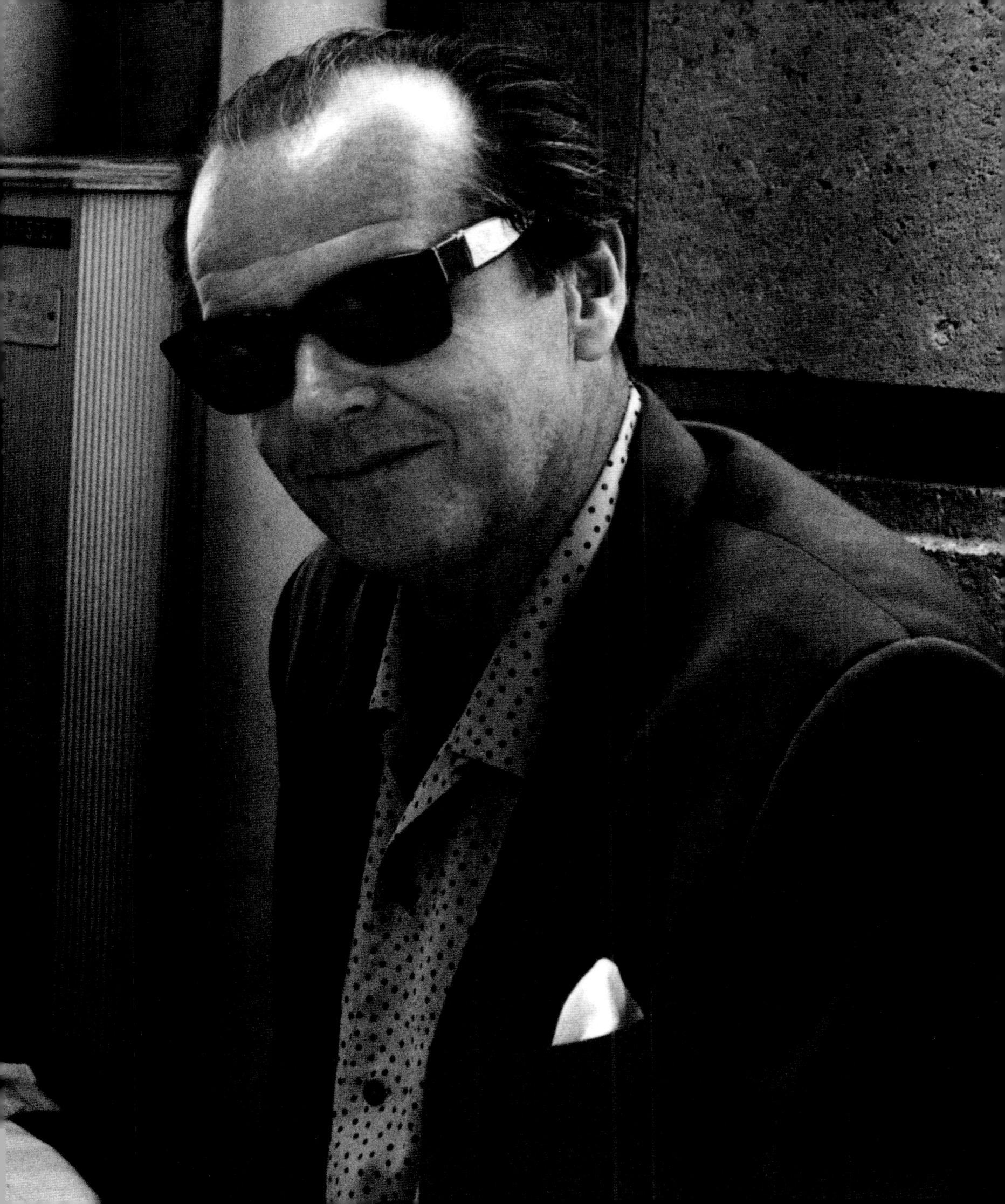

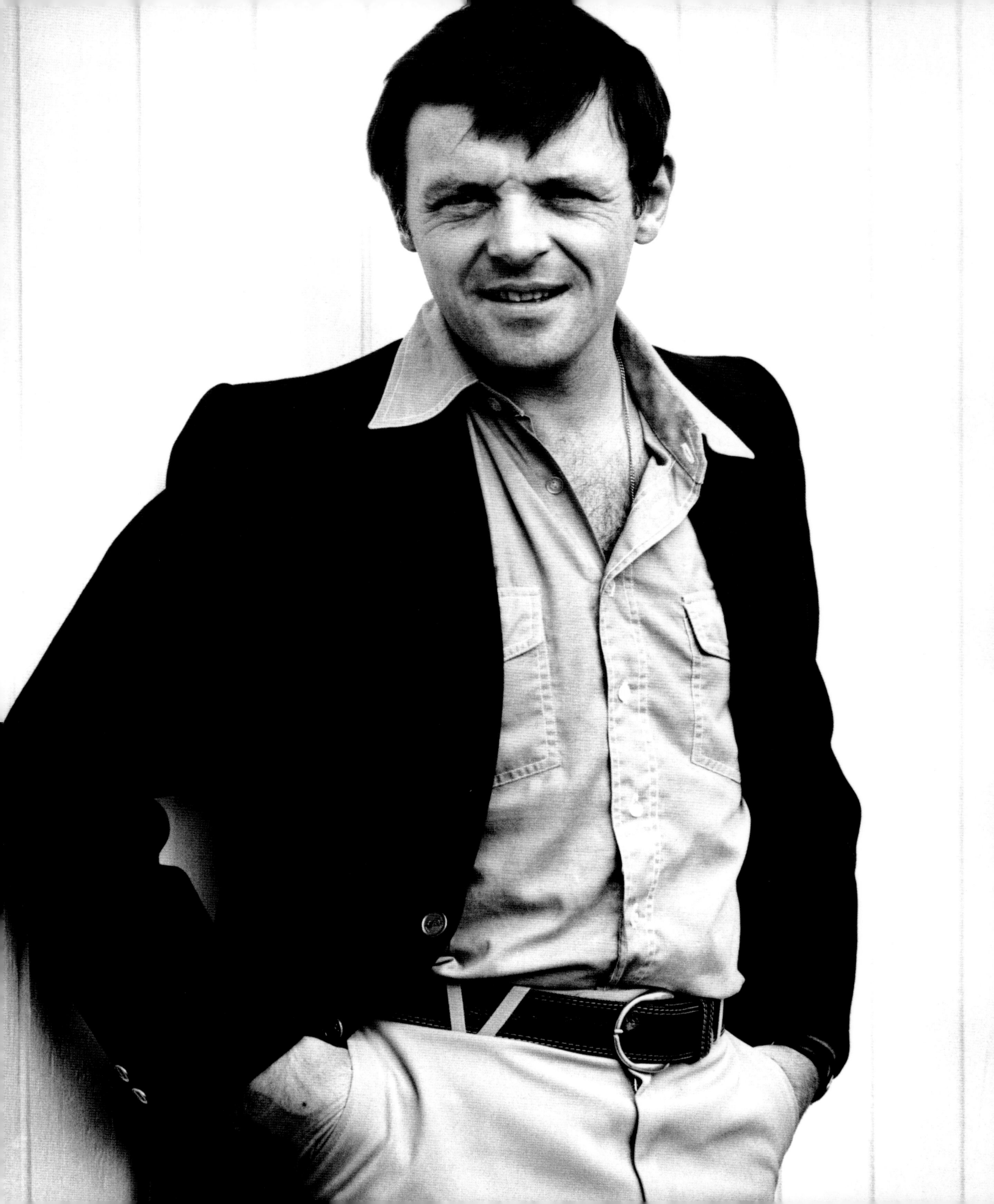

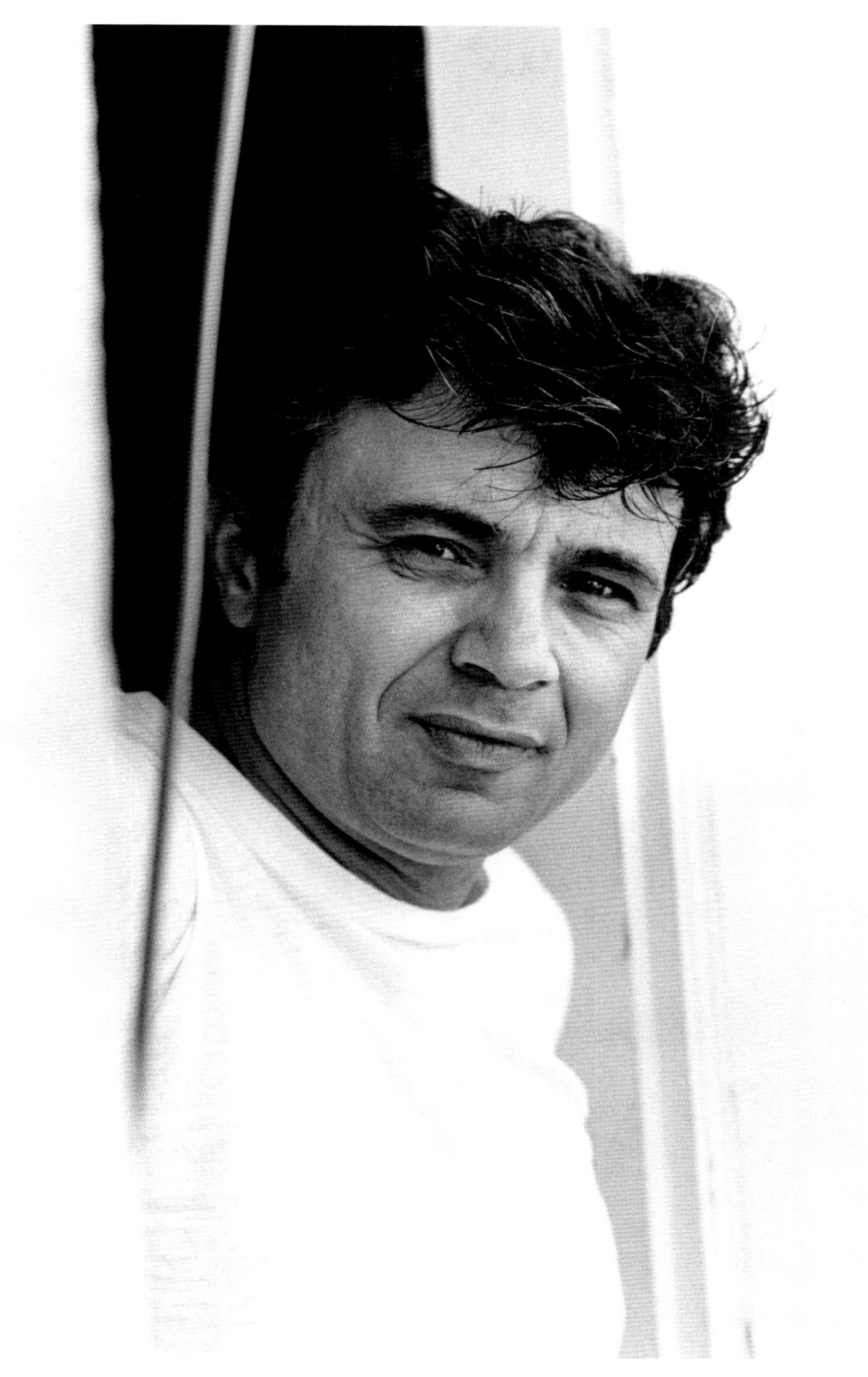

ROBERT BLAKE, LOS ANGELES, 1974

OPPOSITE: ANTHONY HOPKINS, BEVERLY HILLS, 1972

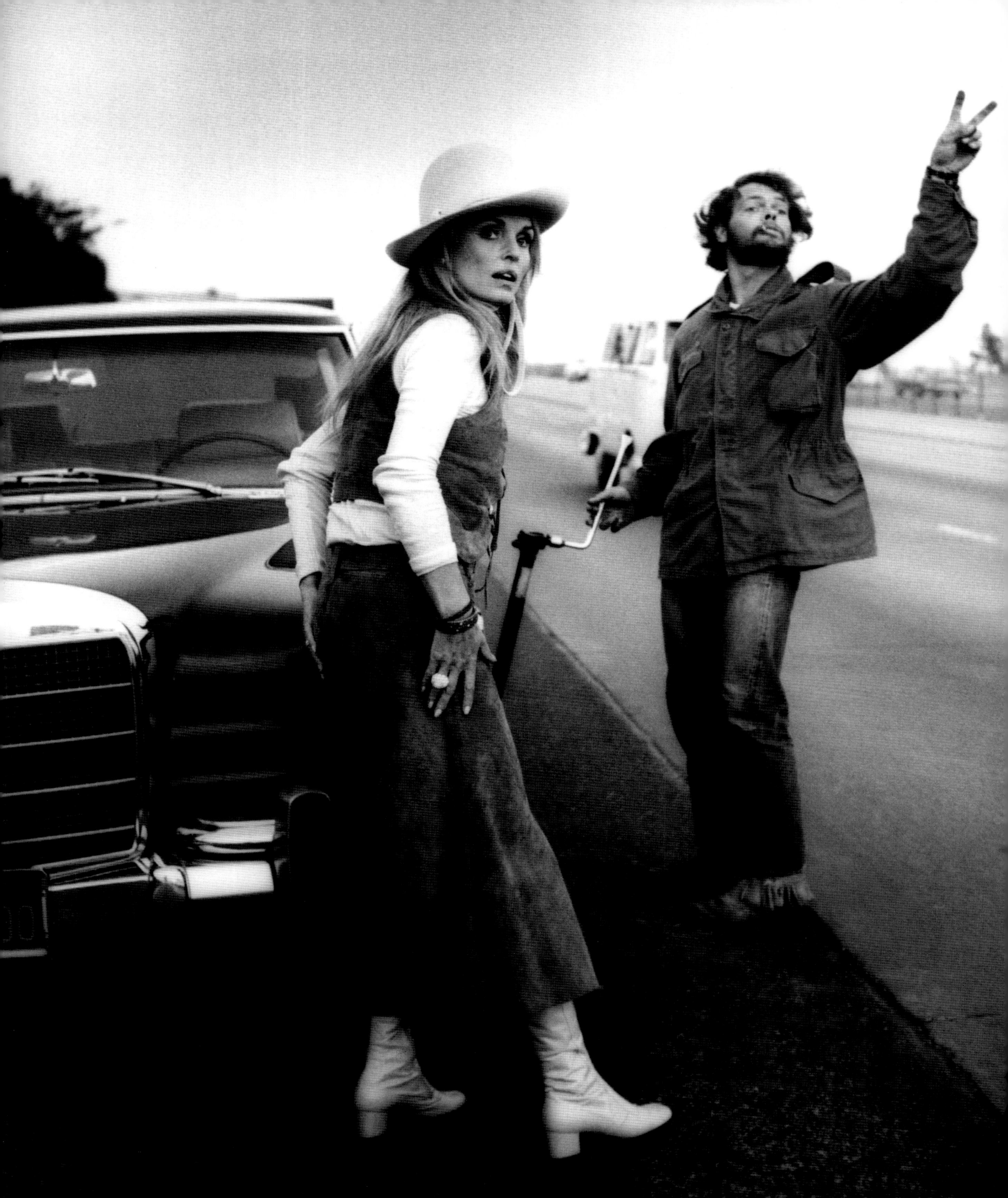

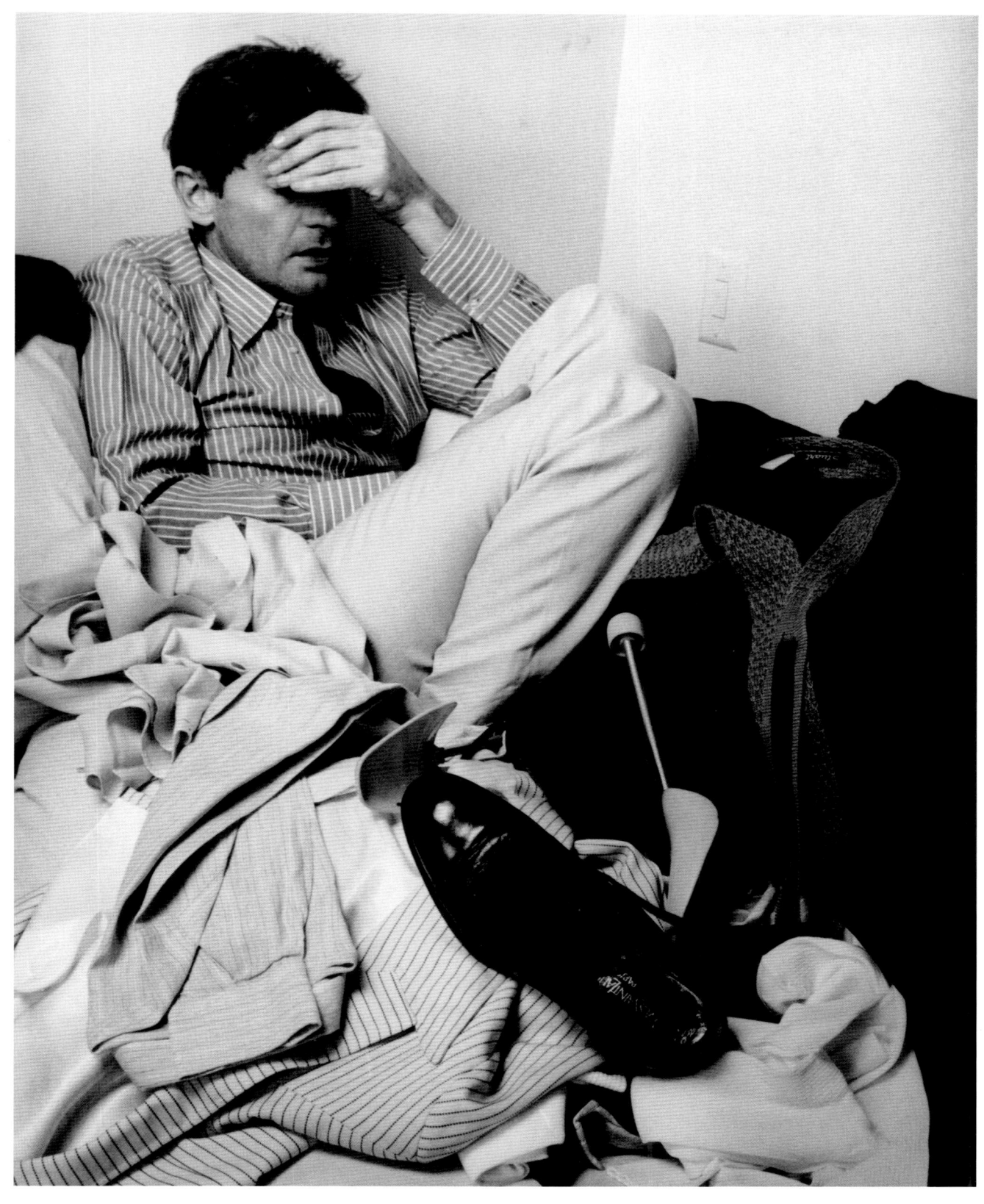

HELMUT BERGER, BEVERLY HILLS, 1984

OPPOSITE: ROSEMARIE STACK AND STRANGER,
DEL MAR, CALIFORNIA, 1970

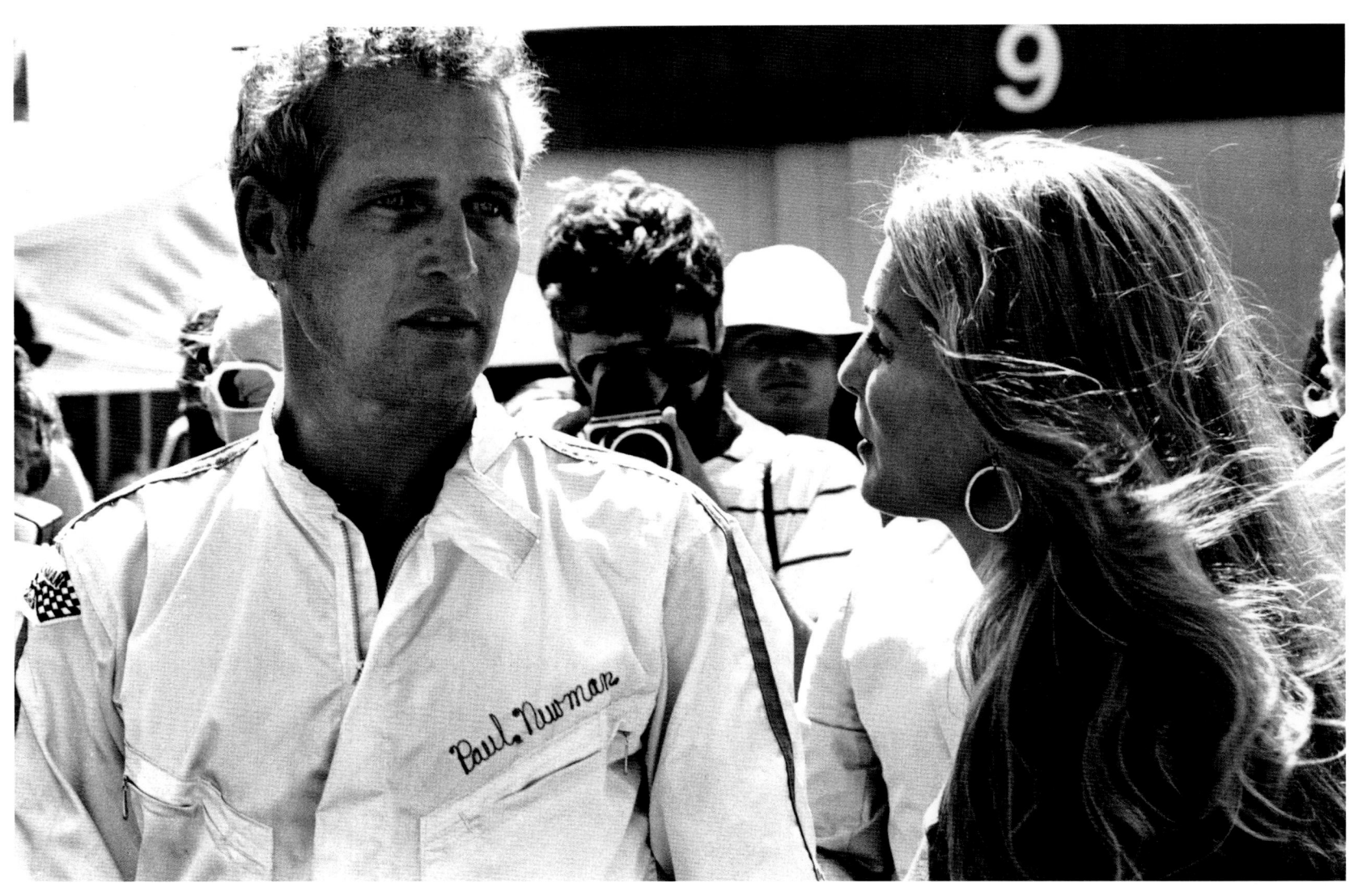
PAUL NEWMAN AND ROSEMARIE STACK, ONTARIO SPEEDWAY RACETRACK, 1973

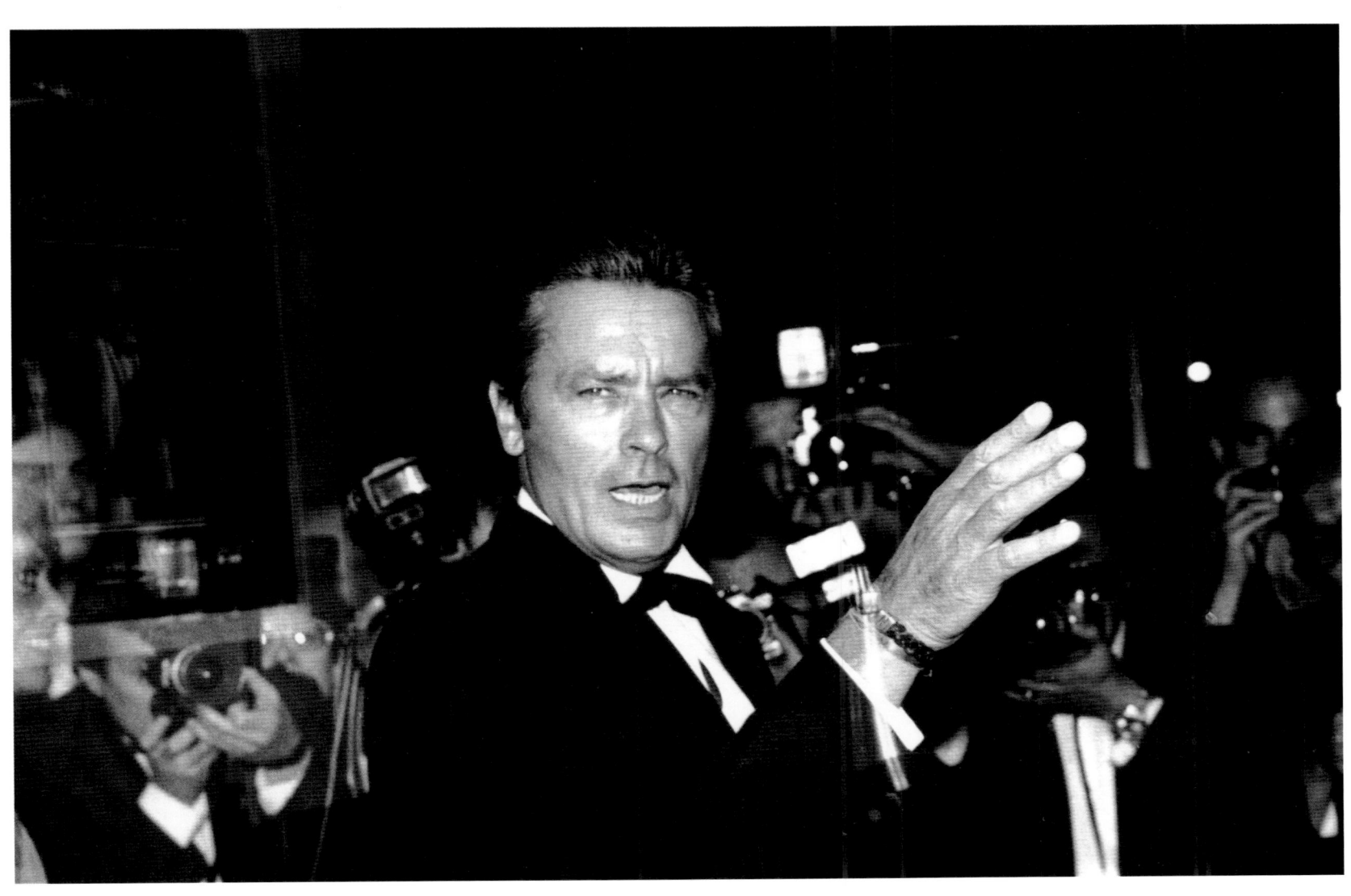

ALAIN DELON, PARIS, 1990

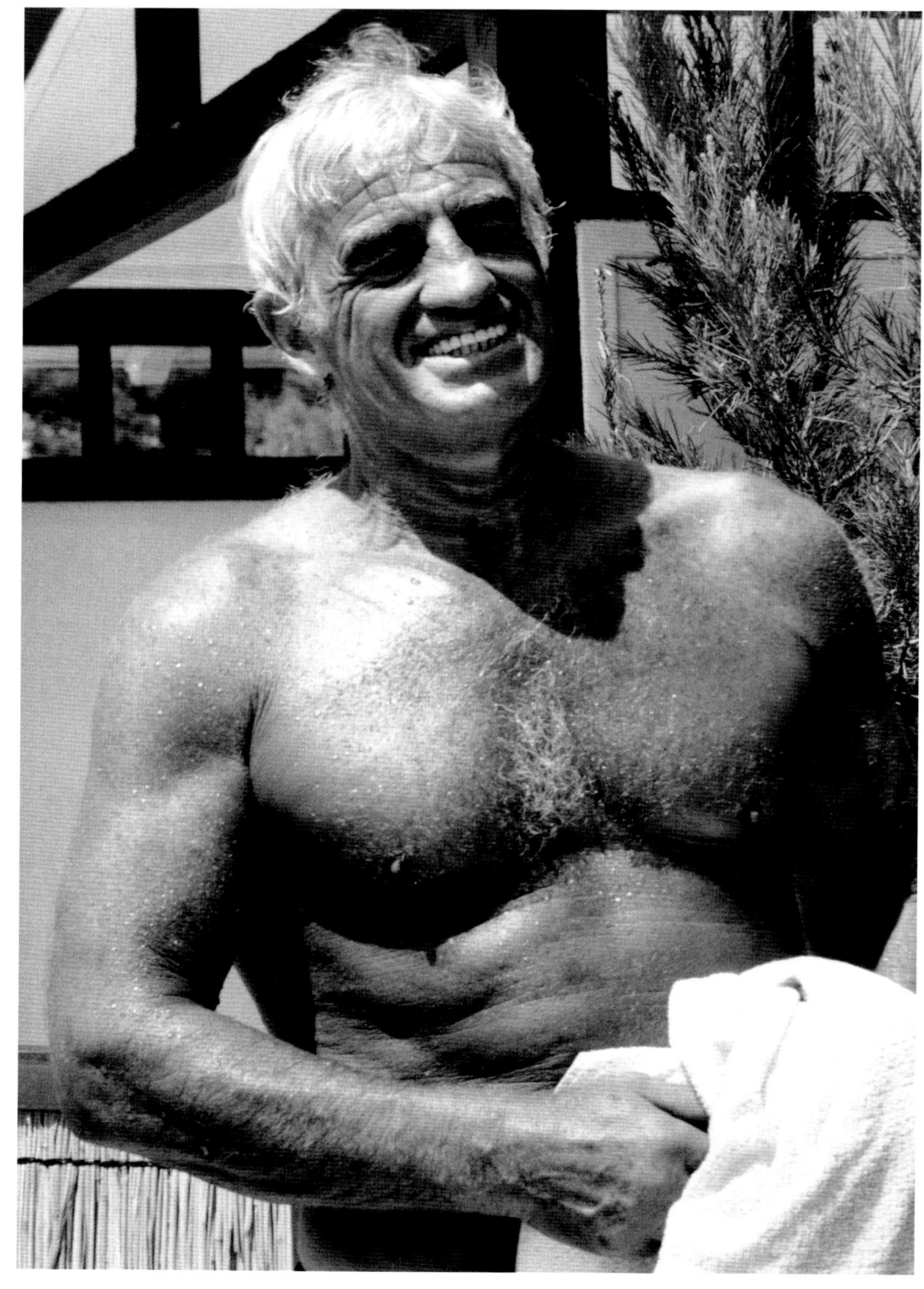

JEAN-PAUL BELMONDO, HÔTEL DU CAP, CAP D'ANTIBES, FRANCE, 1990

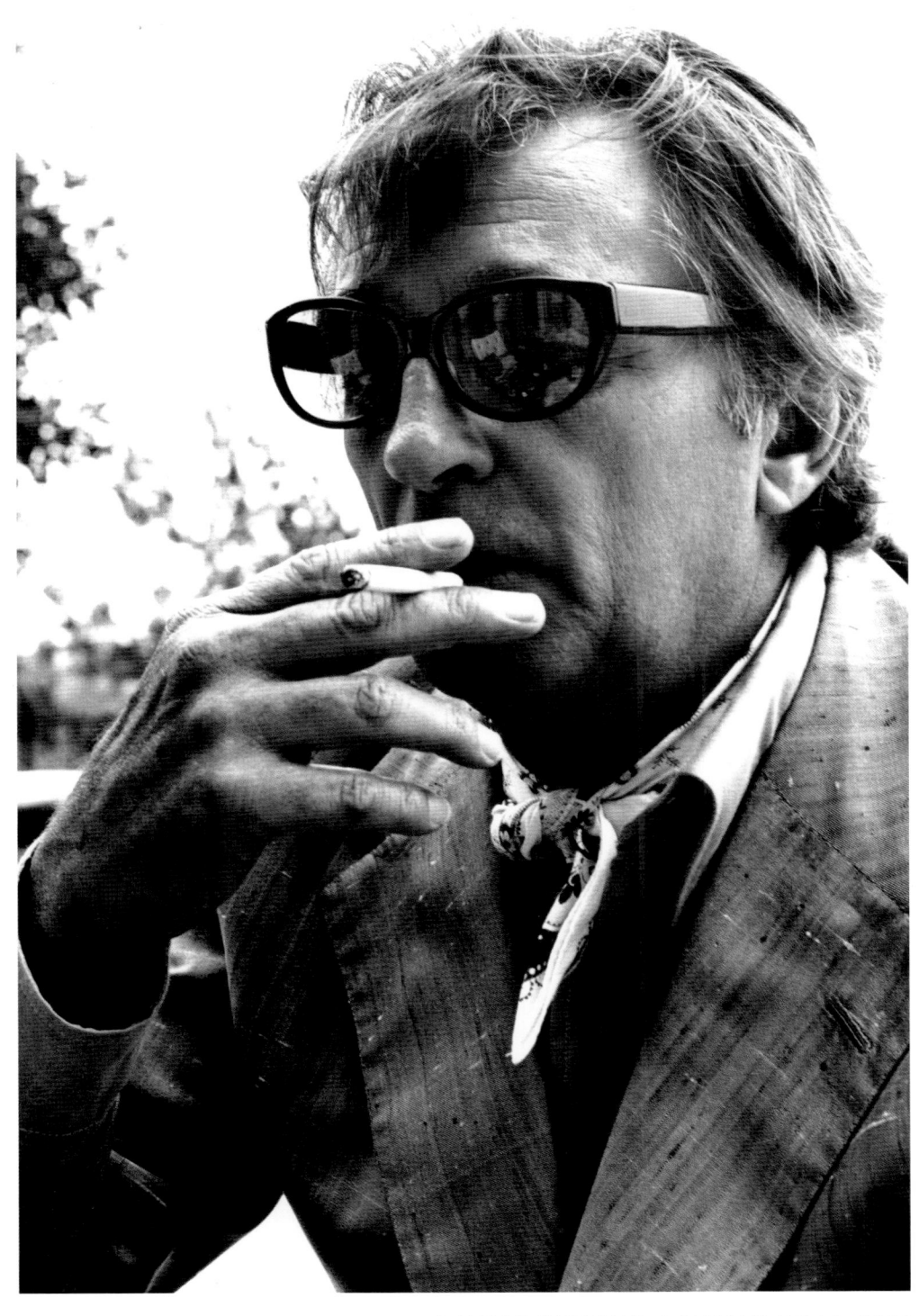

ROBERT MITCHUM, BEVERLY HILLS, 1978

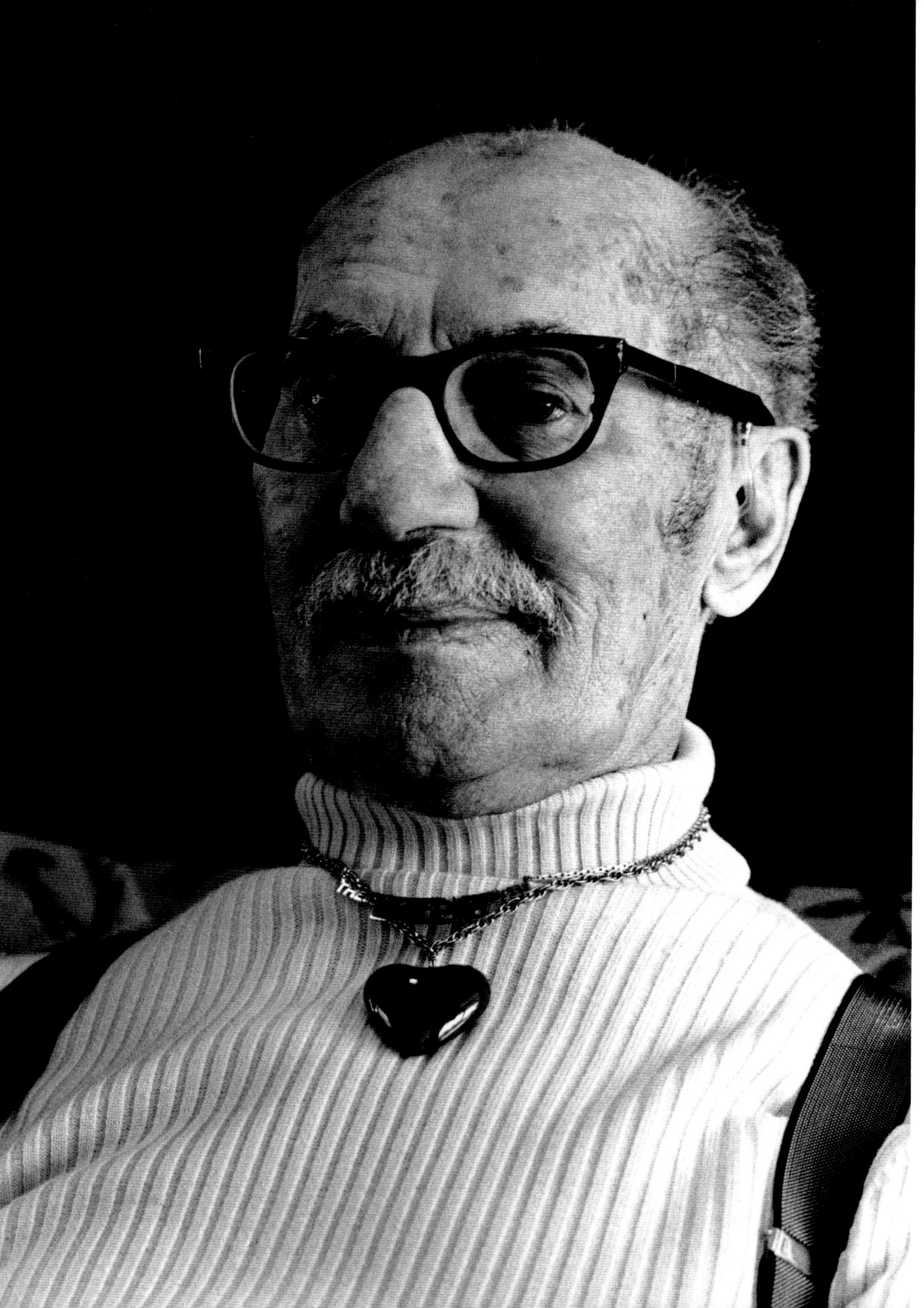

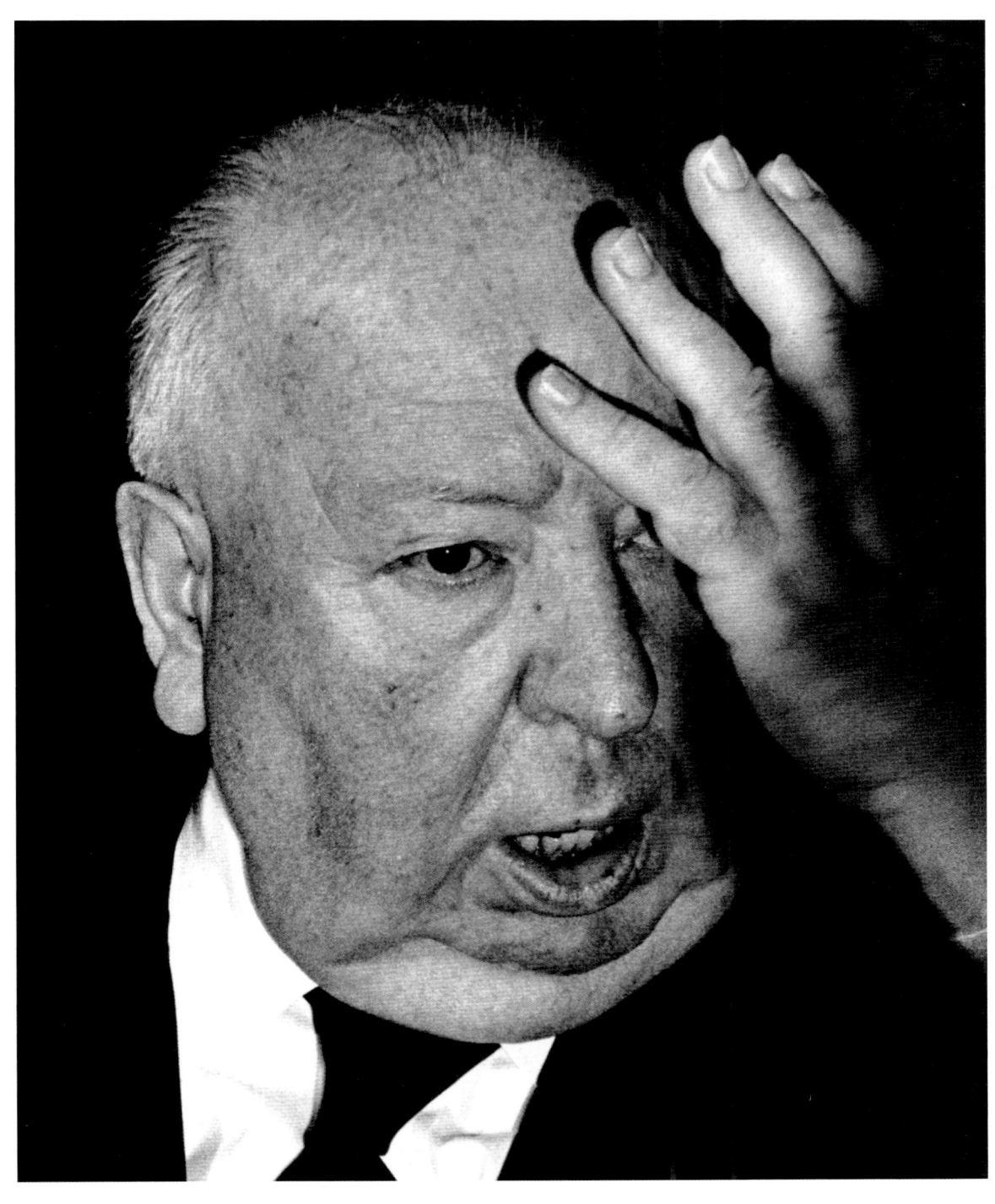

ALFRED HITCHCOCK, BEVERLY HILLS, 1974

OPPOSITE: GROUCHO MARX, BEVERLY HILLS, 1975

OVERLEAF LEFT: STELLA ADLER, LOS ANGELES, 1989

OVERLEAF RIGHT: DAVID BOWIE, LOS ANGELES, 1975

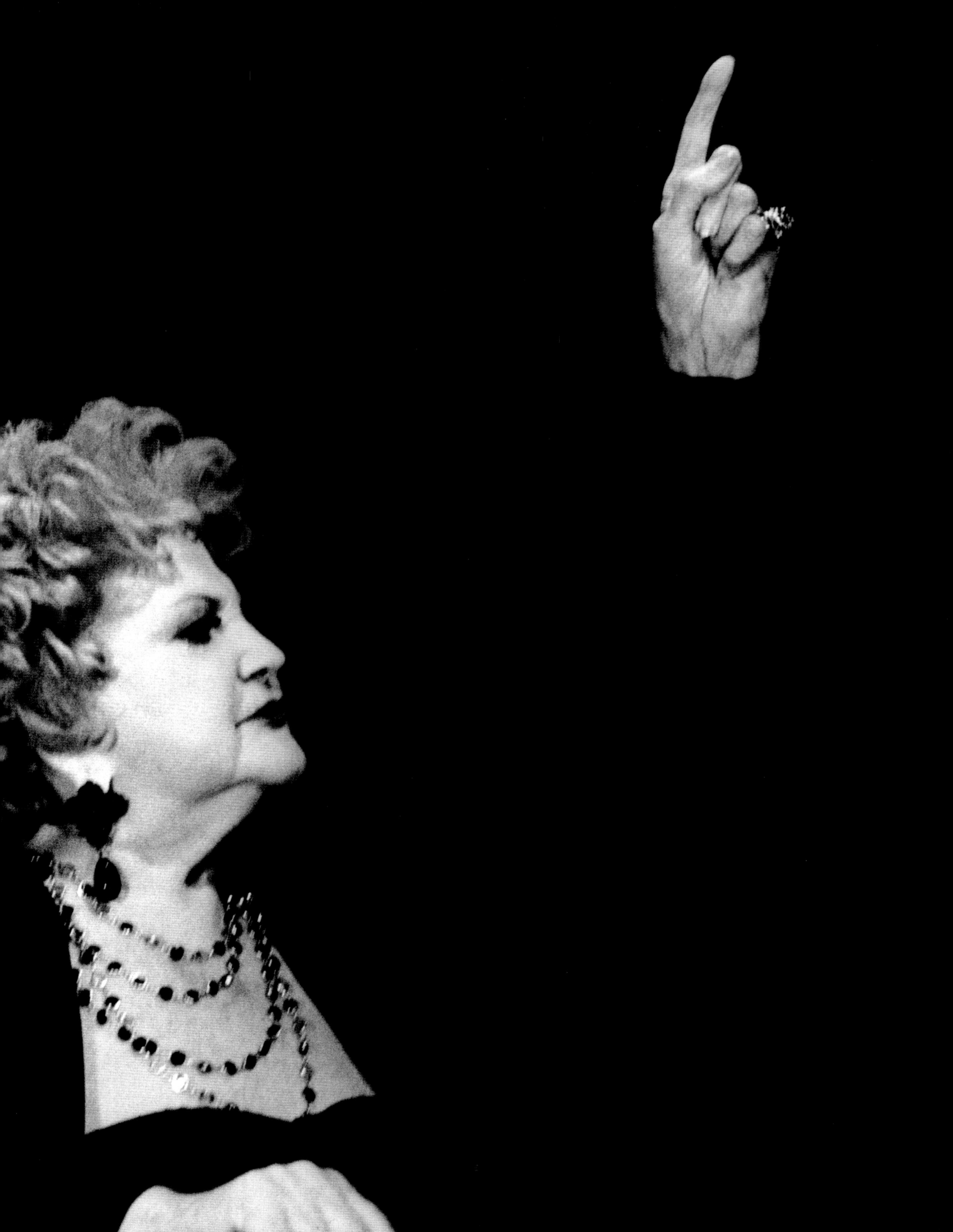

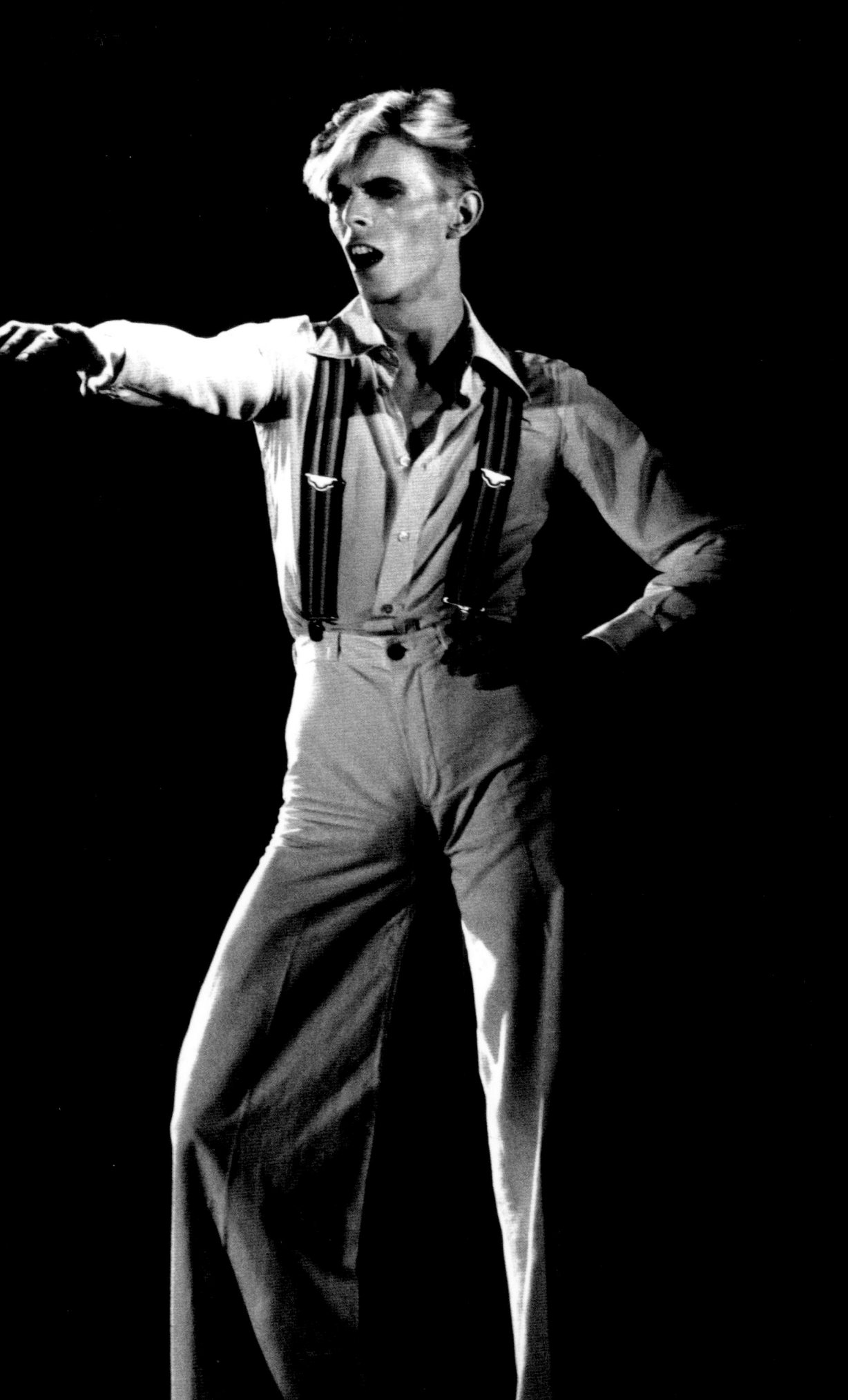

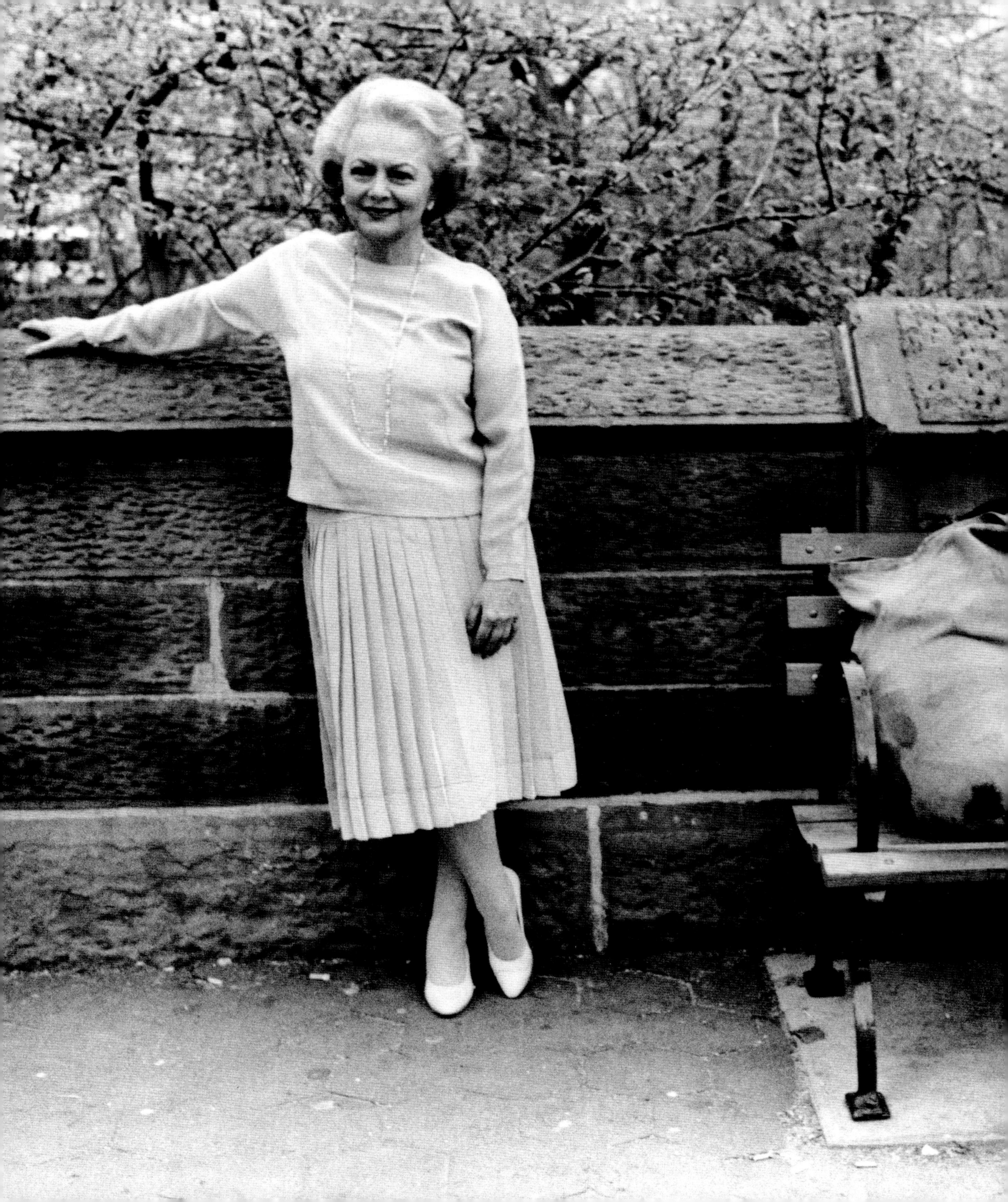

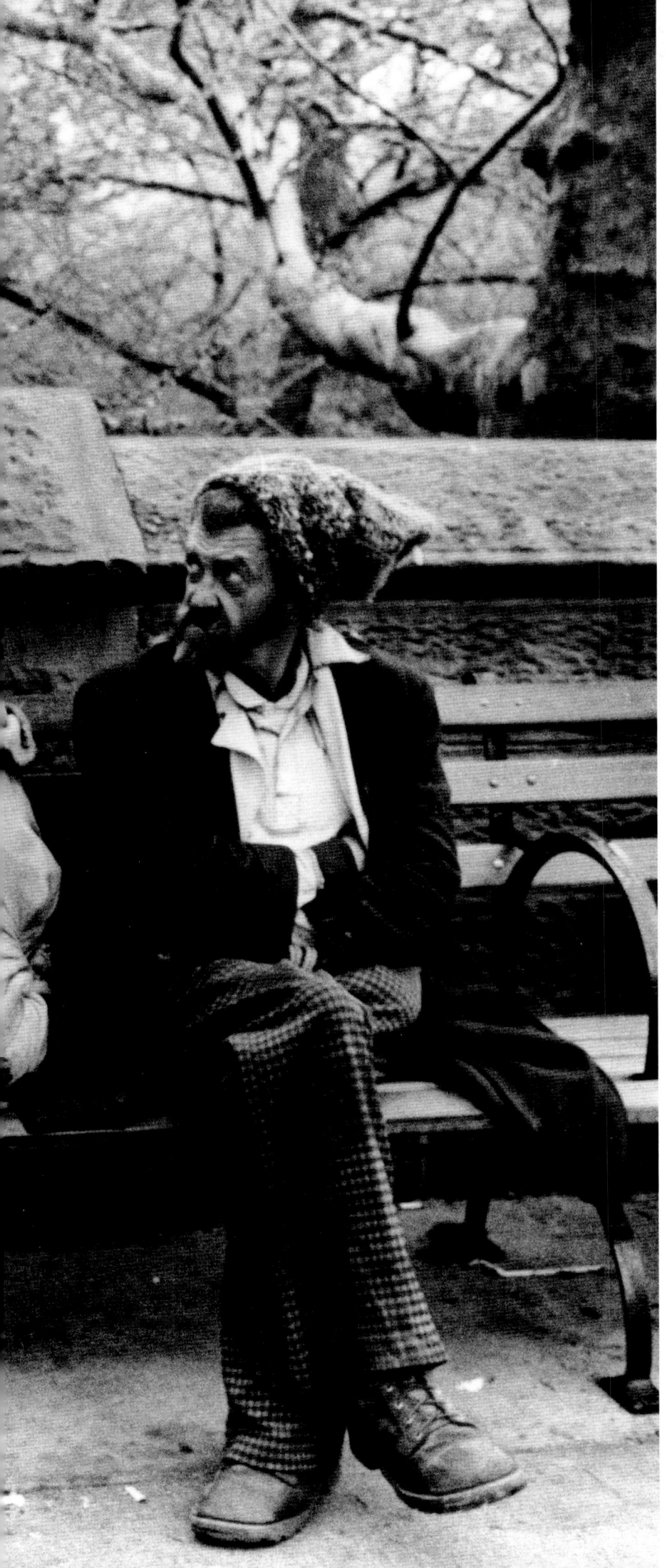

OLIVIA DE HAVILLAND,
CENTRAL PARK, NEW YORK CITY, 1980

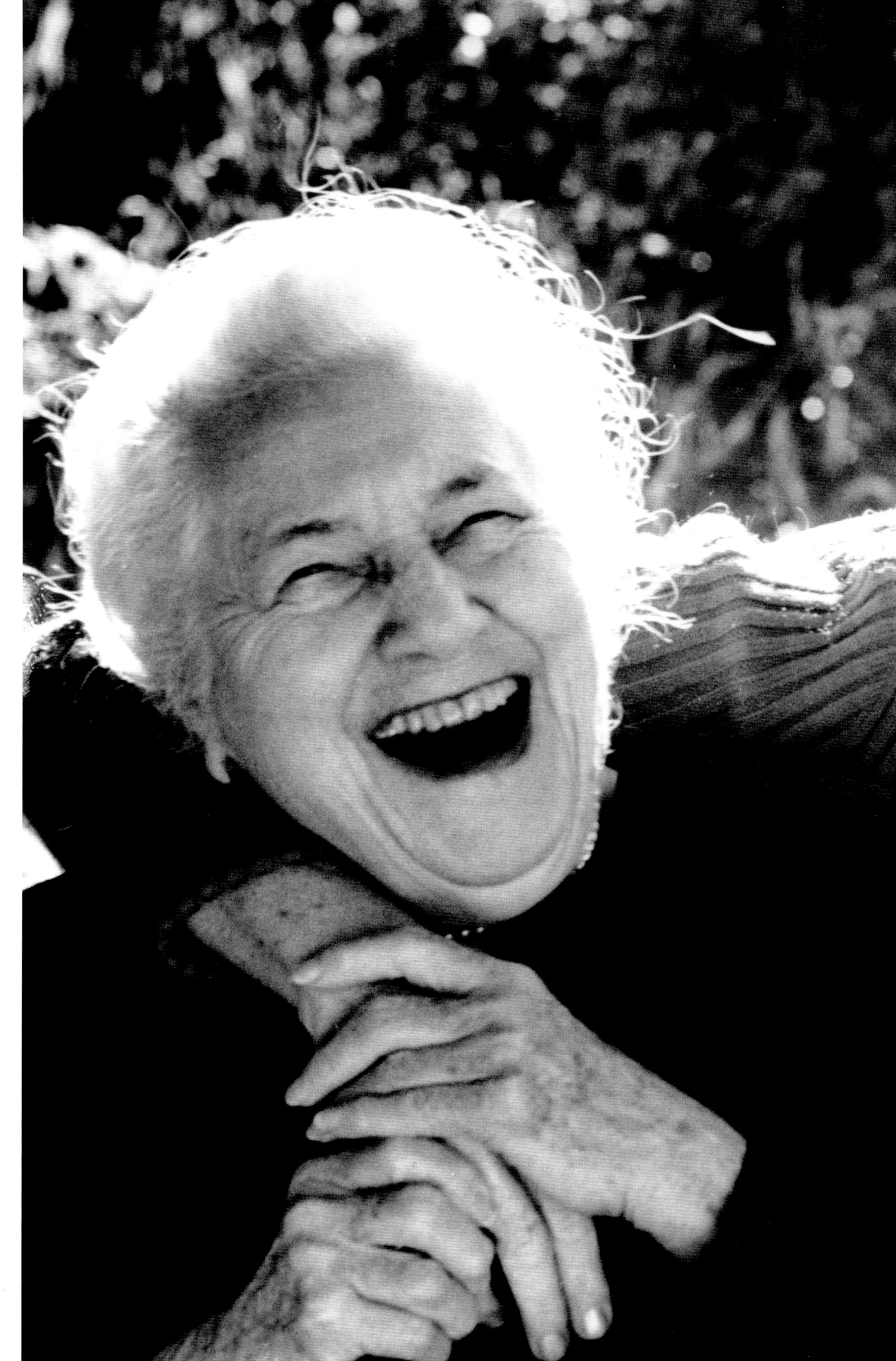

OLIVIA DE HAVILLAND,
HER SISTER,
JOAN FONTAINE,
AND THEIR MOTHER,
LILIAN FONTAINE,
BEVERLY HILLS
HOTEL, 1972

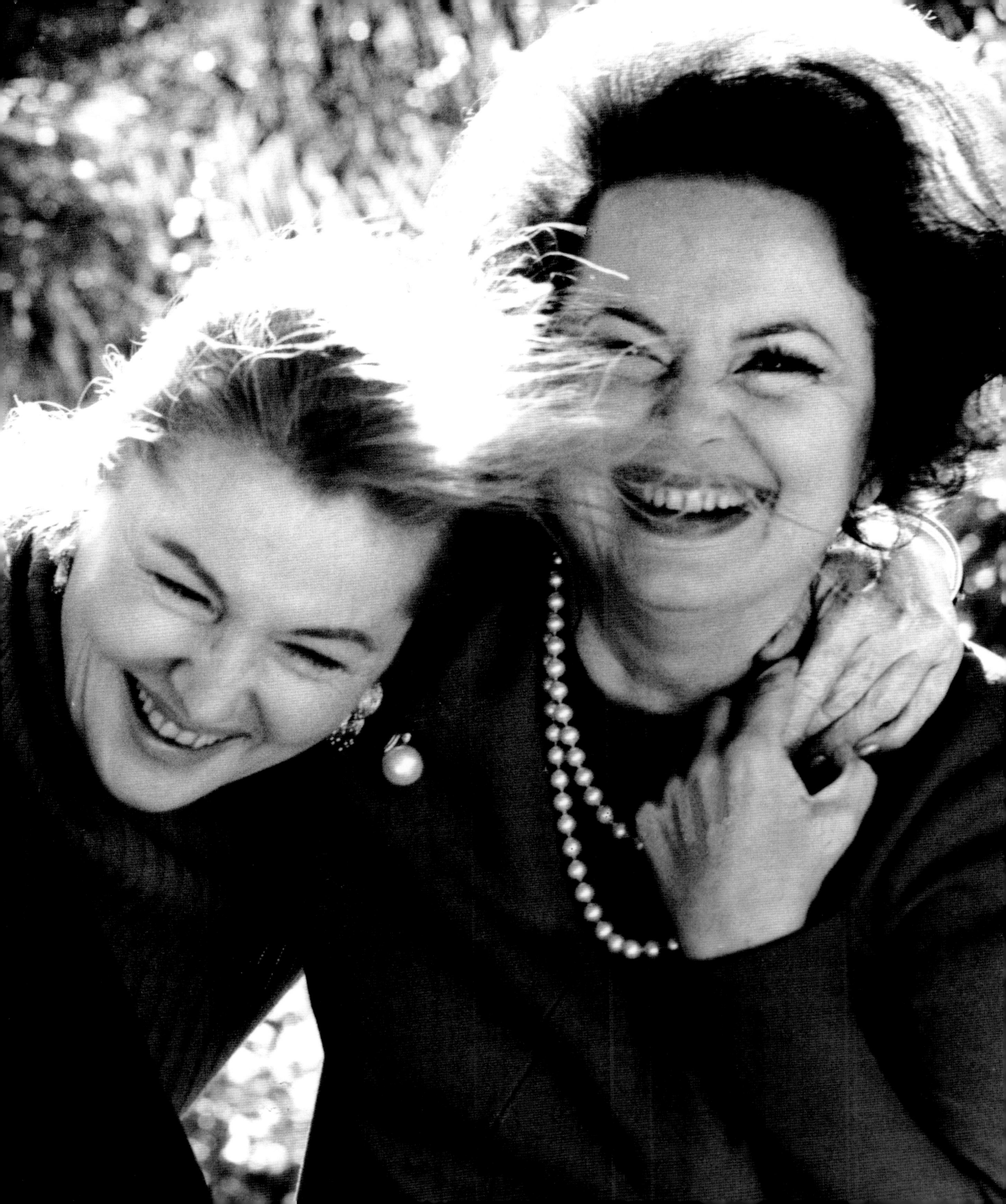

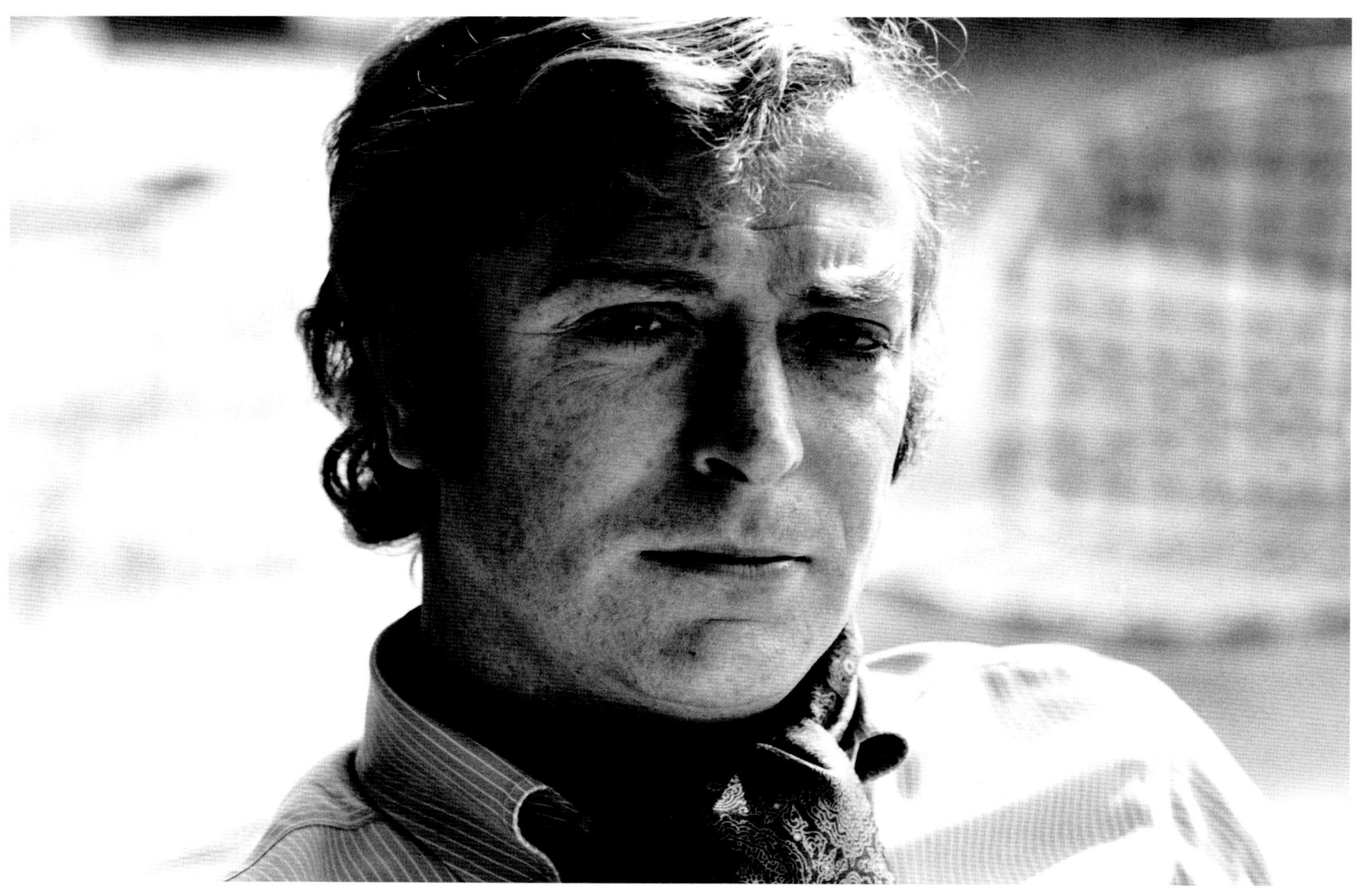

MICHAEL CAINE, BEVERLY HILLS, 1970

OPPOSITE: ANTHONY QUINN, BEL AIR, CALIFORNIA, 1978

OVERLEAF LEFT: SAMMY DAVIS JR., "BOJANGLES," LOS ANGELES, 1970

OVERLEAF RIGHT: LIZA MINNELLI, LAS VEGAS, 1972

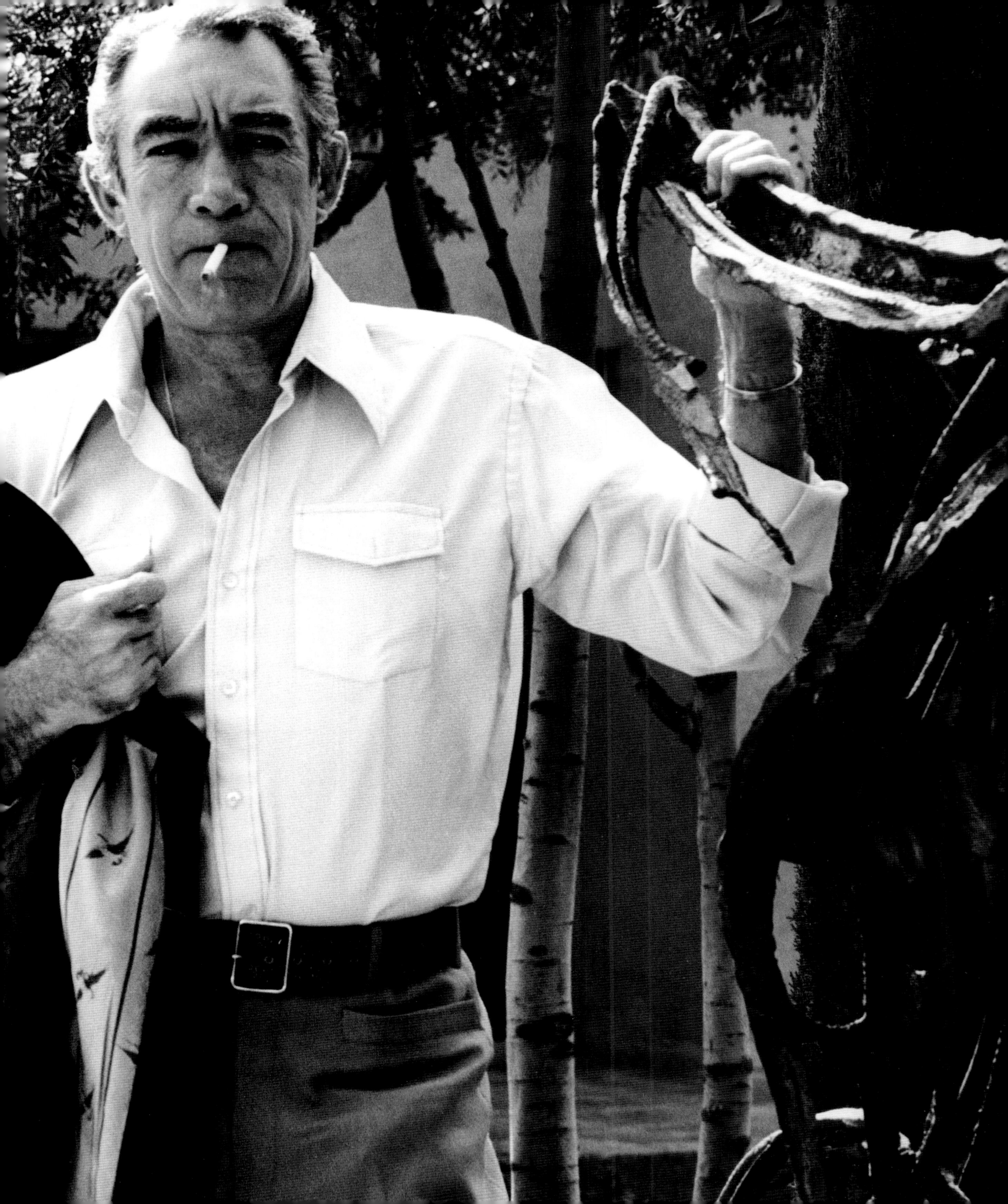

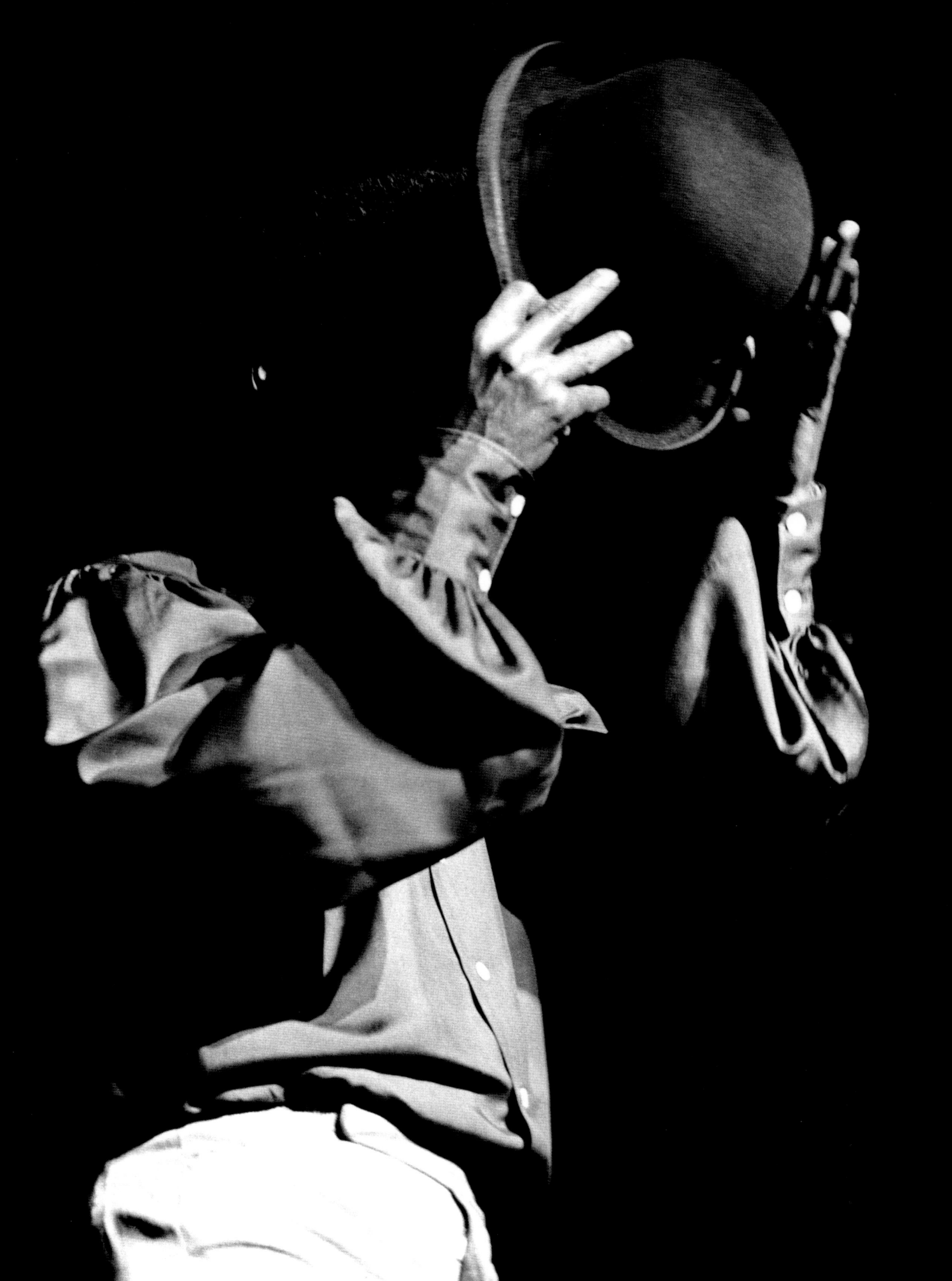

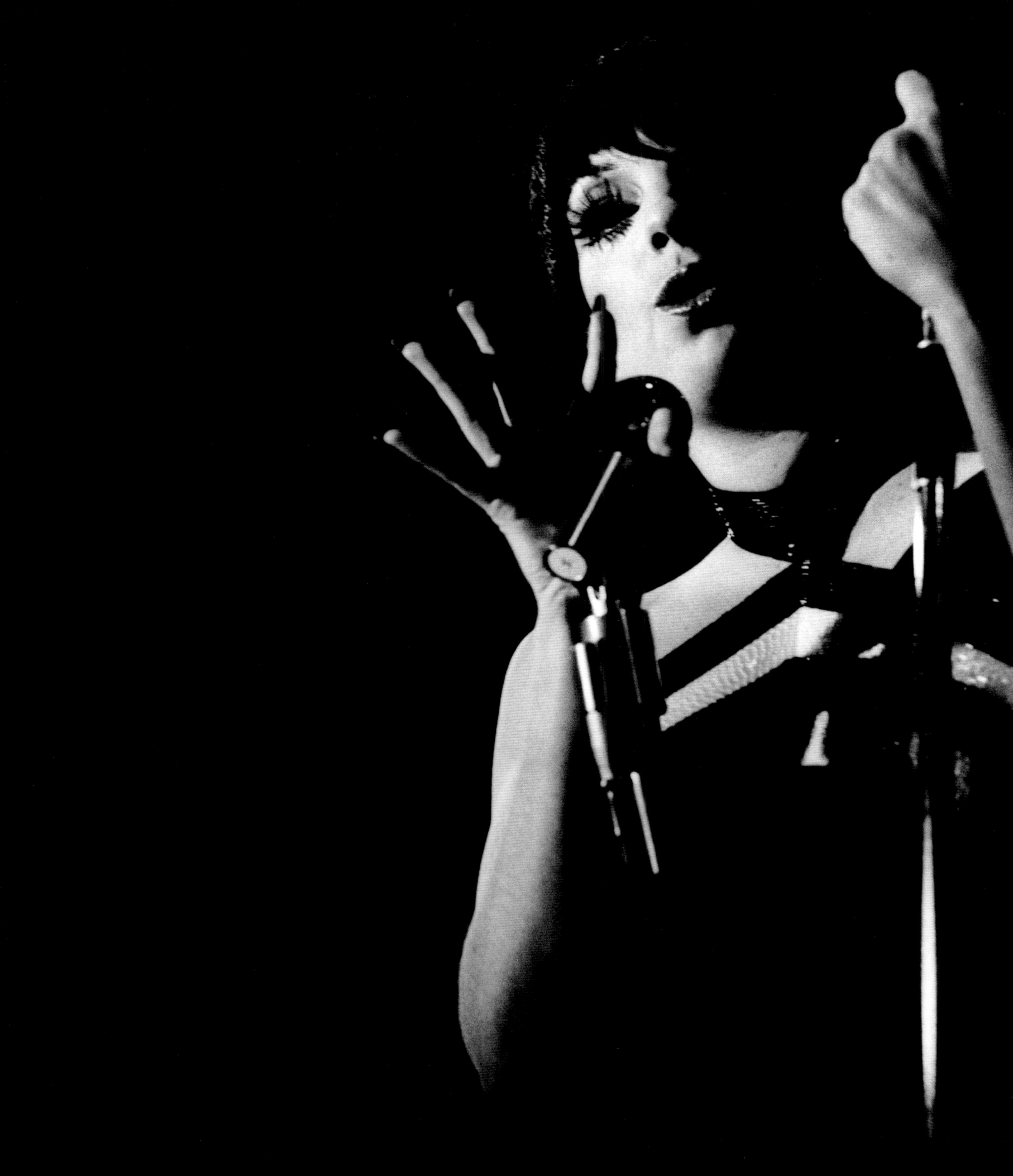

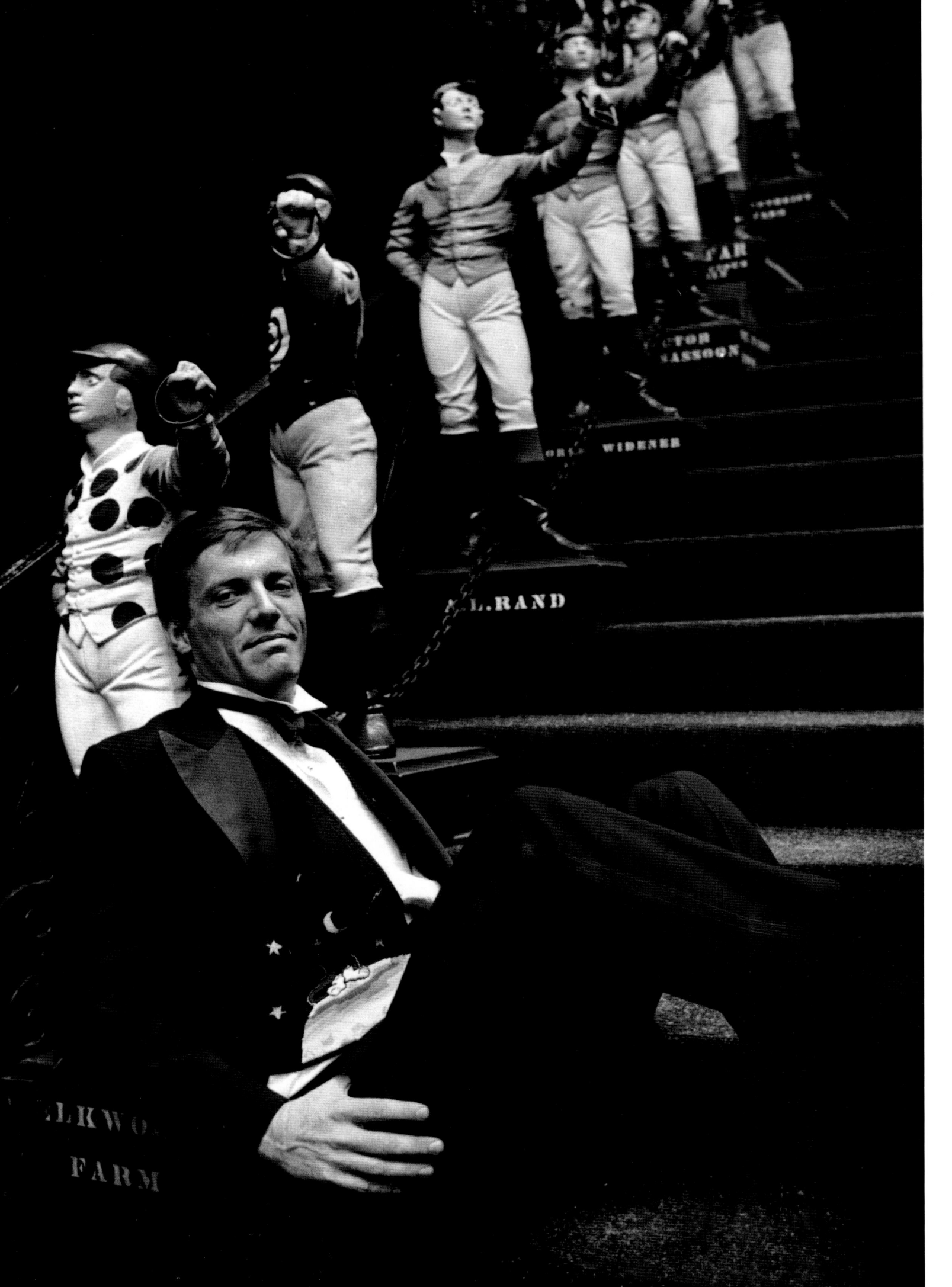

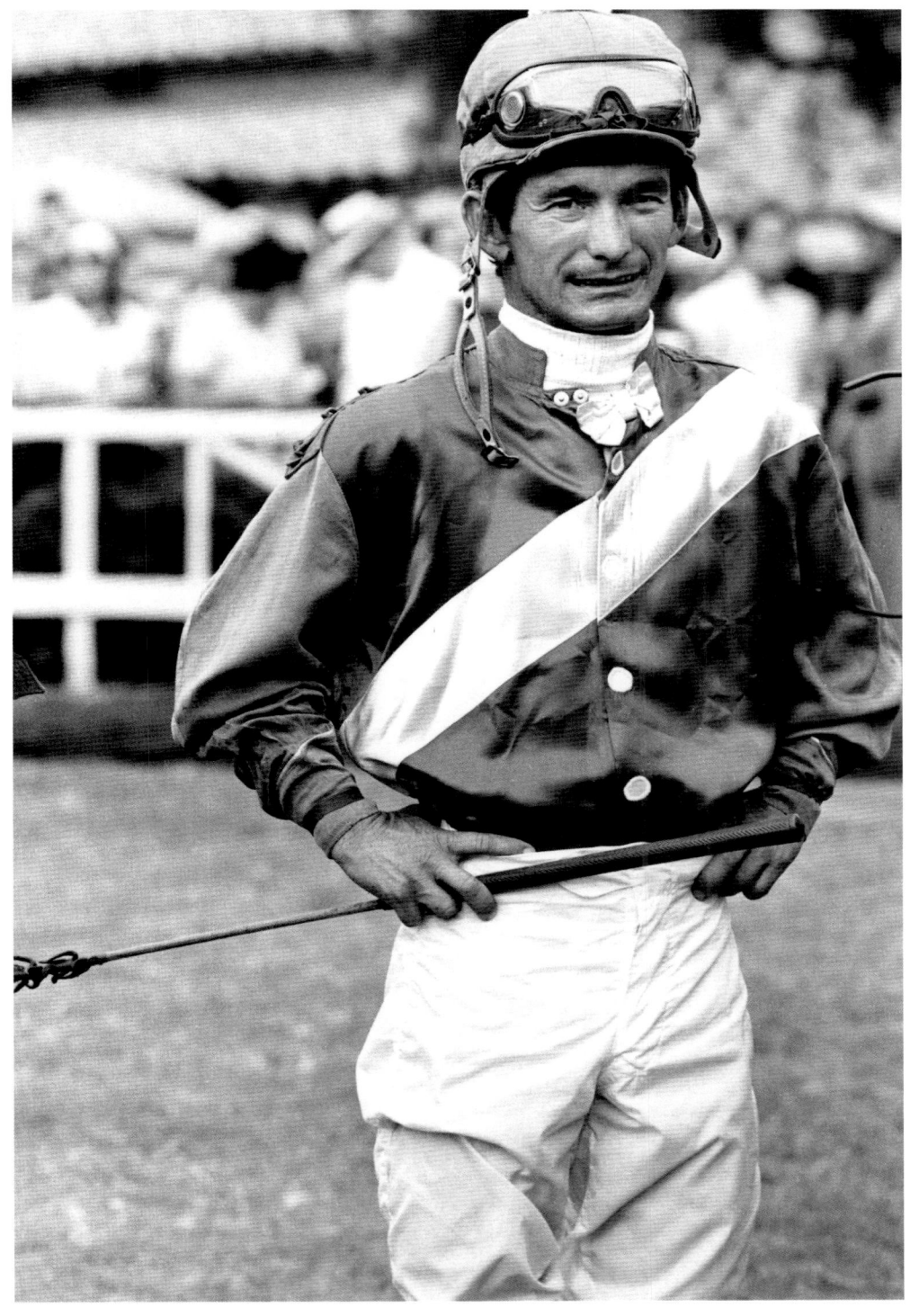

BILL SHOEMAKER, DEL MAR RACETRACK, LOS ANGELES, 1970

OPPOSITE: WILLIAM PITT II, 21 CLUB, NEW YORK CITY, 1983

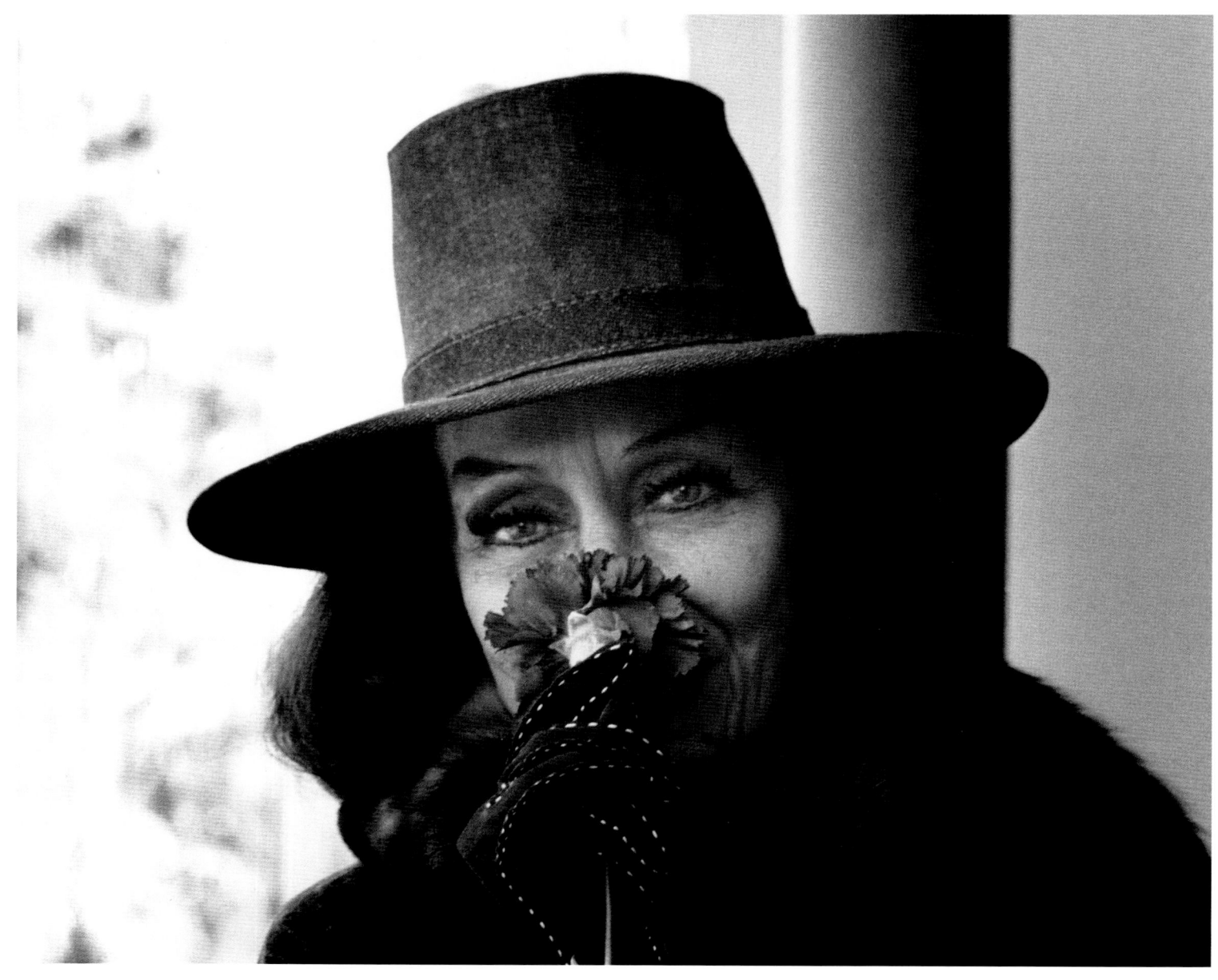

GLORIA SWANSON, BEVERLY HILLS, 1975

OPPOSITE: PRINCE PHILIP, BUDAPEST, HUNGARY, 1984

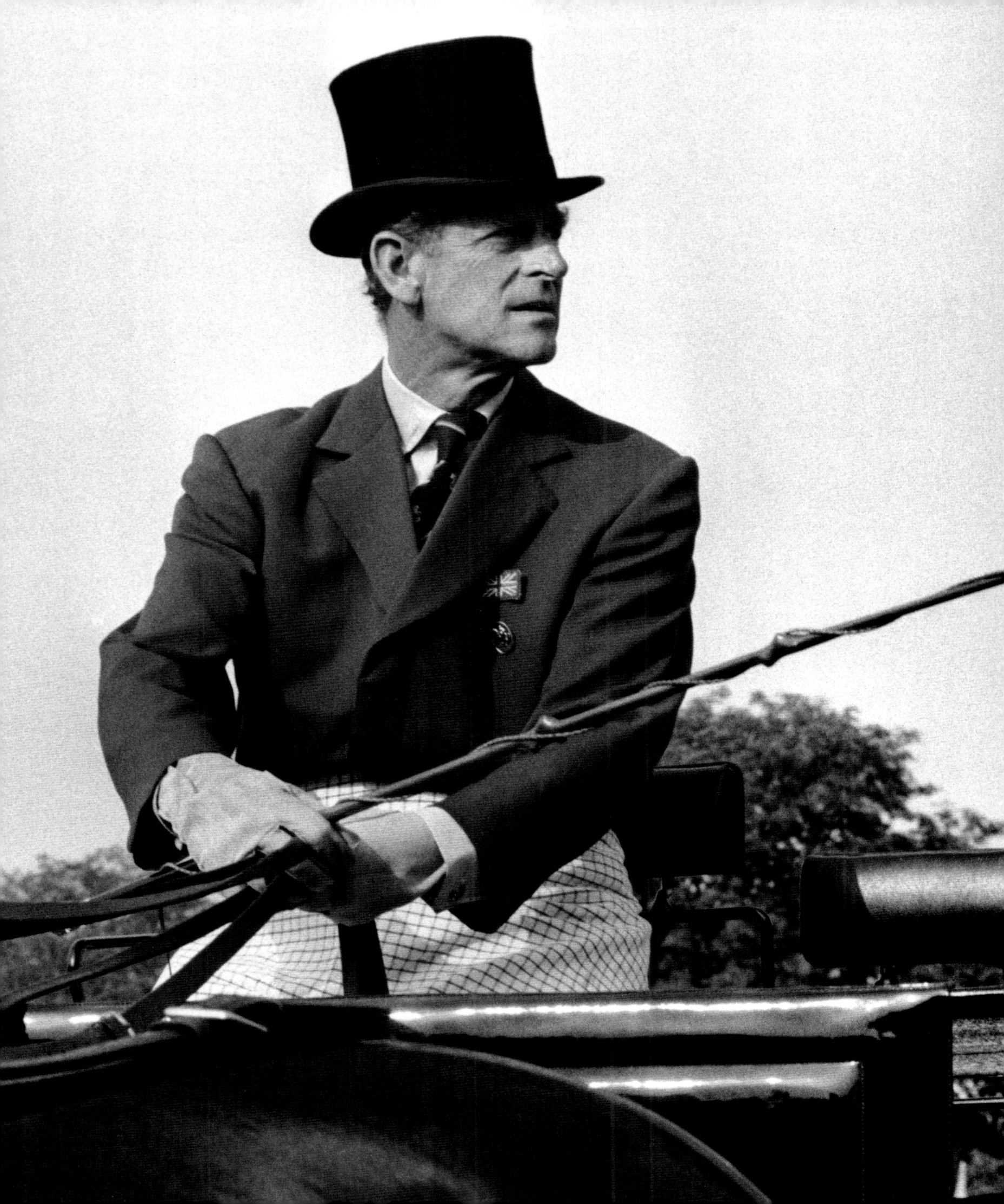

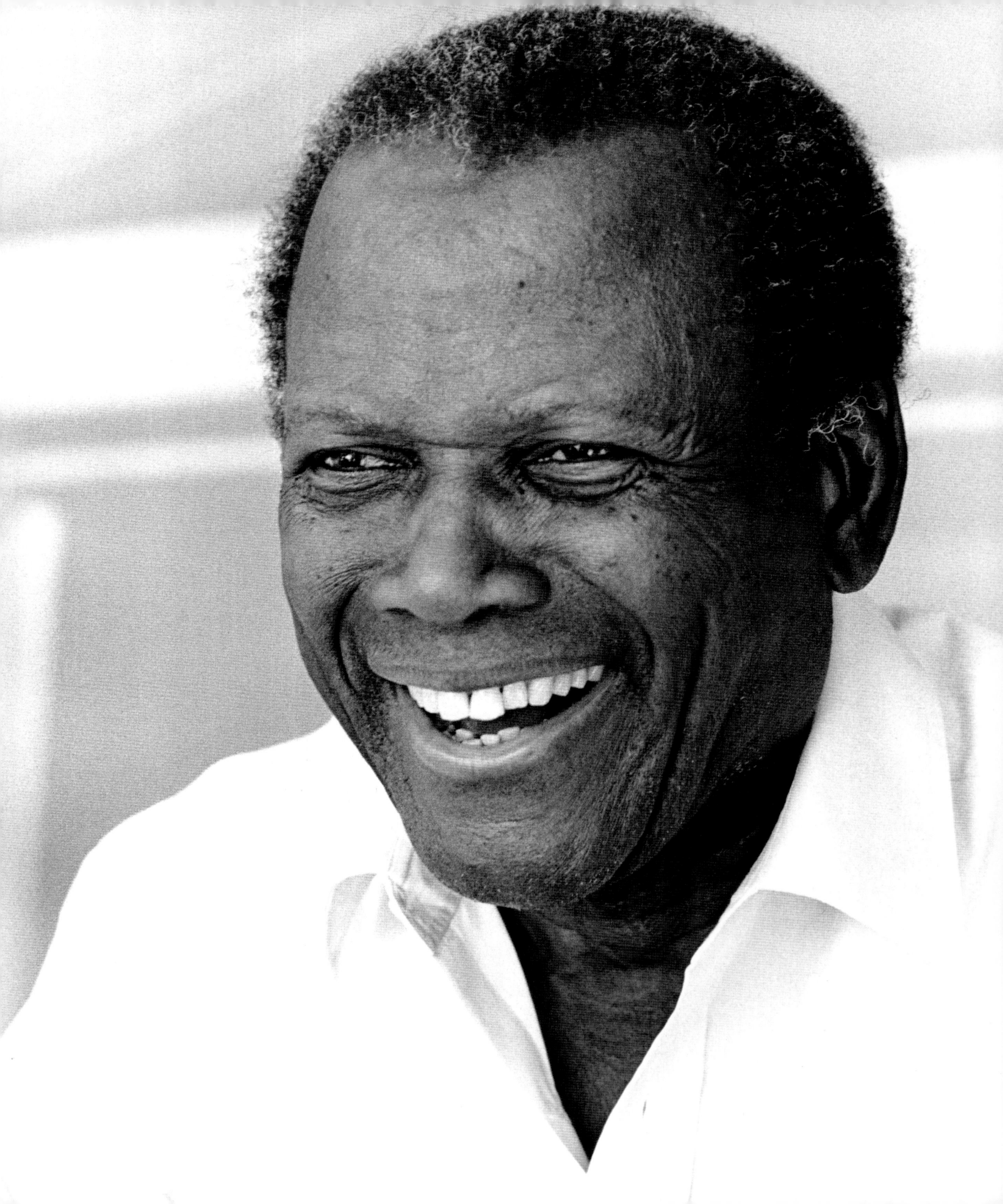

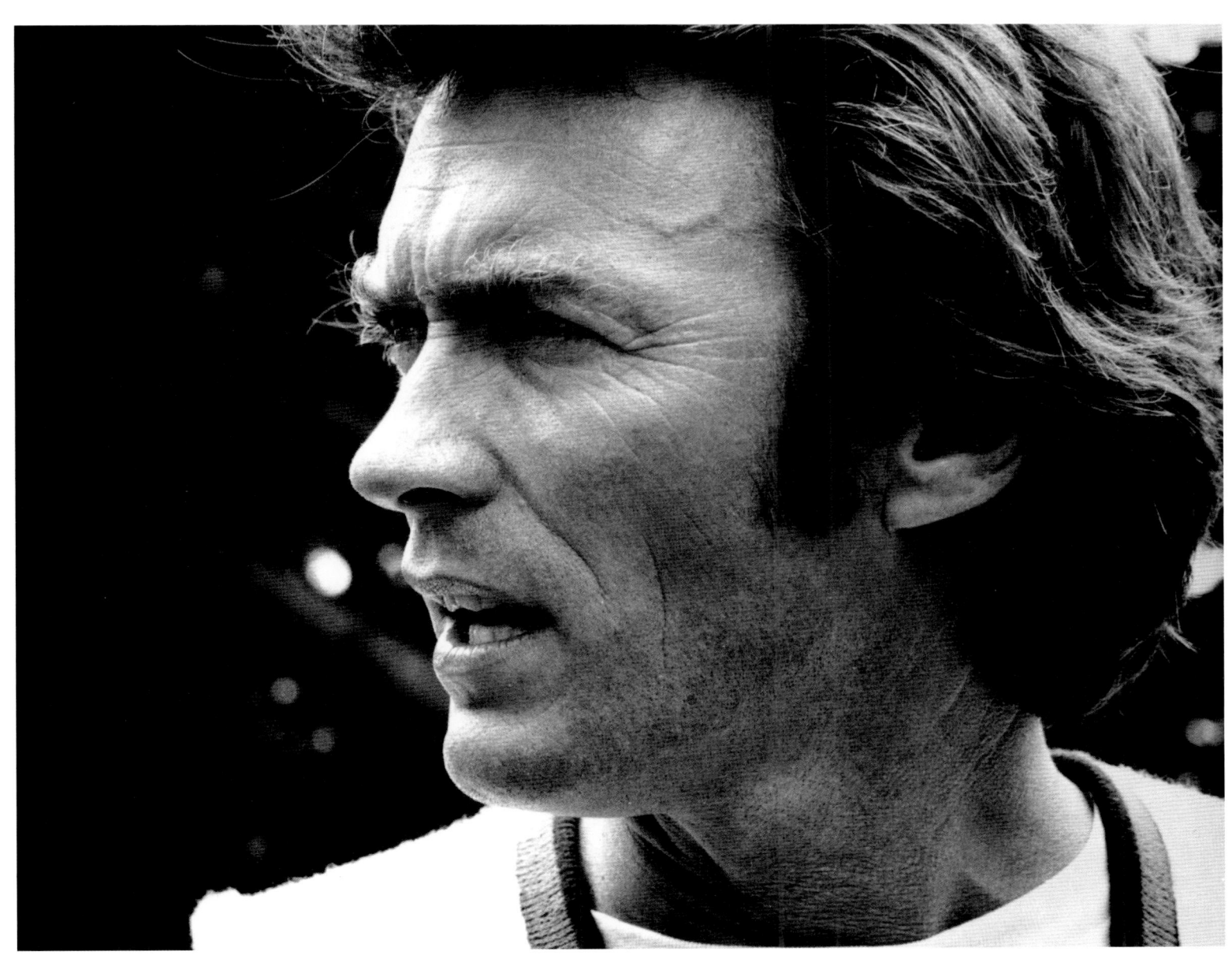

CLINT EASTWOOD, PEBBLE BEACH, CALIFORNIA, 1971

OPPOSITE: SIDNEY POITIER, HÔTEL DU CAP, CAP D'ANTIBES, FRANCE, 2001

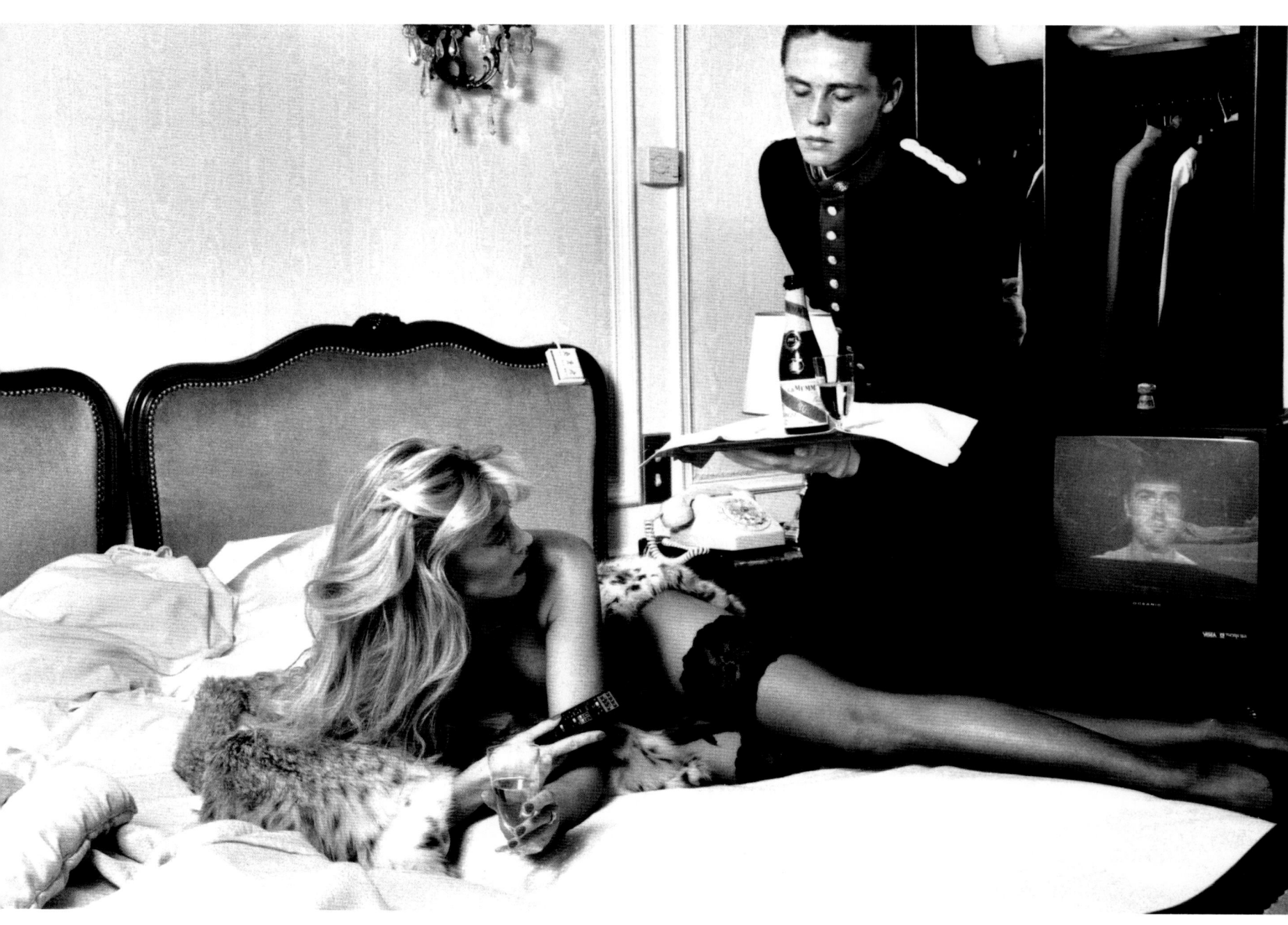

ISABEL KARA, DUCHESS OF SEVILLA, HÔTEL PLAZA ATHÉNÉE, PARIS, 1990

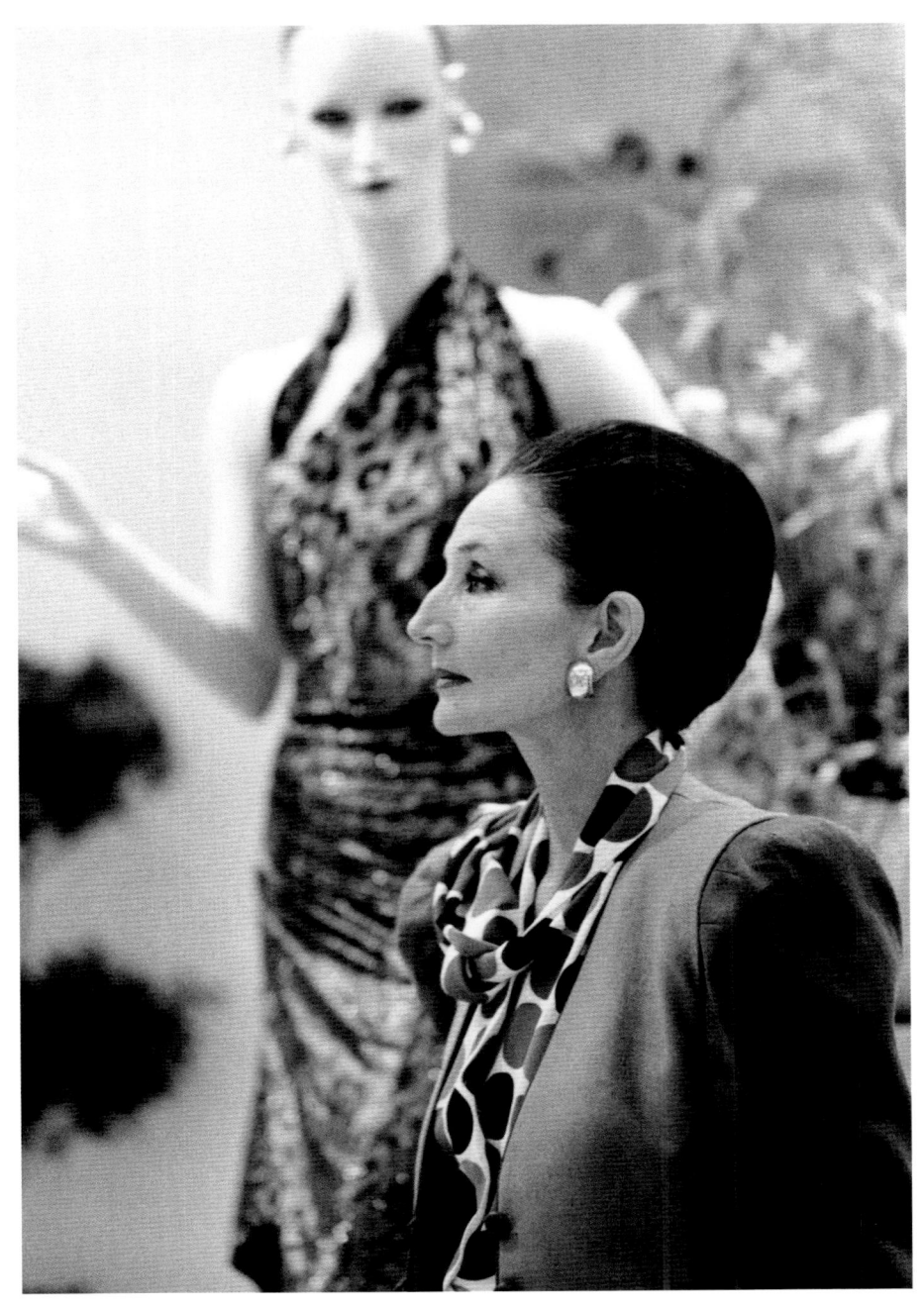

VISCOUNTESS JACQUELINE DE RIBES, BEVERLY HILLS, 1983

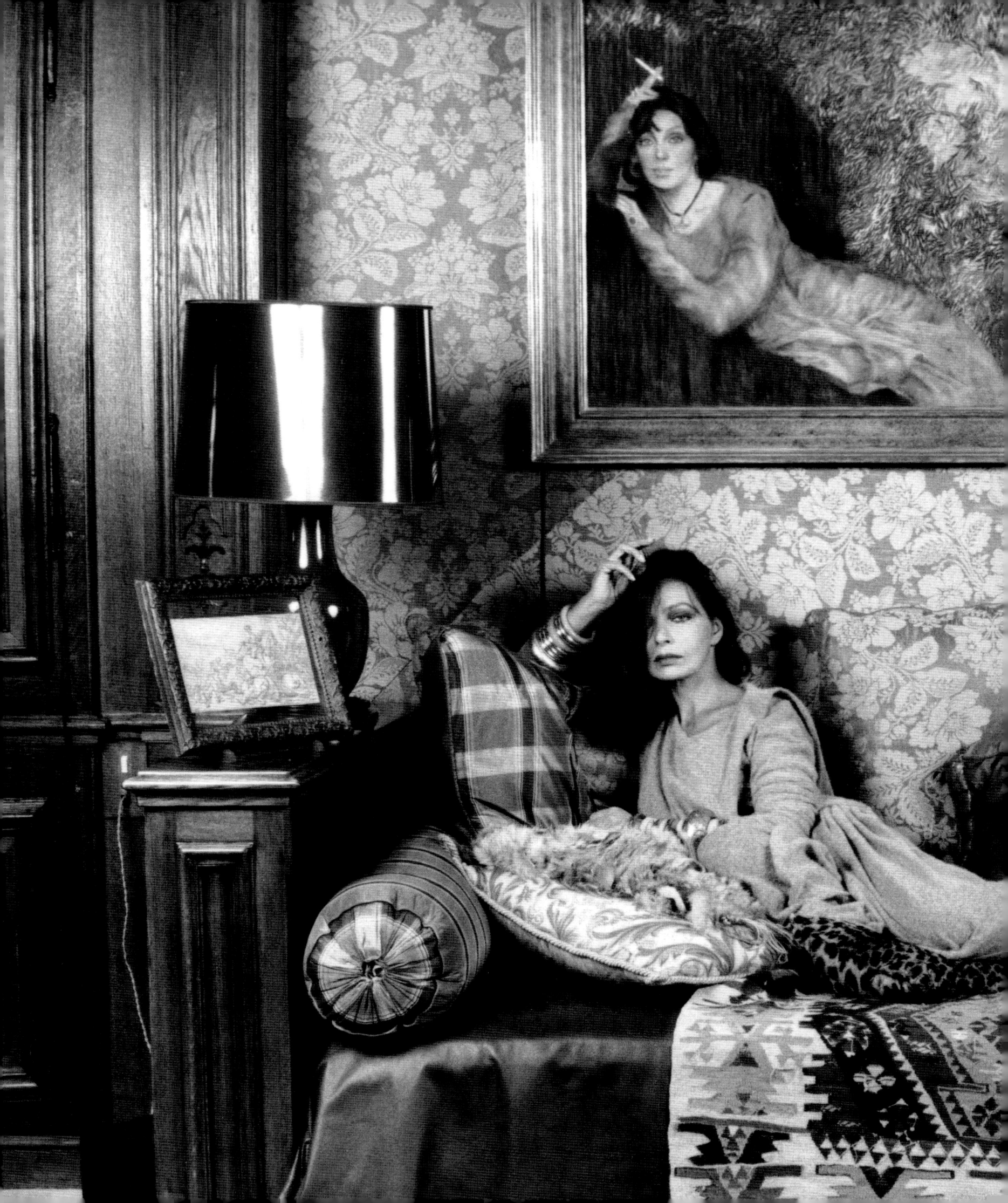

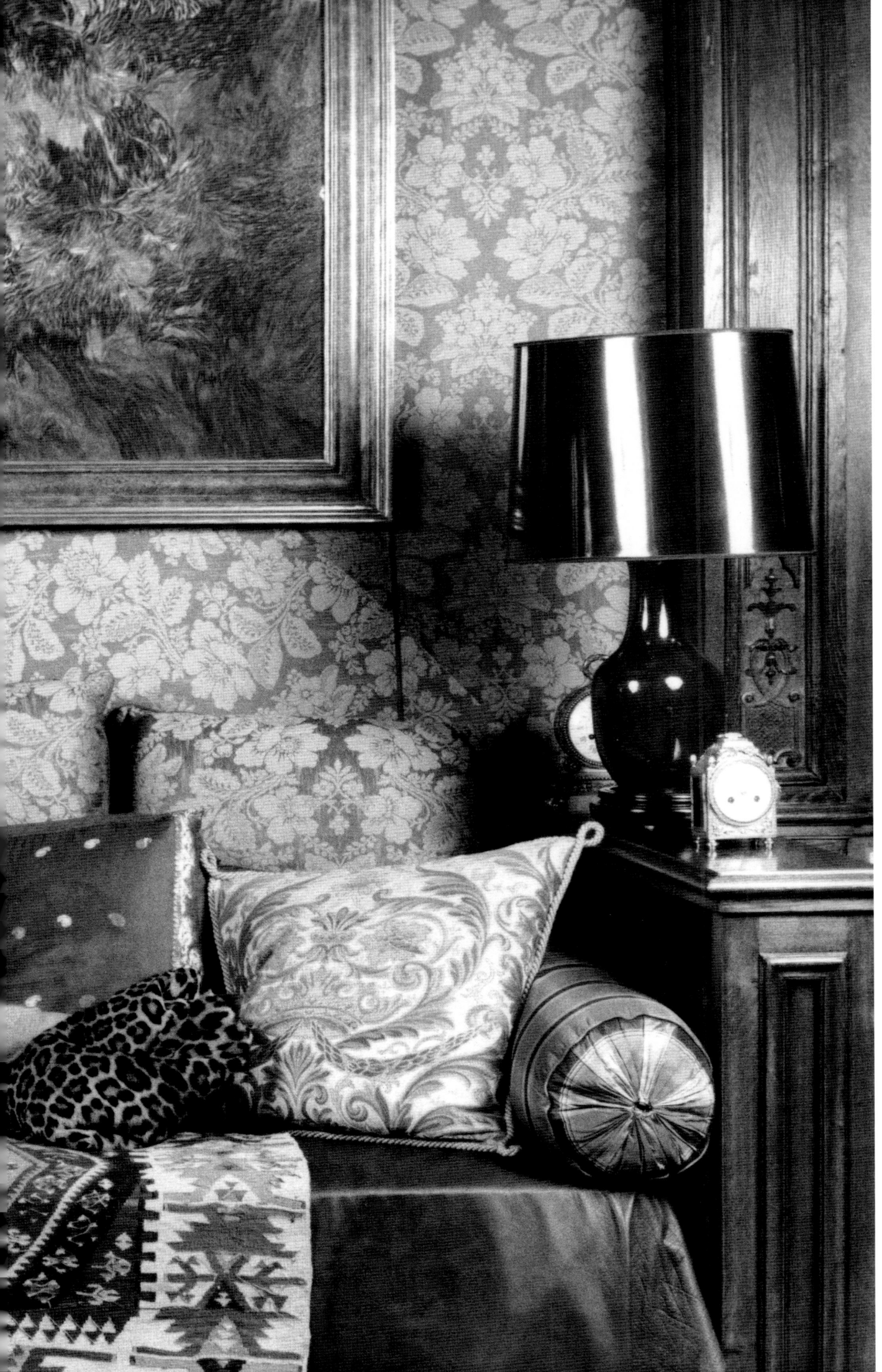

MARIE LAFORÊT AT
HOME, PARIS, 1989

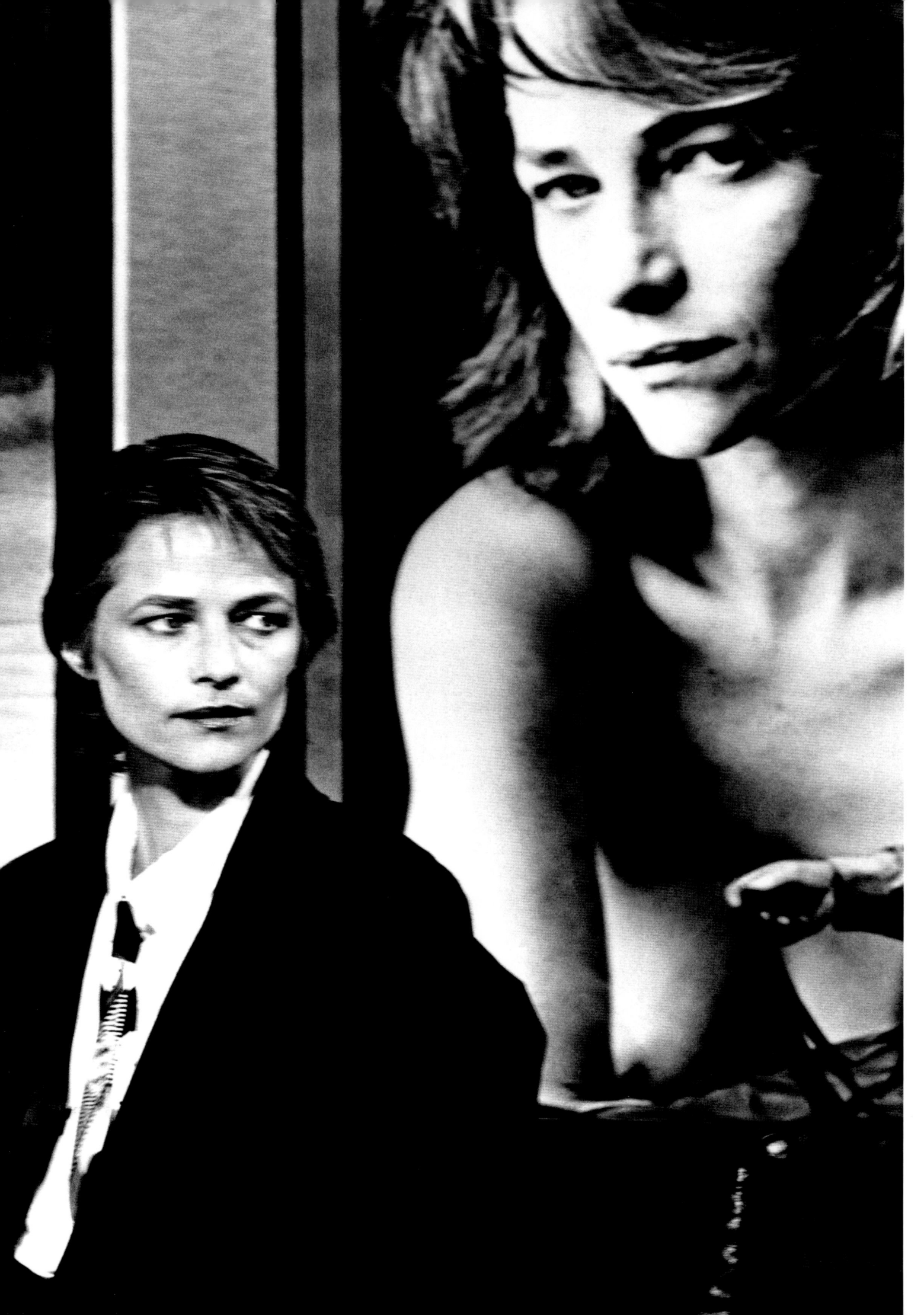

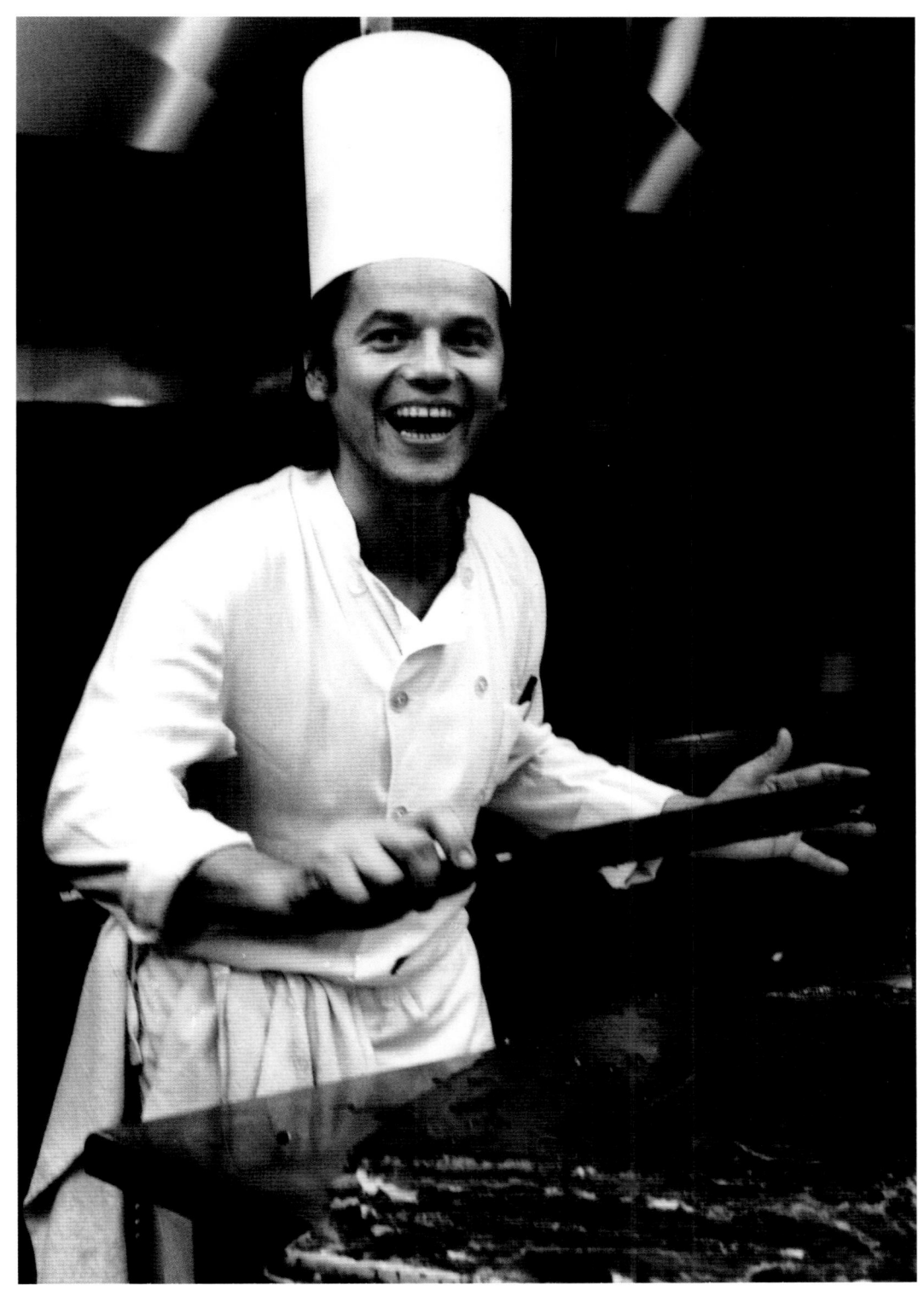

WOLFGANG PUCK, MA MAISON, LOS ANGELES, 1978

OPPOSITE: CHARLOTTE RAMPLING, PARIS, 1985

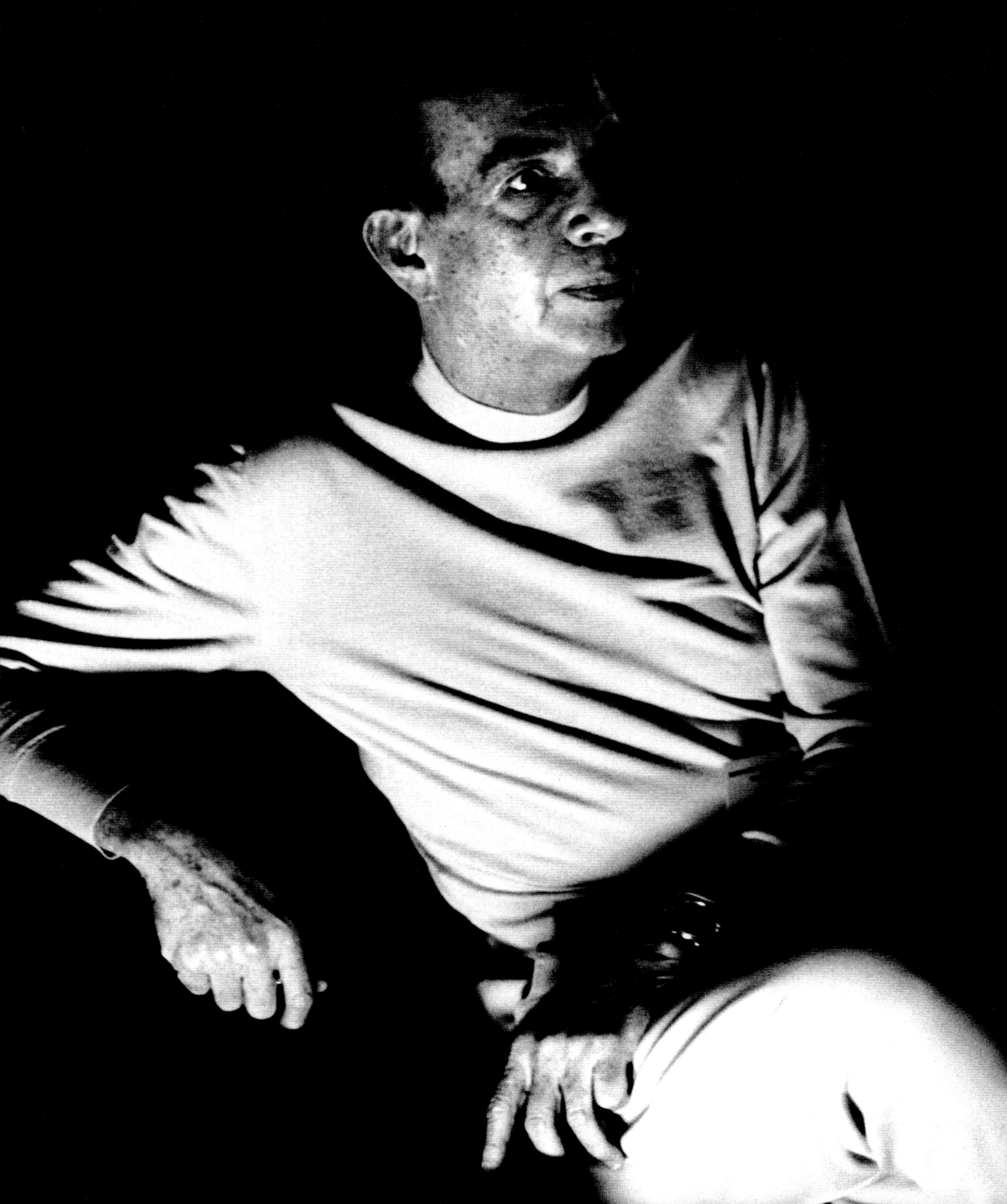

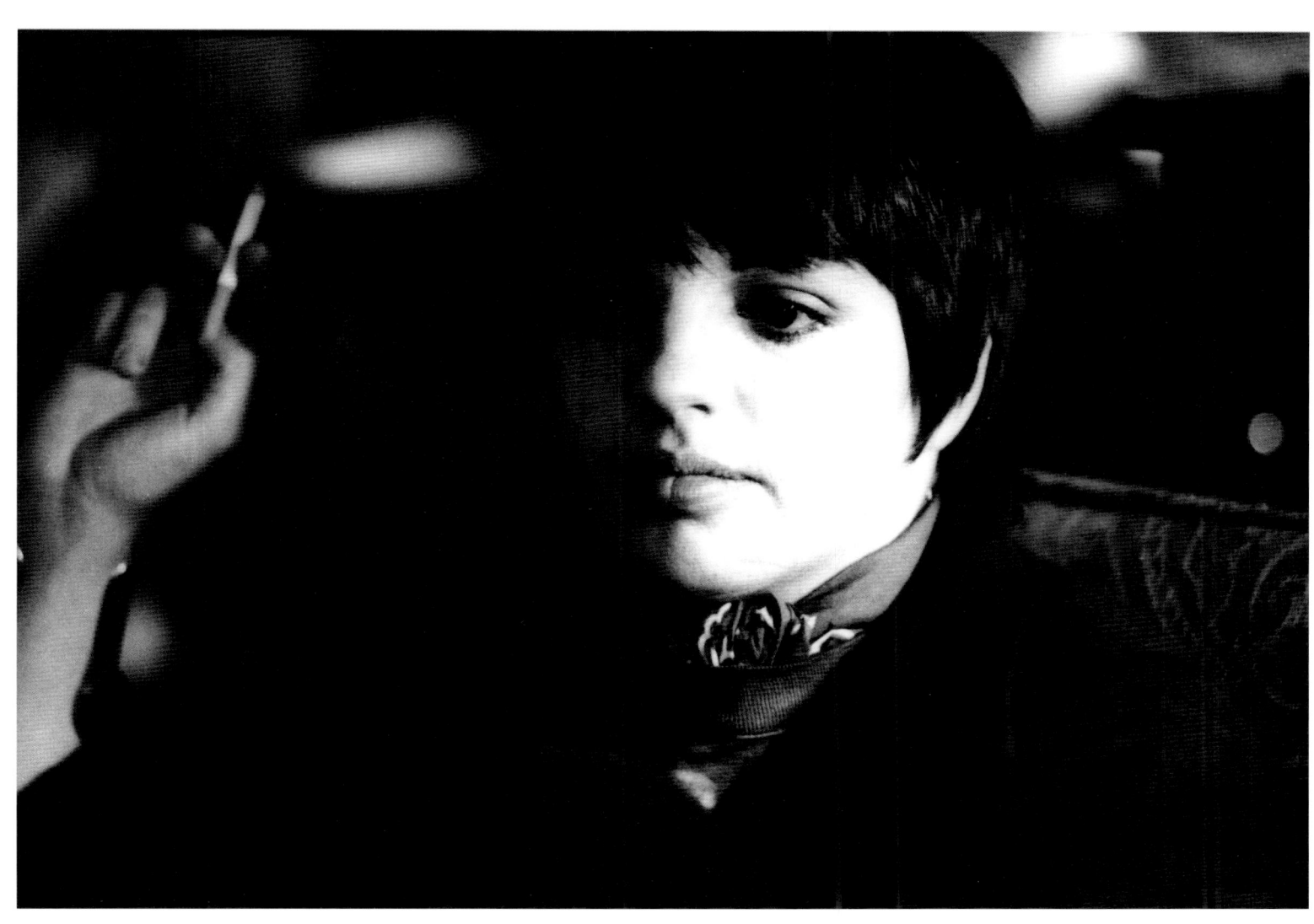

LIZA MINNELLI, BEVERLY HILLS, 1974

OPPOSITE: VINCENTE MINNELLI, LOS ANGELES, 1975

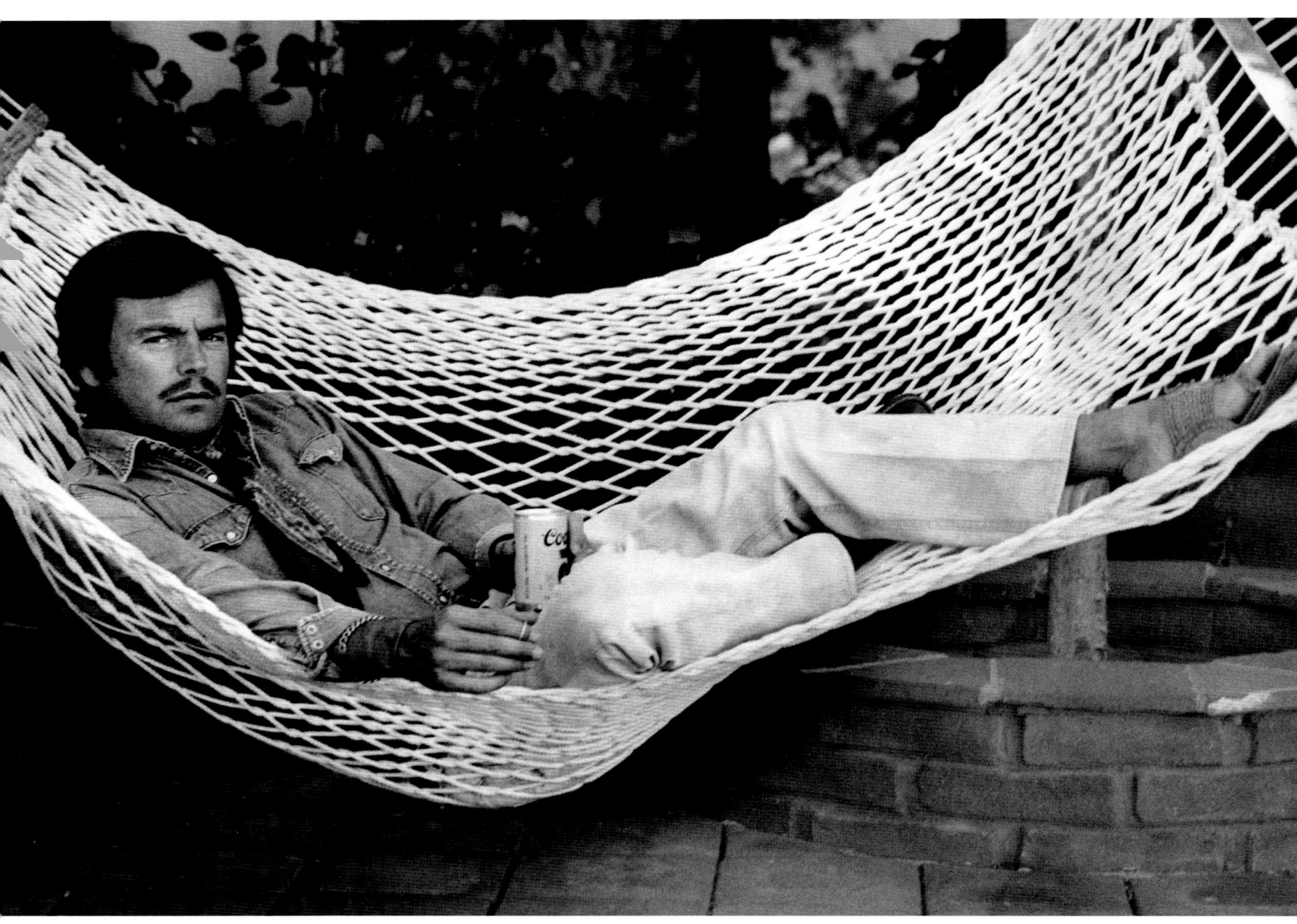

ROBERT WAGNER, PALM SPRINGS, 1973

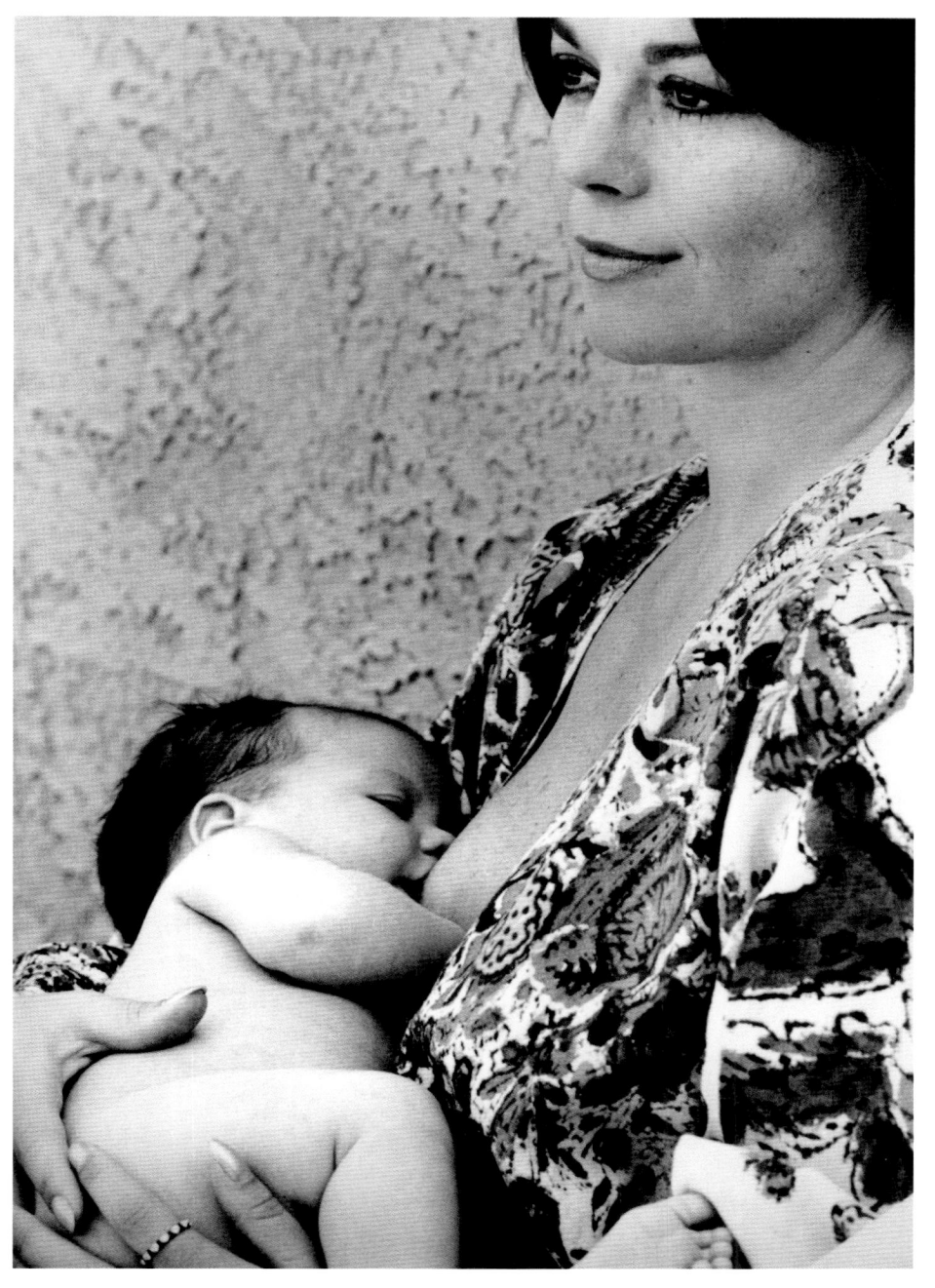
NATALIE WOOD WITH COURTNEY WAGNER, PALM SPRINGS, 1973

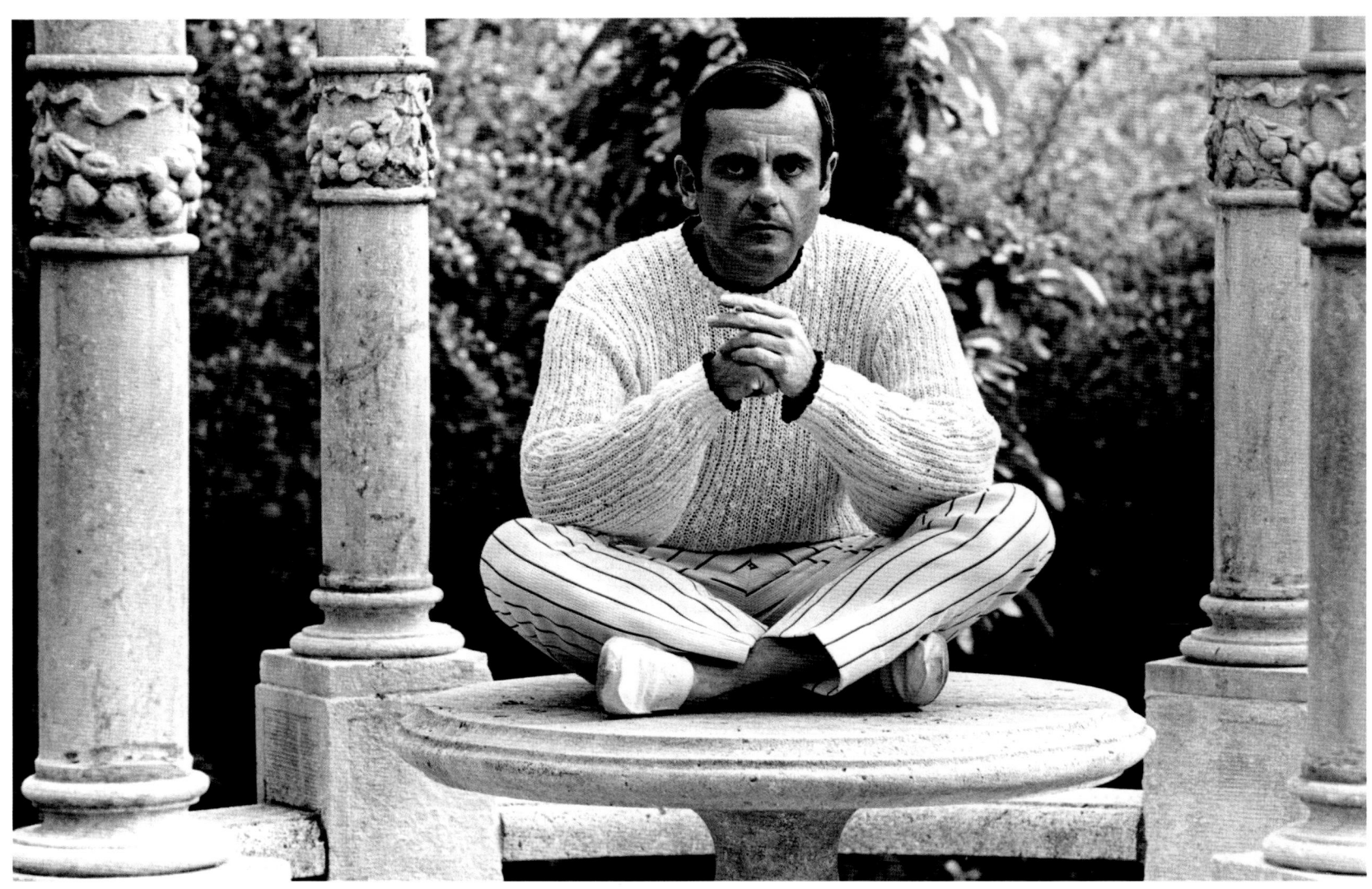

DOMINICK DUNNE, BEVERLY HILLS, 1967

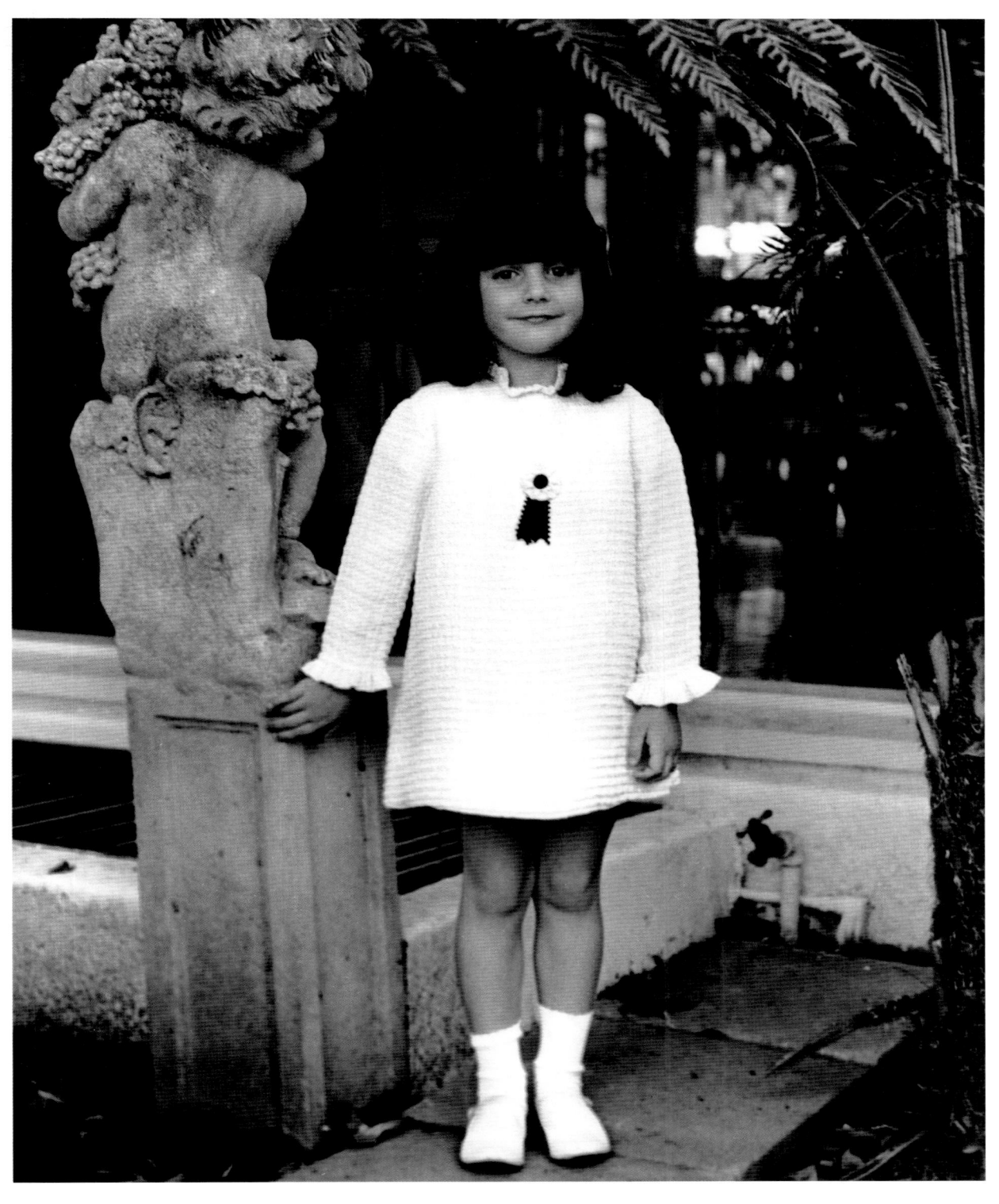

DOMINIQUE DUNNE, BEVERLY HILLS, 1965

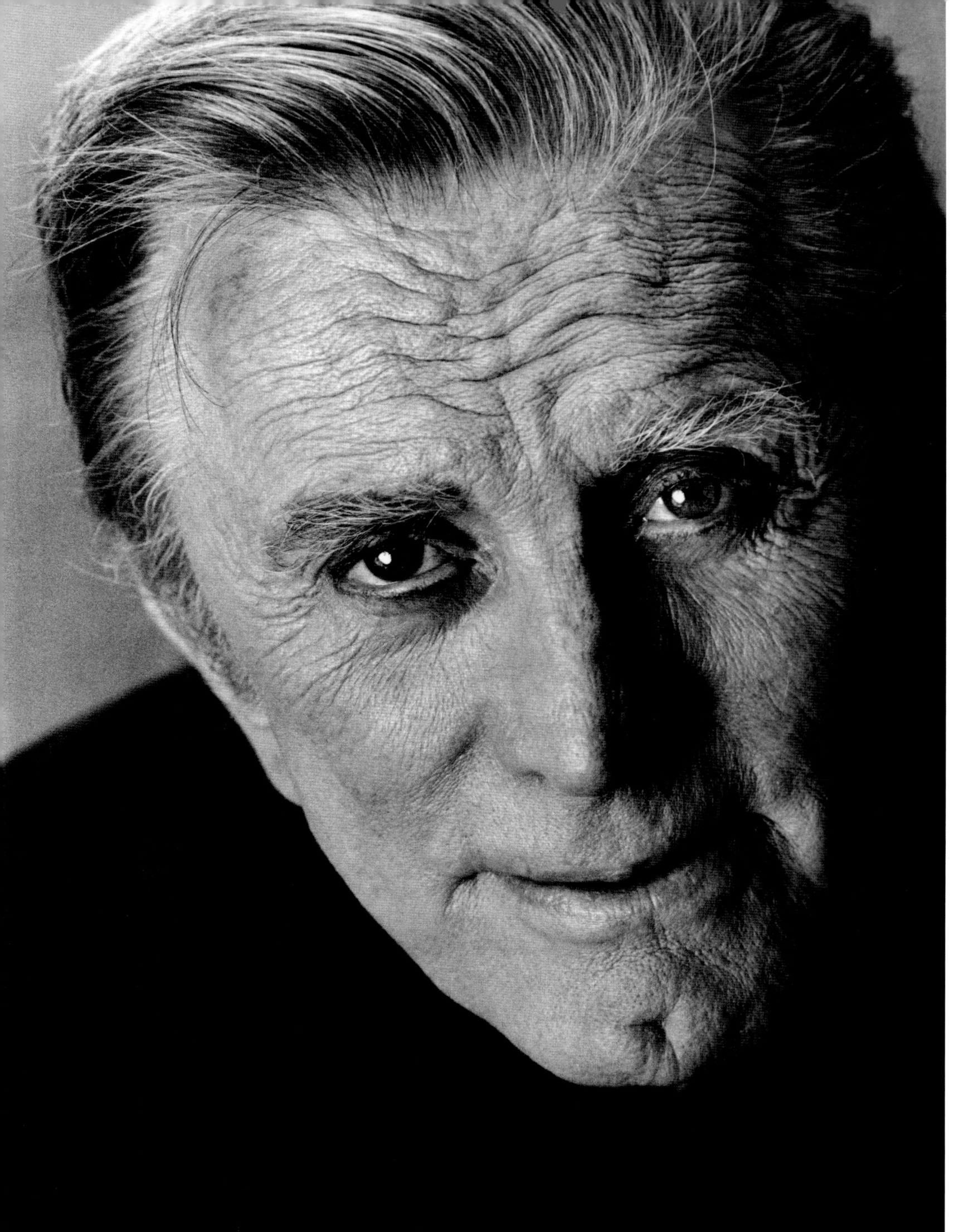

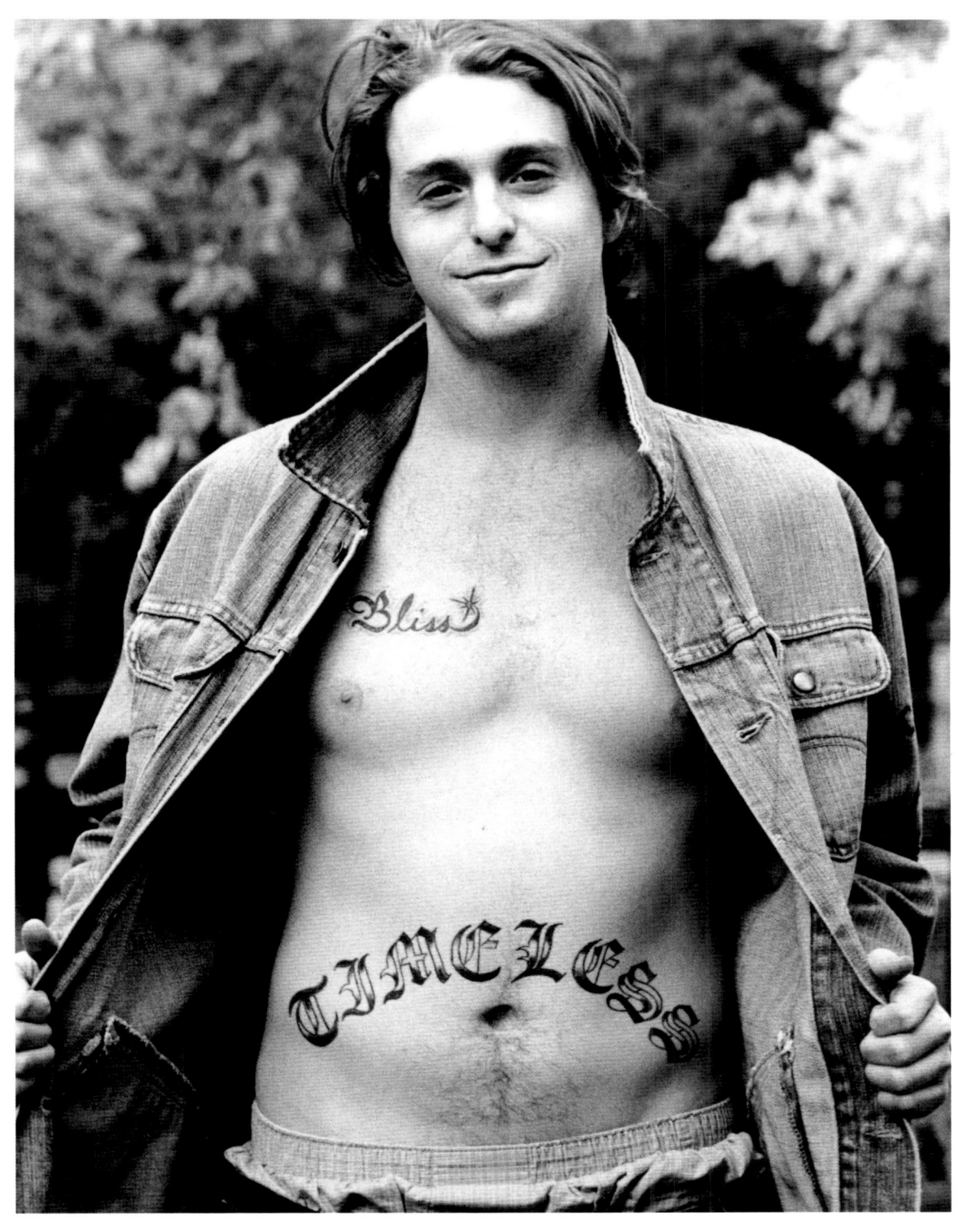

CAMERON DOUGLAS, CENTRAL PARK, NEW YORK CITY, 2002

OPPOSITE: KIRK DOUGLAS, BEVERLY HILLS, 1990

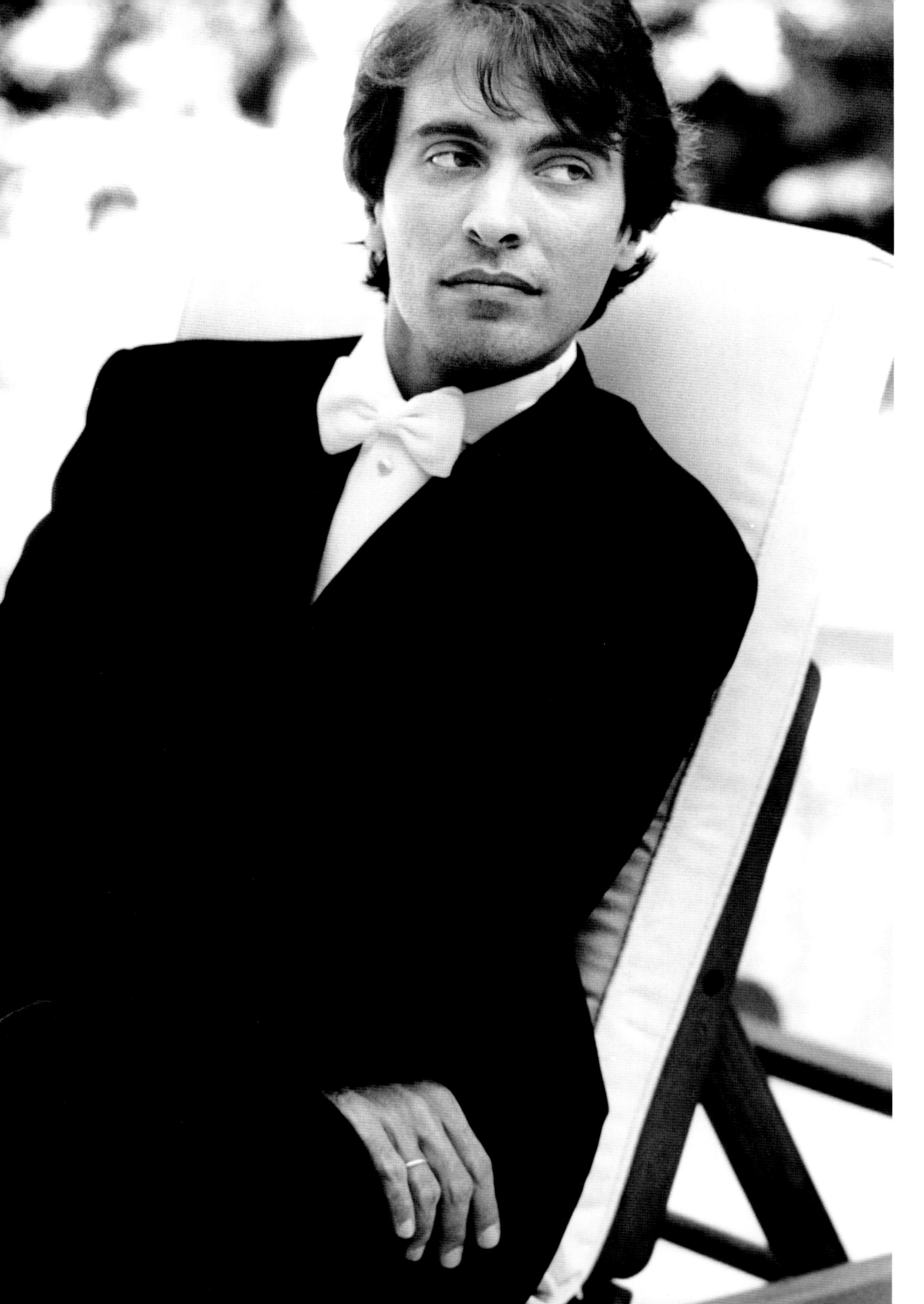

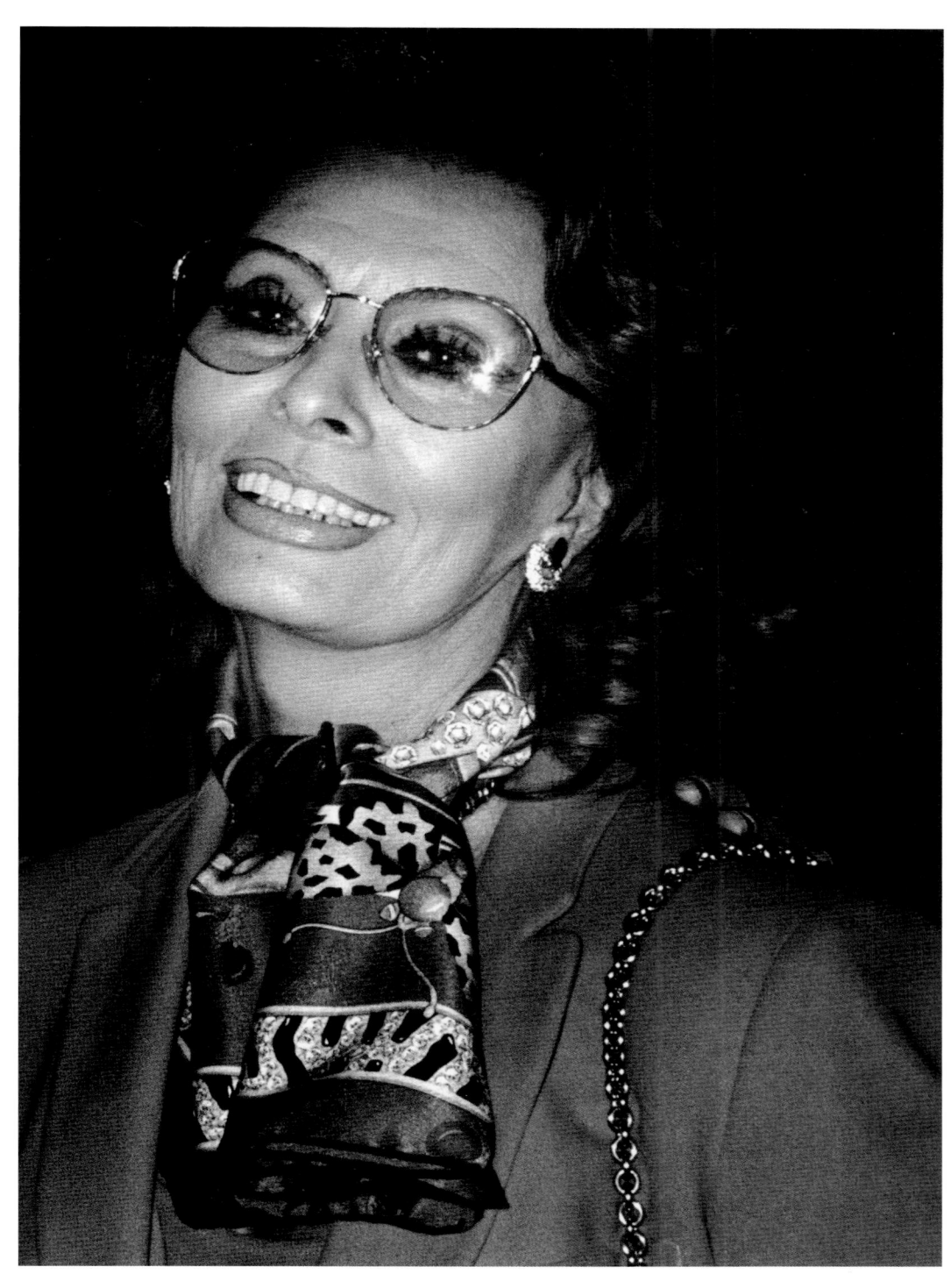

SOPHIA LOREN, MOTHER OF CARLO PONTI JR., NEW YORK CITY, 2000

OPPOSITE: CARLO PONTI JR., BEVERLY HILLS, 2001

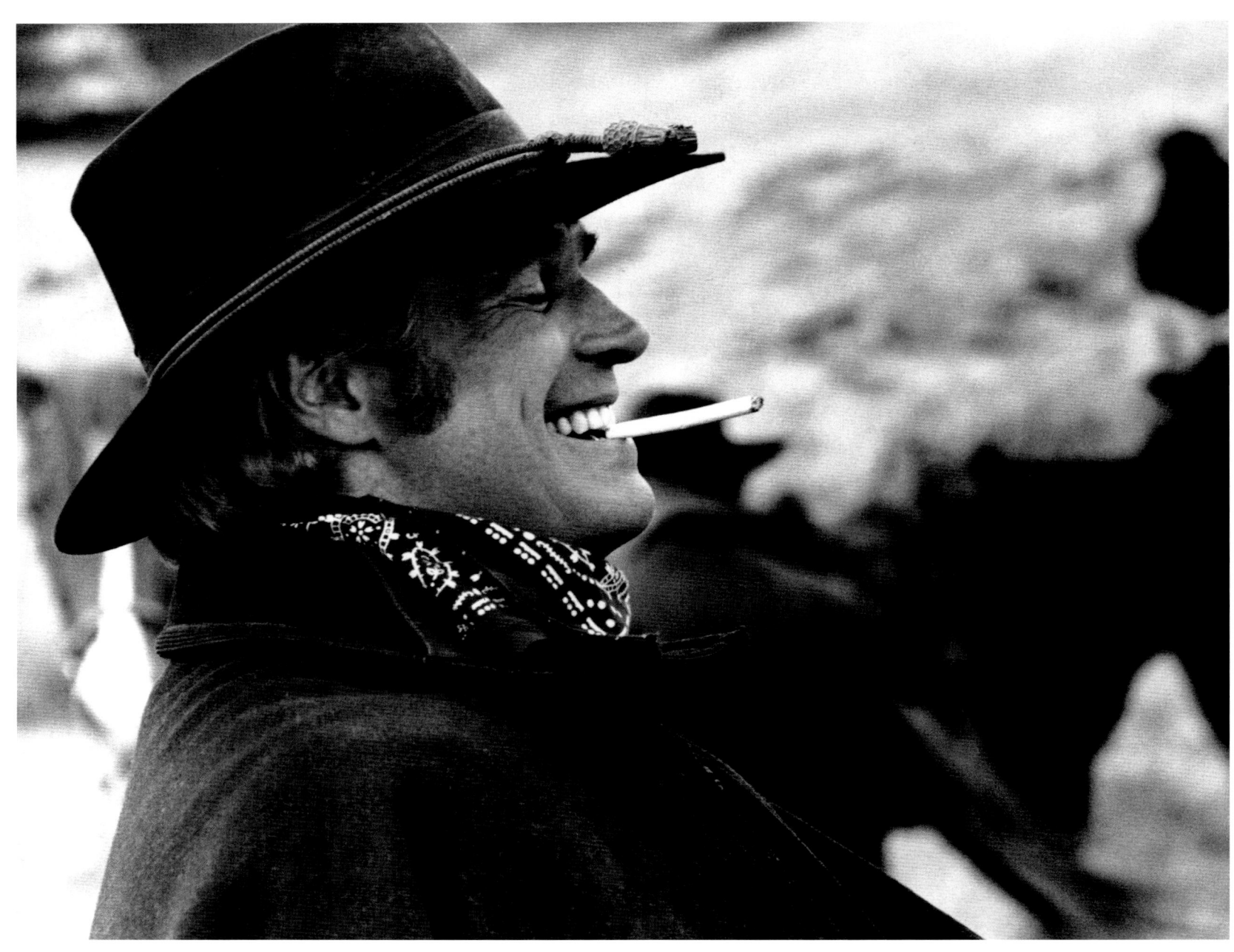
GEORGE PEPPARD, *THE BRAVOS* ON LOCATION, FLAGSTAFF, ARIZONA, 1971

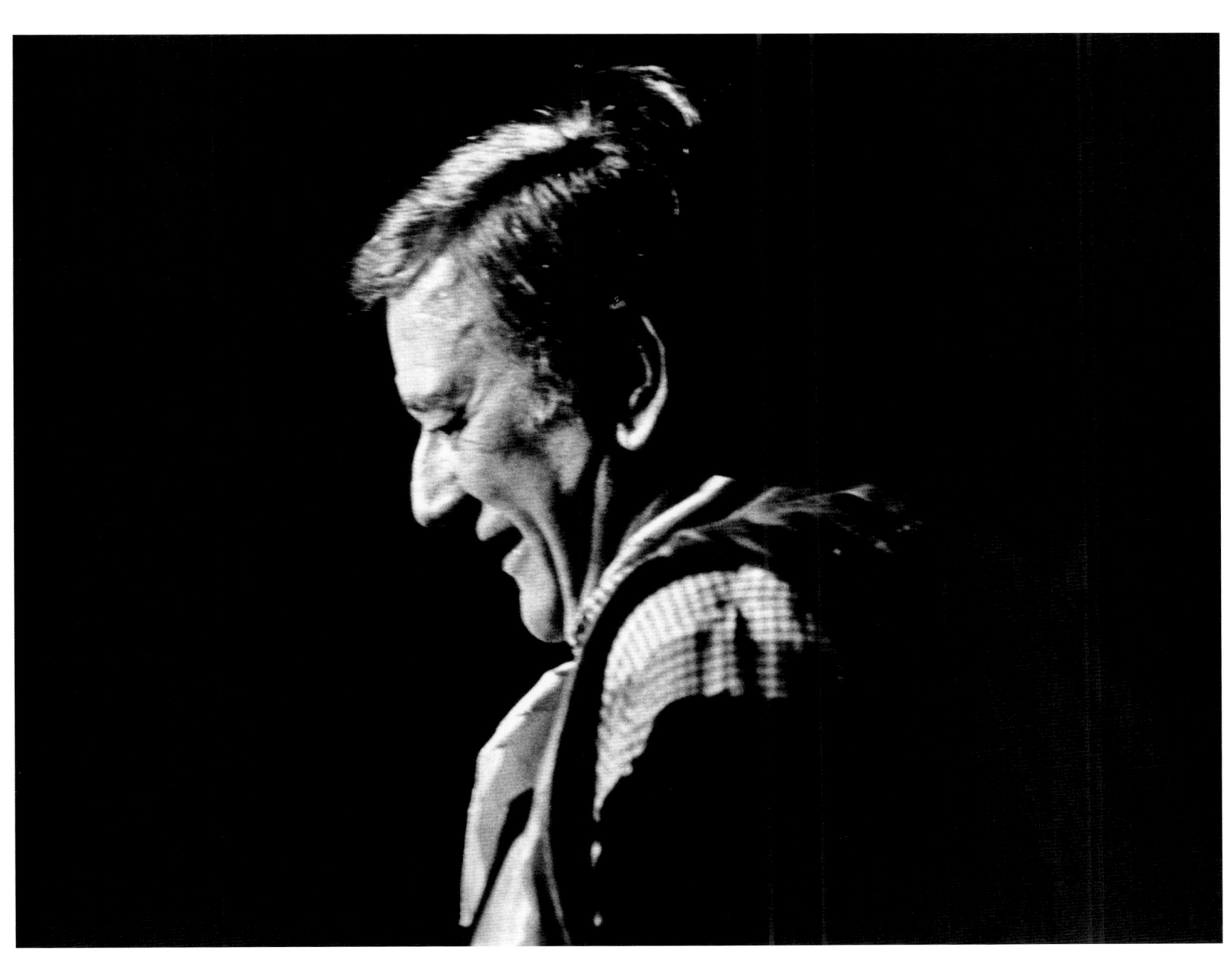

JOHN WAYNE, LOS ANGELES, 1970

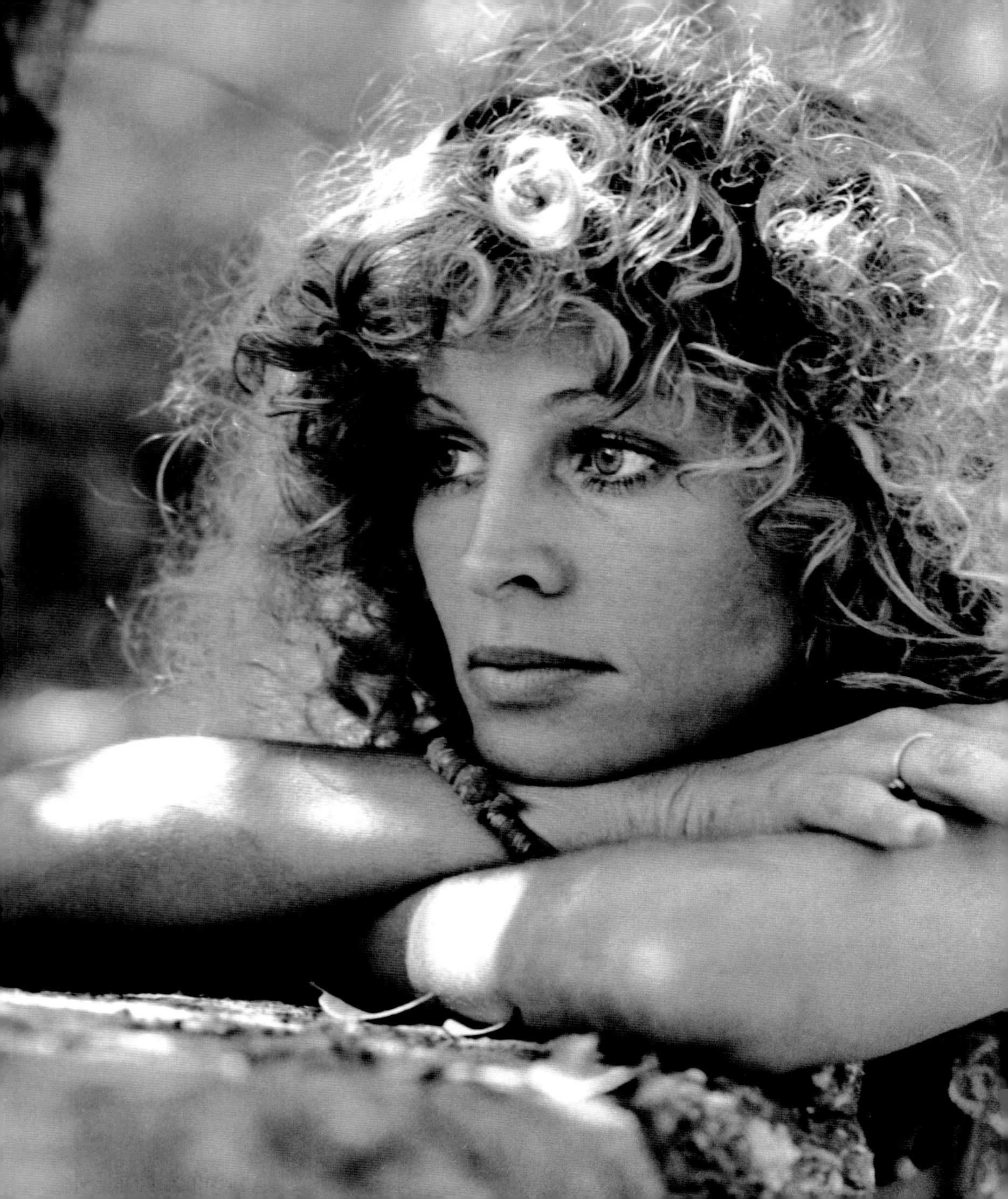

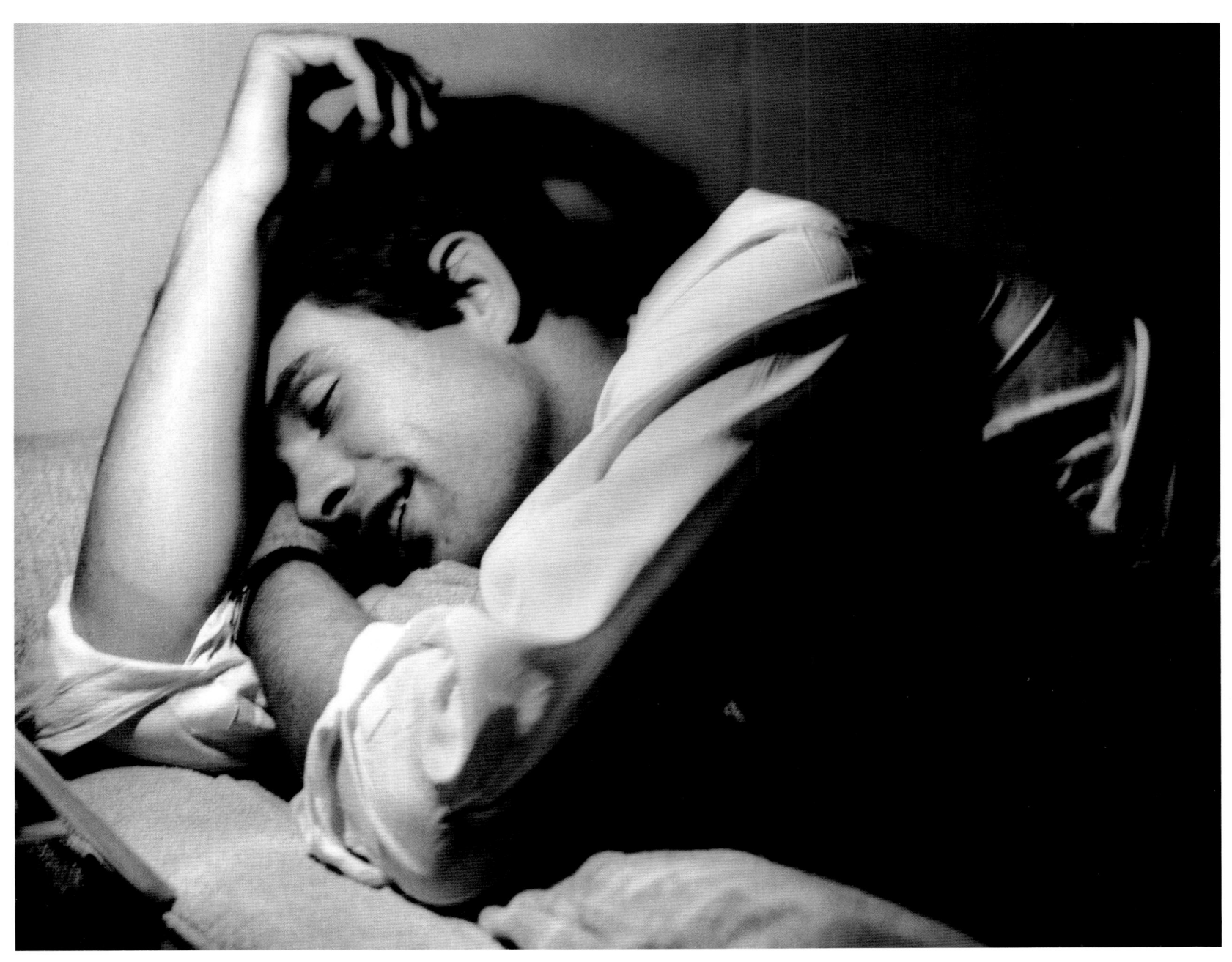

WARREN BEATTY, BEVERLY HILLS, 1967

OPPOSITE: JULIE CHRISTIE, BEVERLY HILLS, 1974

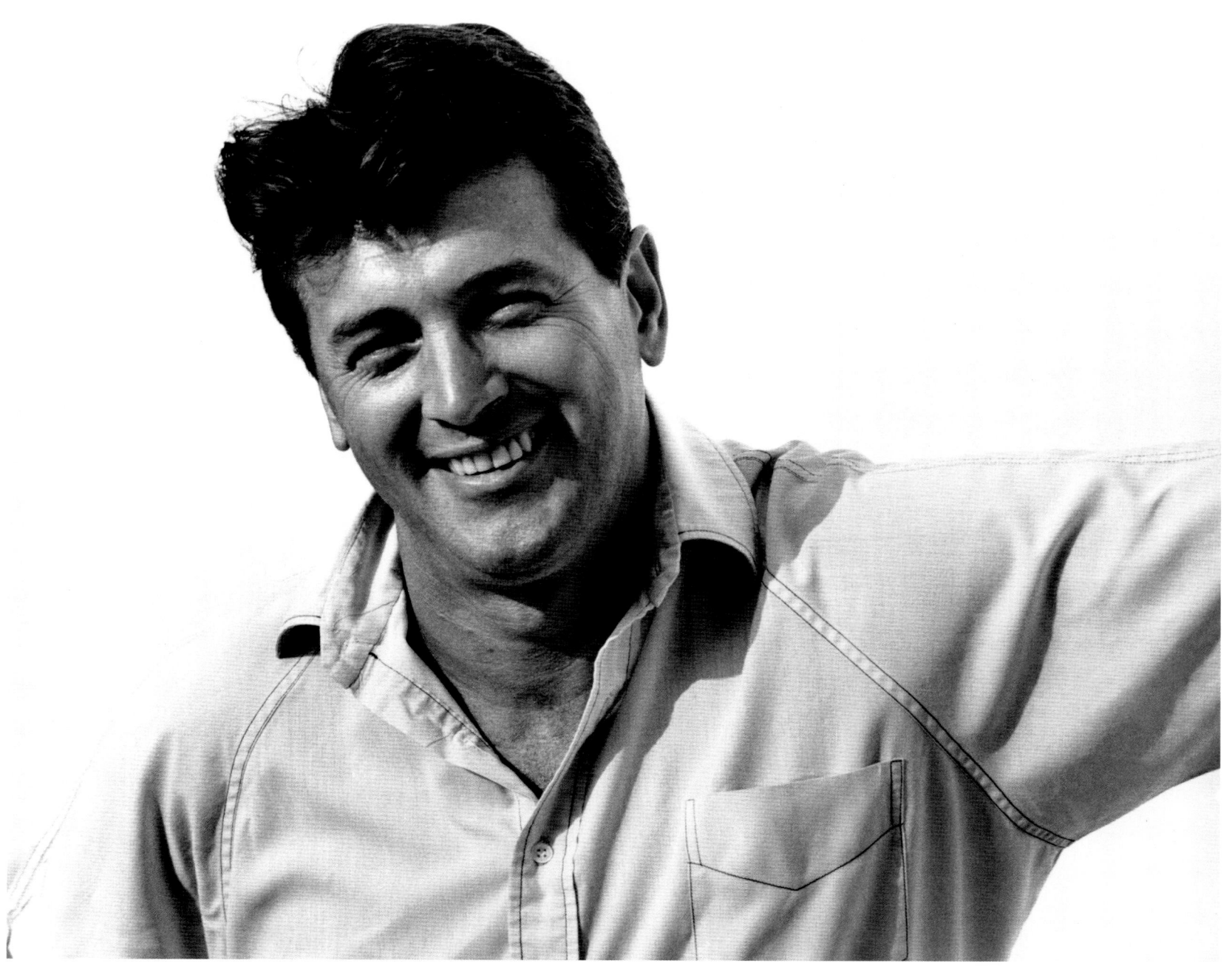

ROCK HUDSON, BEVERLY HILLS, 1966

OPPOSITE: DORIS DAY, BEVERLY HILLS, 1973

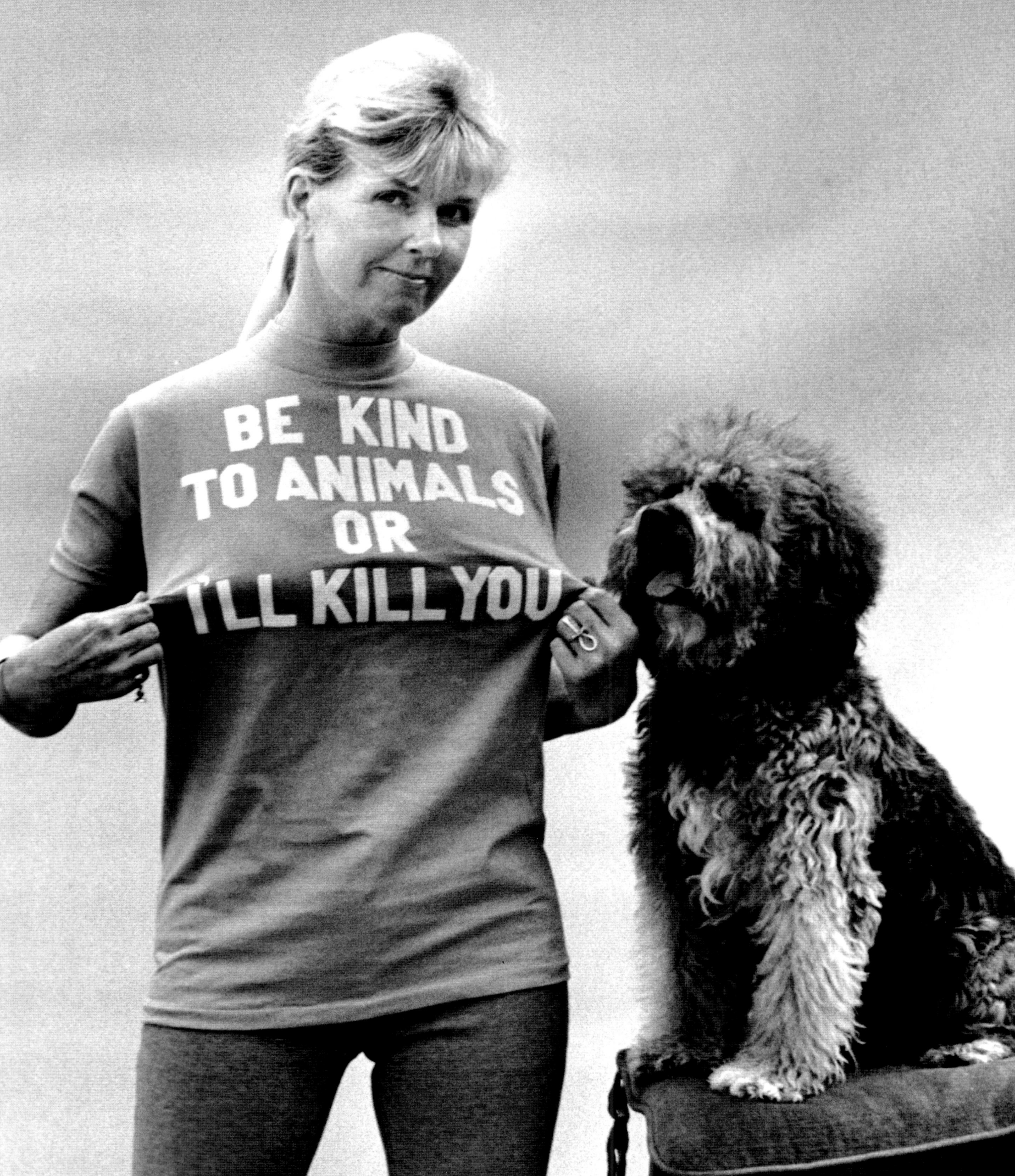

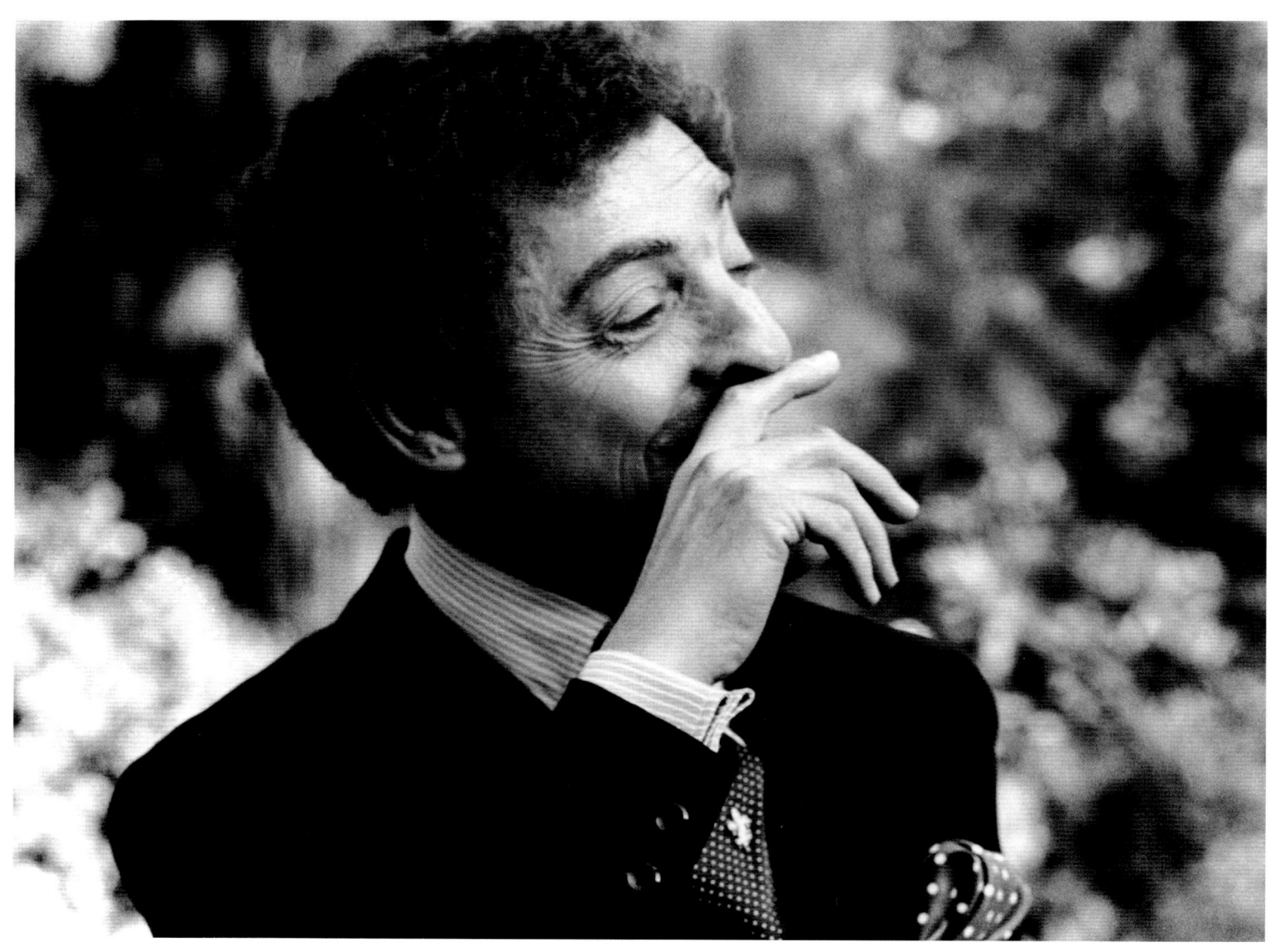

JAMES GALANOS, BEVERLY HILLS, 1966

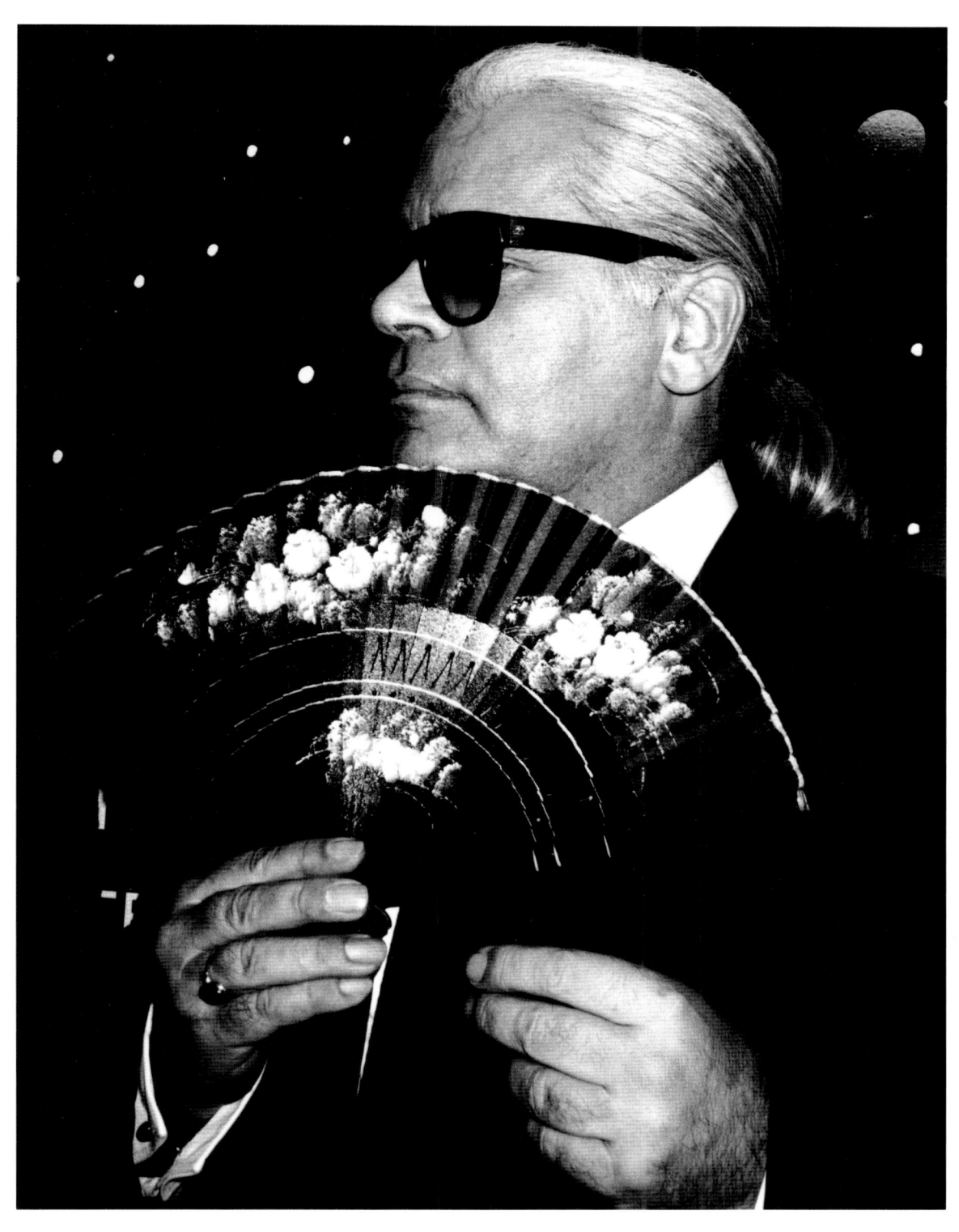

KARL LAGERFELD, PARIS, 1995

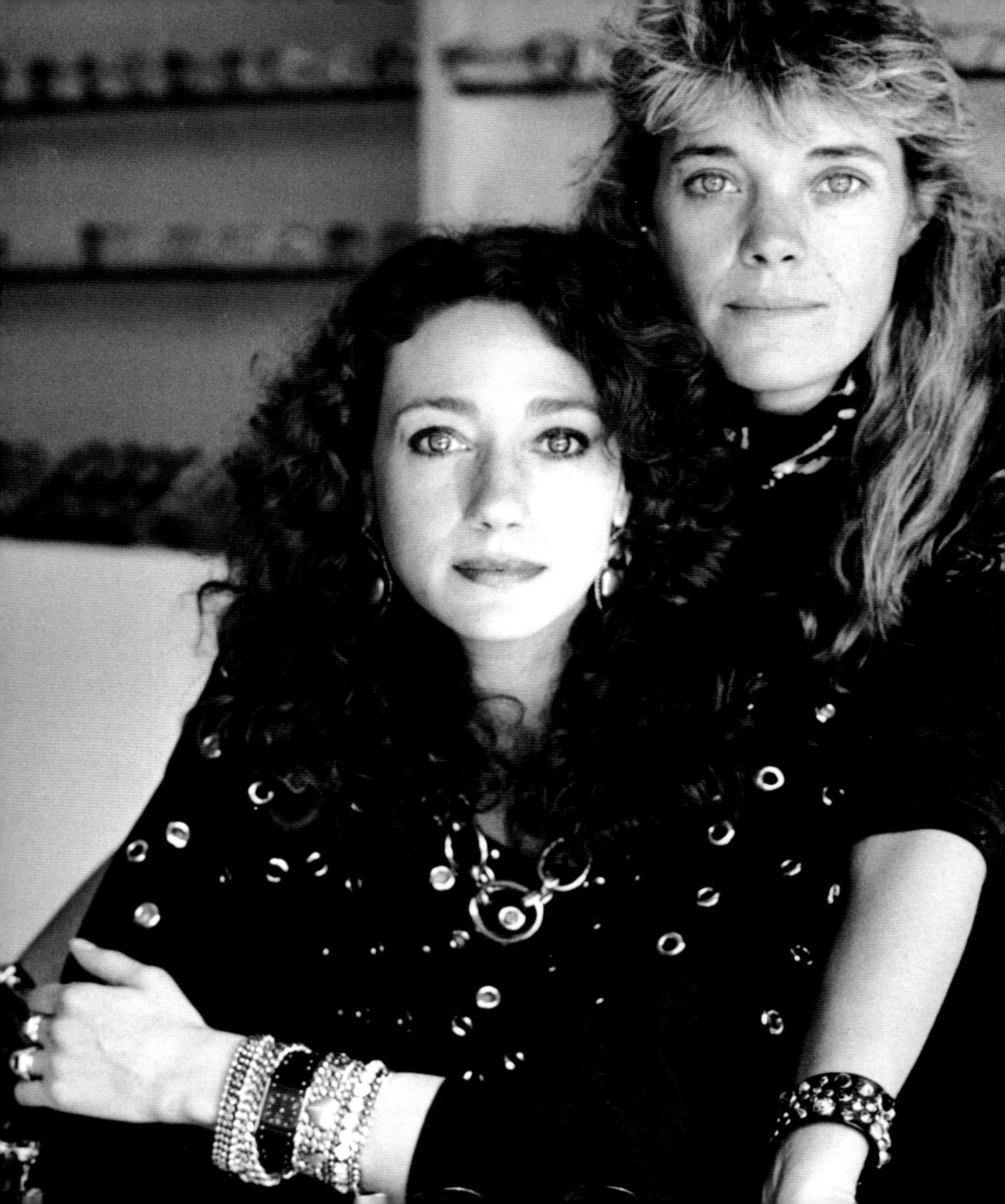

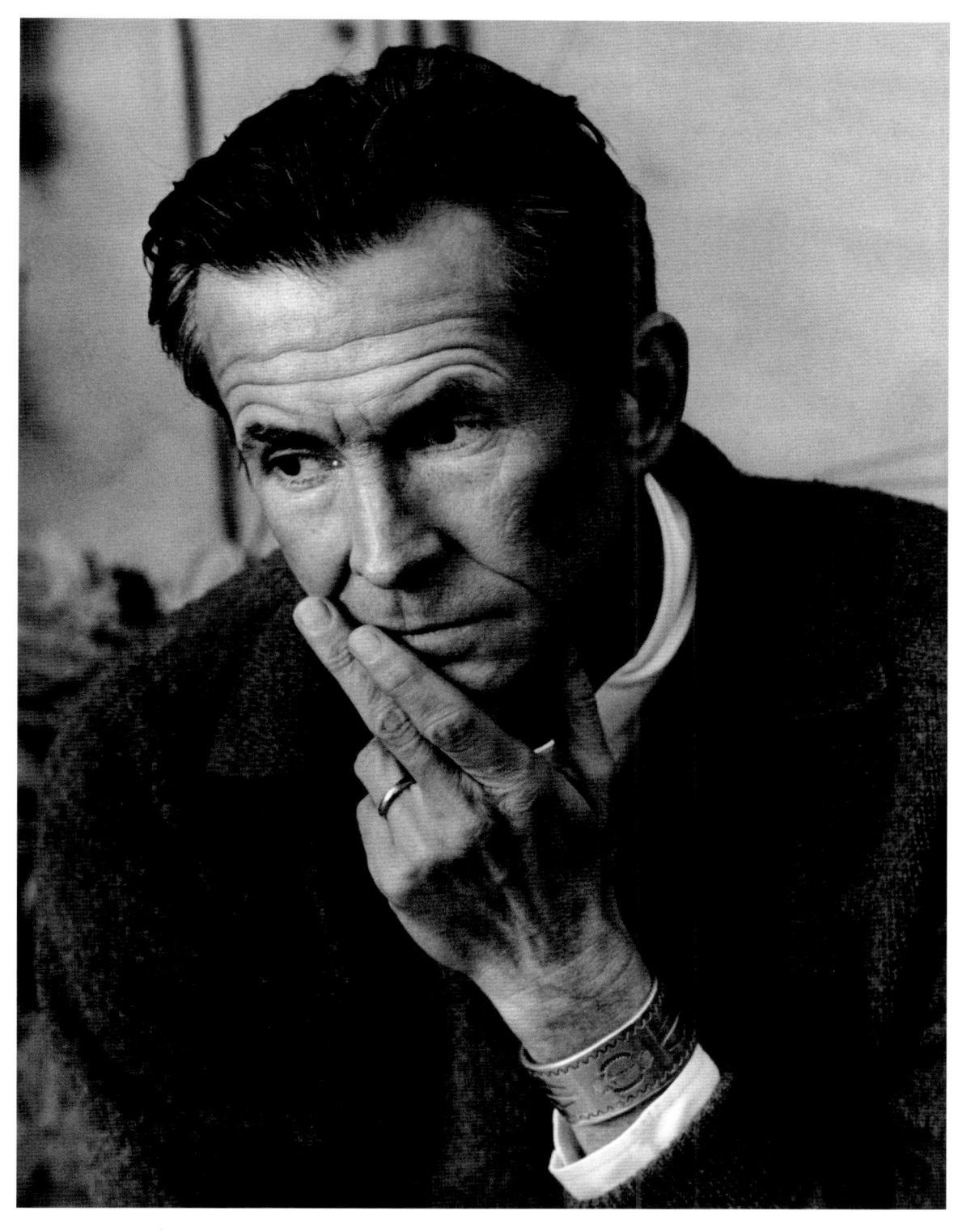

ANTHONY PERKINS, LOS ANGELES, 1984

OPPOSITE: MARISA BERENSON, BERRY BERENSON, LOS ANGELES, 1984

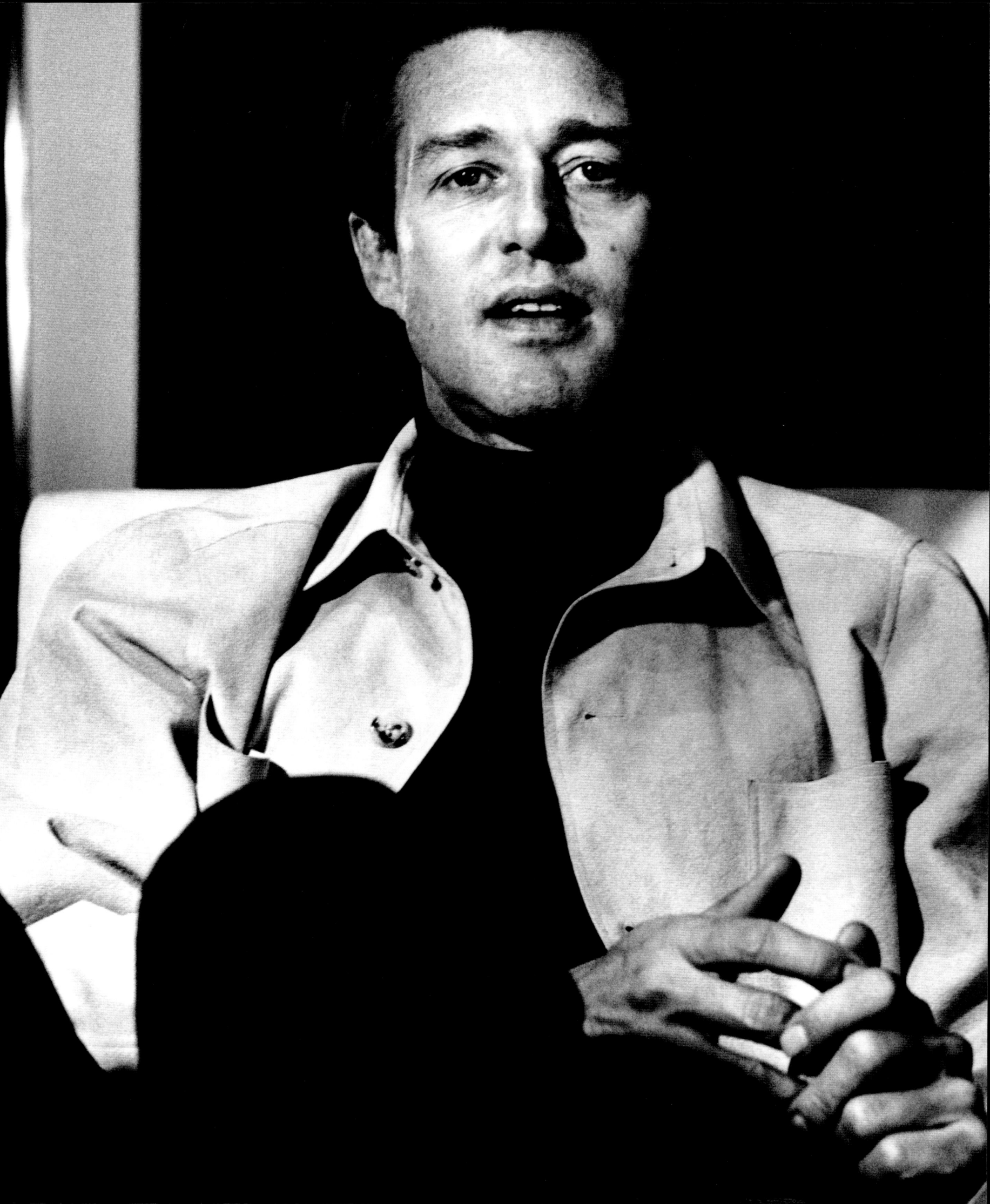

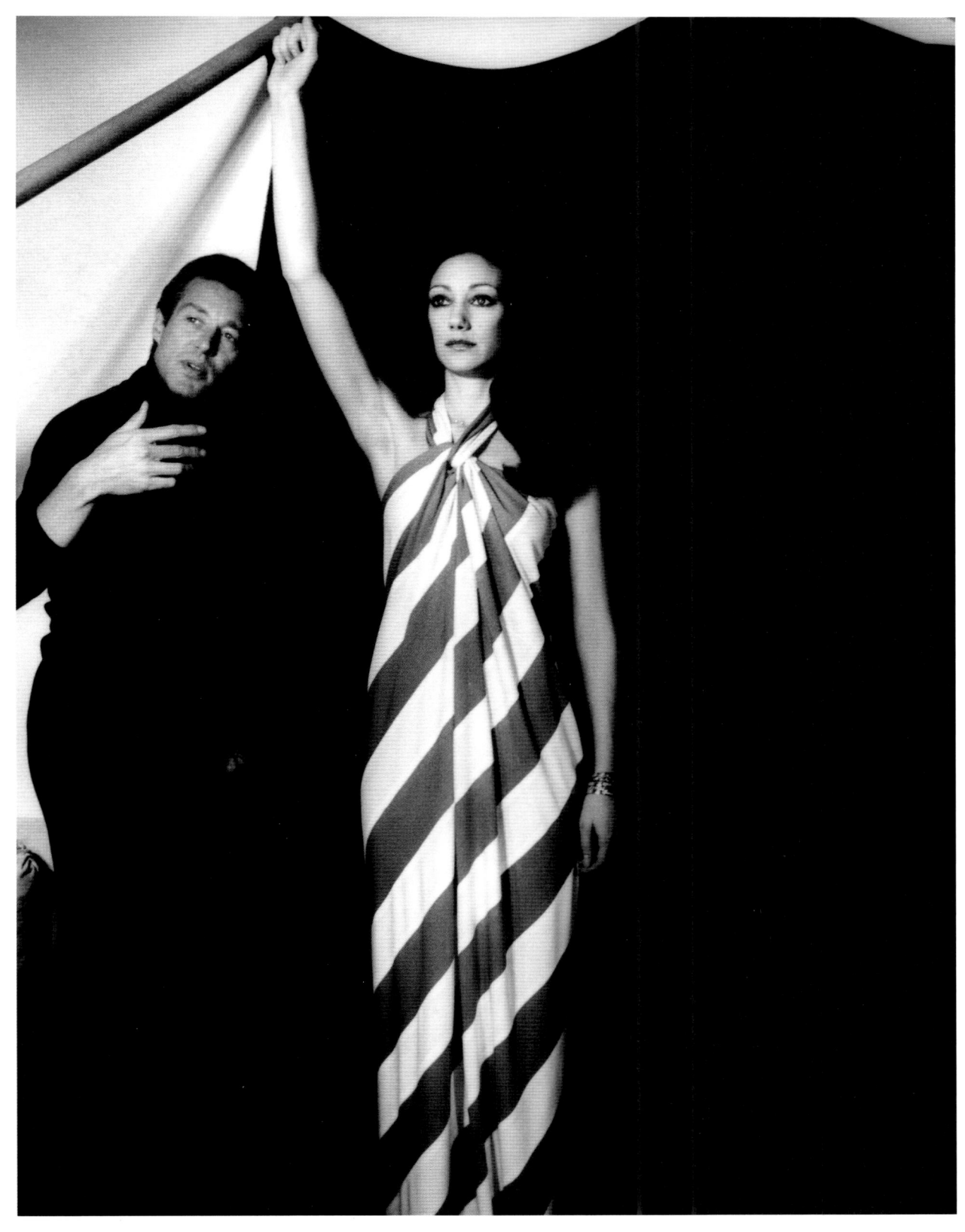

HALSTON AND MARISA BERENSON, NEW YORK CITY, 1975

OPPOSITE: HALSTON, NEW YORK CITY, 1975

OVERLEAF: VALENTINA SCHLEE, VENICE-LIDO, ITALY, 1959

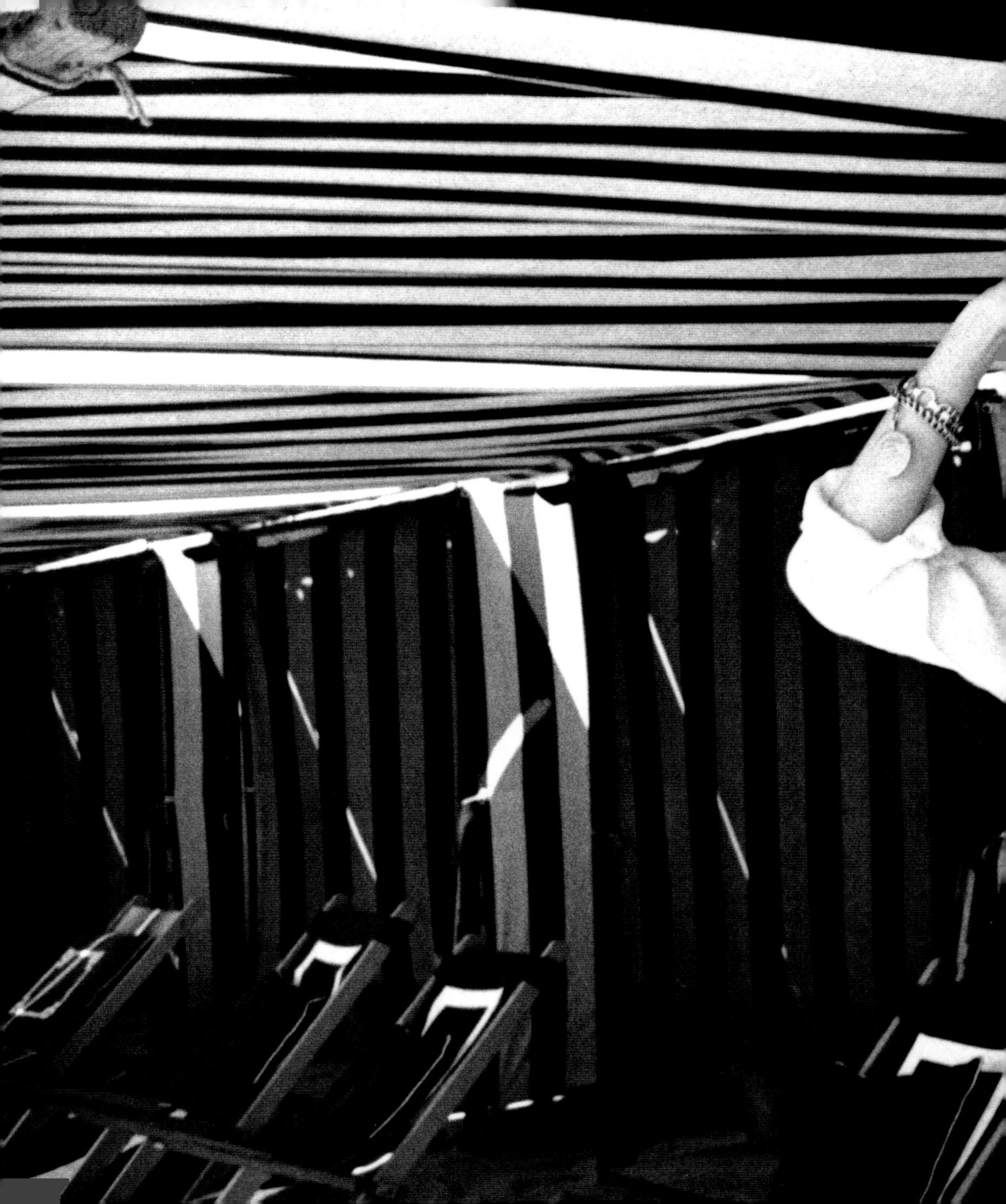

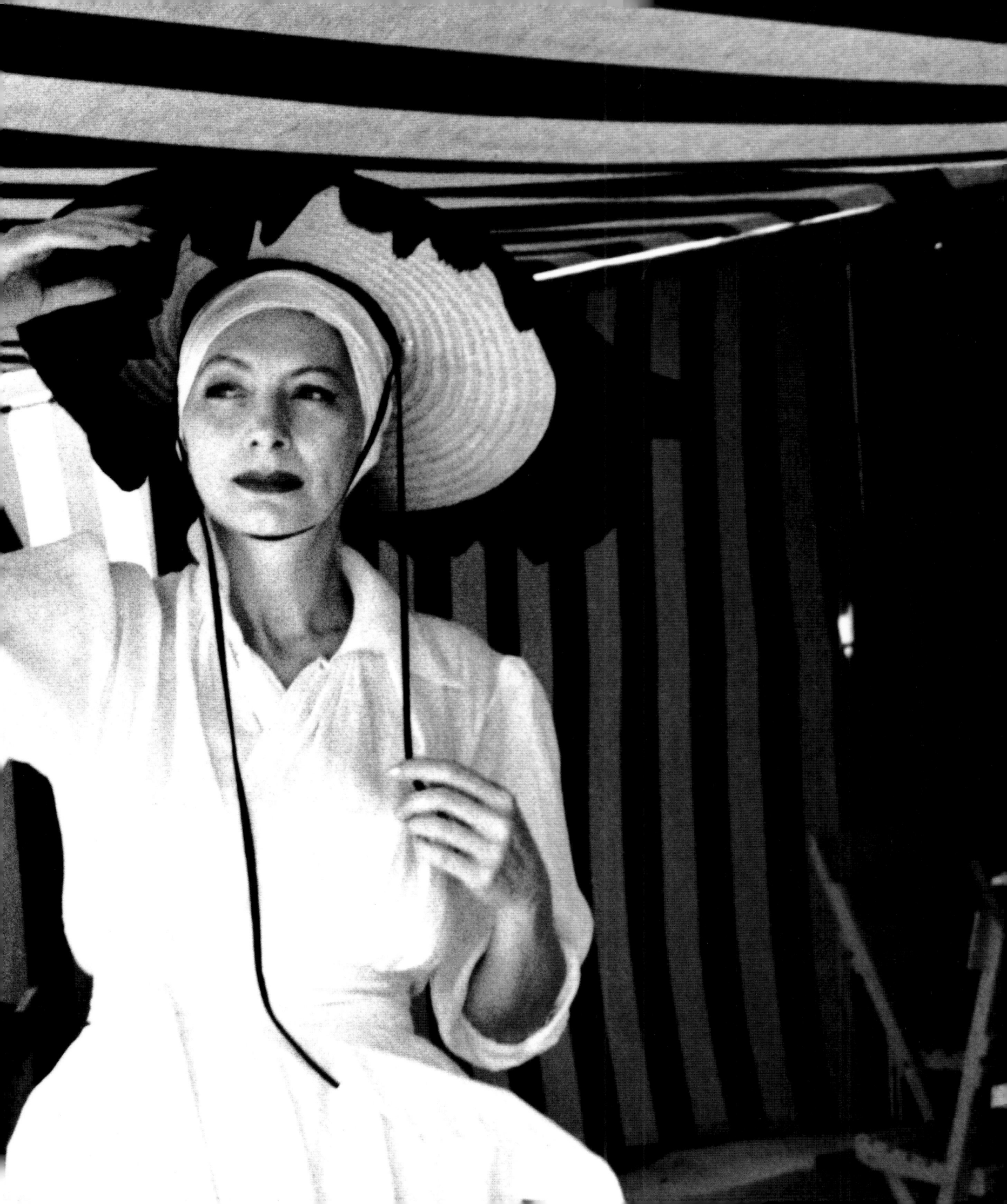

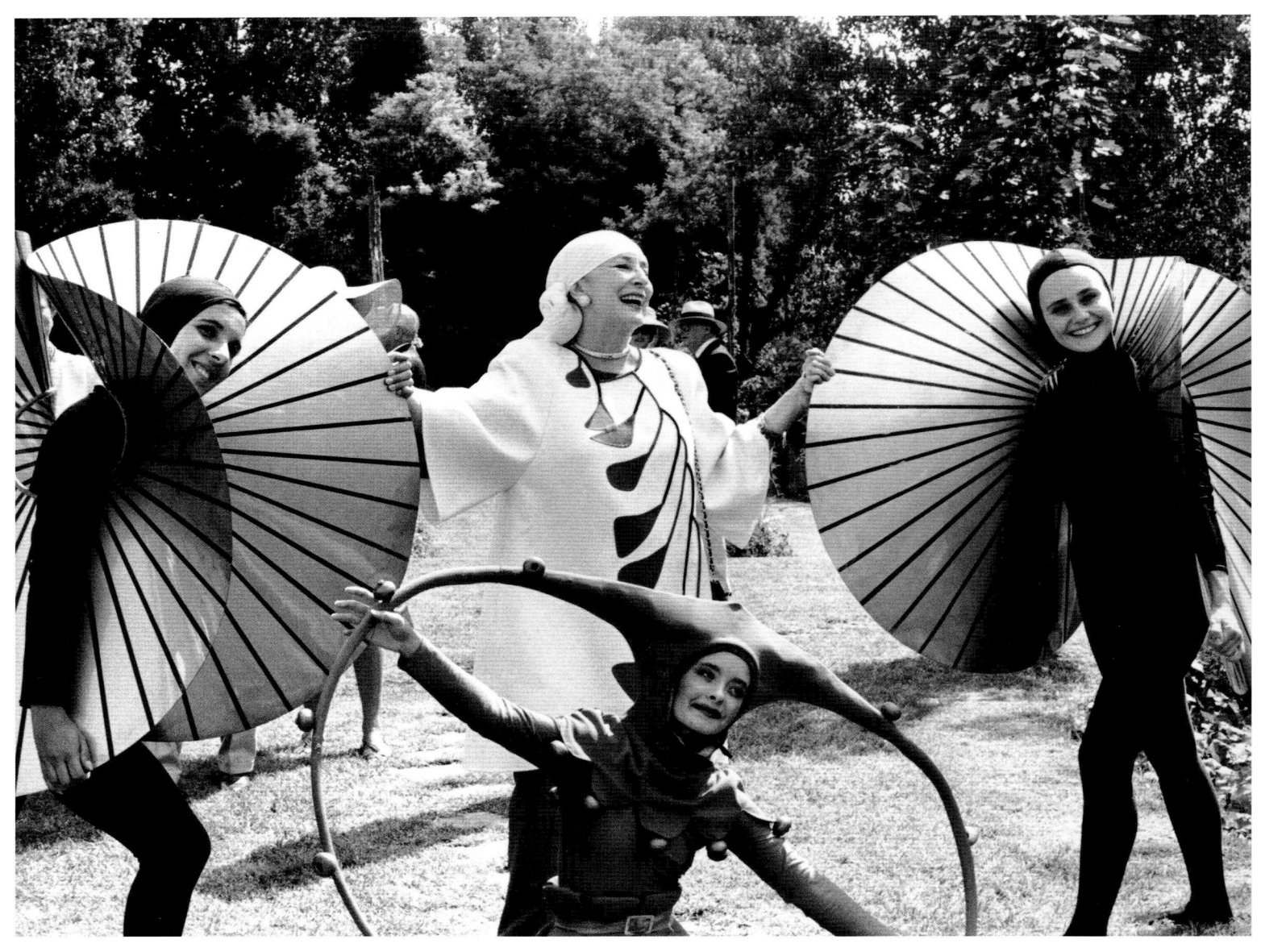

VALENTINA CORTESE, VENICE, ITALY, 1996

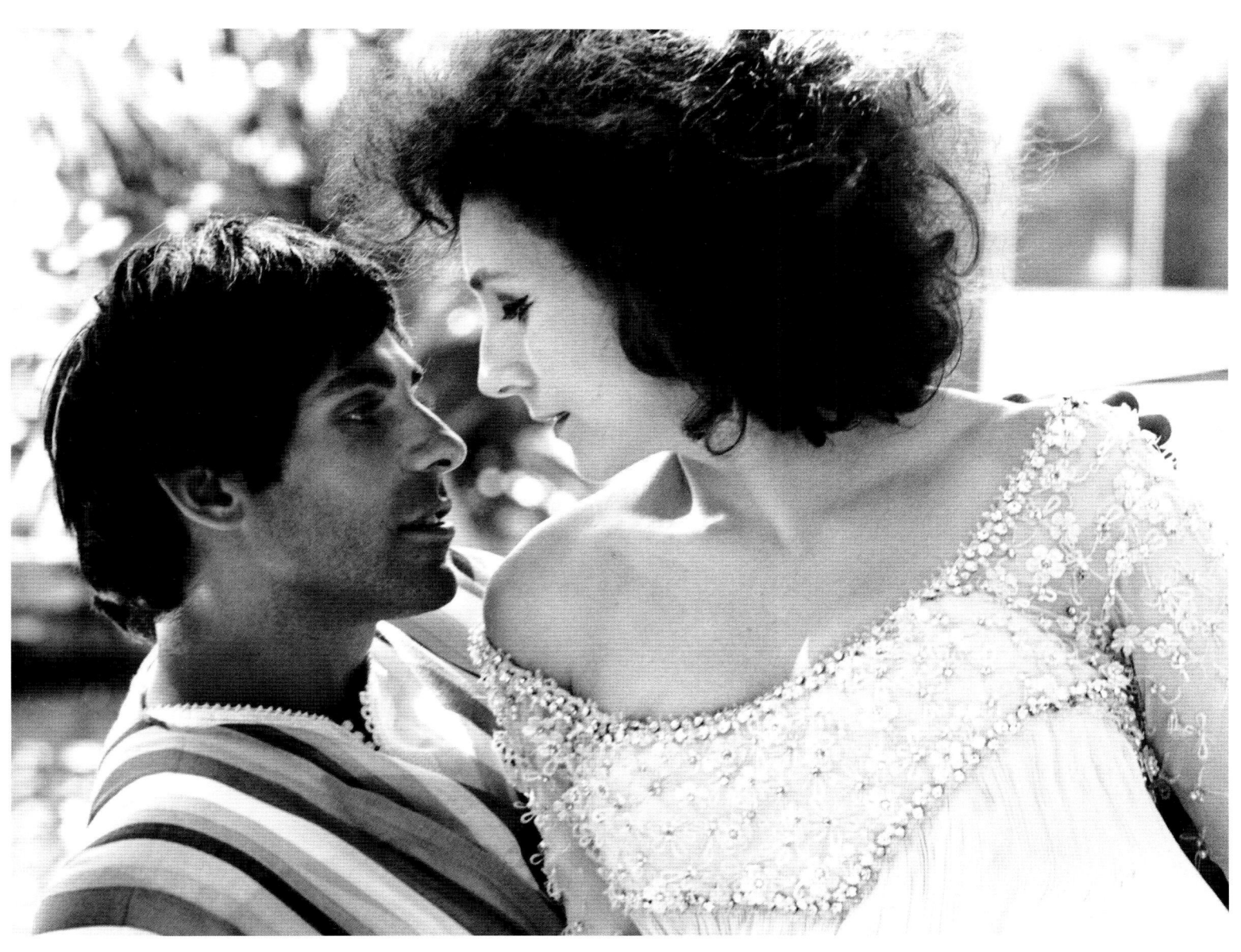

VALENTINA CORTESE AND RICHARD CARUSO, BEL AIR, CALIFORNIA, 1967

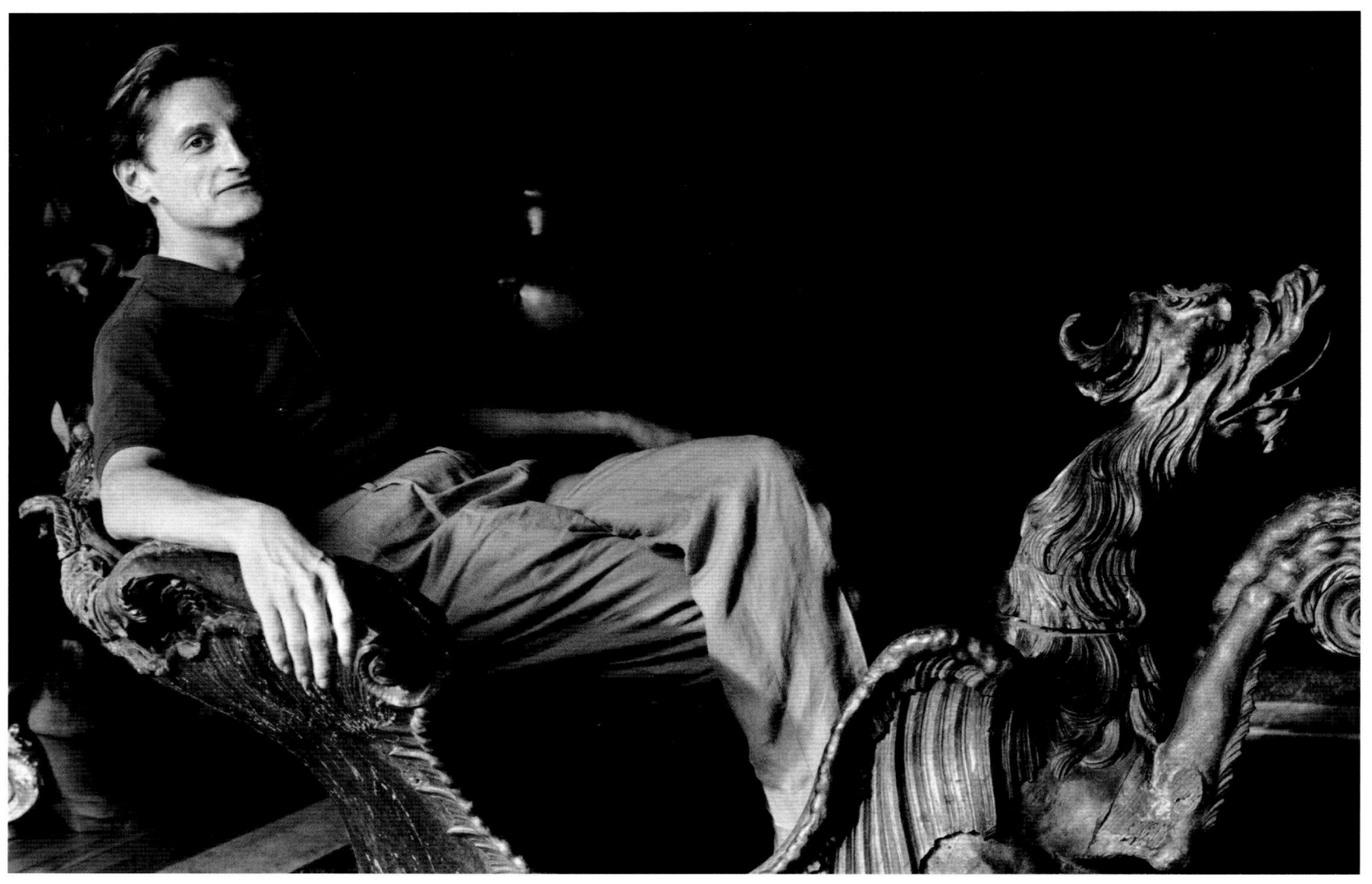

HAMISH BOWLES, PALAZZO BRANDOLINI, VENICE, ITALY, 1999

OPPOSITE: VERUSCHKA WITH A NEEDLEPOINT SELF-PORTRAIT, VENICE BIENNALE, ITALY, 2001

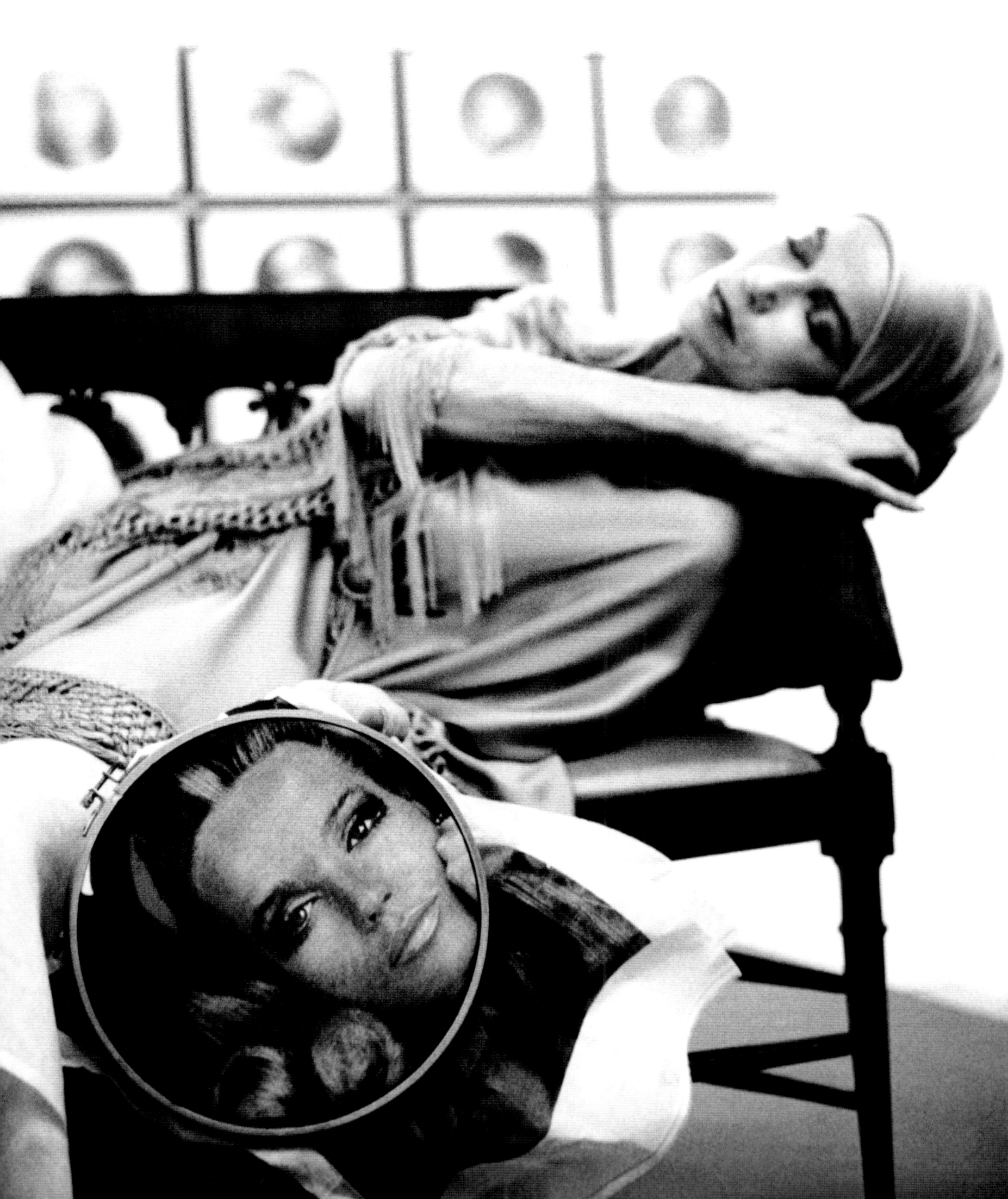

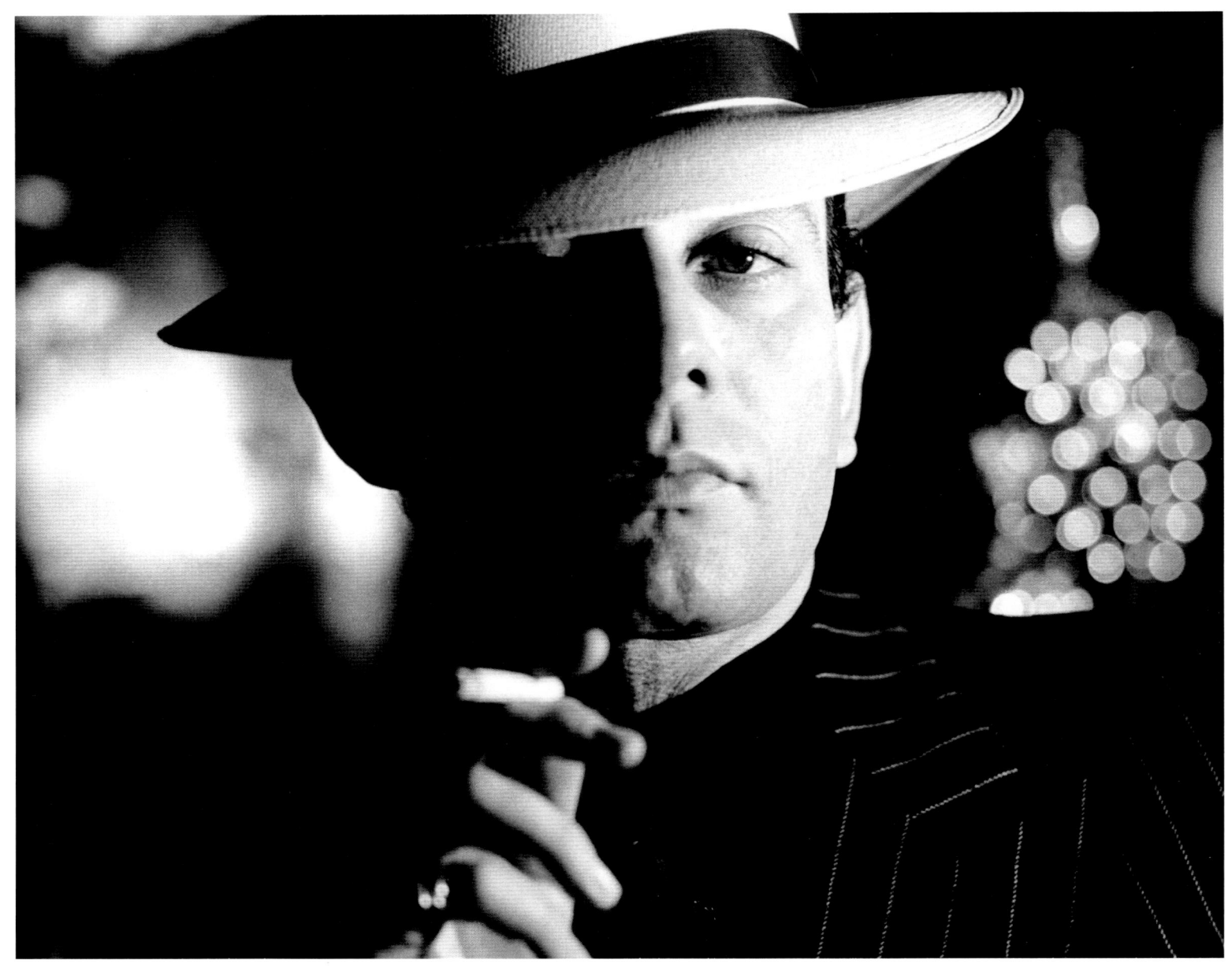

KENNETH JAY LANE, NEW YORK CITY, 1967

OPPOSITE: NAN KEMPNER, VENICE, ITALY, 1999

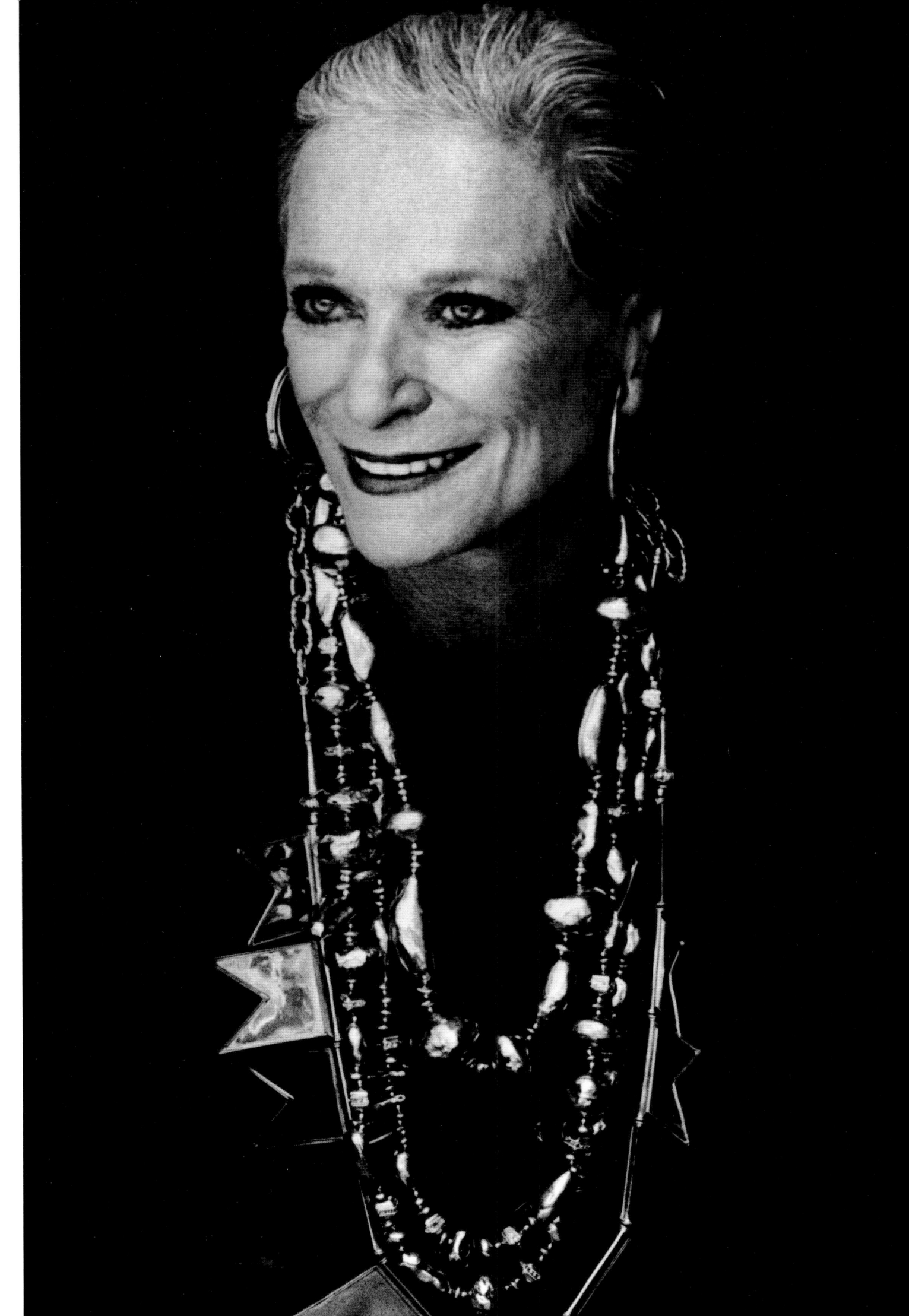

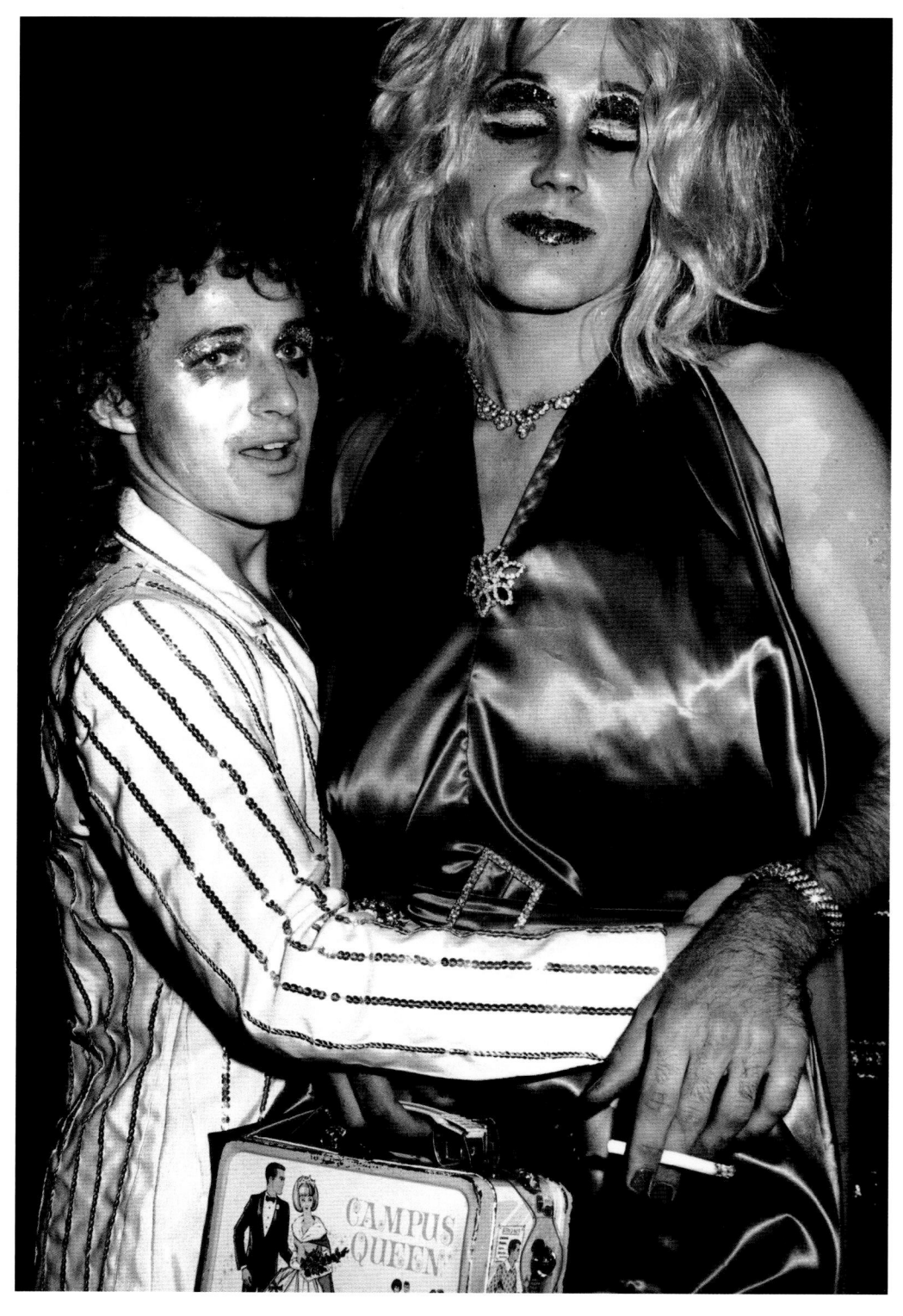

BOY WITH MARILYN MONROE IMPERSONATOR, LOS ANGELES, 1972

OPPOSITE: JAMES COBURN WITH HIS PET MONKEY, BEVERLY HILLS, 1971

OVERLEAF LEFT: DON STROUD, BEVERLY HILLS, 1967

OVERLEAF RIGHT: TEENAGER, HAVANA, CUBA, 1999

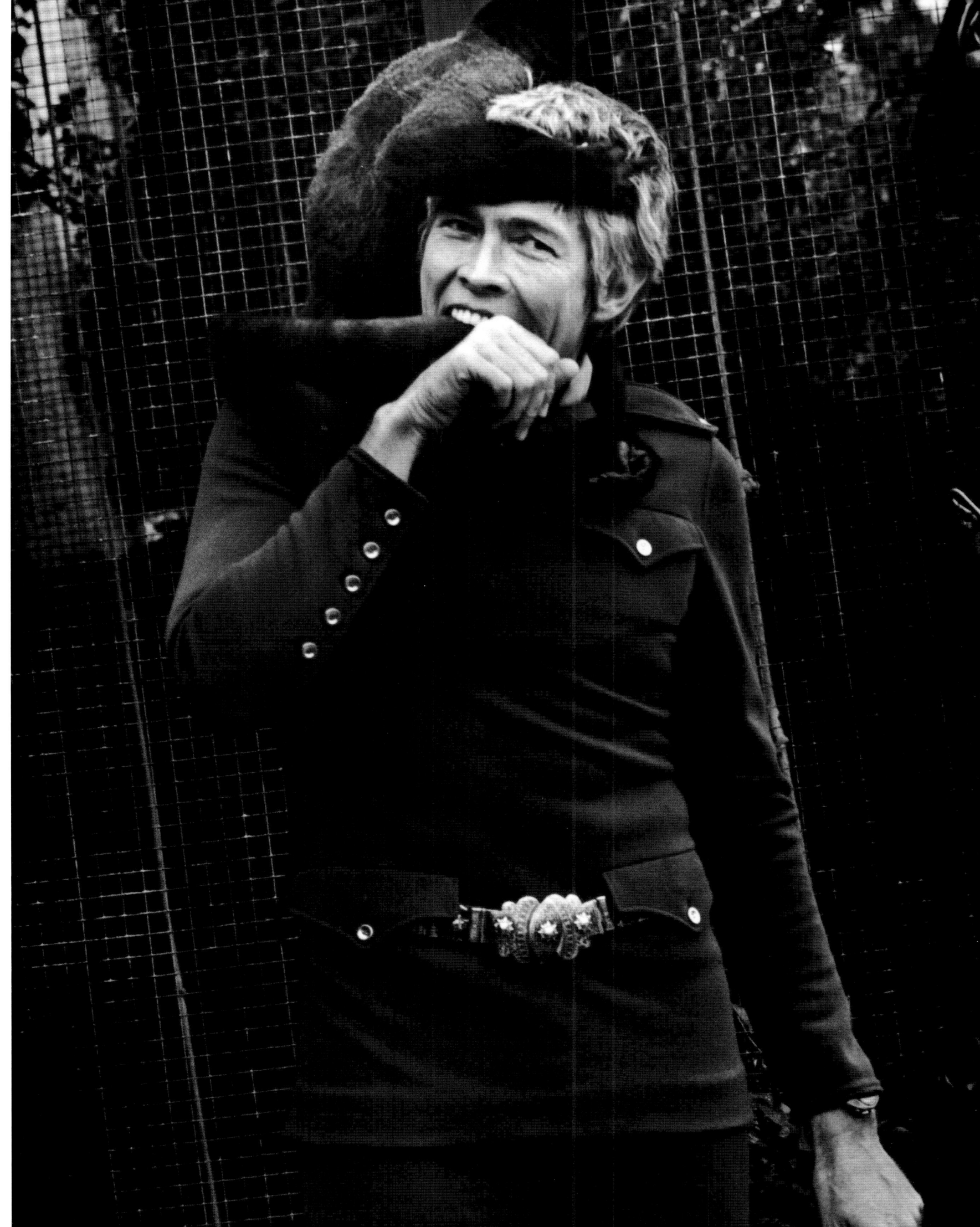

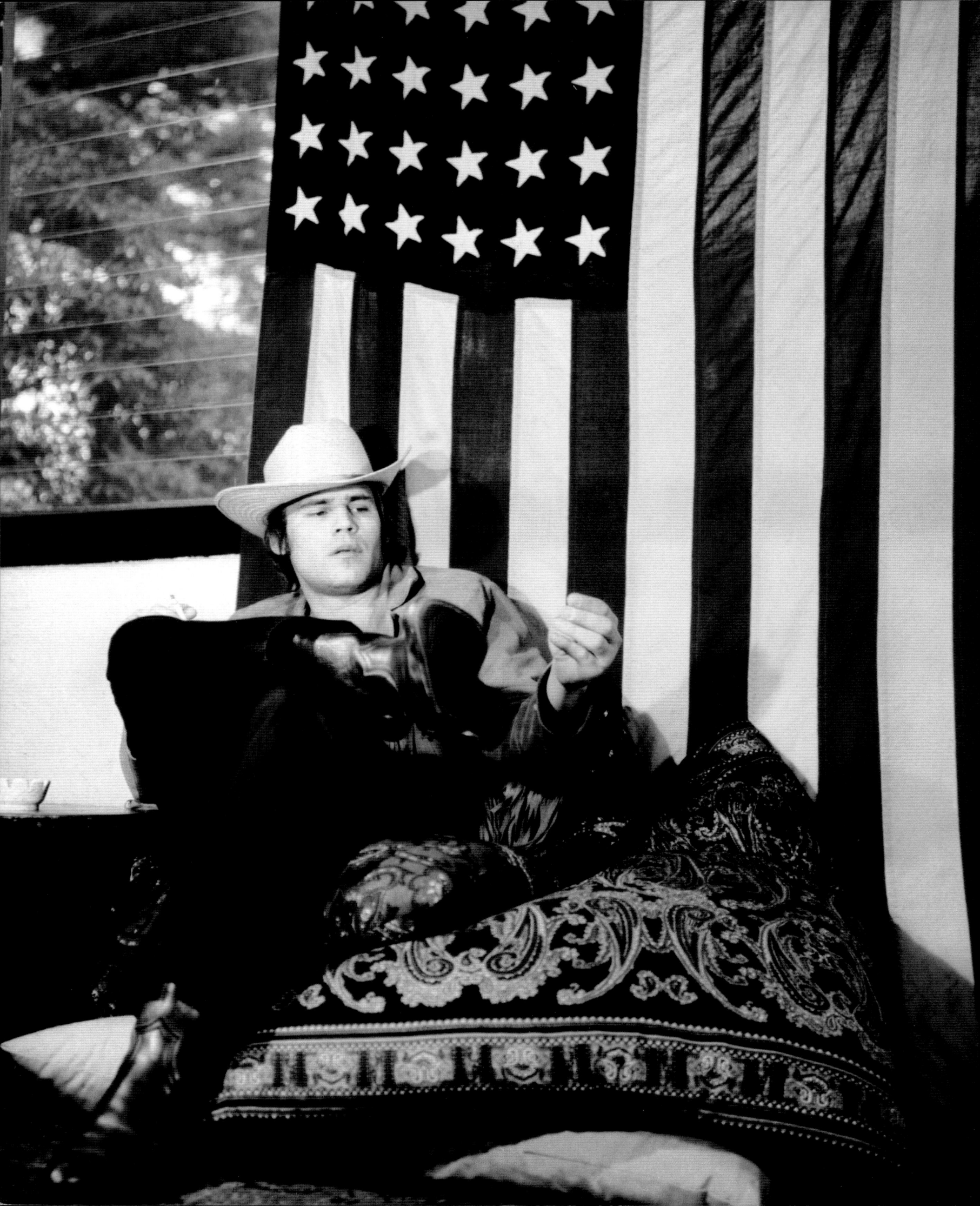

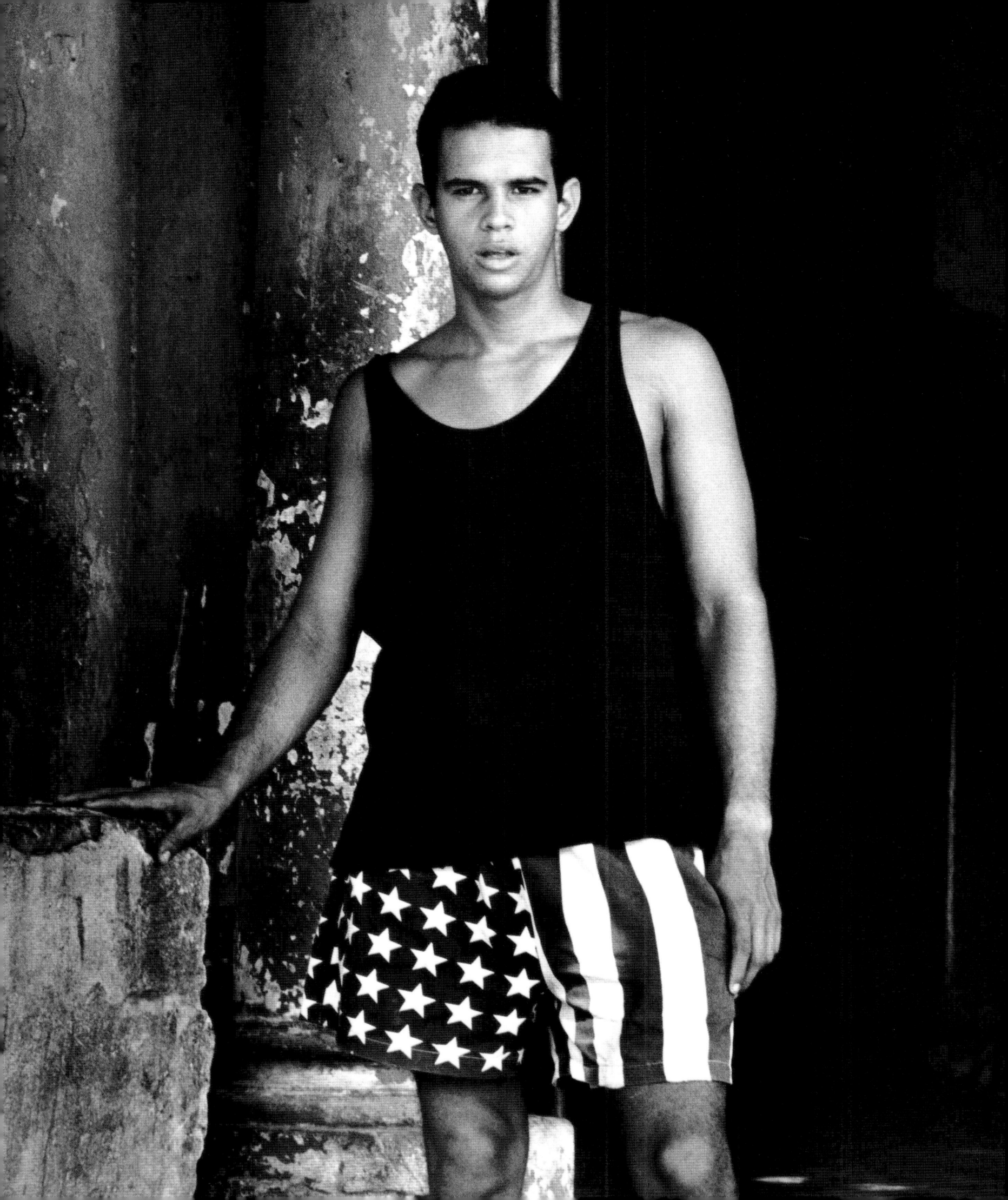

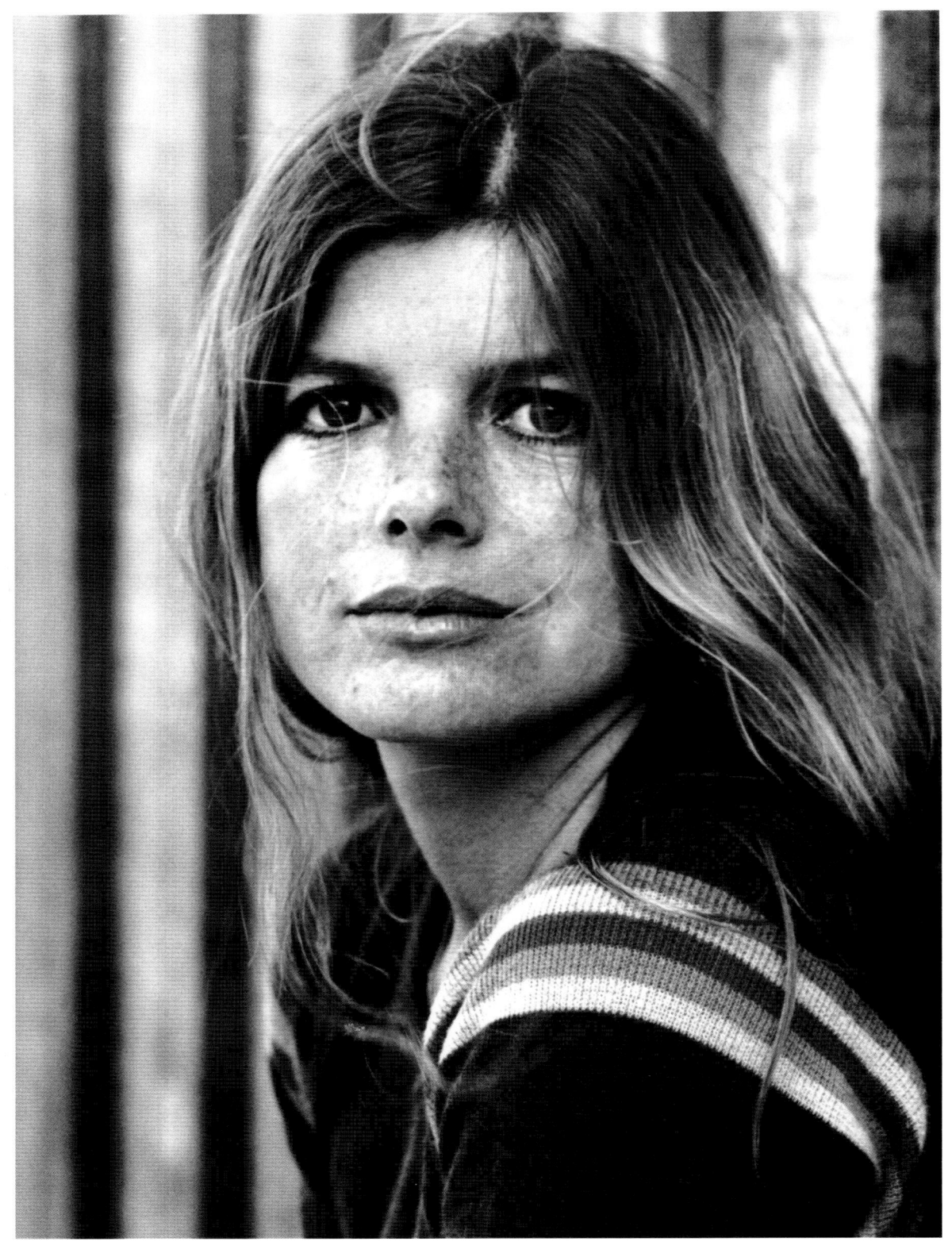

KATHERINE ROSS, TRANCAS BEACH, CALIFORNIA, 1975

OPPOSITE: ADOLPHUS CAMBIASO, ARGENTINE
TEN-GOALER, PALM BEACH POLO, 1999

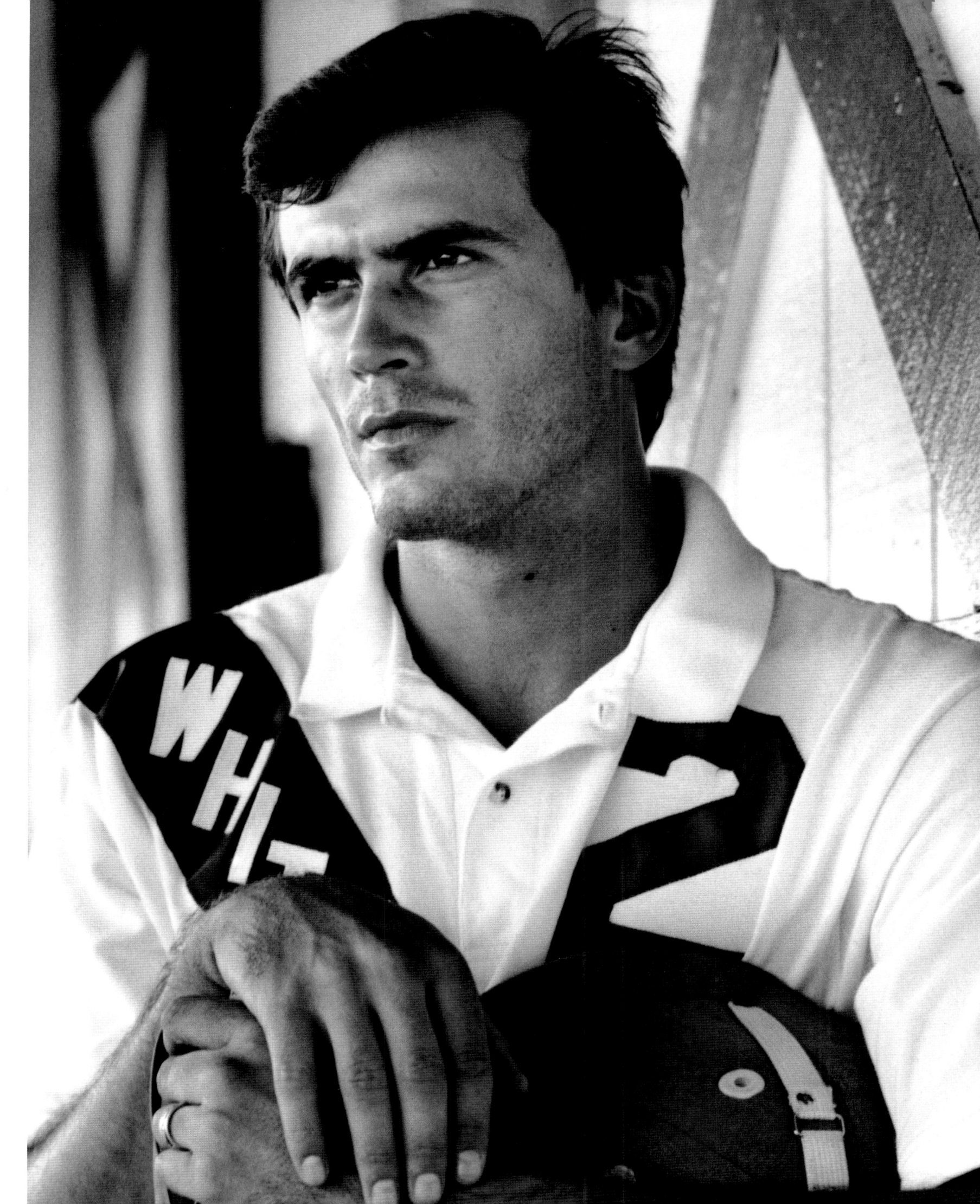

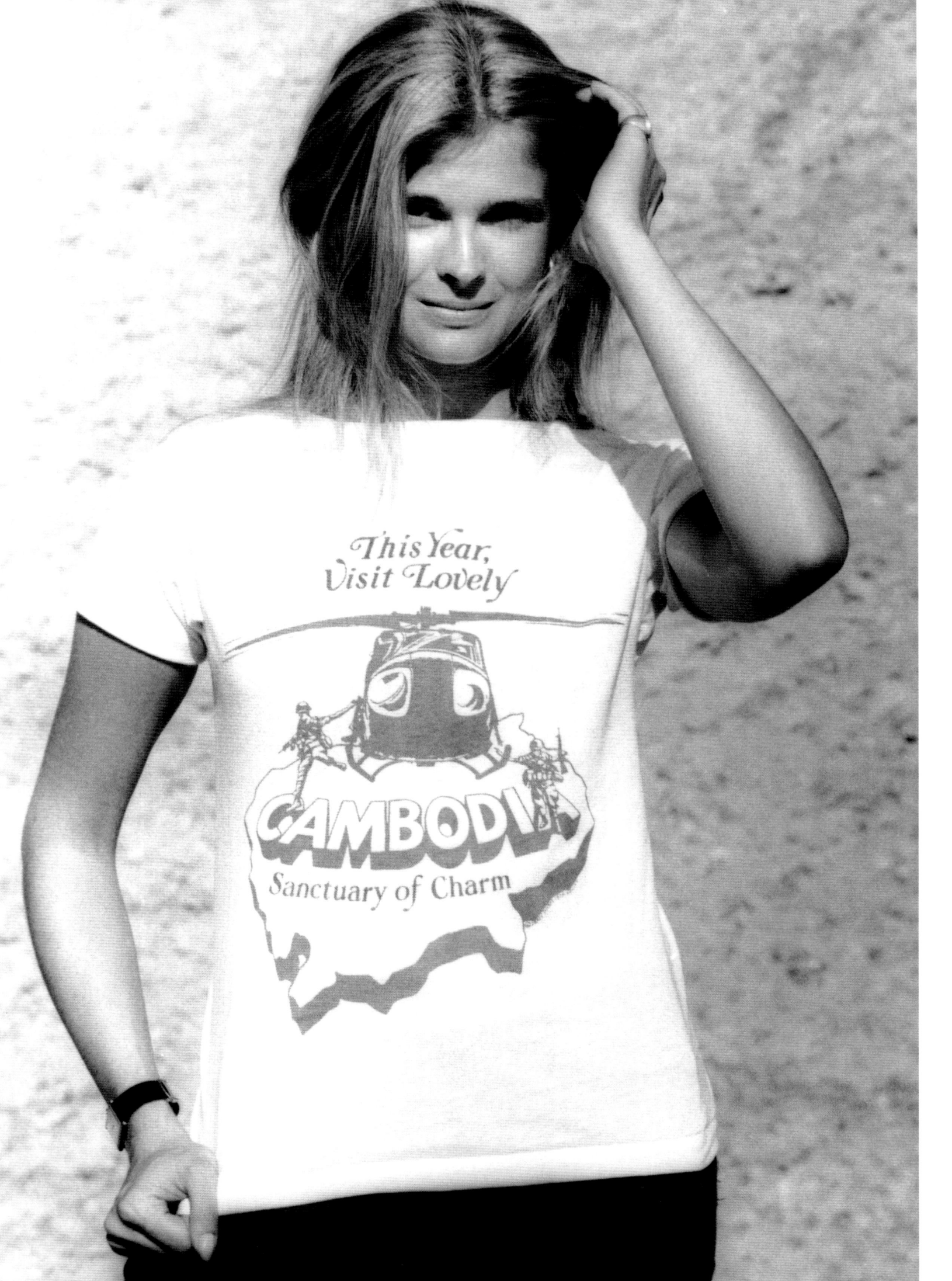

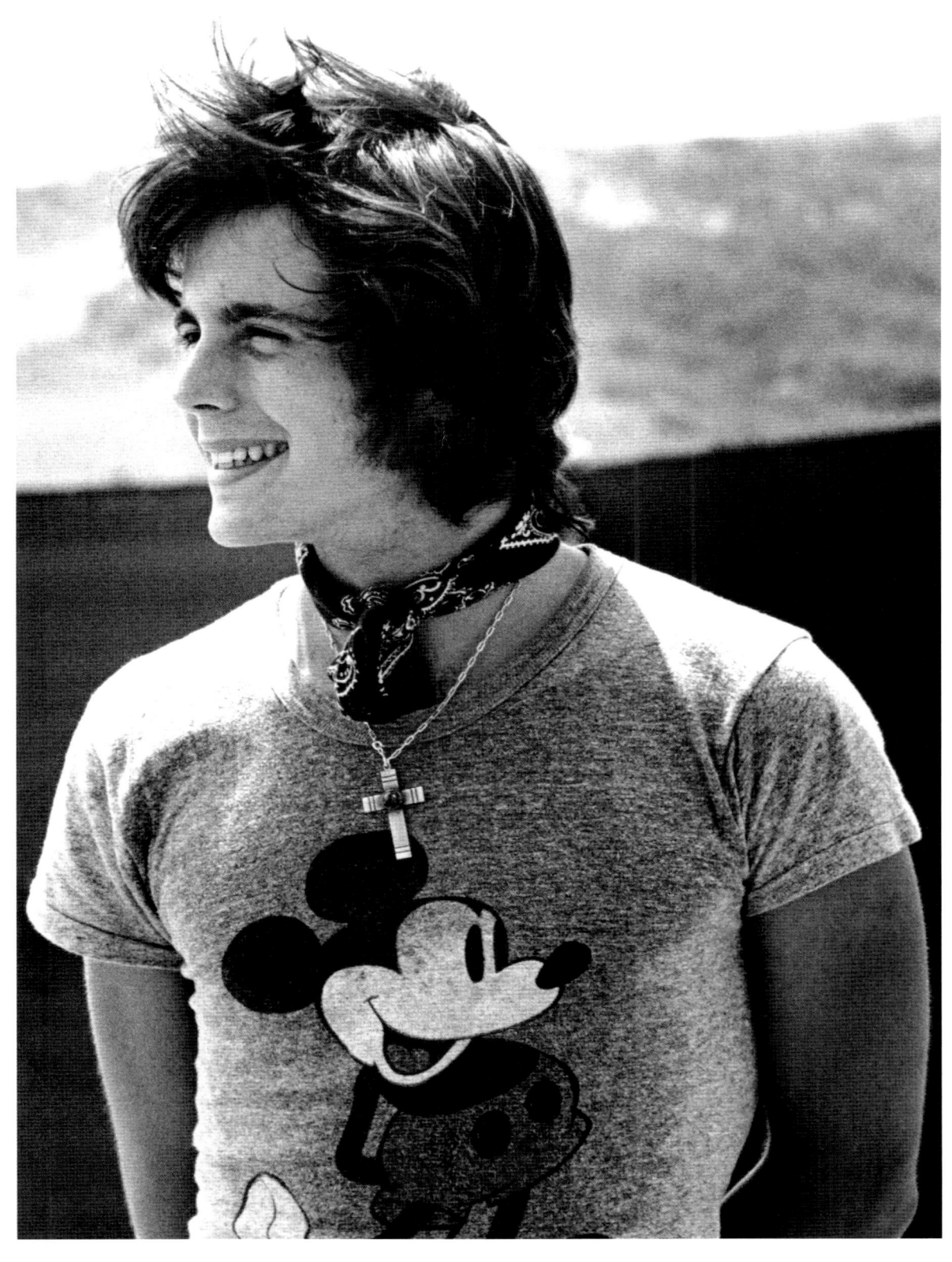

DESI ARNAZ JR., BEVERLY HILLS, 1973

OPPOSITE: CANDICE BERGEN, BEVERLY HILLS, 1971

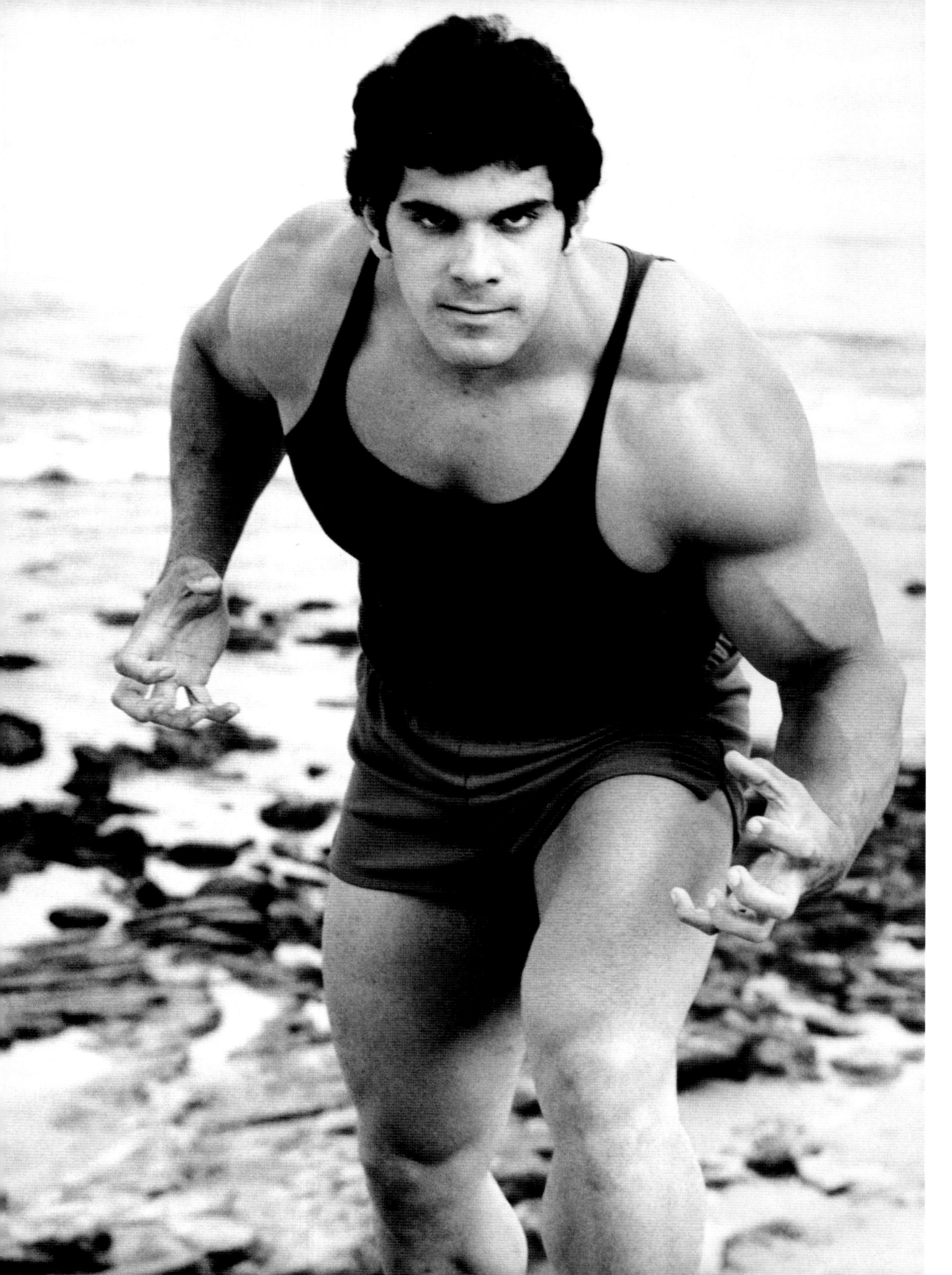

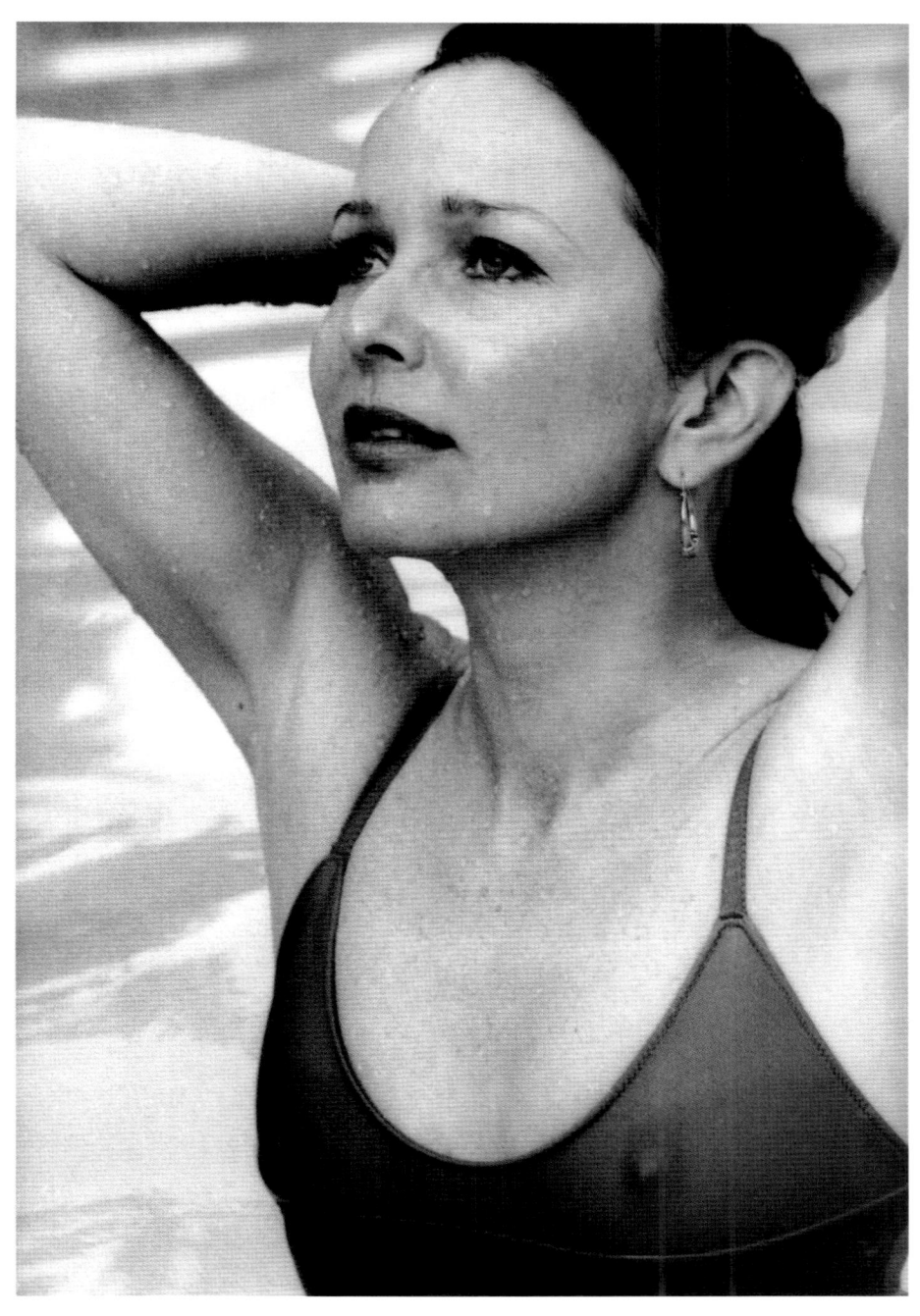

BROOKE HAYWARD, LA COSTA, CALIFORNIA, 1977

OPPOSITE: LOU FERRIGNO, "THE INCREDIBLE HULK," MALIBU, 1978

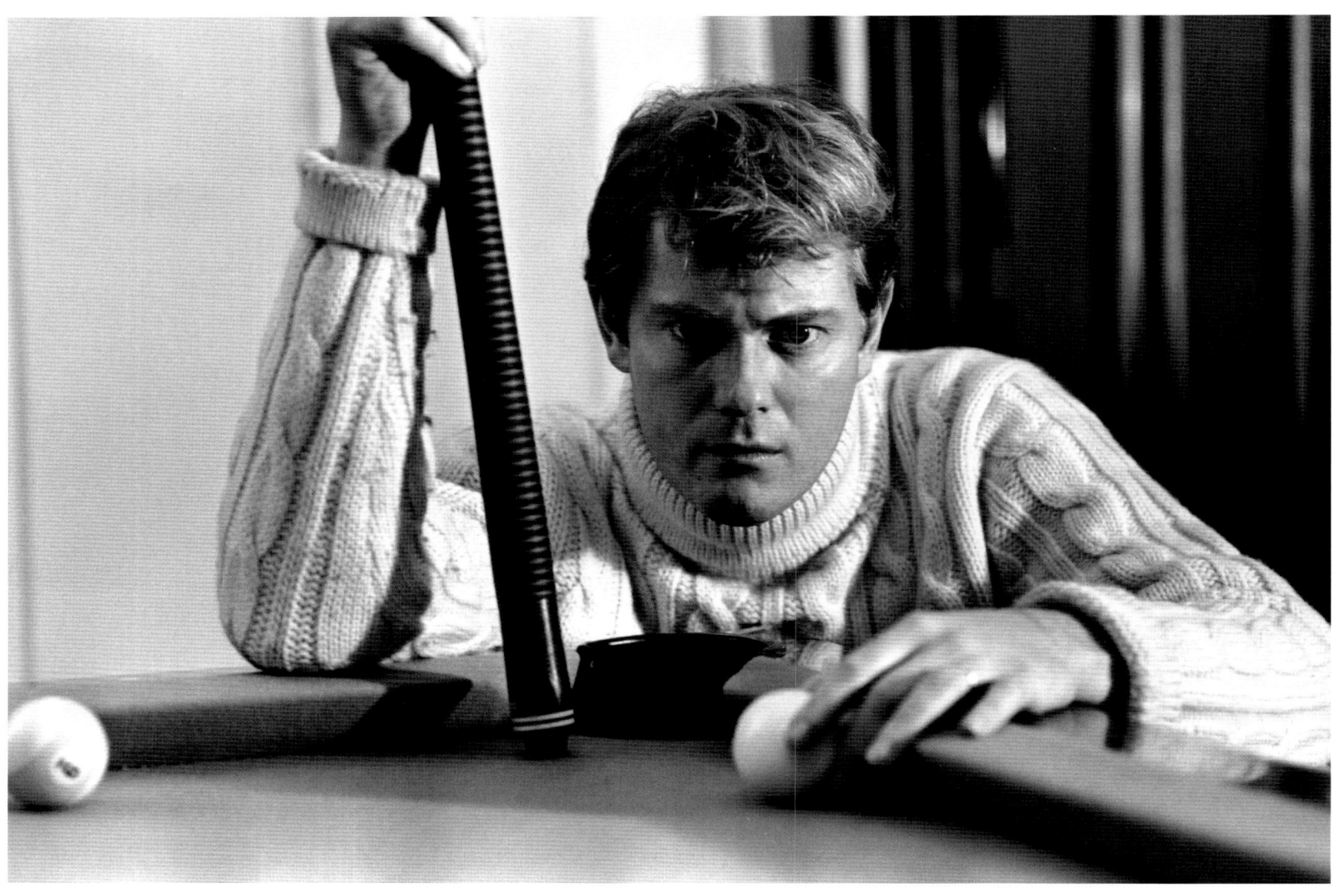

TROY DONAHUE, BEVERLY HILLS, 1966

OPPOSITE: DAVID HASSELHOFF, BEVERLY HILLS, 1983

OVERLEAF LEFT: MALCOLM MCDOWELL, NEW YORK CITY, 1973

OVERLEAF RIGHT: MELANIE GRIFFITH, LOS ANGELES, 1974

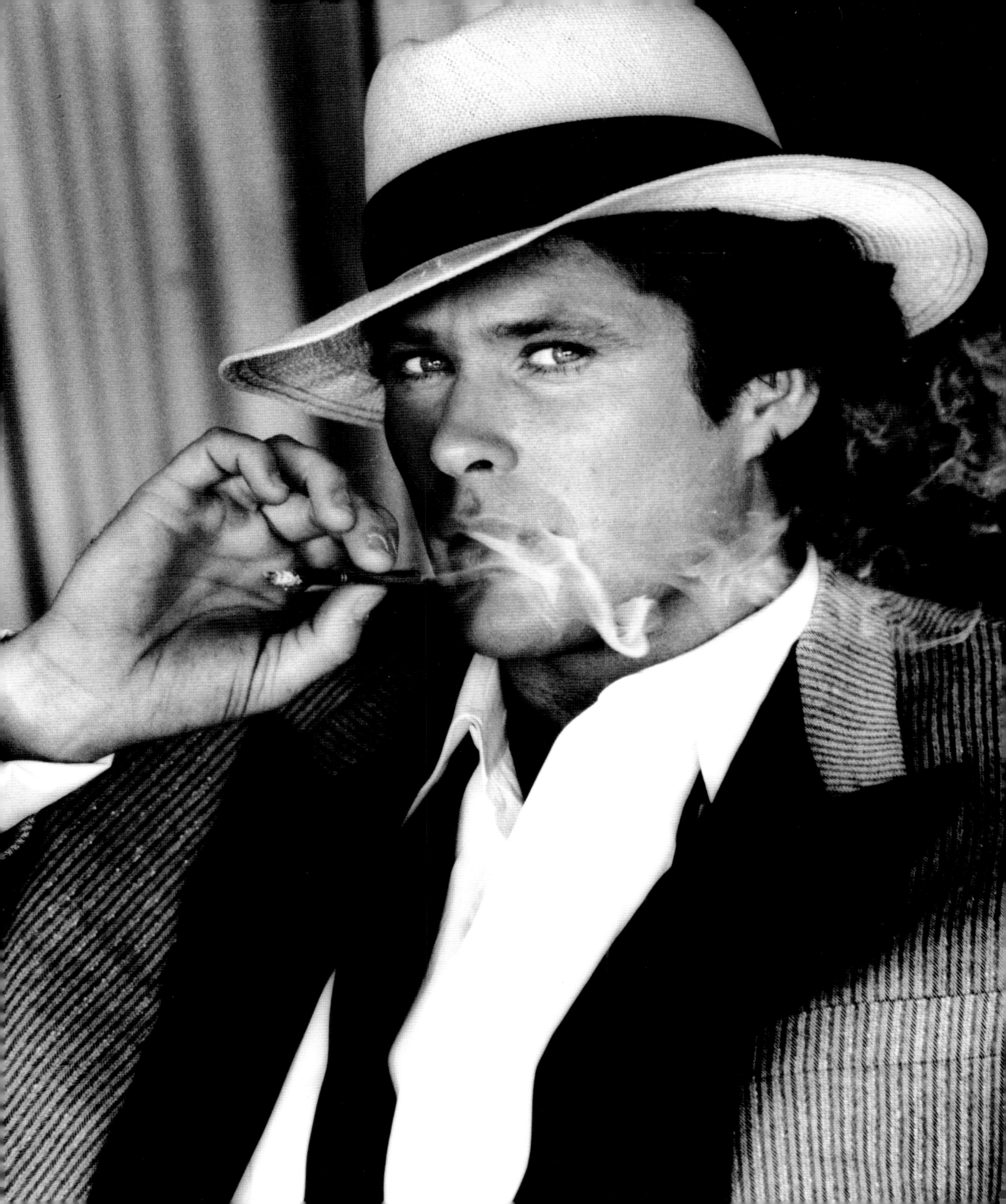

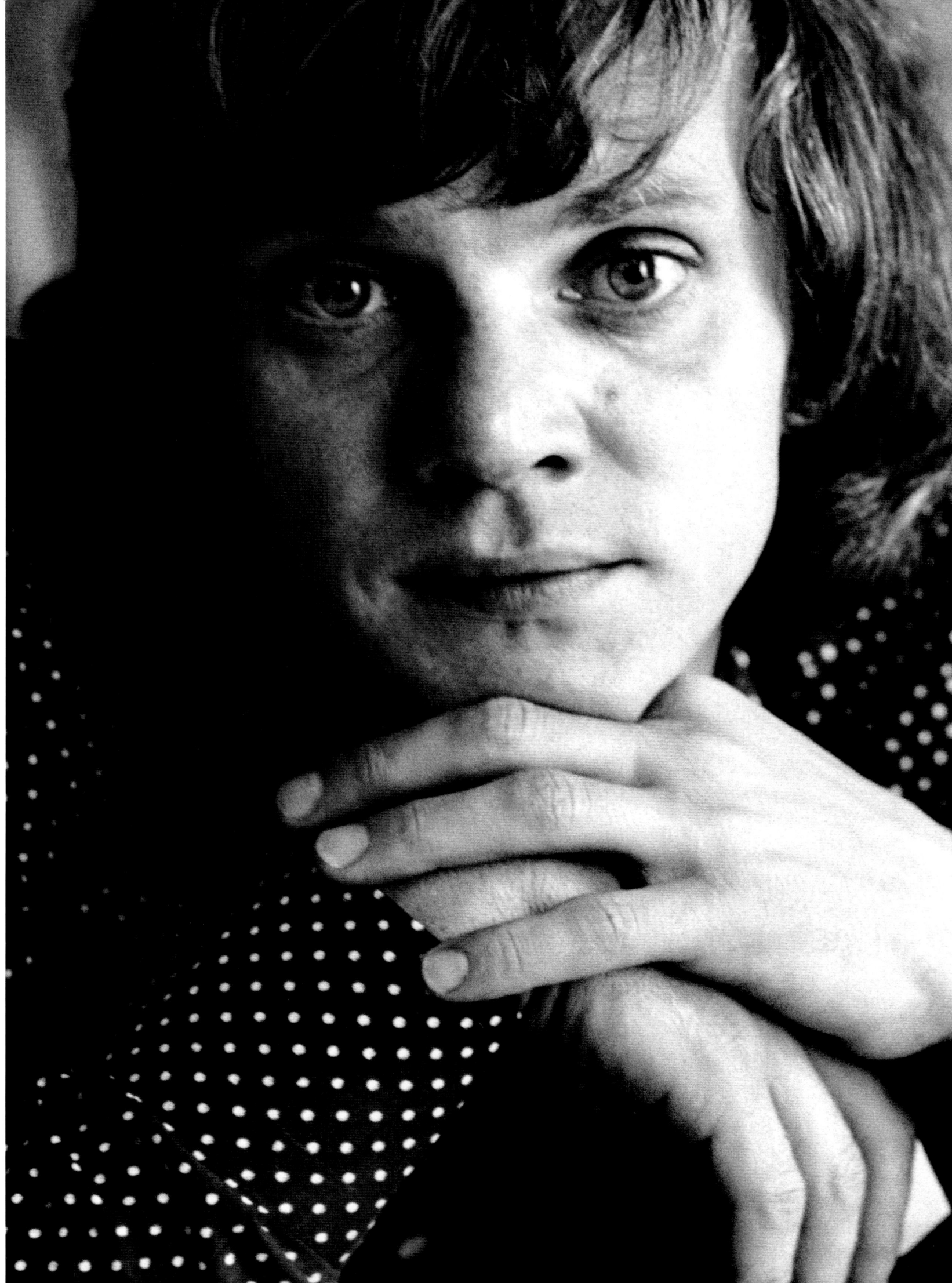

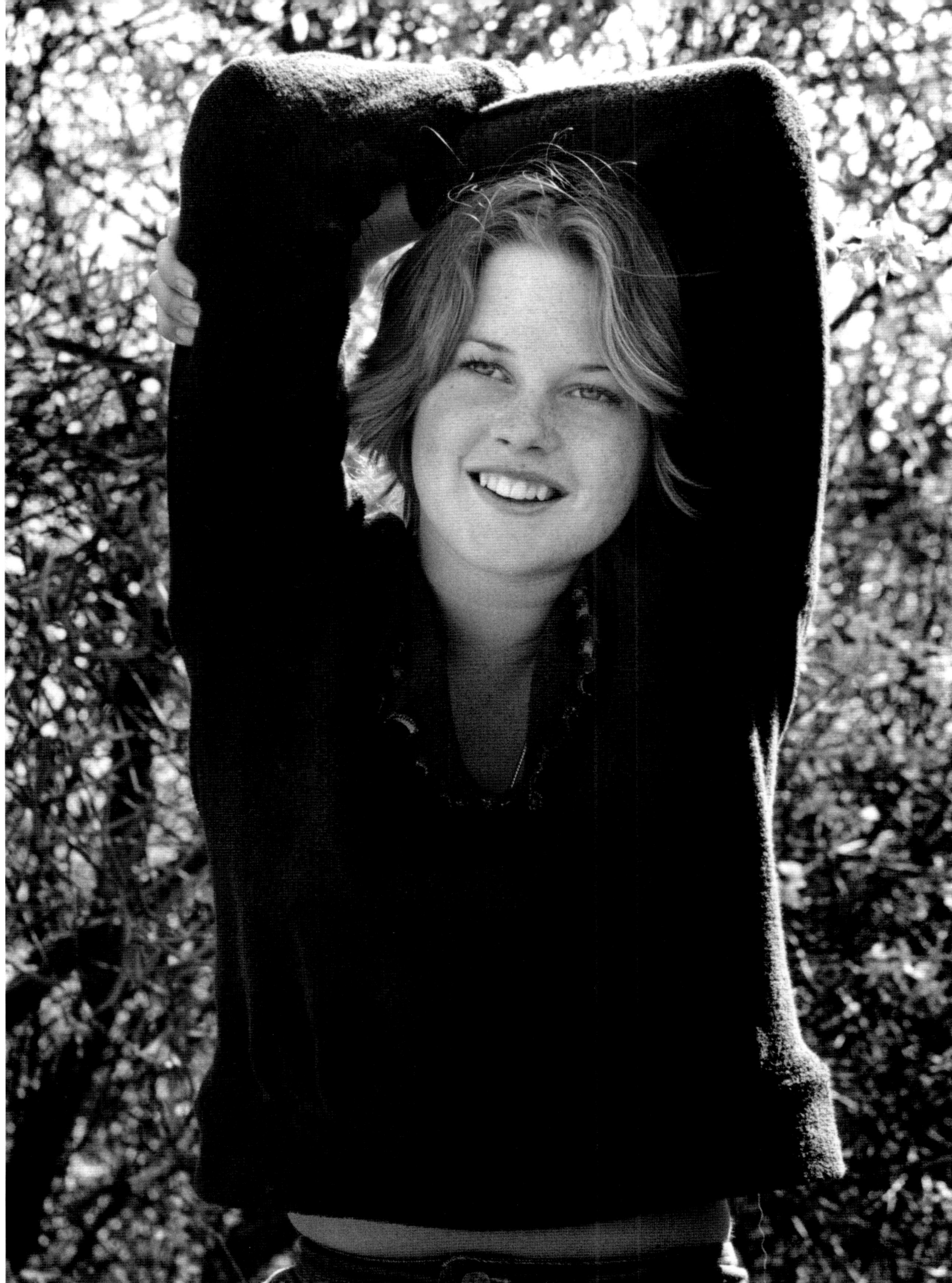

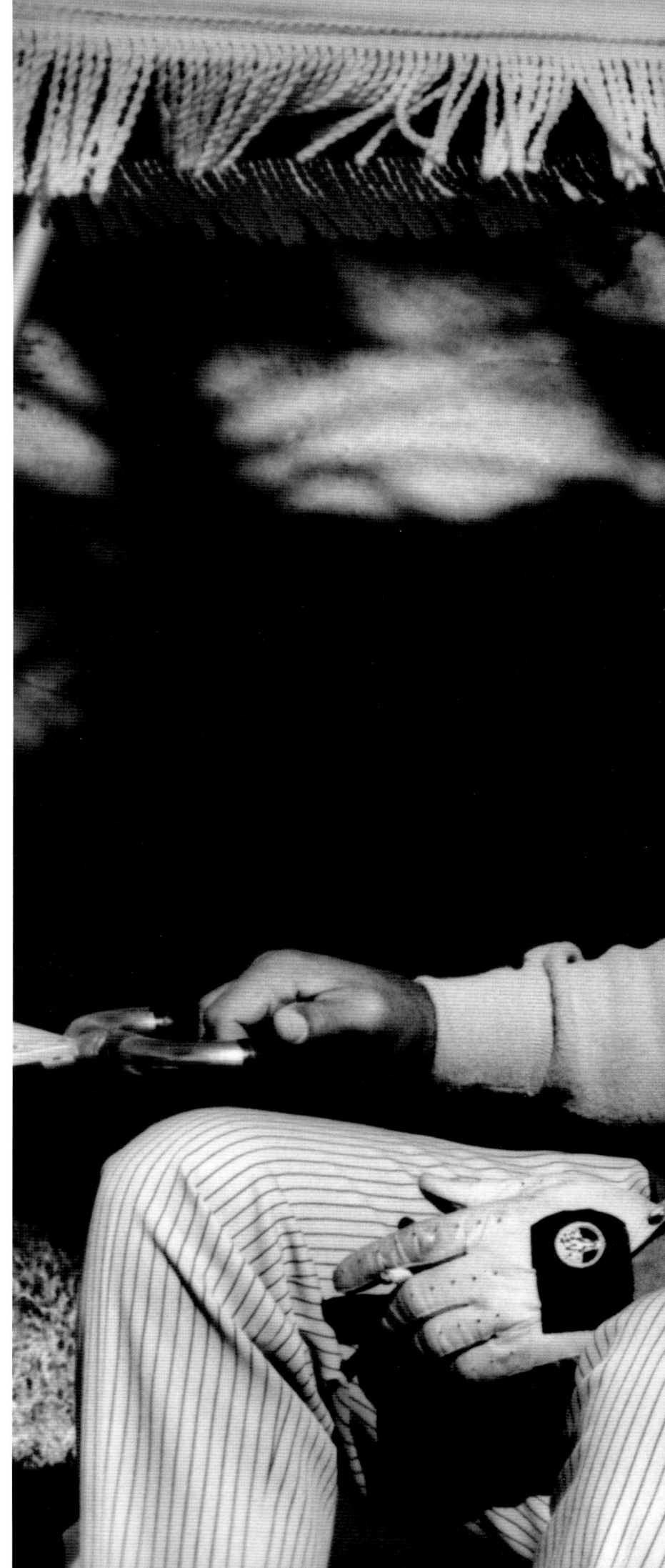

JOE LOUIS, PALM SPRINGS, 1972

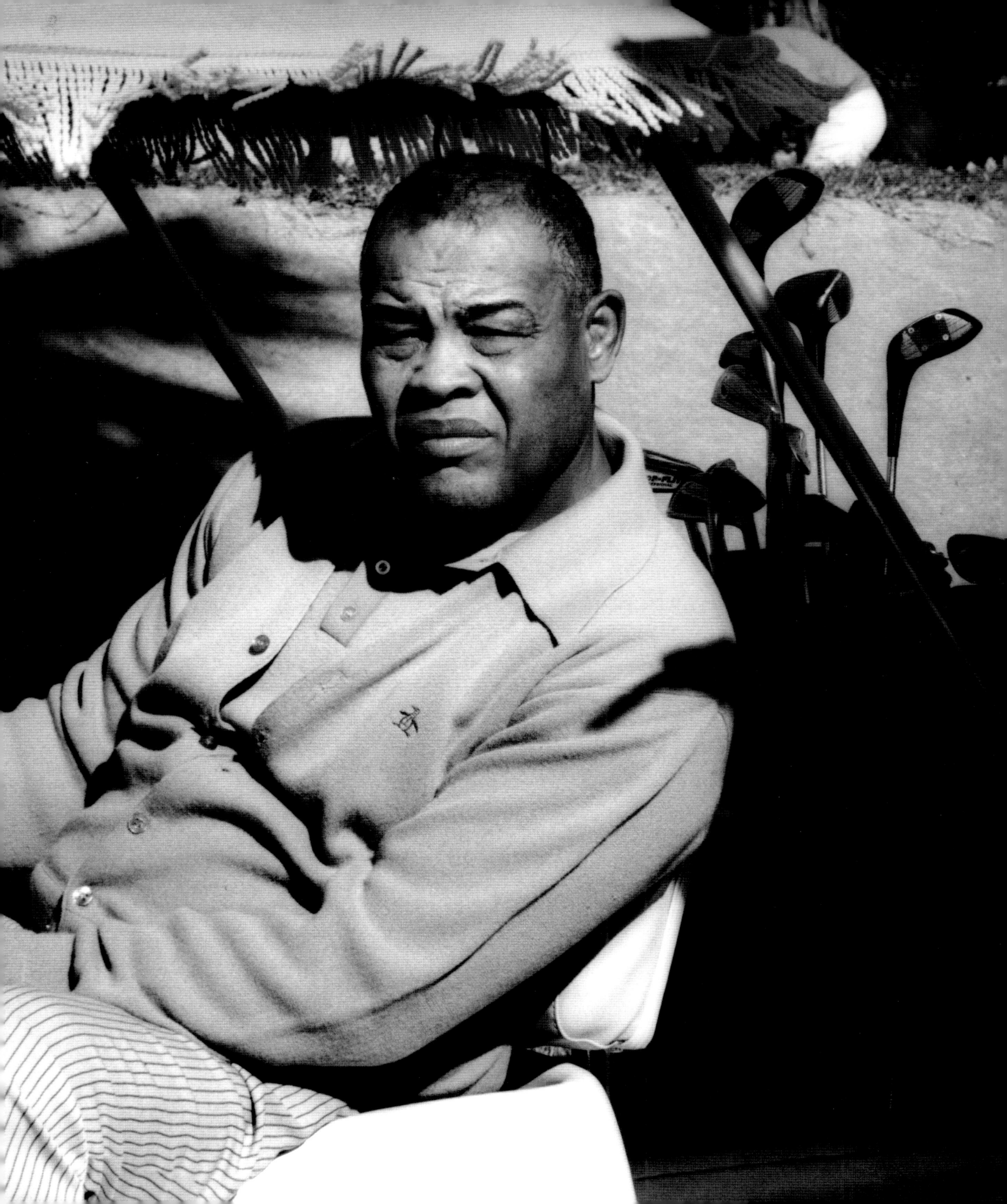

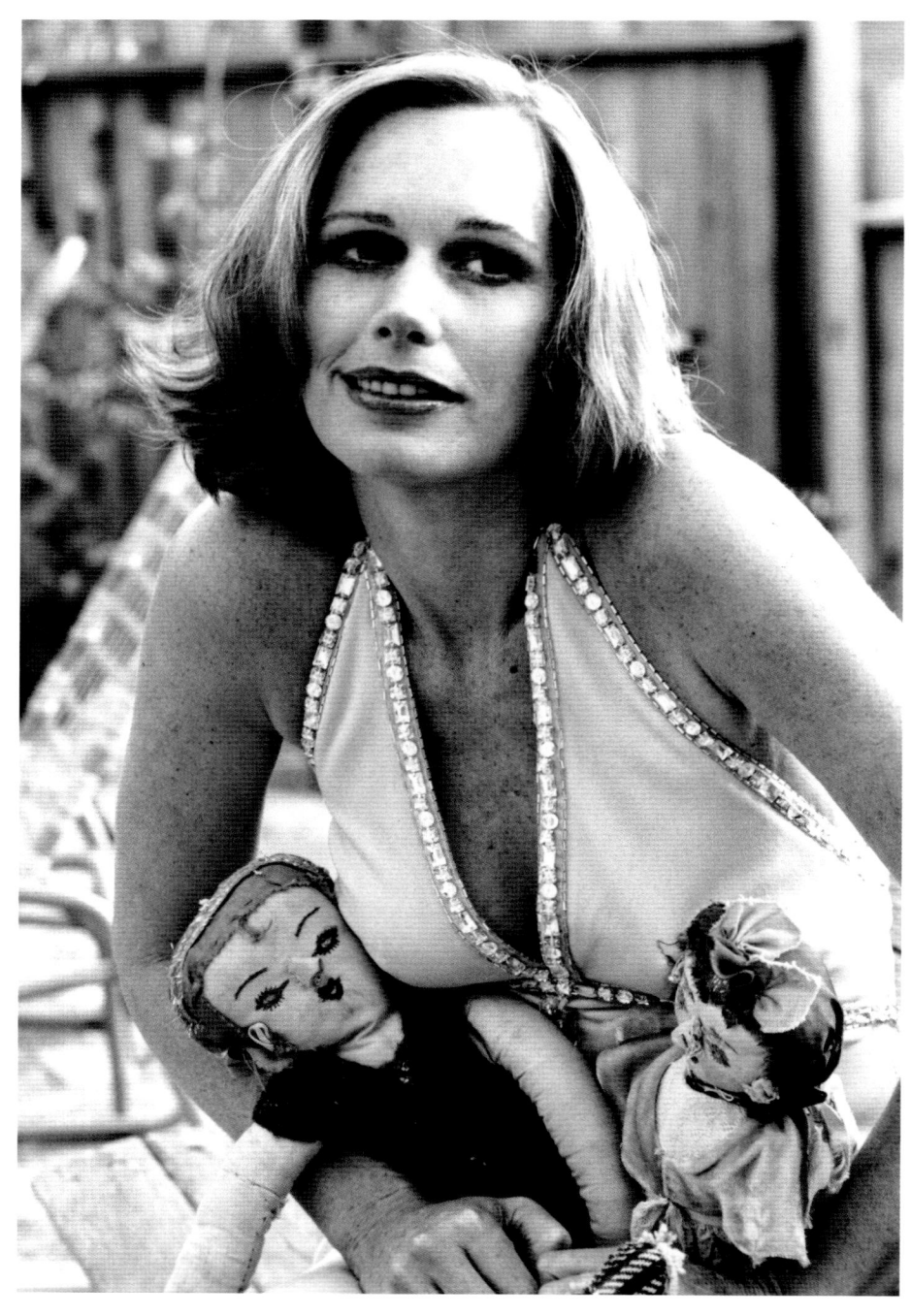

SALLY KELLERMAN, LOS ANGELES, 1974

OPPOSITE: SISSY SPACEK, SANTA FE, NEW MEXICO, 1974

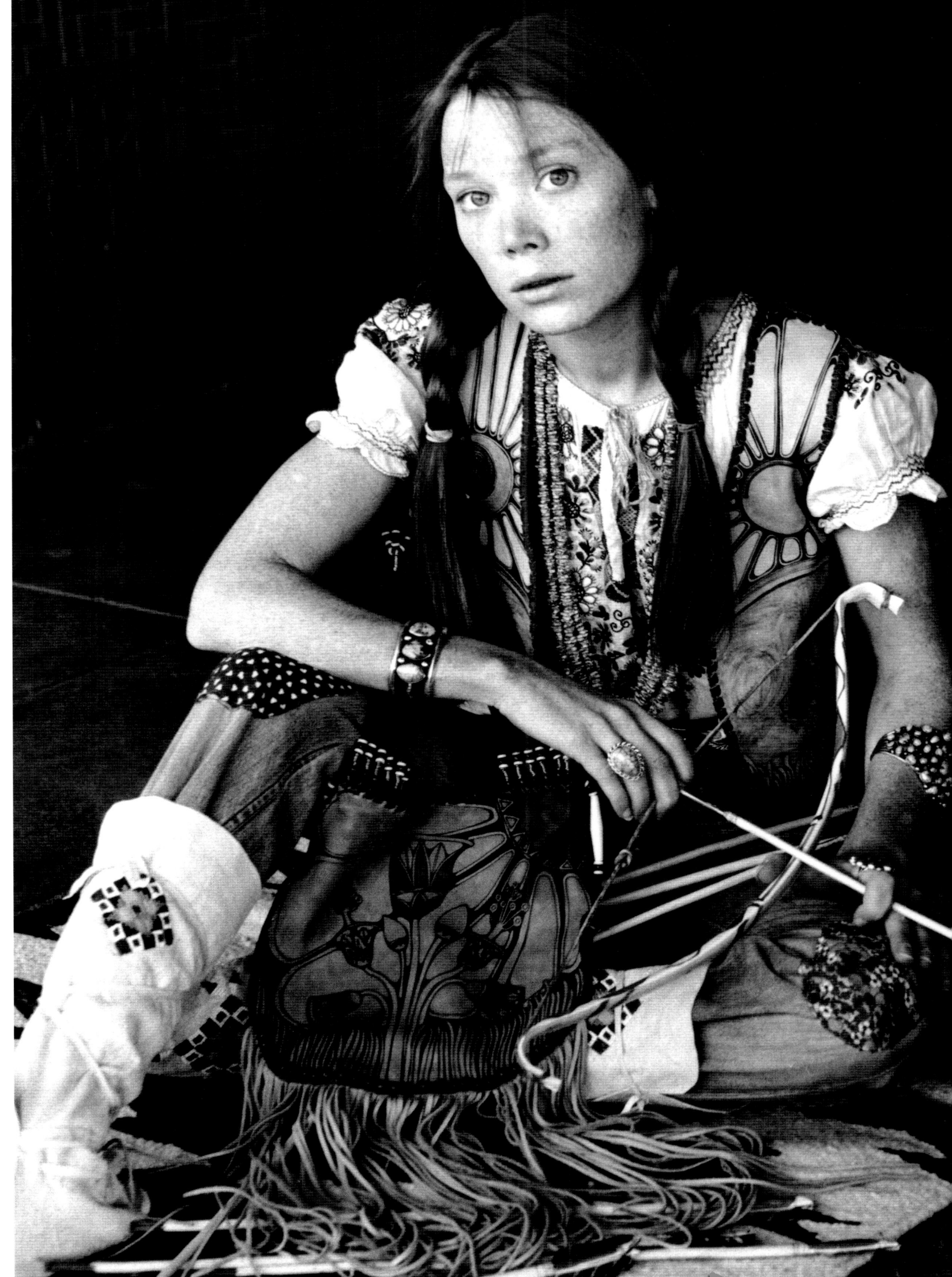

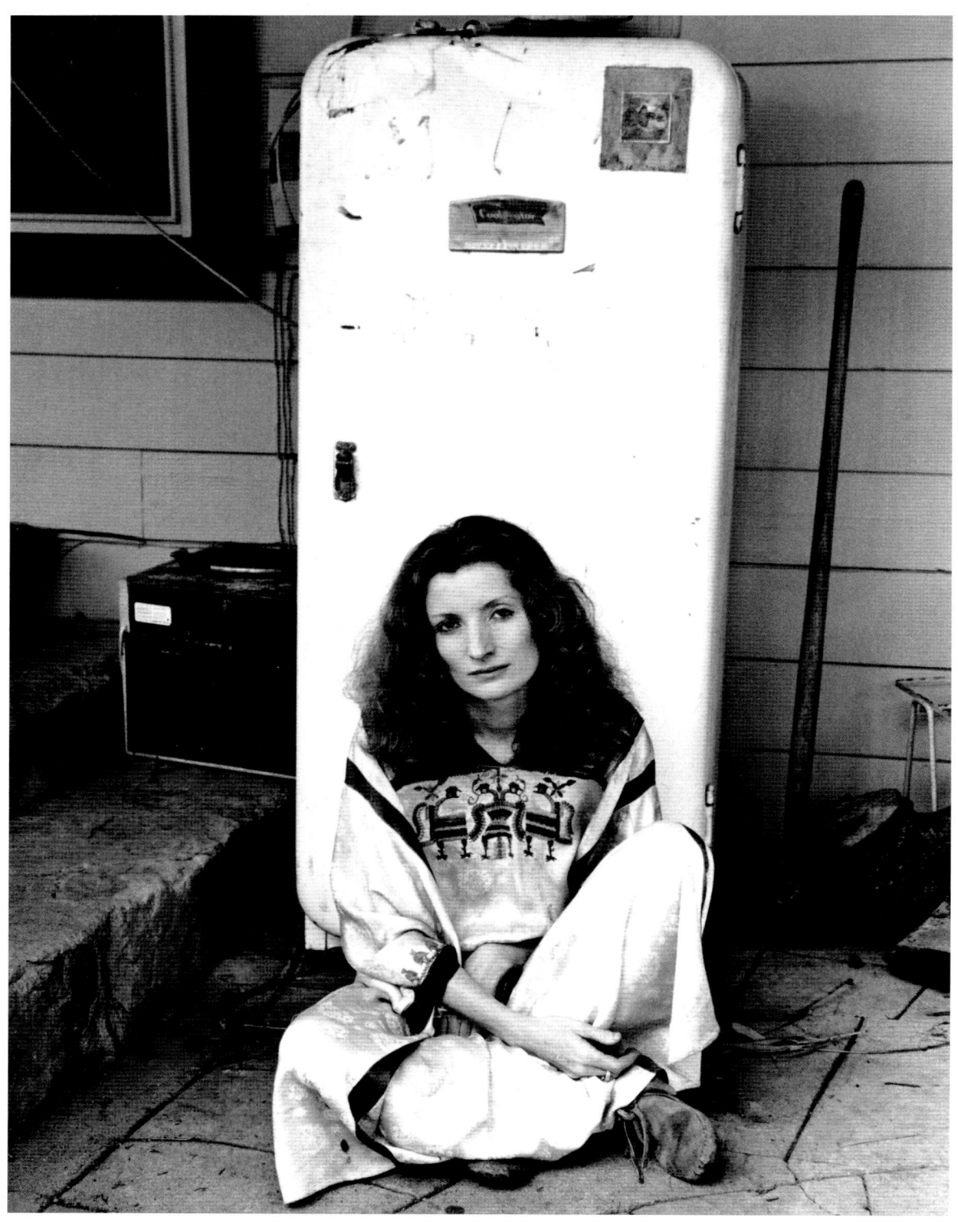

VIVA, TOPANGA CANYON, LOS ANGELES, 1974

OPPOSITE: PETER MARTINS WITH ALEXANDER CALDER
SCULPTURE, LINCOLN CENTER, NEW YORK CITY, 1983

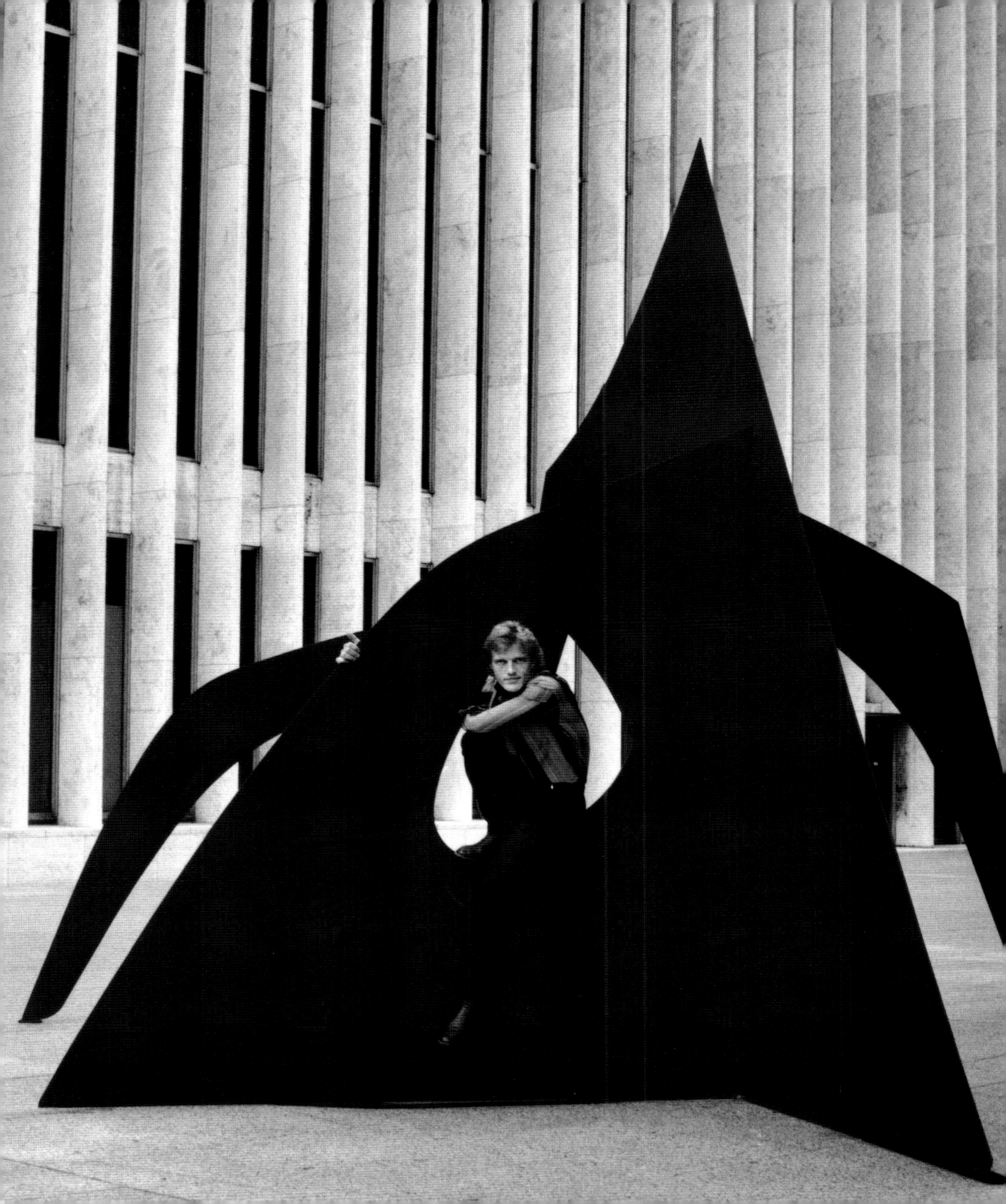

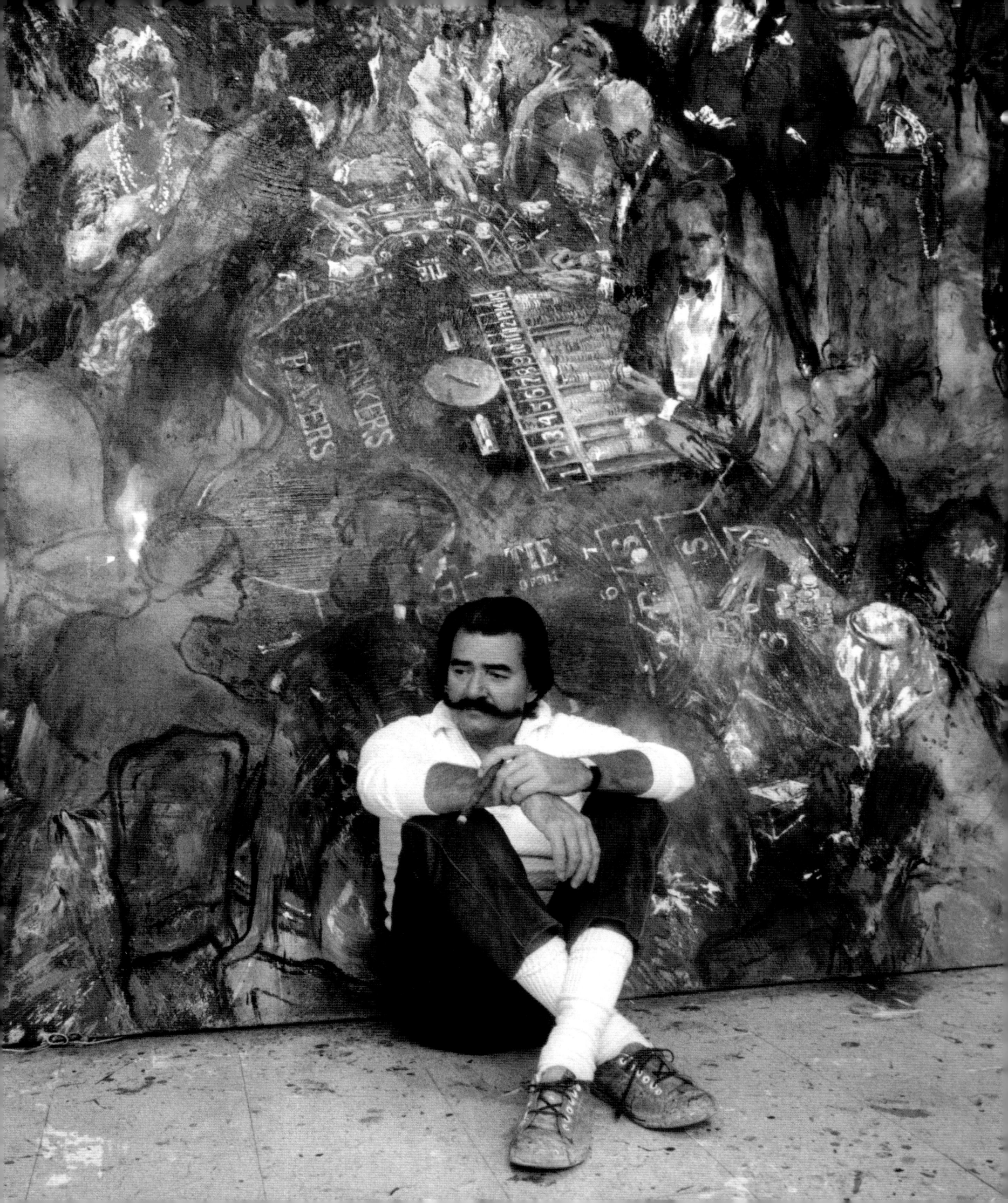

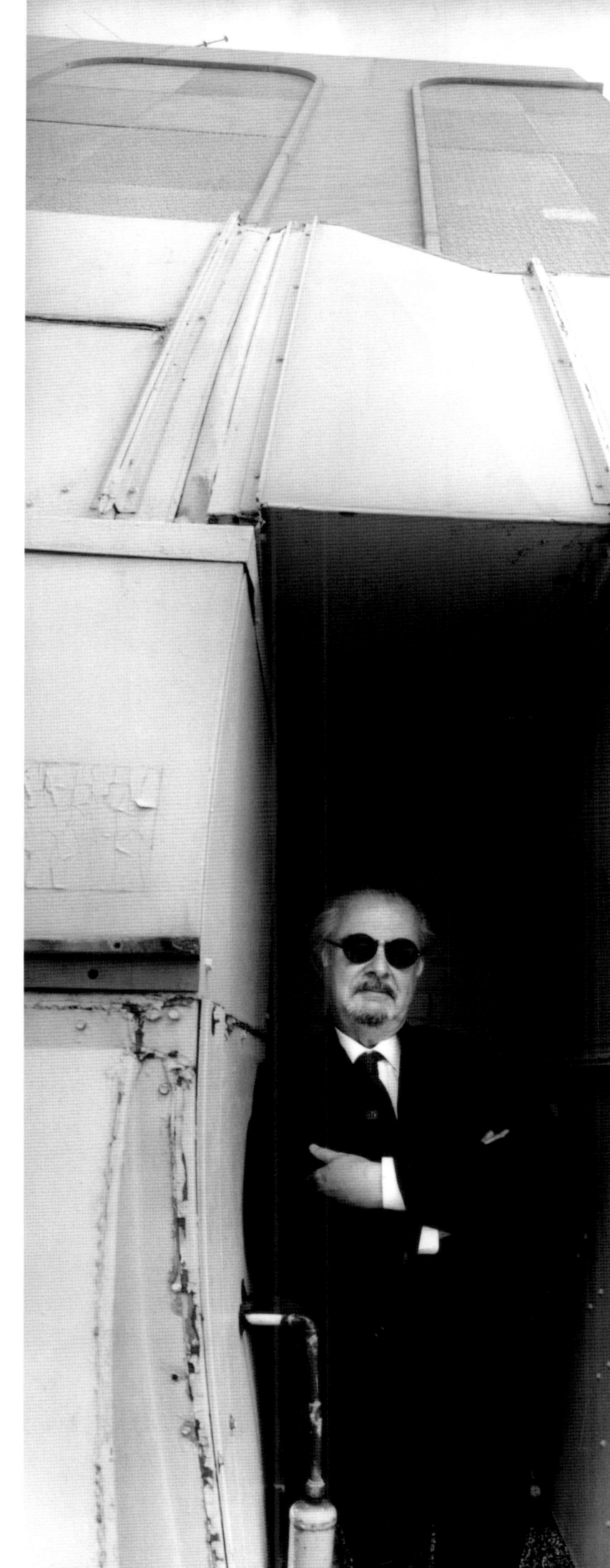

OPPOSITE: LEROY NEIMAN, NEW YORK CITY, 1987

RIGHT: FERNANDO BOTERO, NEW YORK CITY, 1999

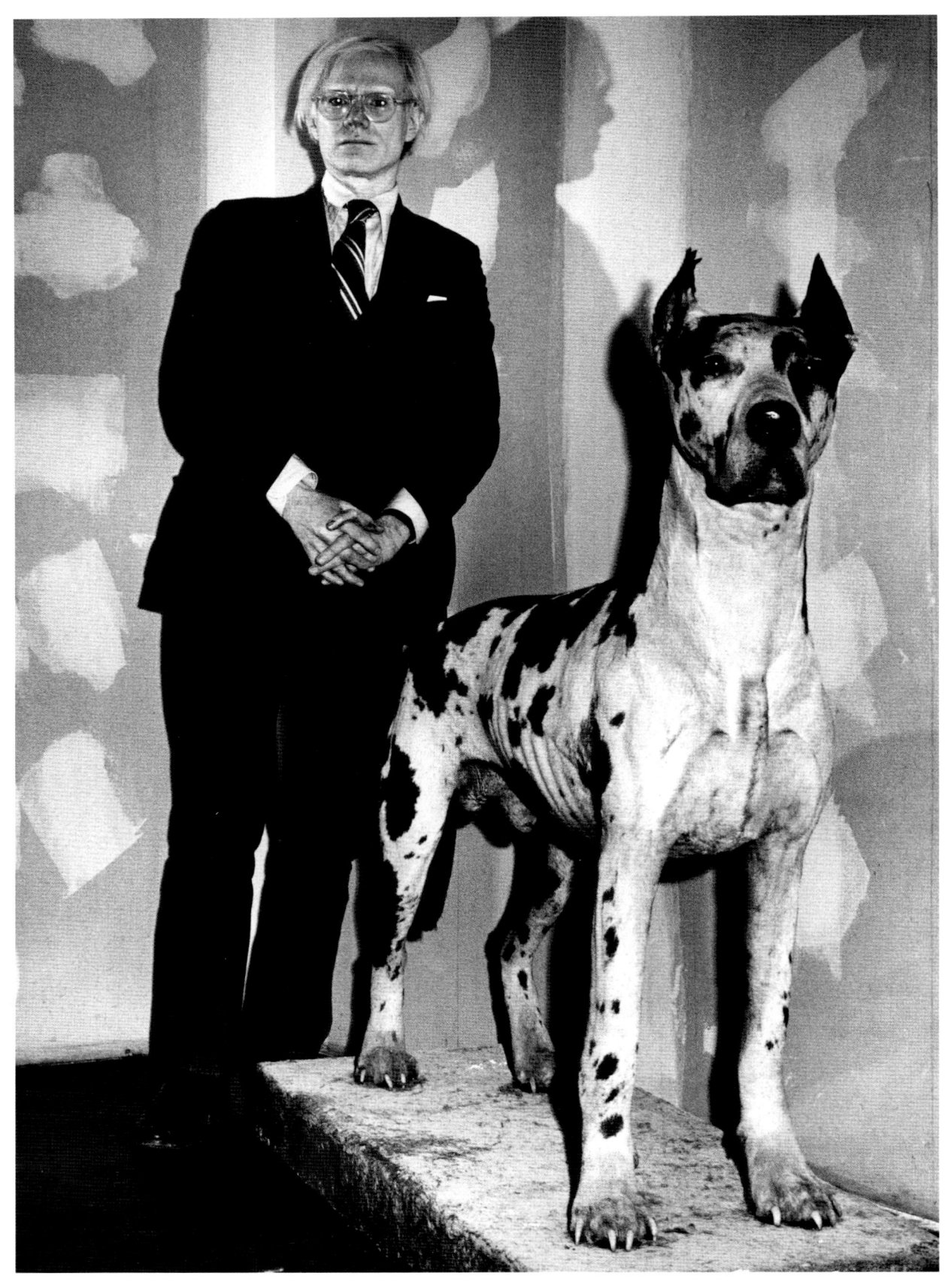

ANDY WARHOL WITH STUFFED DOG, NEW YORK CITY, 1974

OPPOSITE: ALICE NEEL WITH SELF-PORTRAIT, NEW YORK CITY, 1981

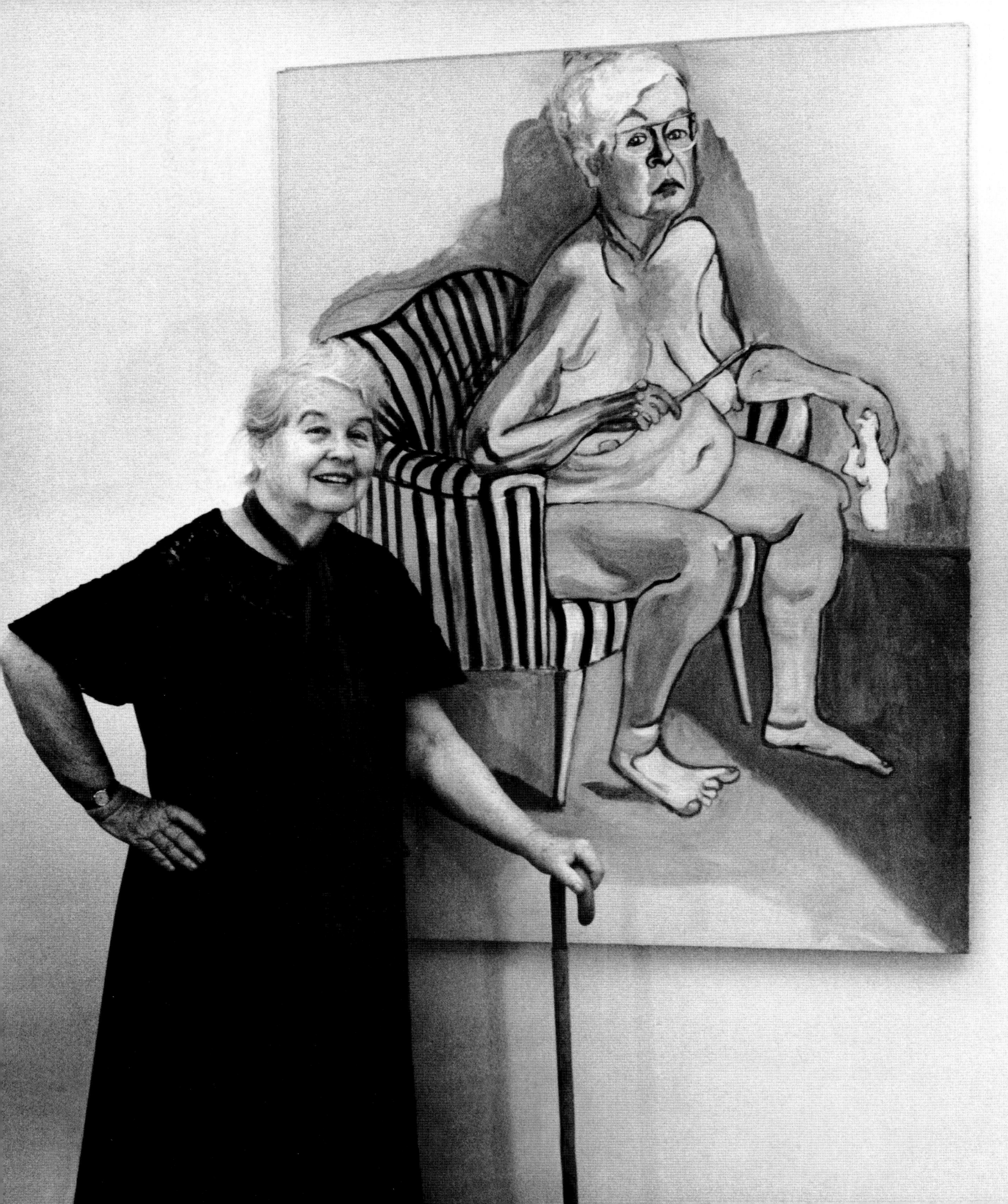

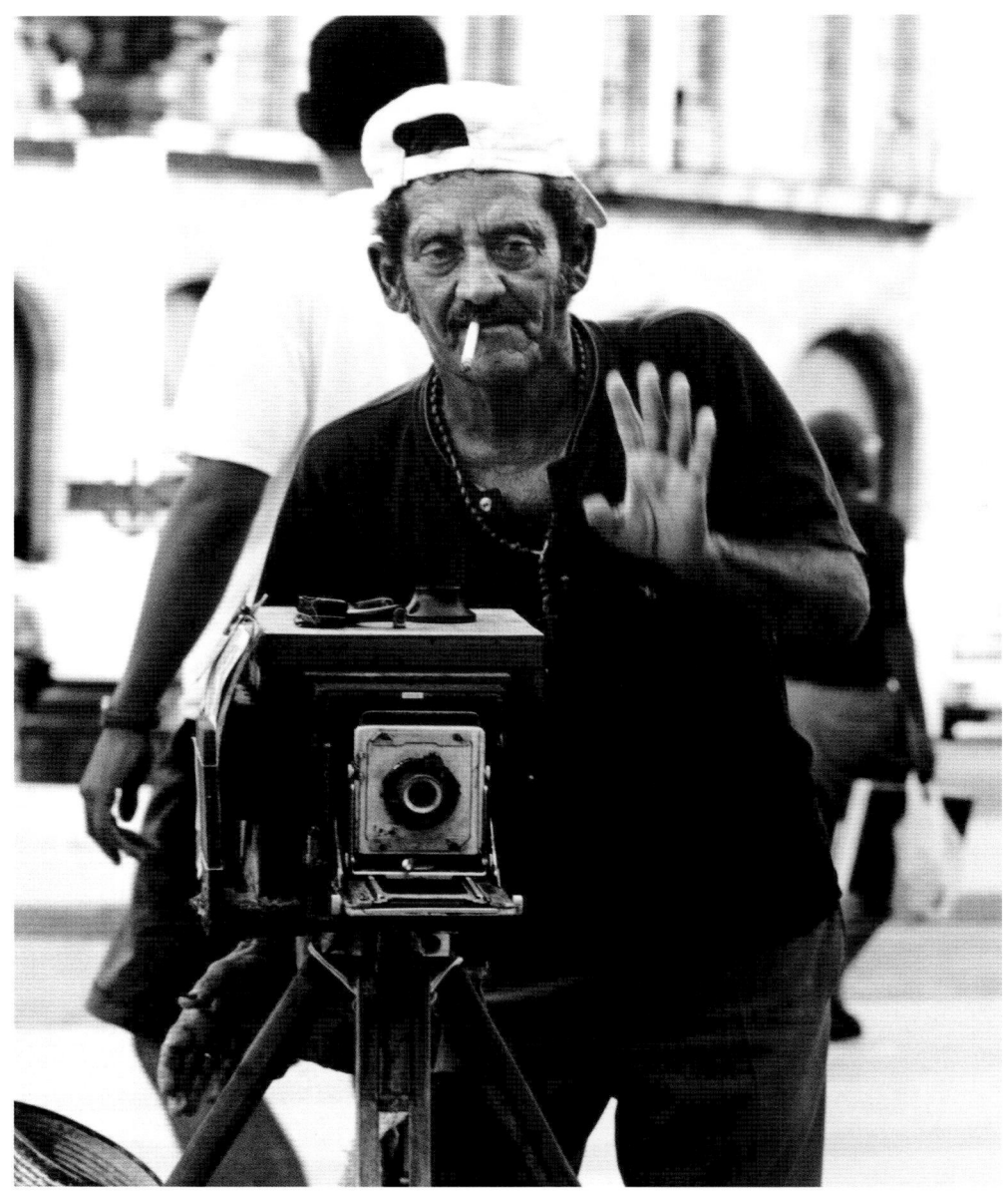

STREET PHOTOGRAPHER, HAVANA, CUBA, 1999

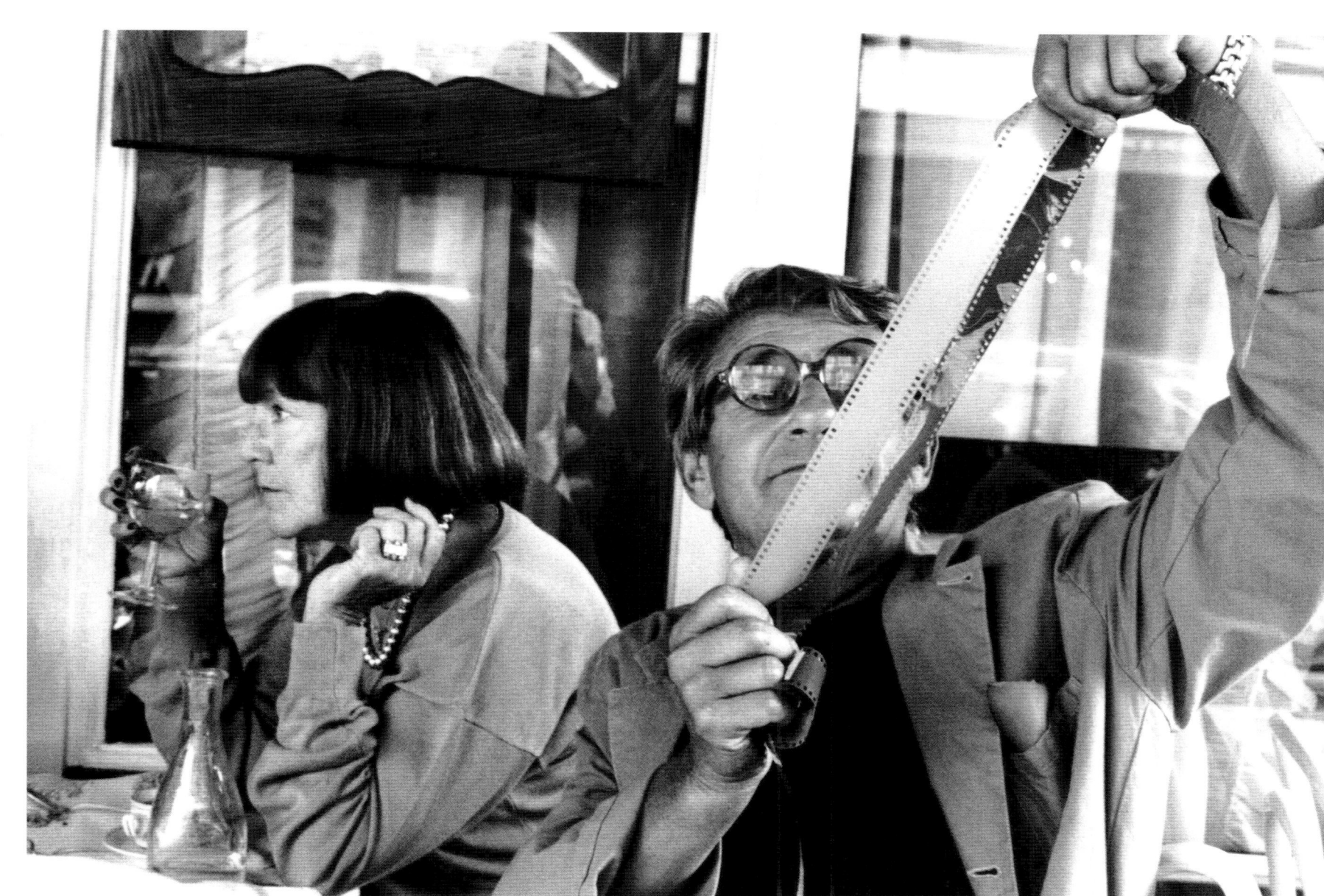

JUNE AND HELMUT NEWTON, PARIS, 1990

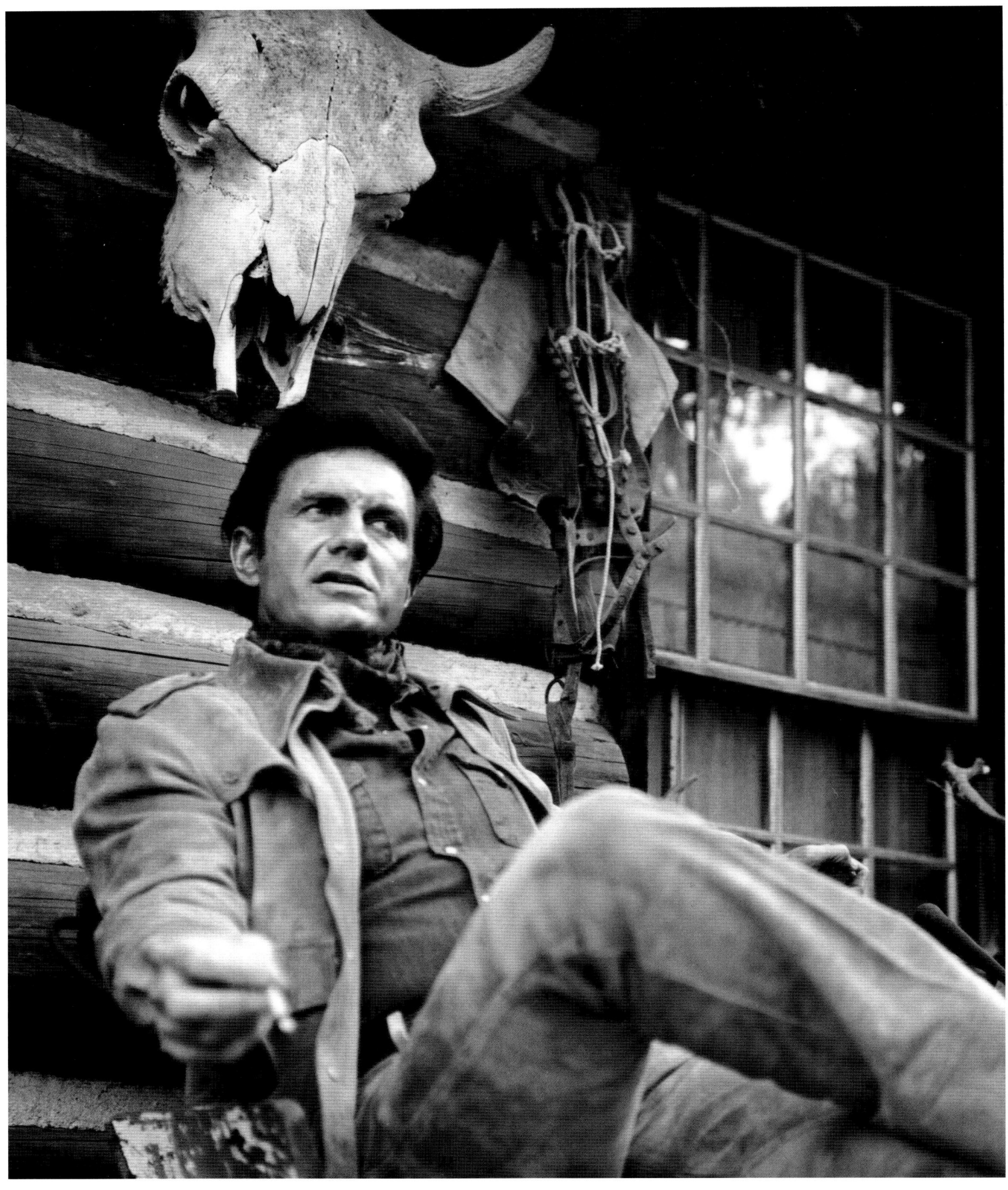

CLIFF ROBERTSON, LOS ANGELES, 1971

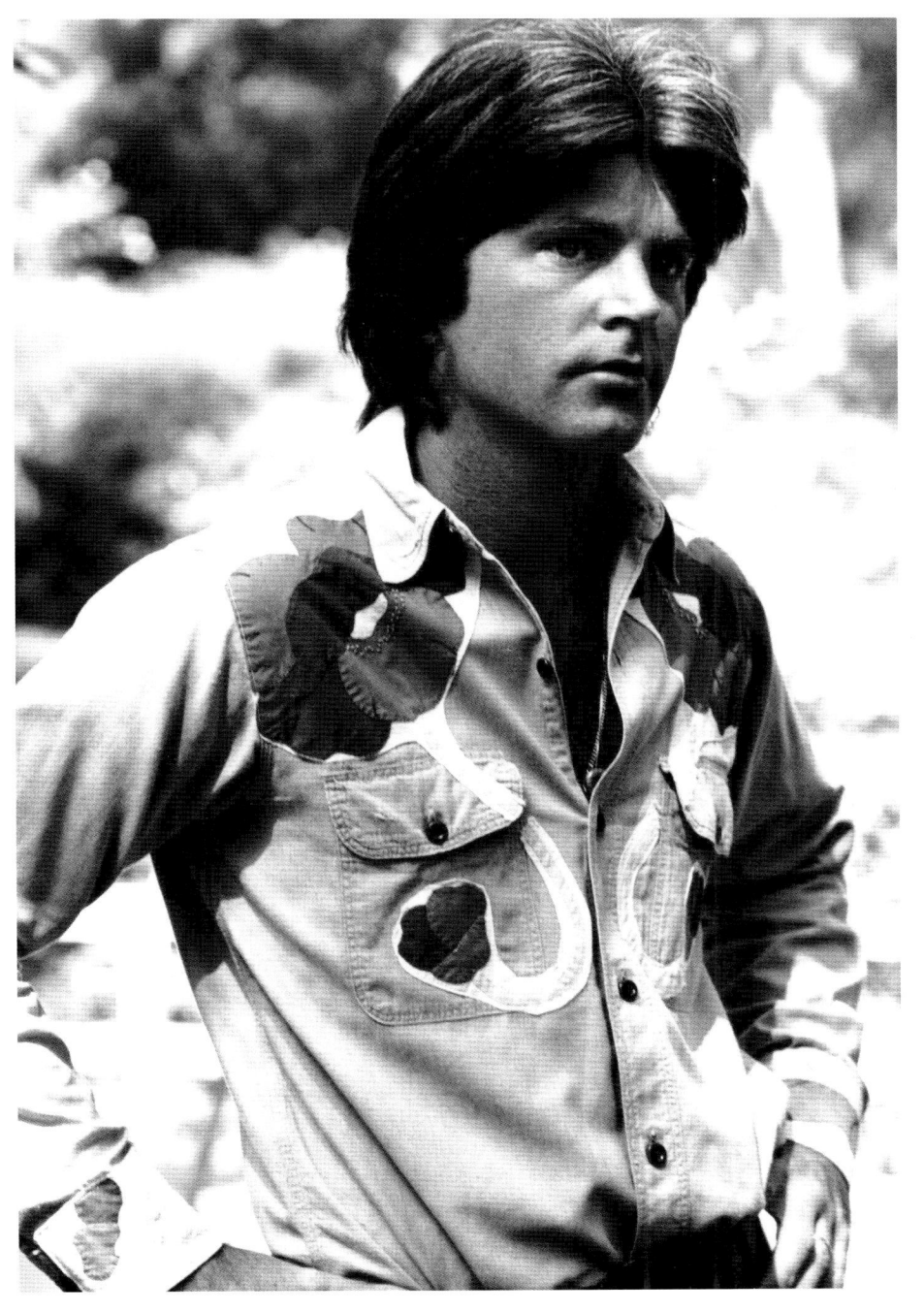

RICK NELSON, LOS ANGELES, 1973

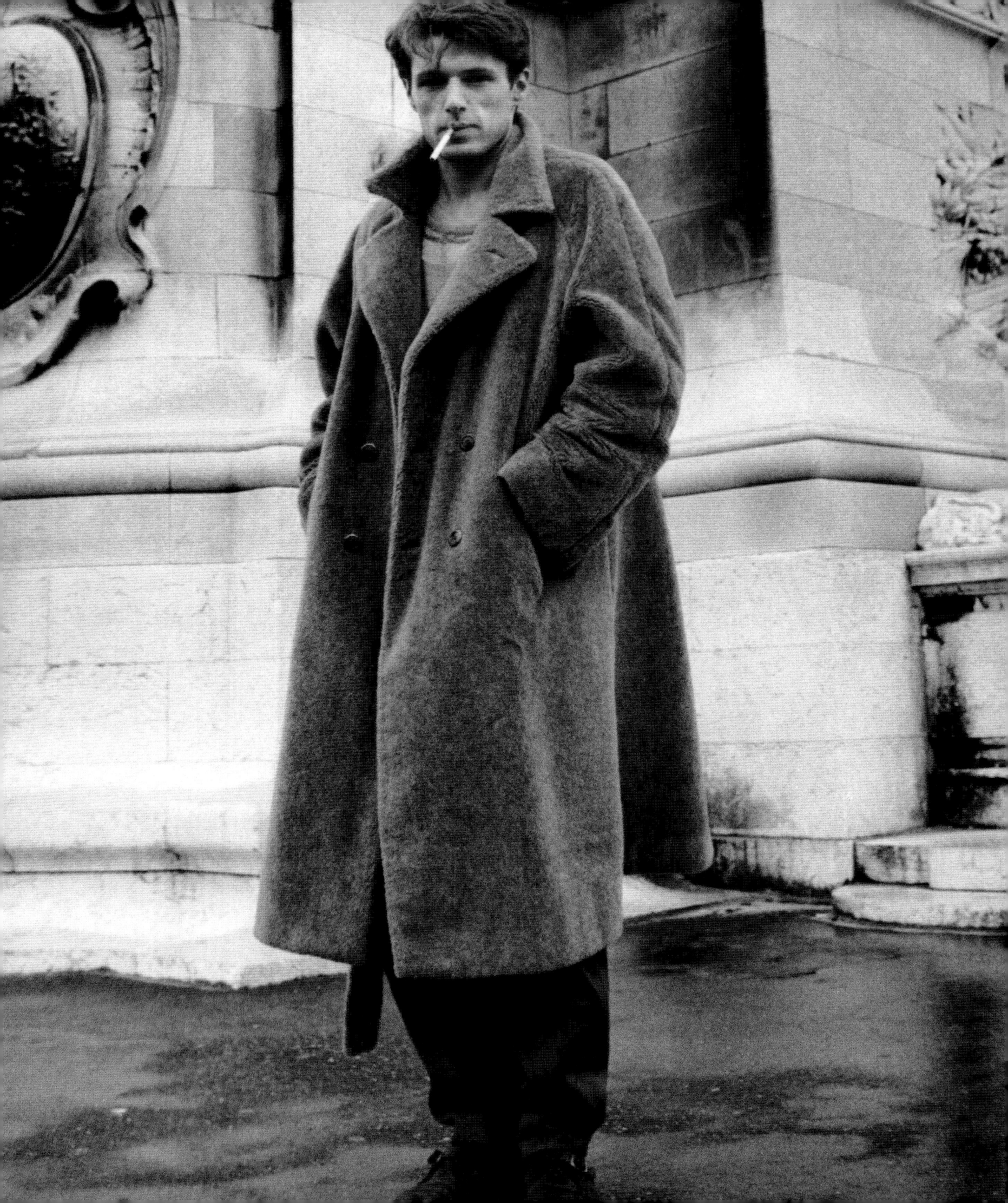

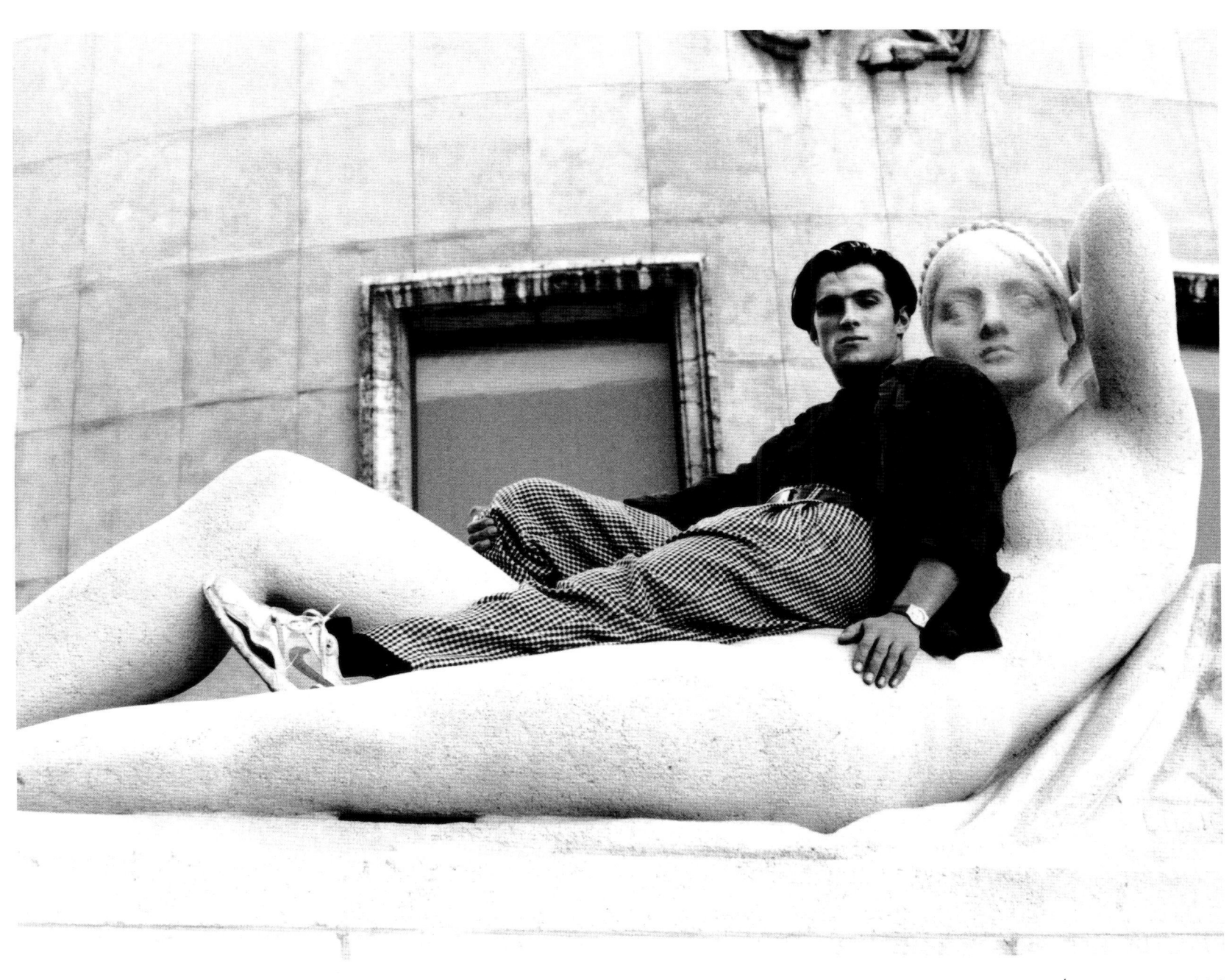

GWENEL, TROCADÉRO, PARIS, 1990

OPPOSITE: LAMBERT WILSON, PONT ALEXANDRE TROIS, PARIS, 1983

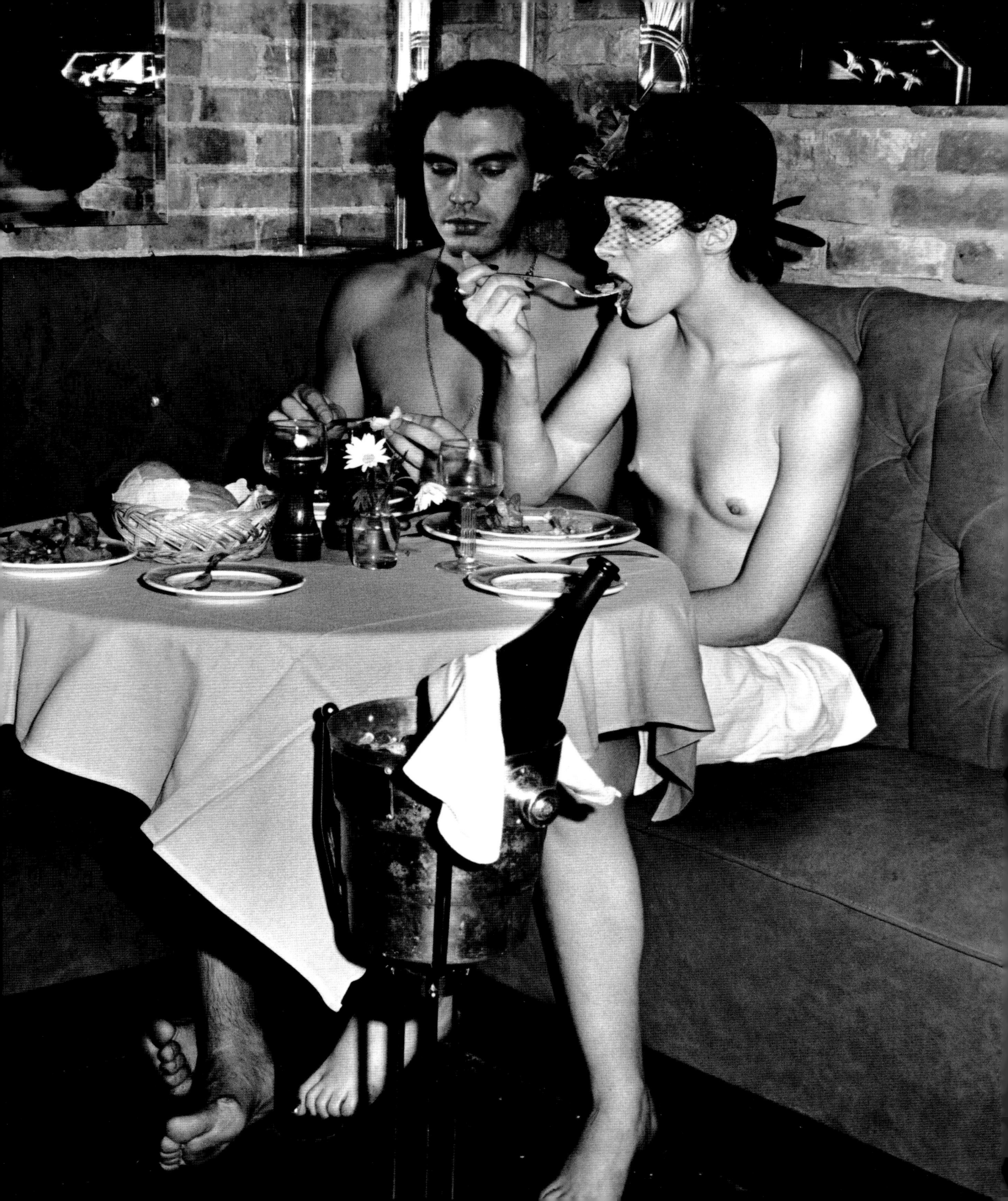

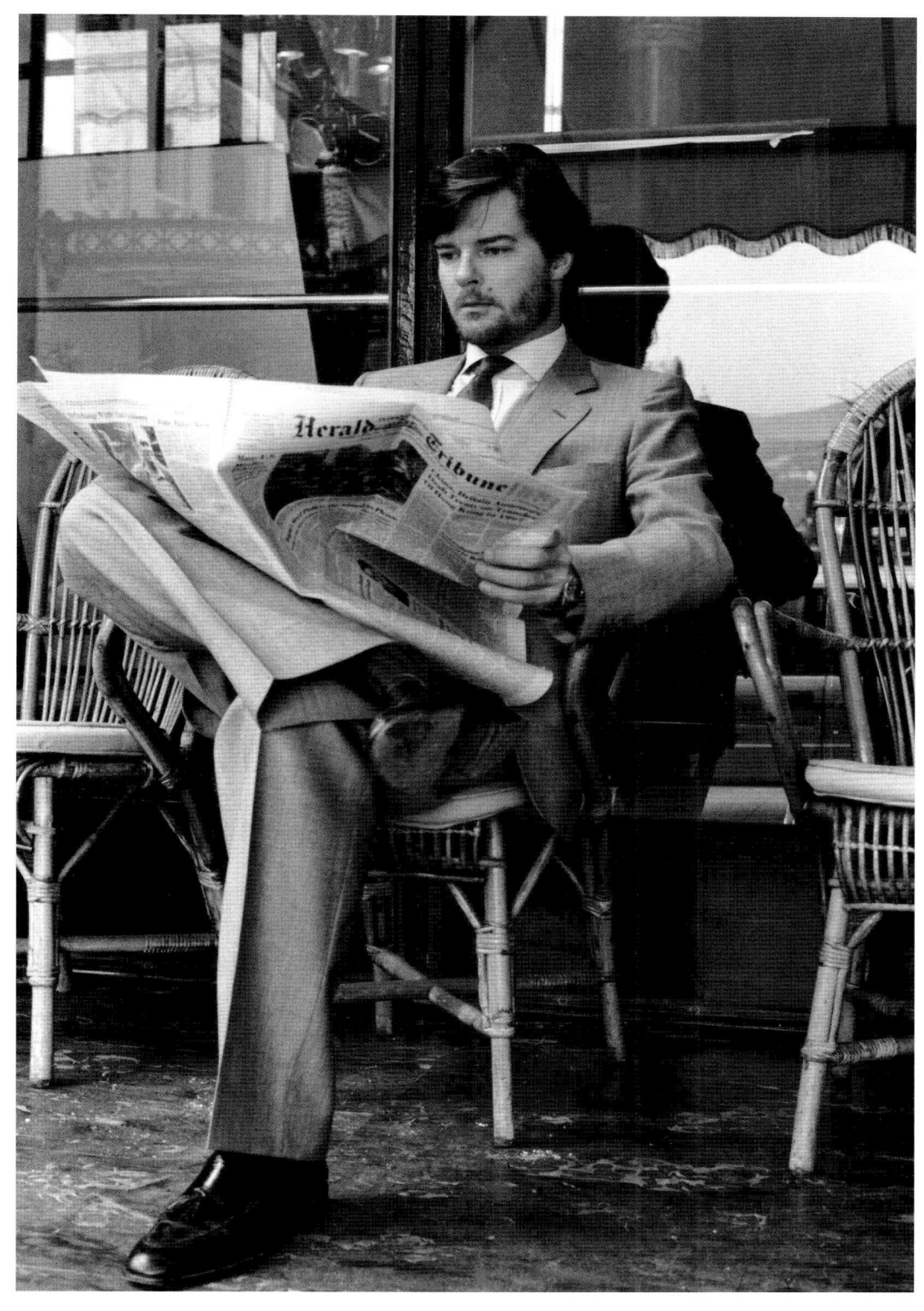

ROBERTO ROSSELLINI, MONTE CARLO, 1984

OPPOSITE: NAKED LUNCH, NEW YORK CITY, 1974

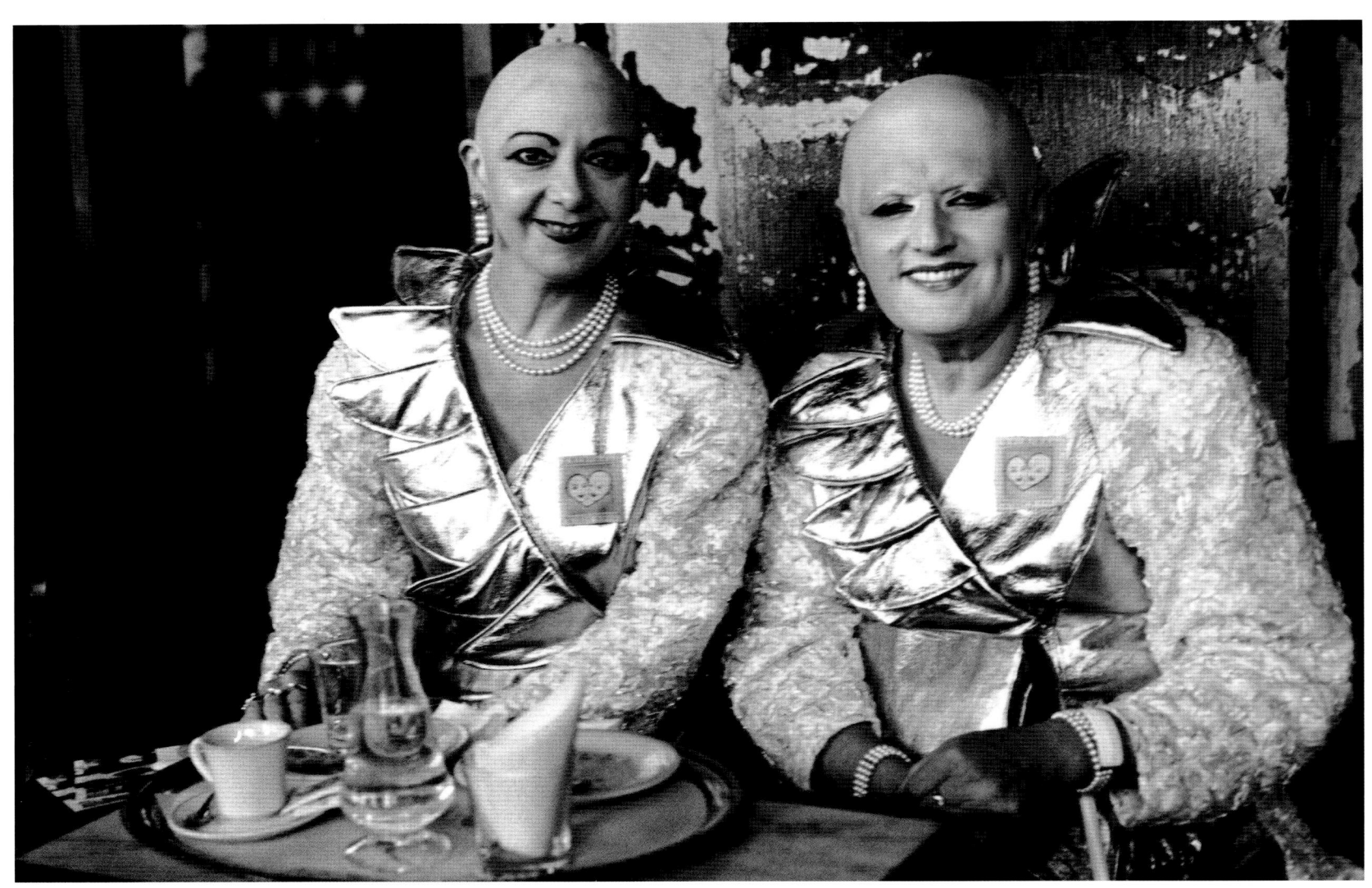
WIFE AND HUSBAND, CAFE FLORIAN, VENICE, ITALY, 1999

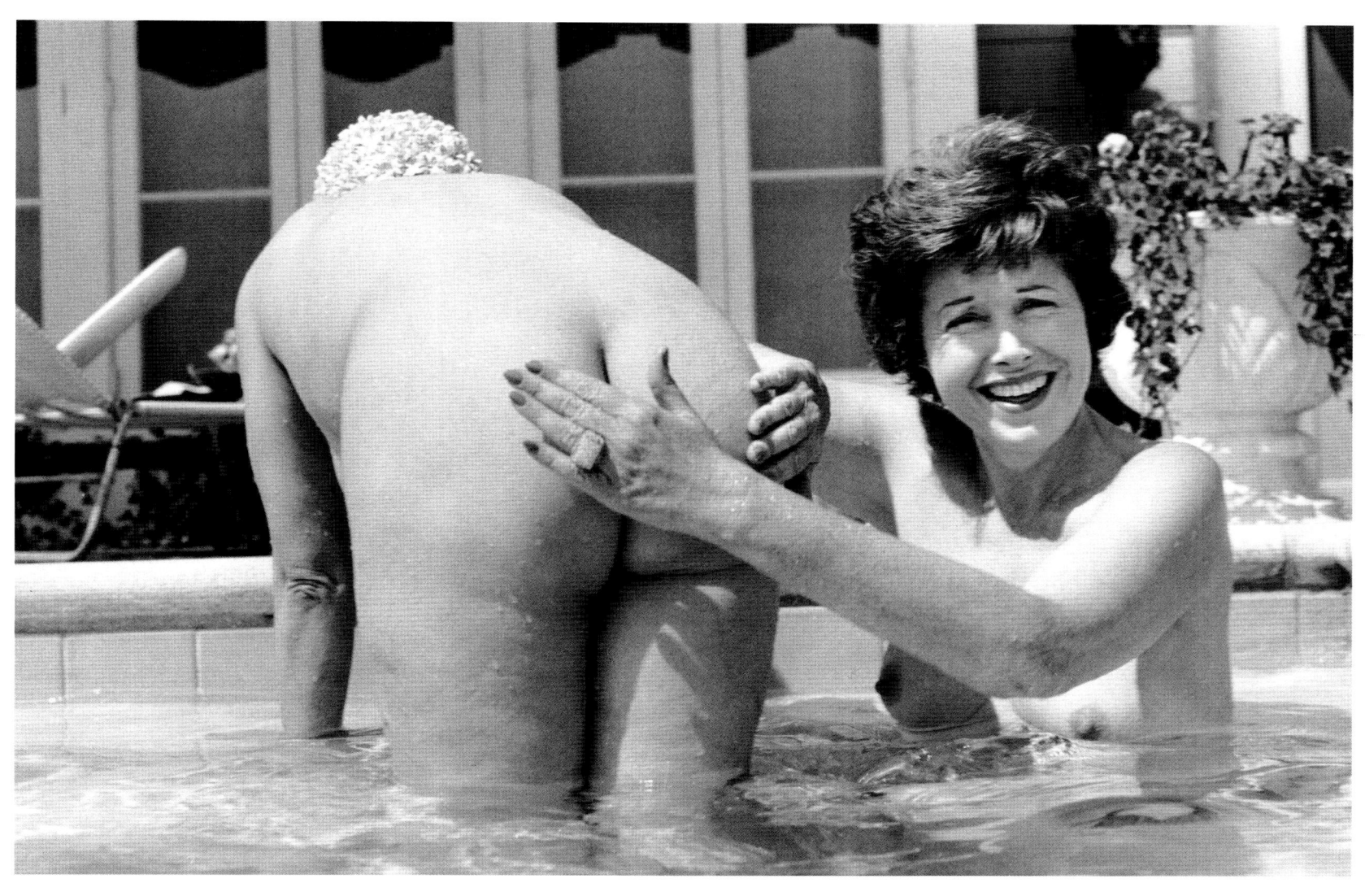

BATHING BEAUTIES, SOUTHAMPTON, NEW YORK, 1962

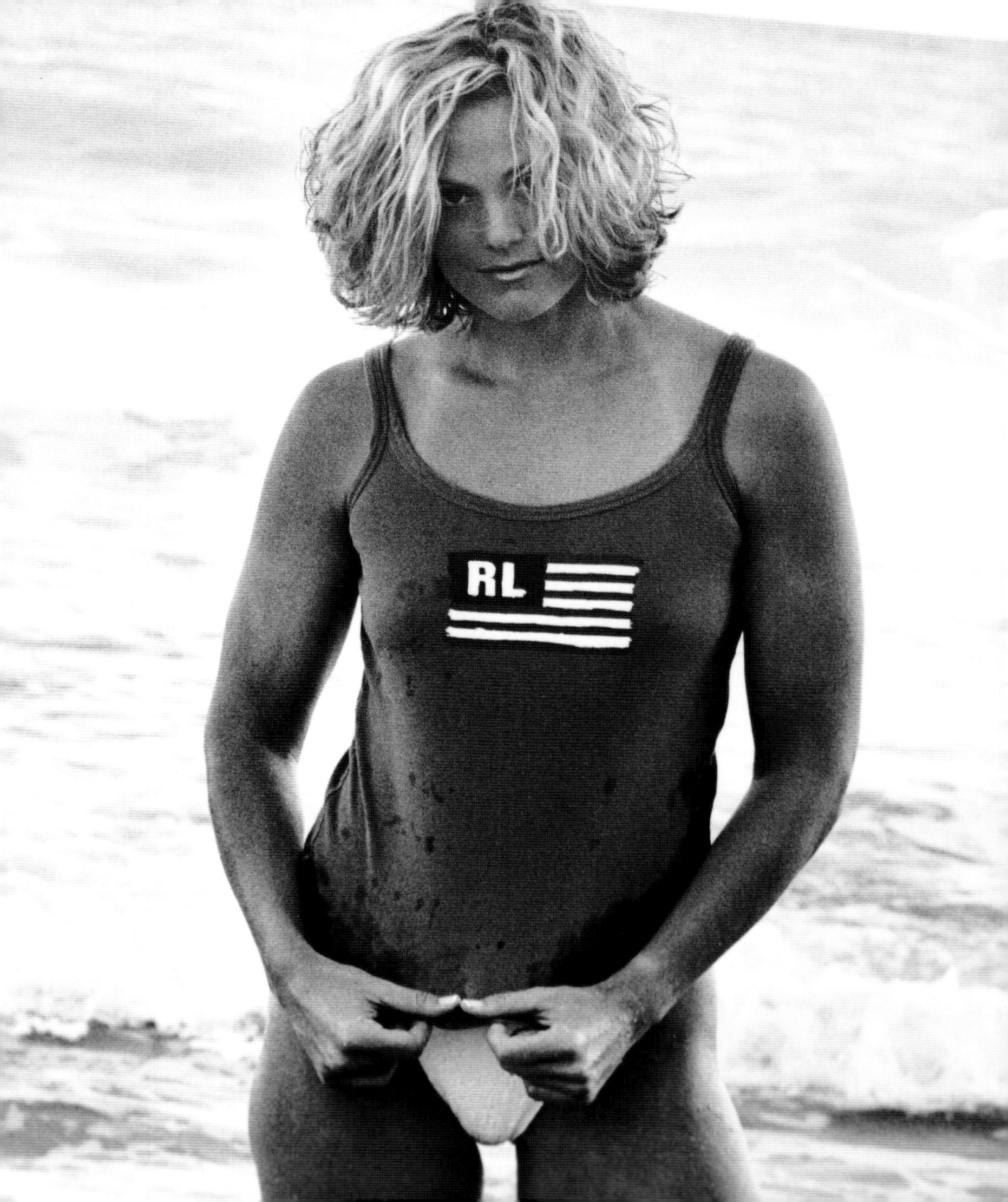

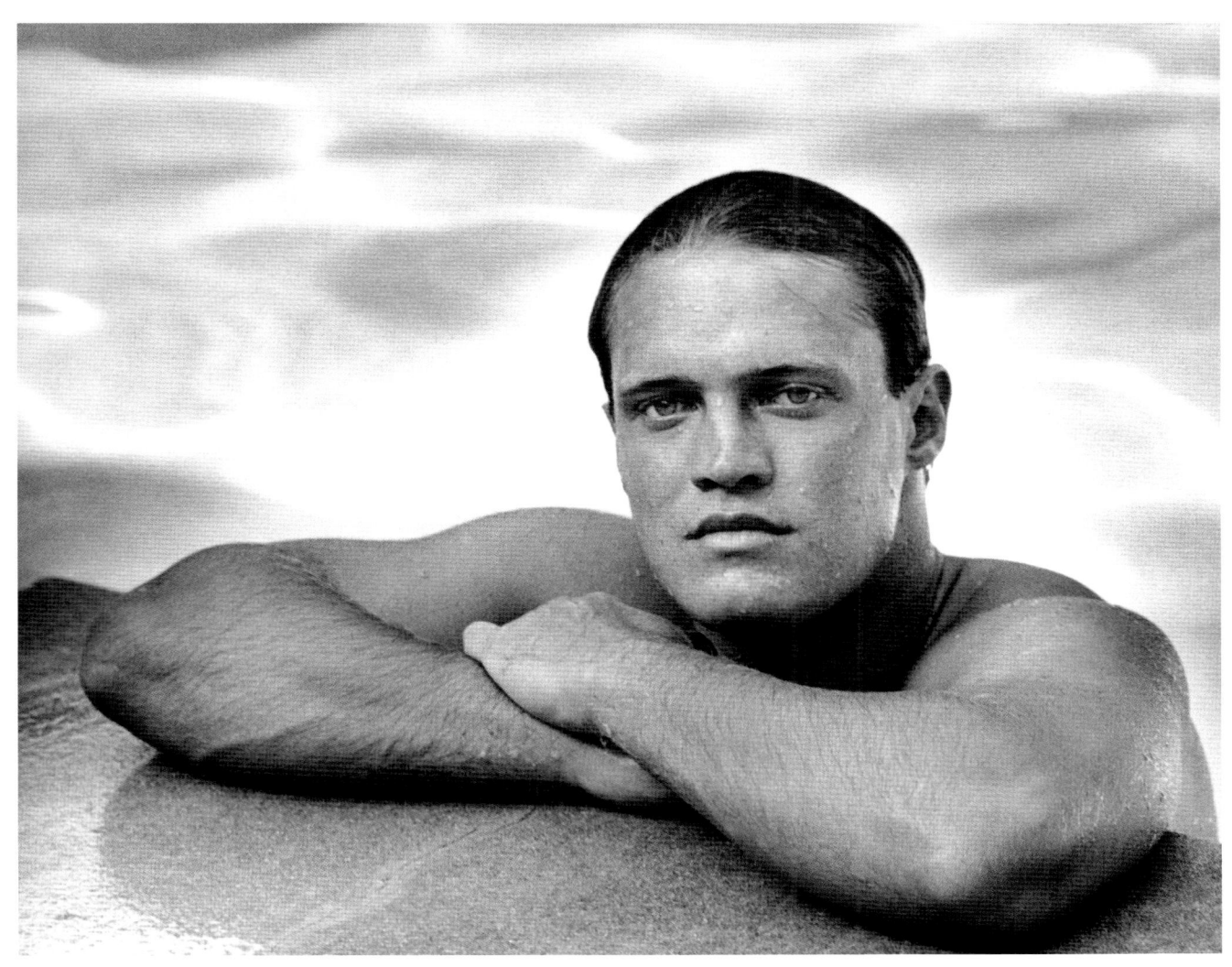

KRIS BERGEN, BEVERLY HILLS, 1984

OPPOSITE: DARA TORRES, NINE-TIME OLYMPIC MEDALIST, PALM BEACH, 2001

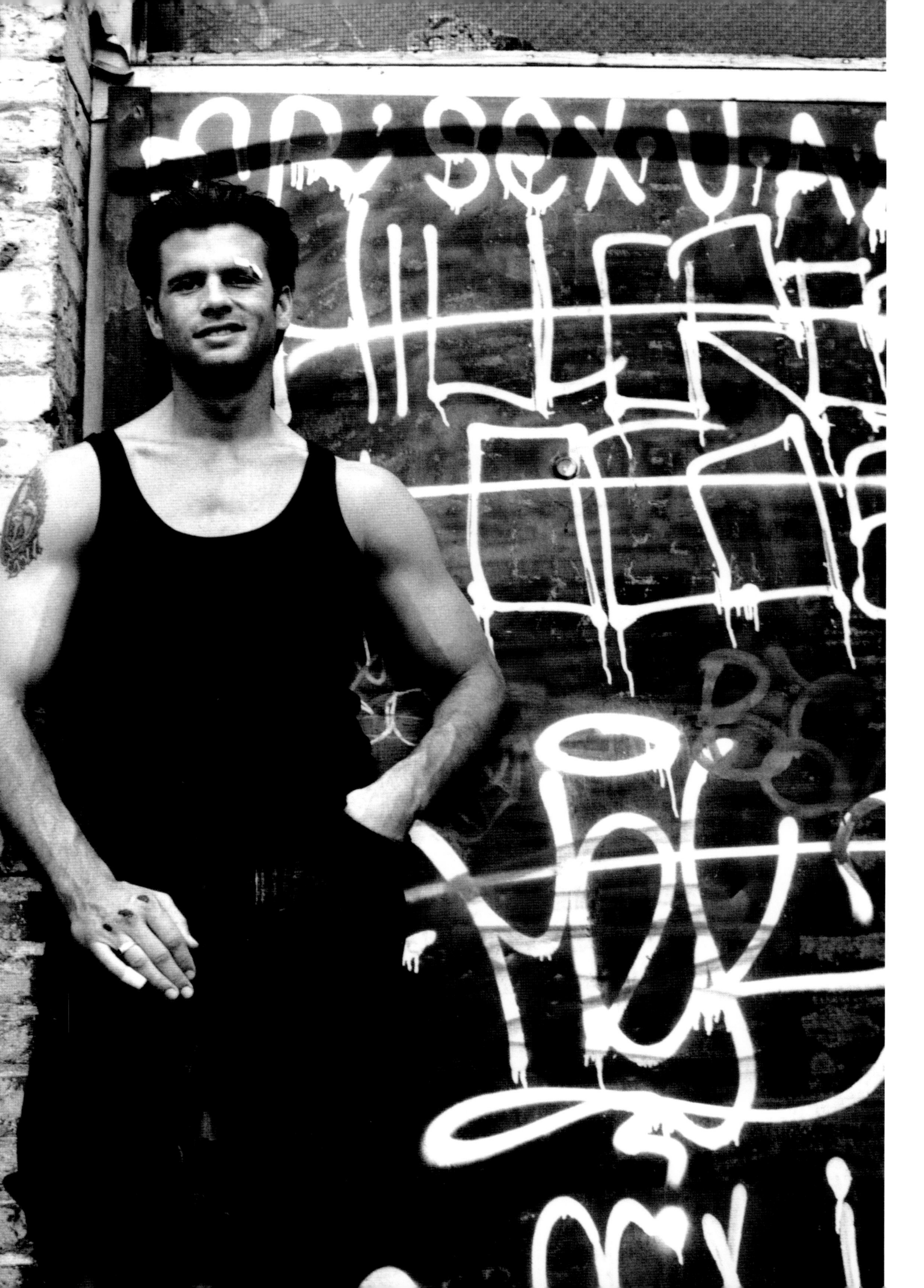

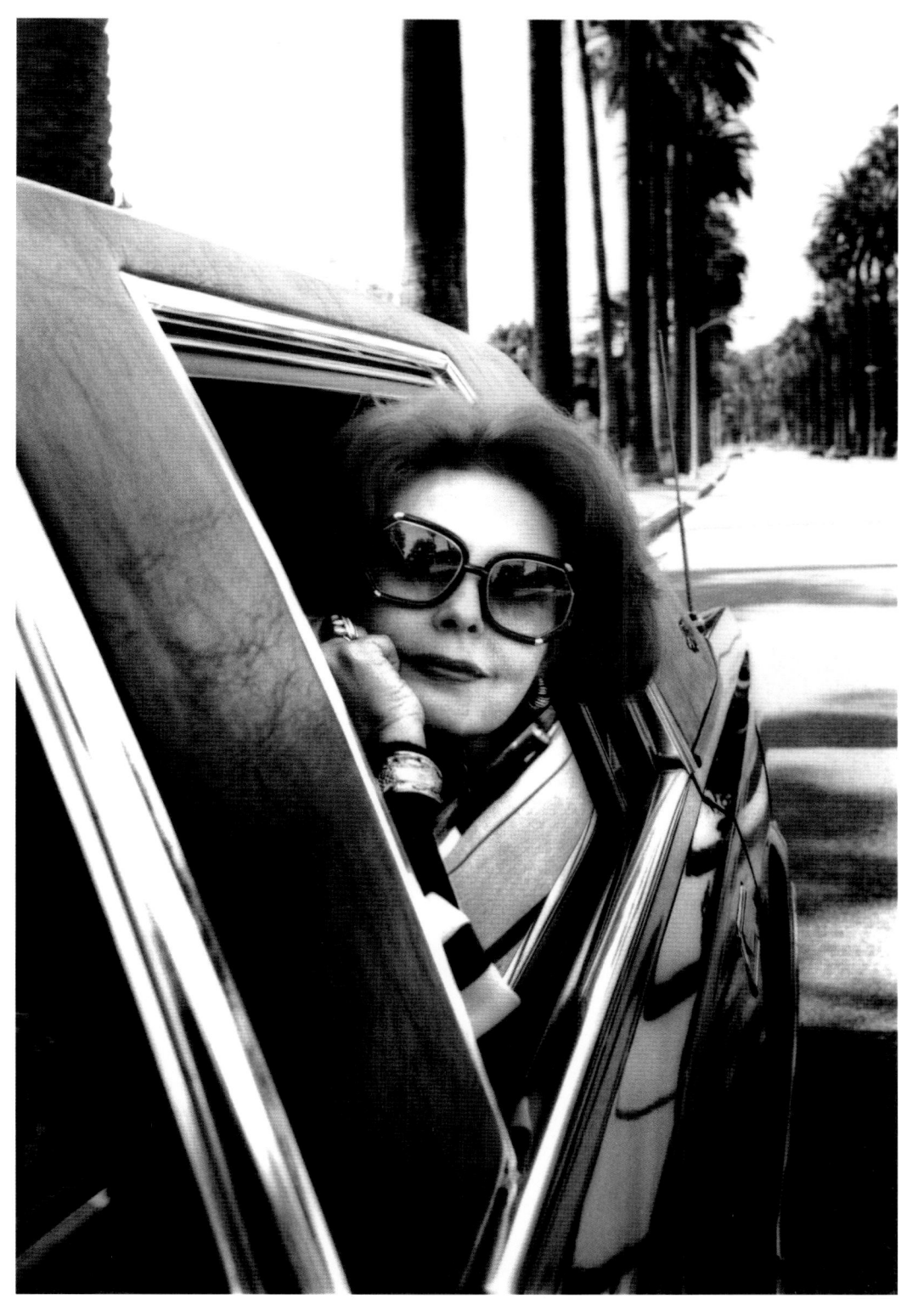

ARLENE DAHL, MOTHER OF LORENZO LAMAS, BEVERLY HILLS, 1987

OPPOSITE: LORENZO LAMAS, LOS ANGELES, 1989

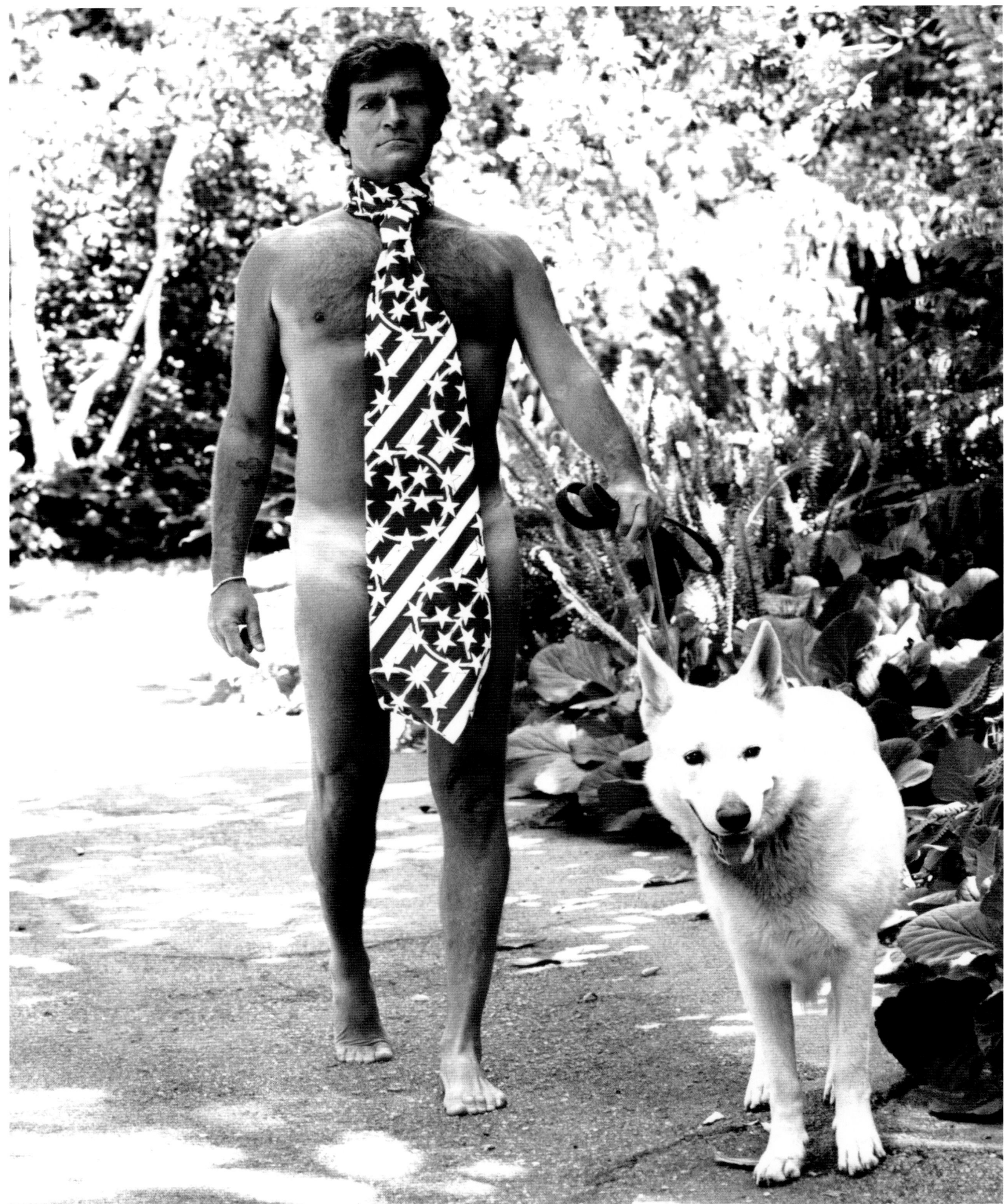

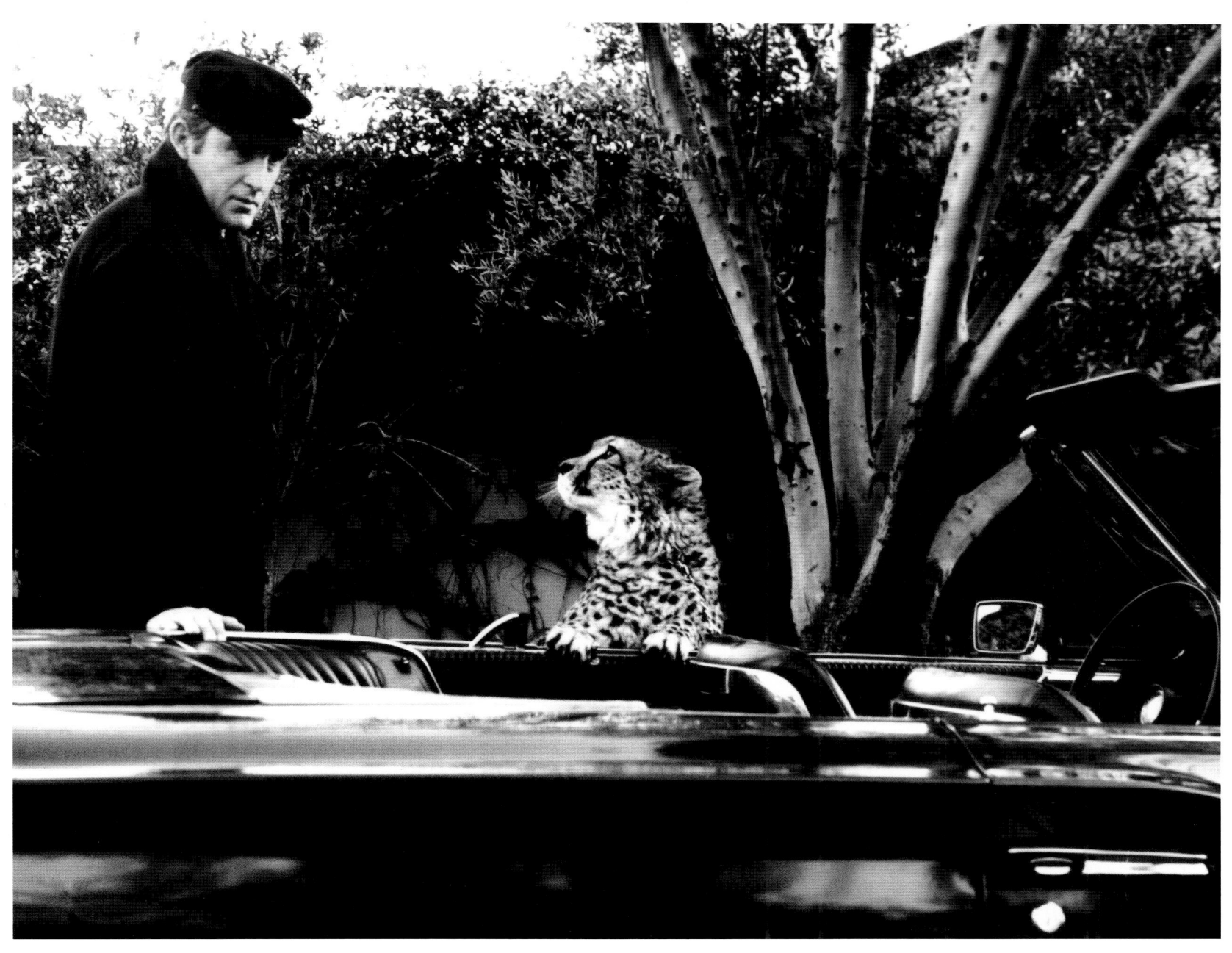

JACQUES BERGERAC AND HIS CHEETAH, BEVERLY HILLS, 1967

OPPOSITE: HUGH O'BRIEN AND HIS DOG, BEVERLY HILLS, 1974

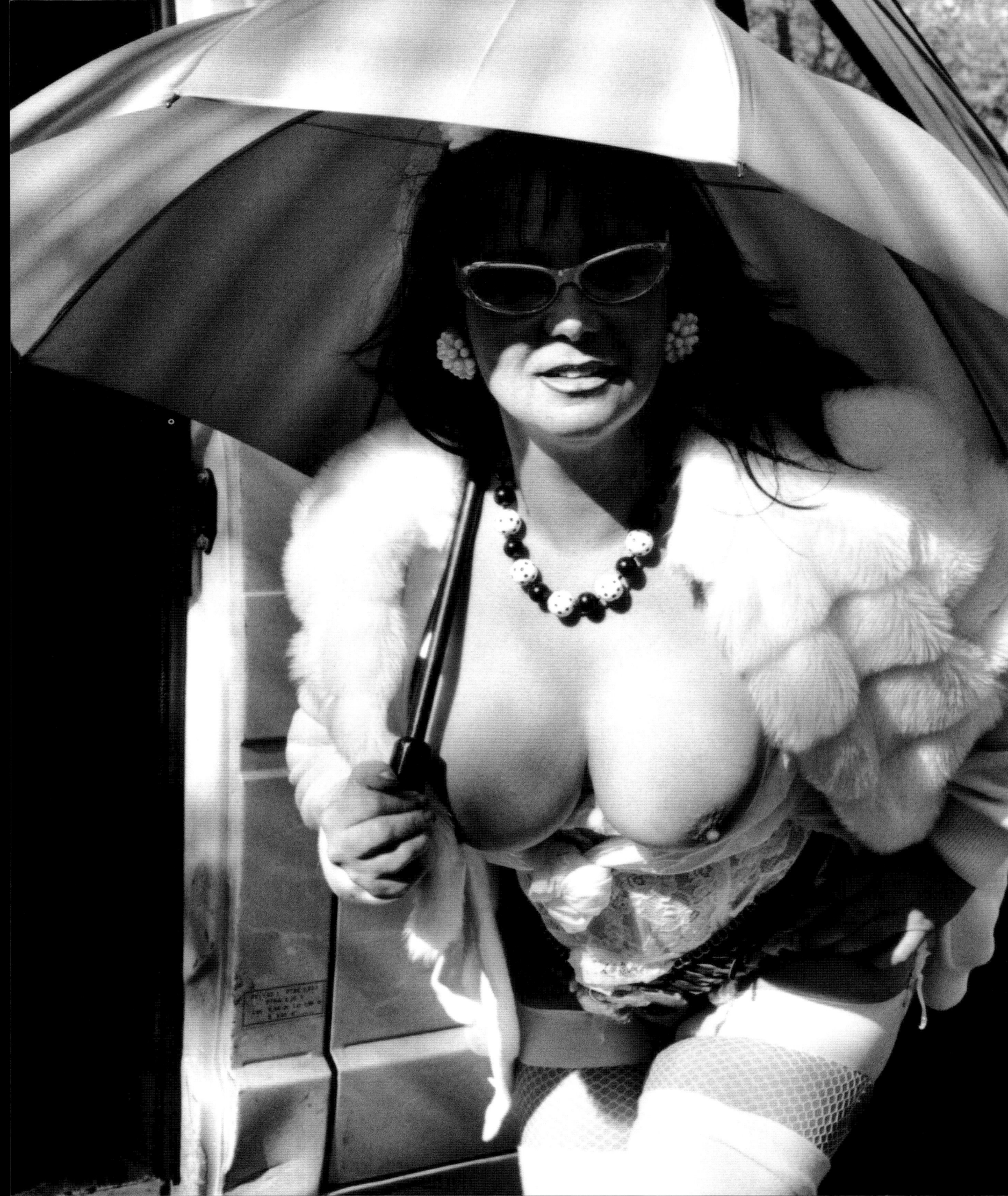

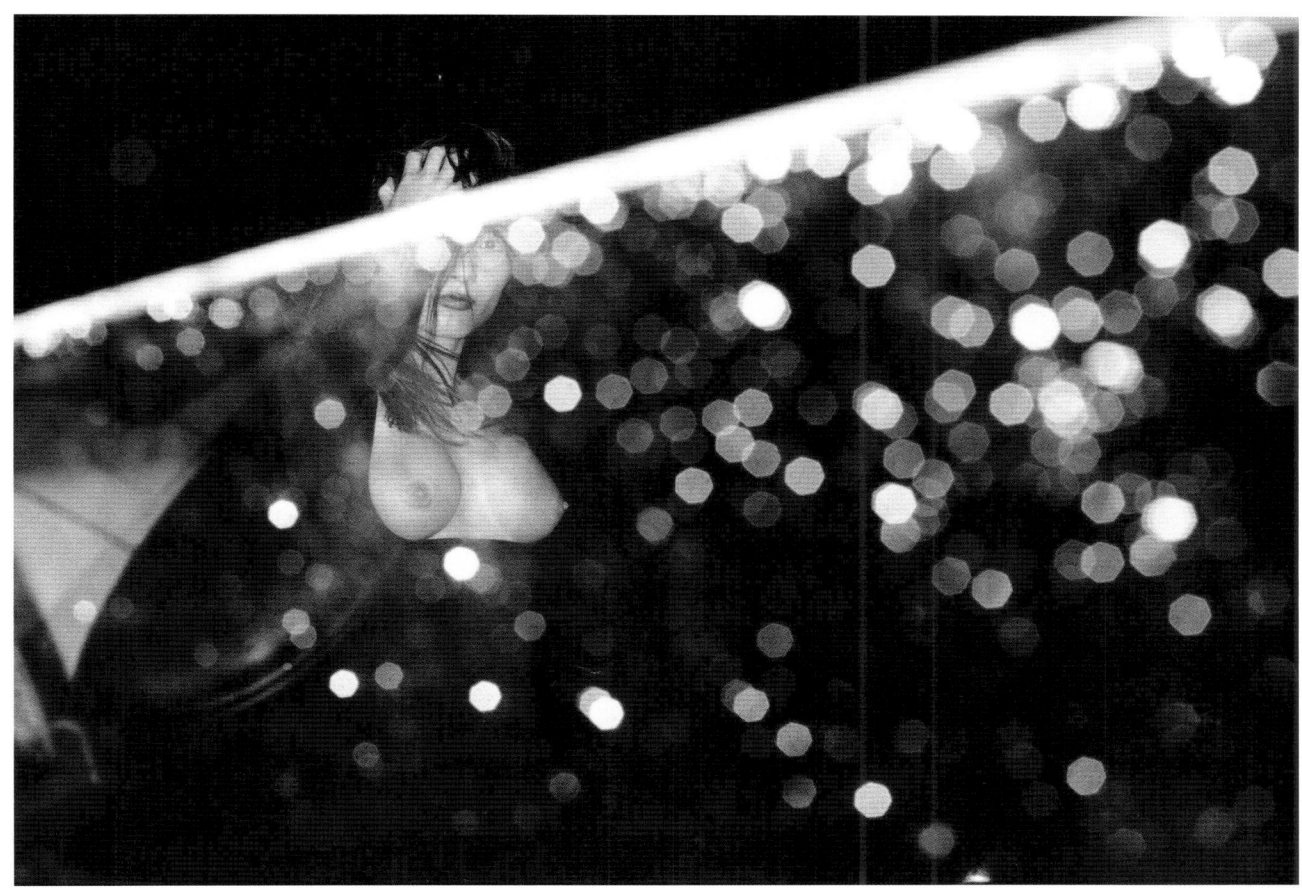

TRANSVESTITE, BOIS DE BOULOGNE, PARIS, 1990

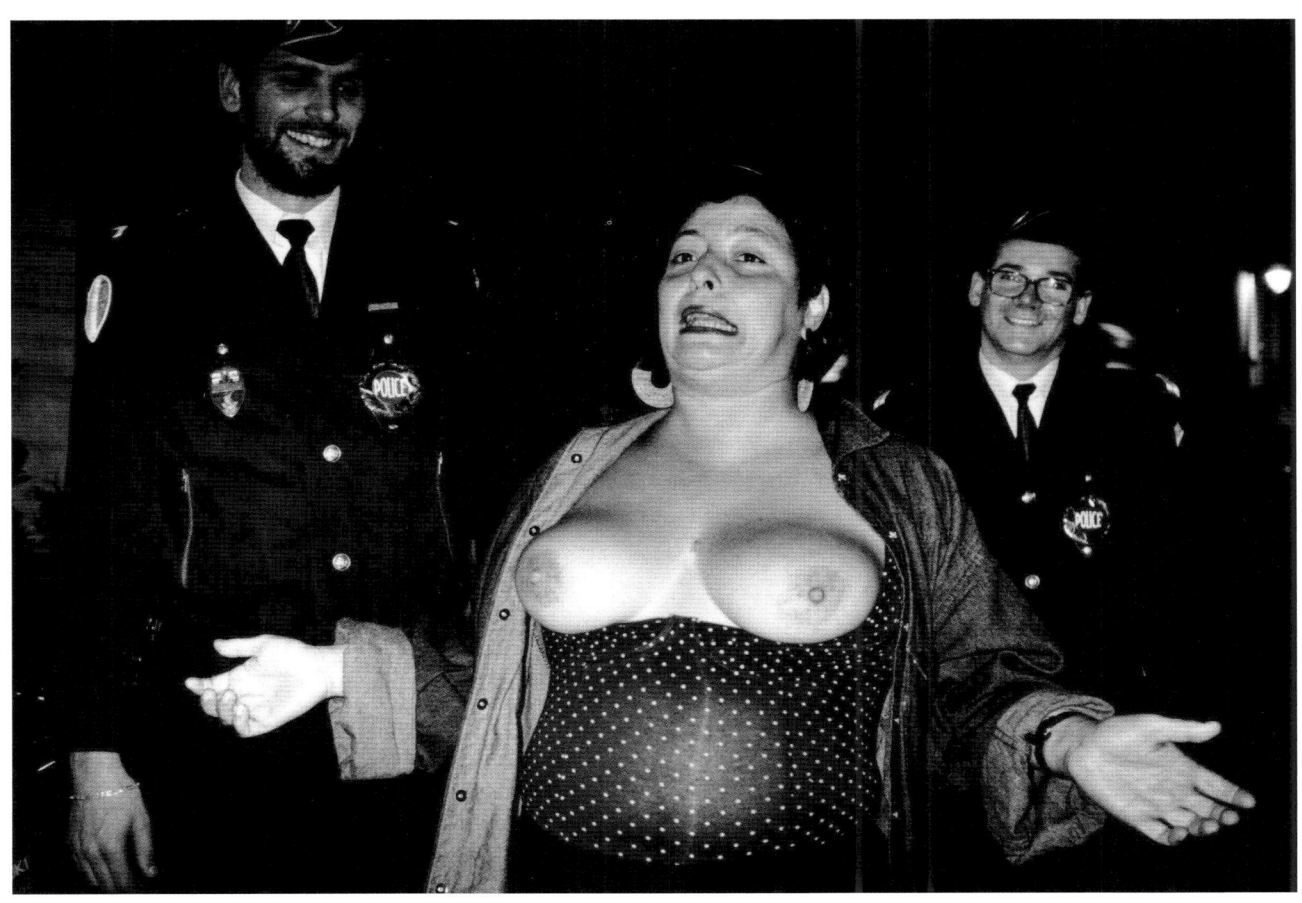

GENDARMES WITH "FANNY," CAPTAIN BANANA CLUB, PARIS, 1990

OPPOSITE: ELISE PROSTITUTE, BOIS DE BOULOGNE, PARIS, 1989

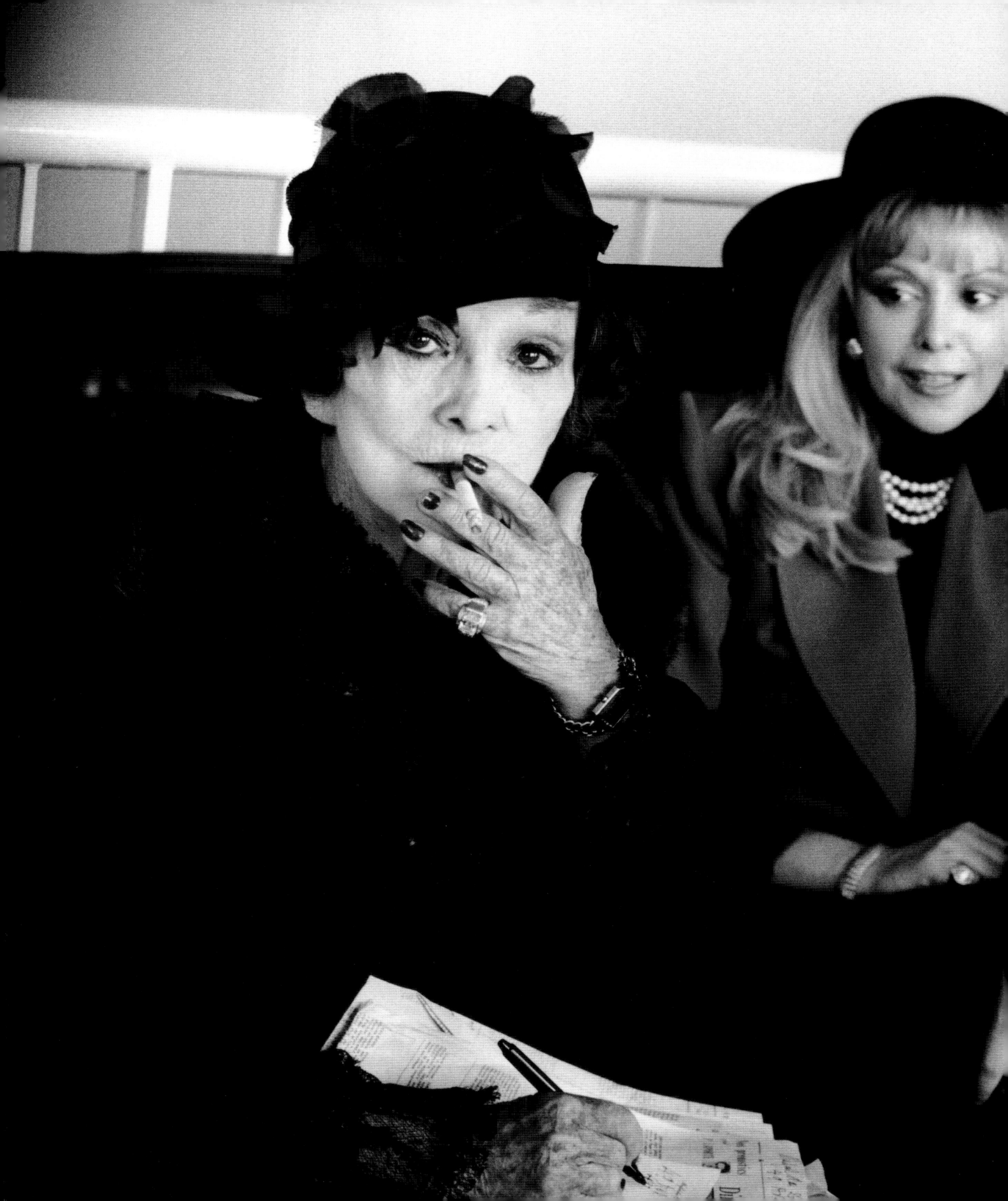

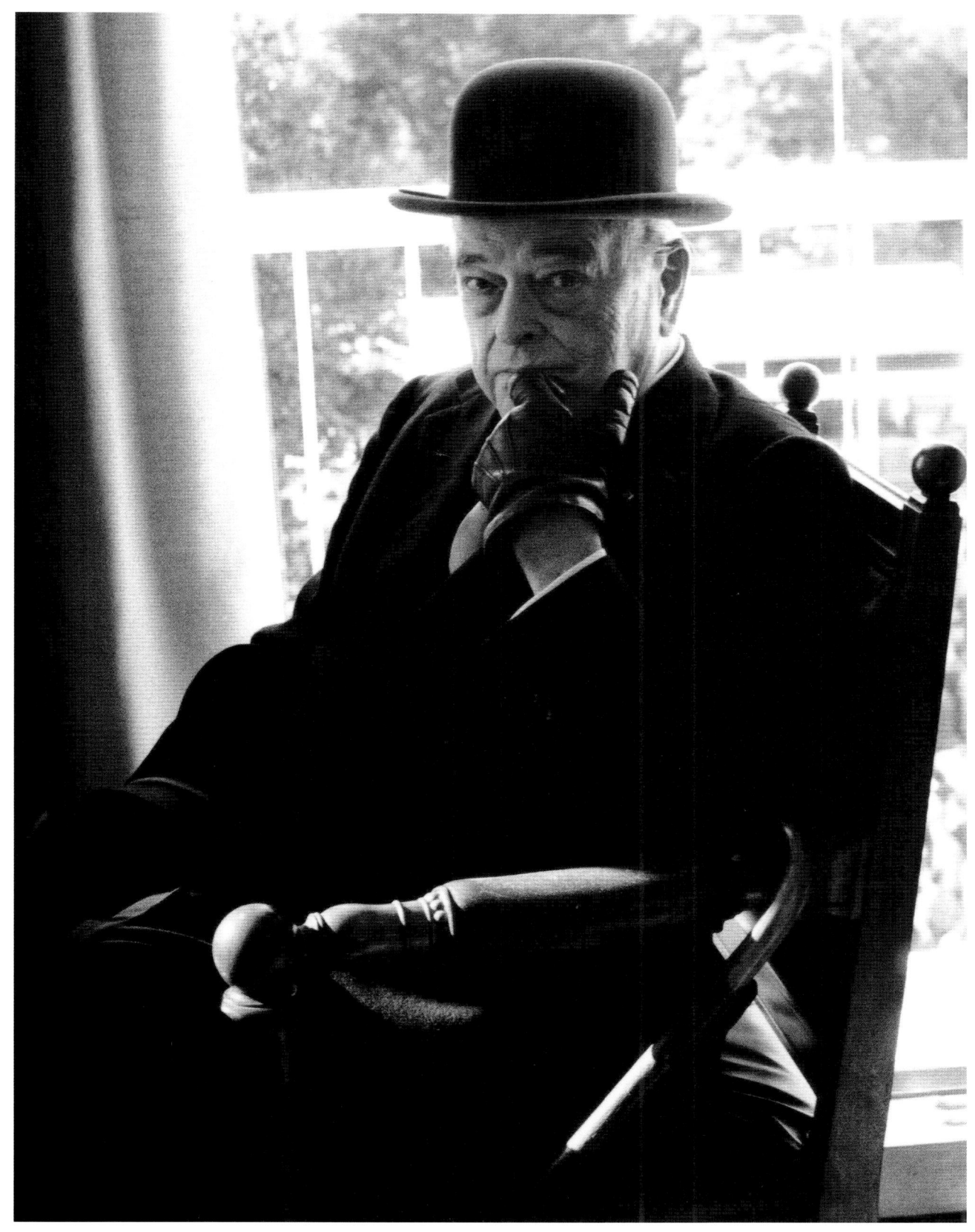

GENTLEMAN, ARC DE TRIOMPHE RACE, PARIS, 1990

OPPOSITE: LADIES, ARC DE TRIOMPHE RACE, PARIS, 1990

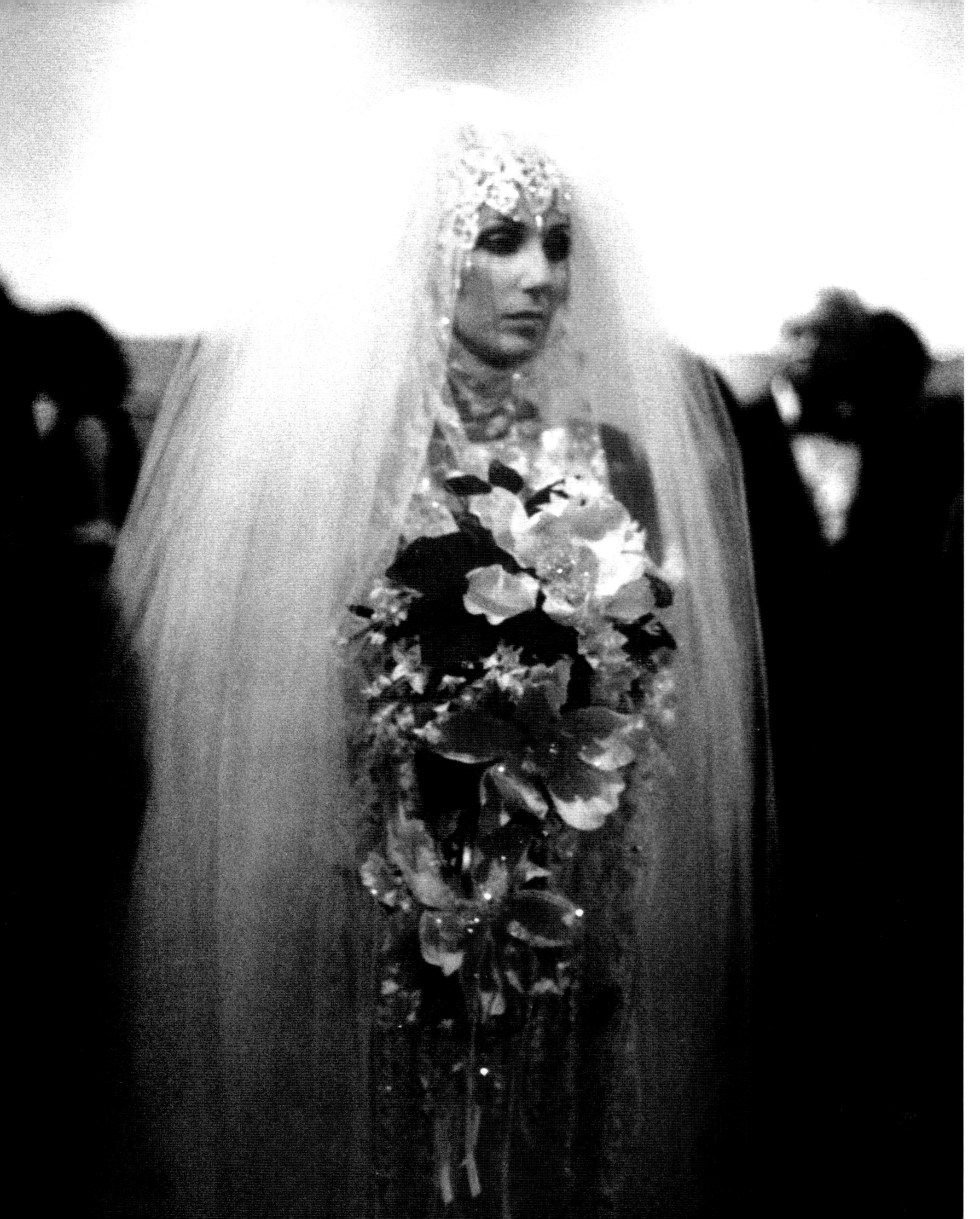

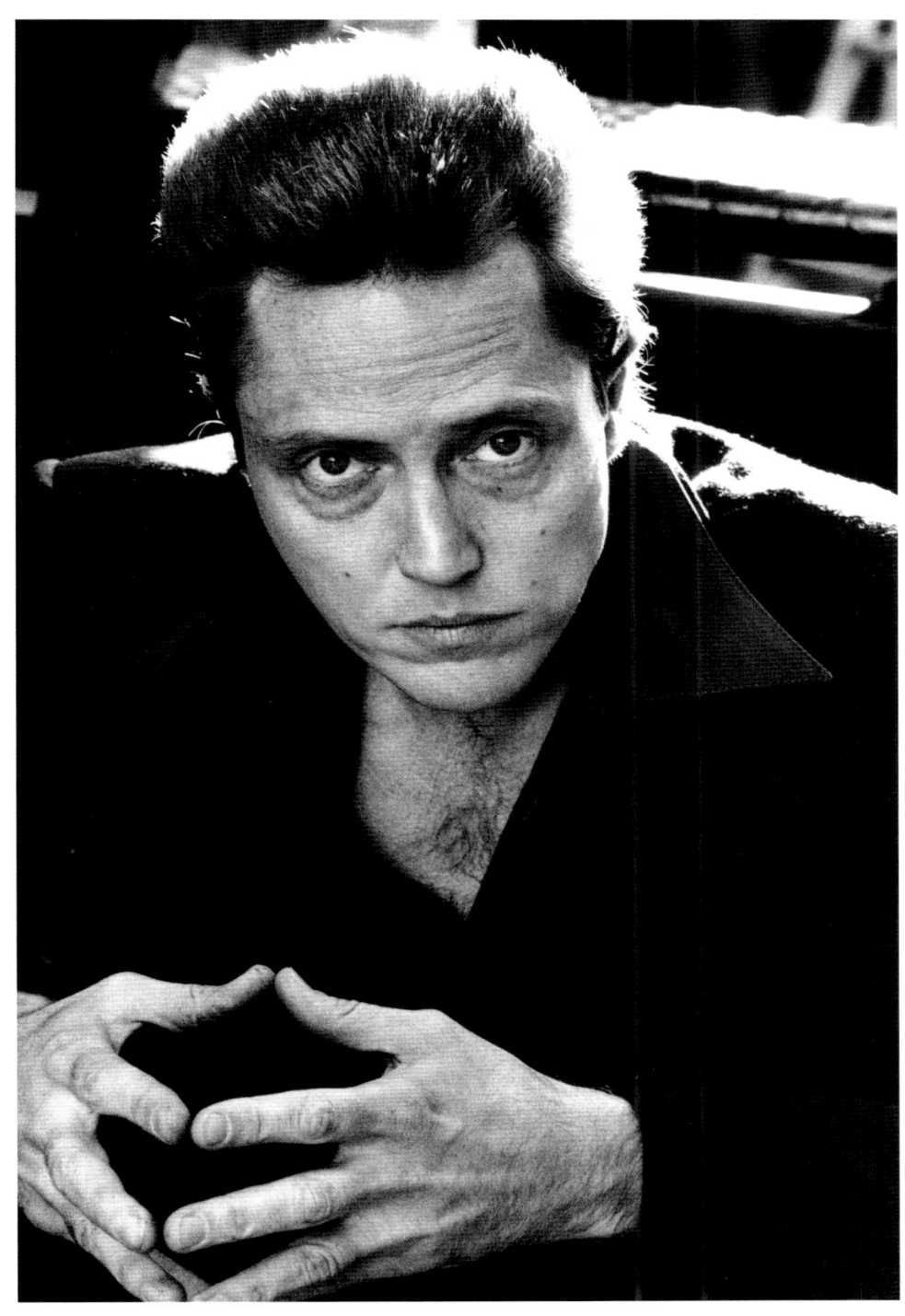

CHRISTOPHER WALKEN, NEW YORK CITY, 1983

OPPOSITE: CHER, NEW YORK CITY, 1982

OVERLEAFT LEFT: JONATHAN FREEMAN AND MYLINDA HULL, *42ND STREET*, NEW YORK CITY, 2002

OVERLEAF RIGHT: TWIGGY, *MY ONE AND ONLY*, NEW YORK CITY, 1983

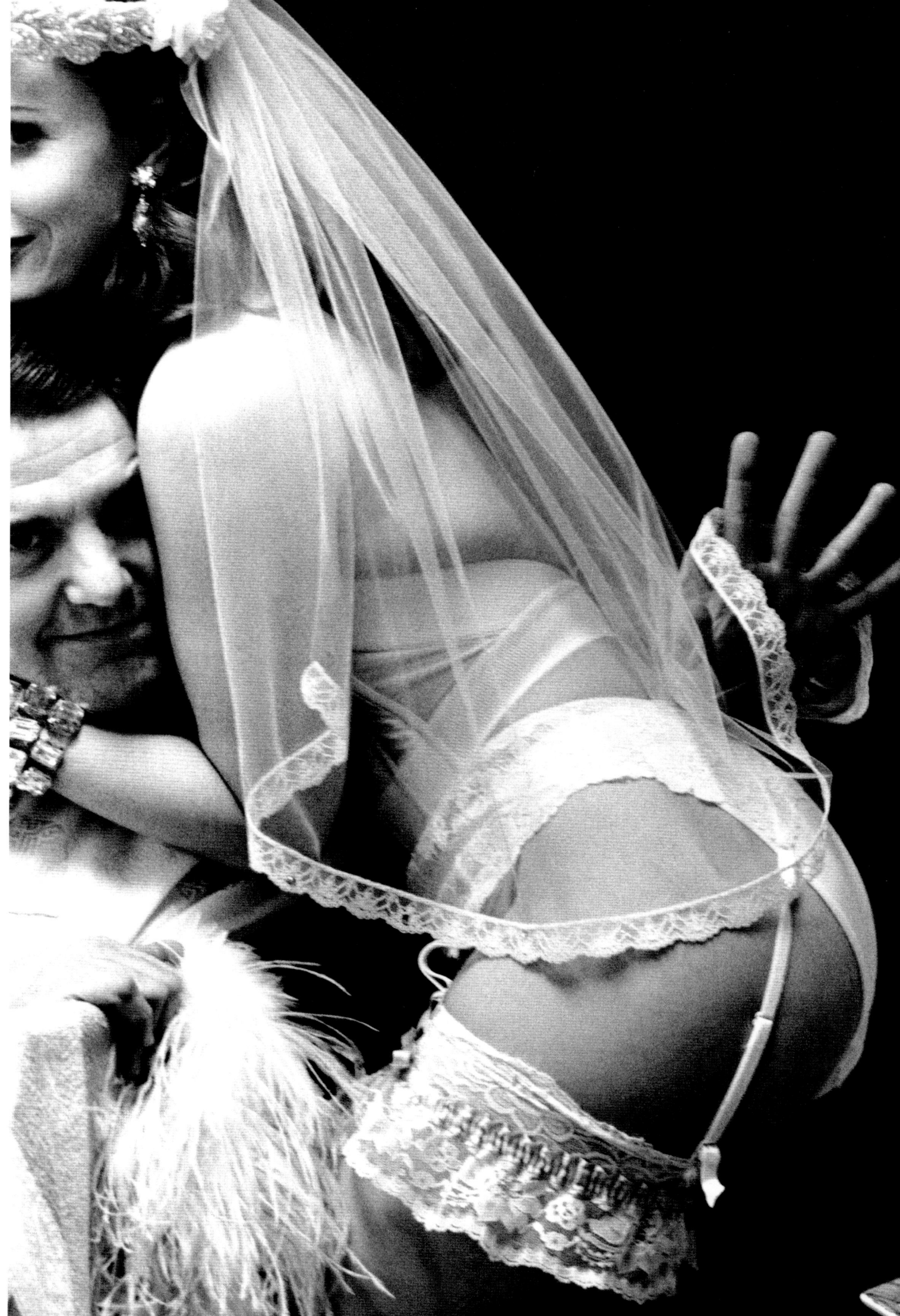

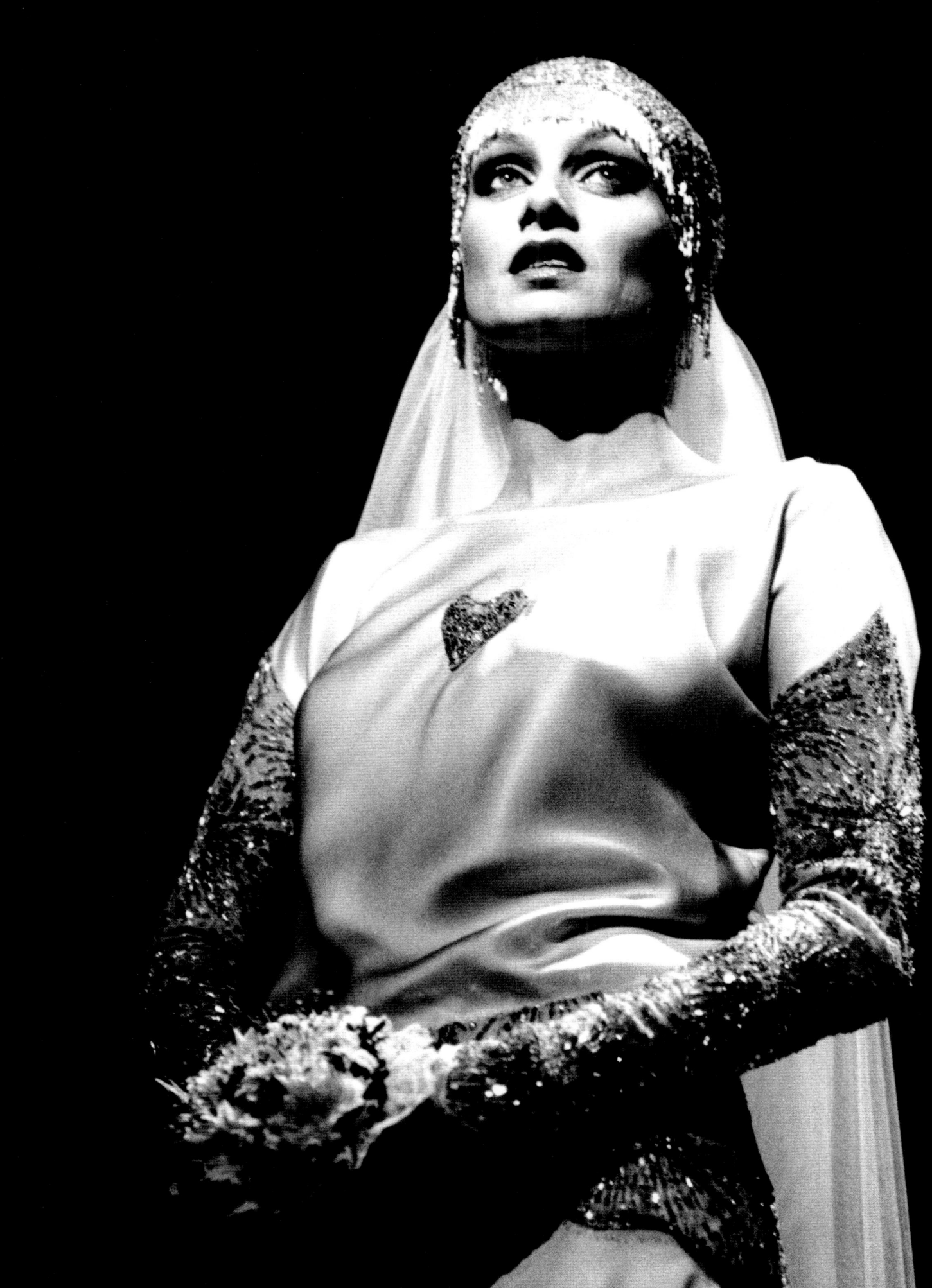

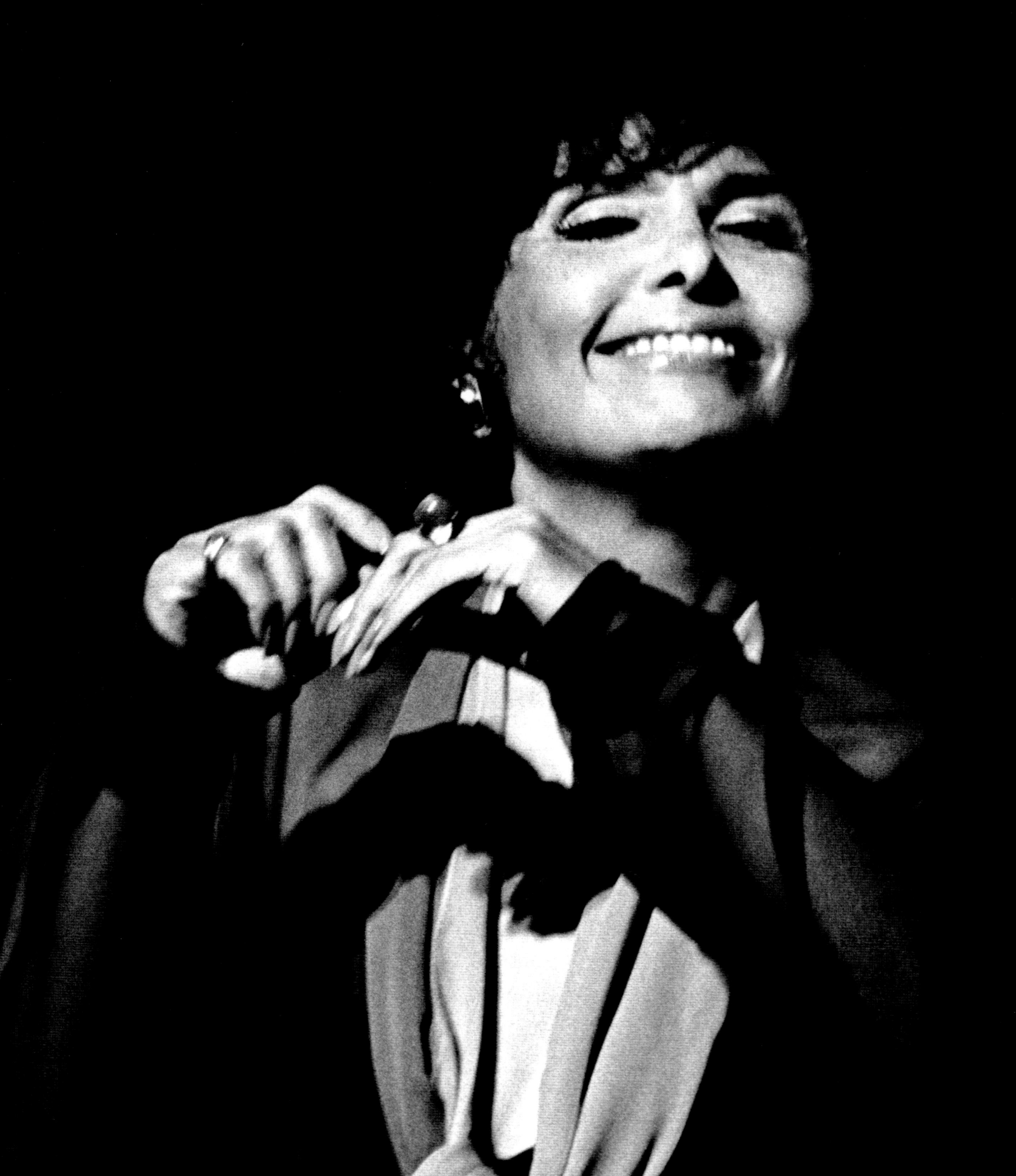

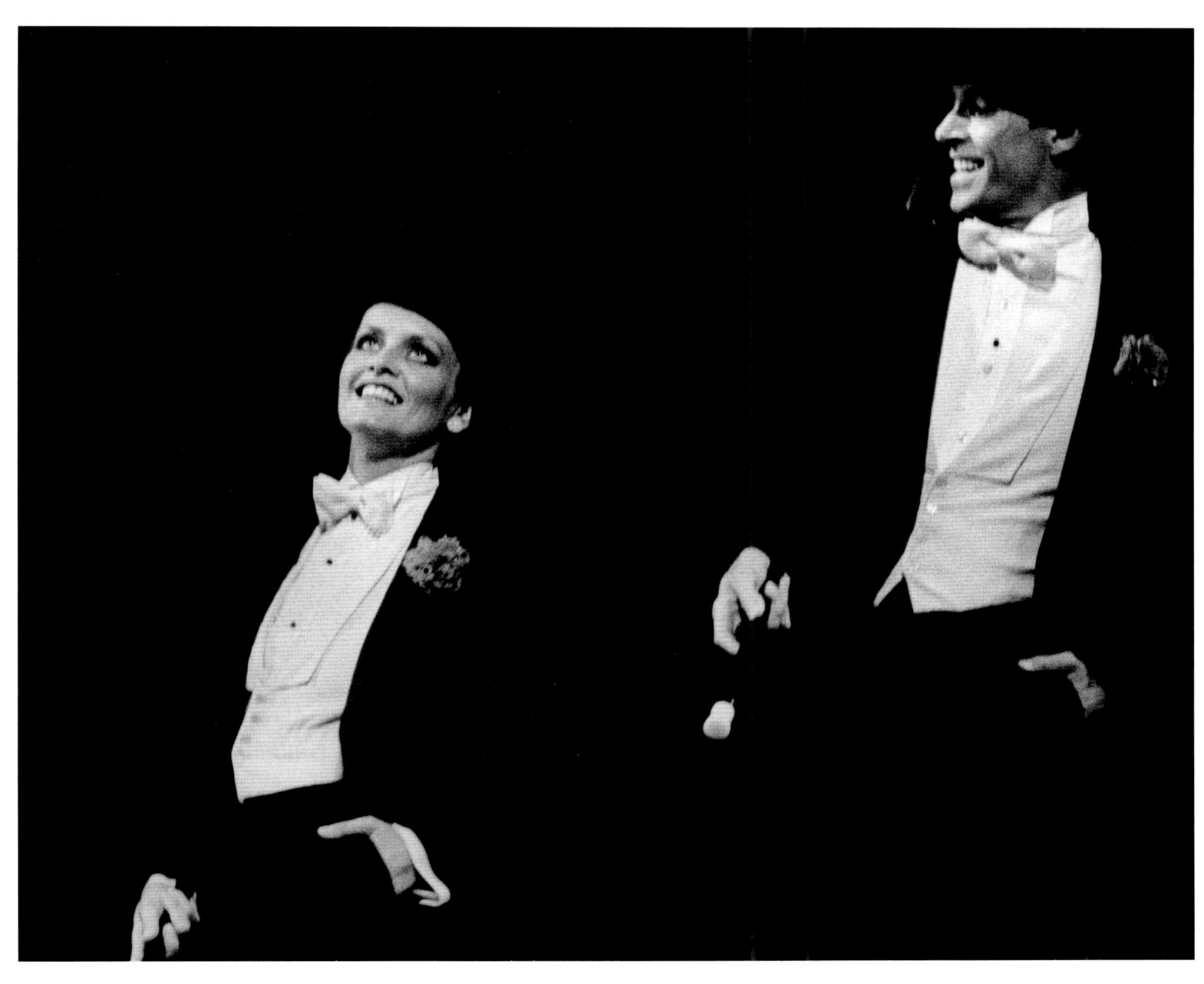

TWIGGY AND TOMMY TUNE, *MY ONE AND ONLY*, NEW YORK CITY, 1983

OPPOSITE: LENA HORNE, NEW YORK CITY, 1972

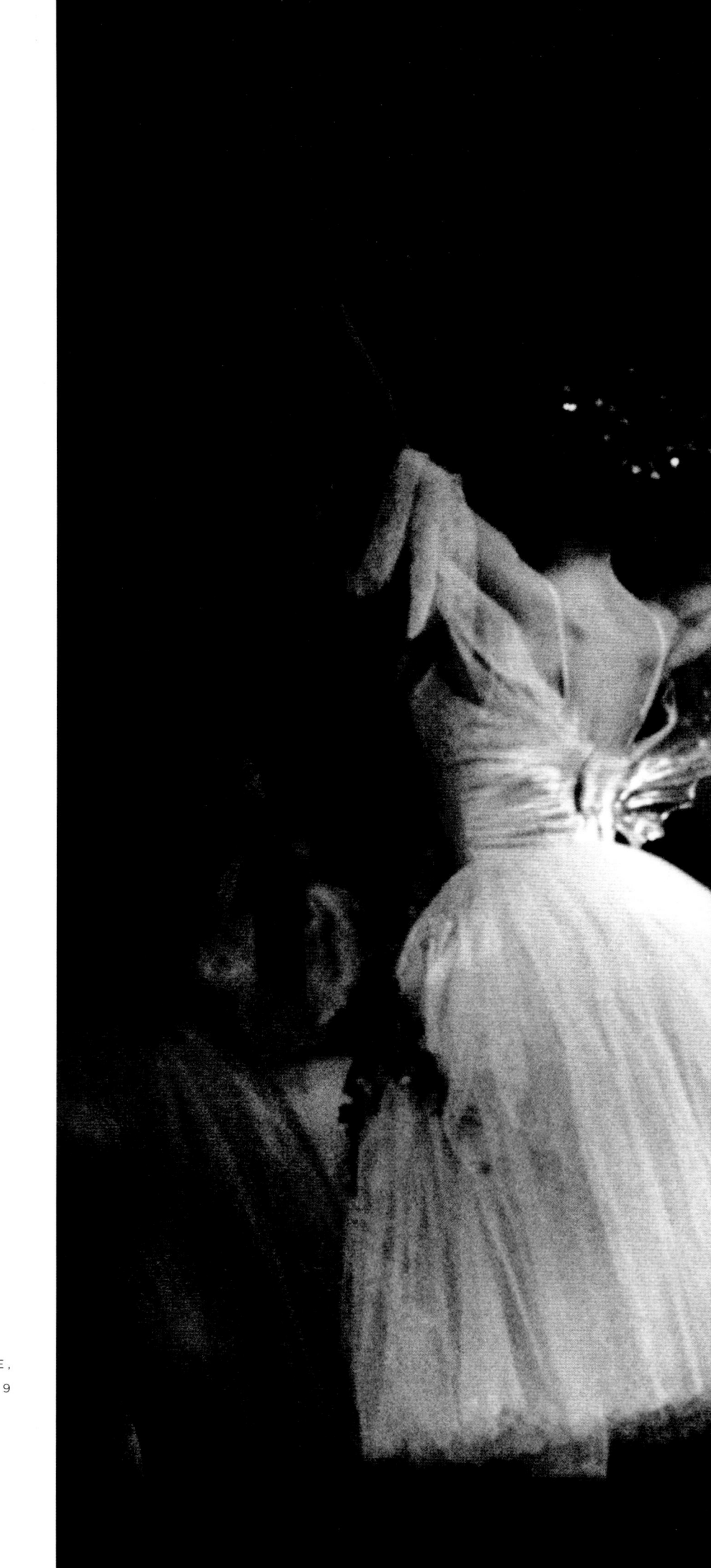

RUDOLF NUREYEV AND MARGOT FONTAYNE, *GISELLE*, SHRINE AUDITORIUM, LOS ANGELES, 1969

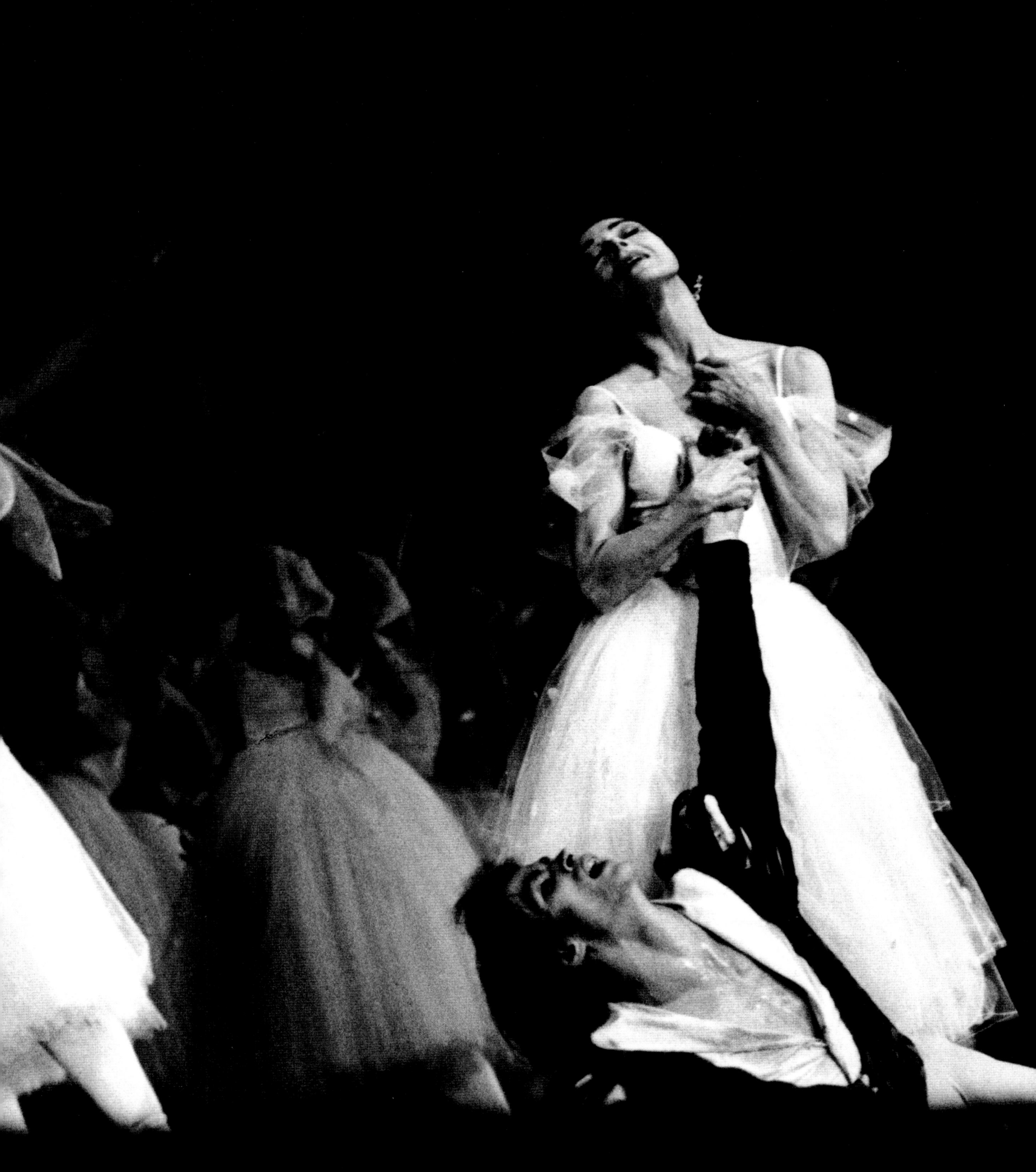

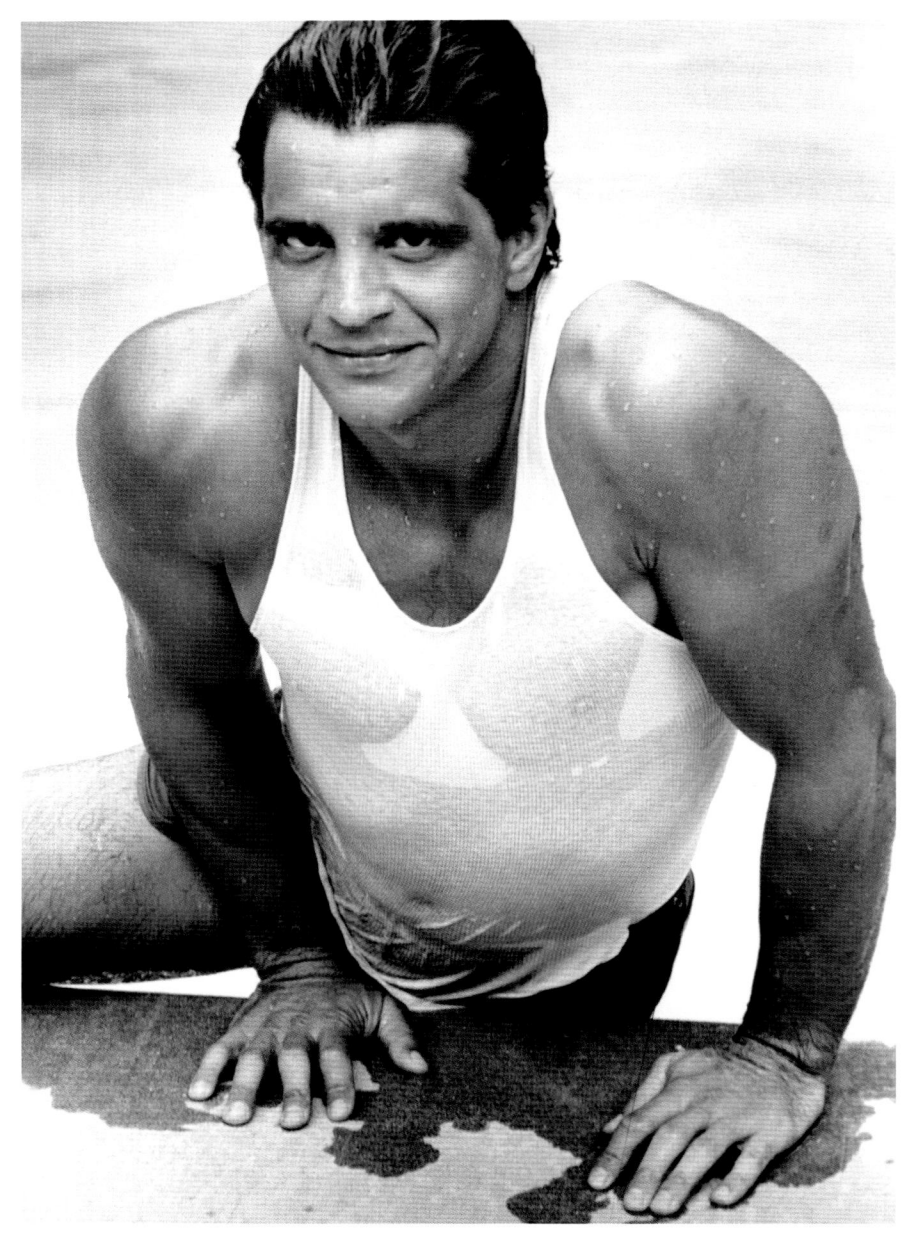

ED MARINARO, BEVERLY HILLS, 1983

OPPOSITE: RUDOLF NUREYEV, *GISELLE*, SHRINE AUDITORIUM, LOS ANGELES, 1969

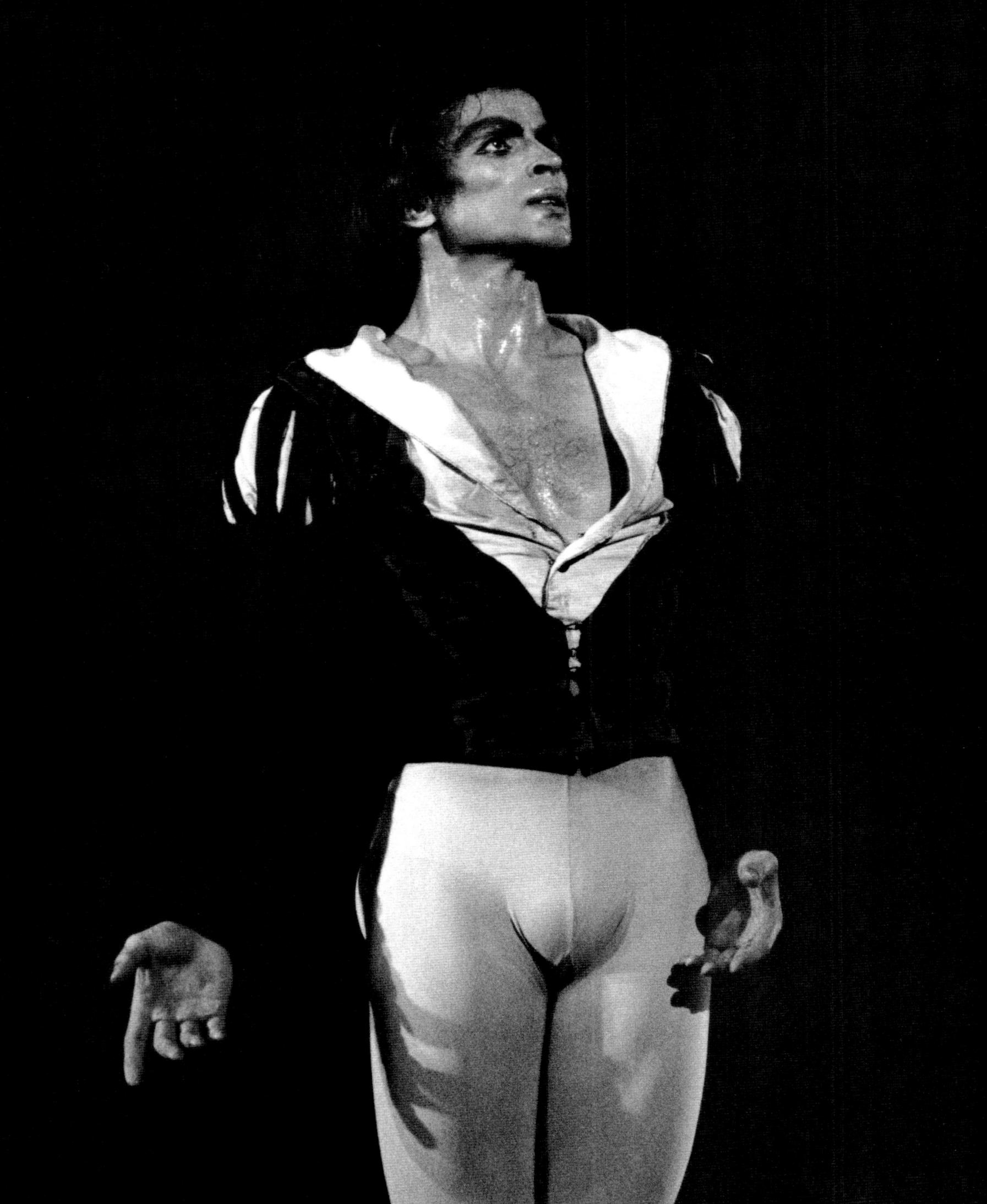

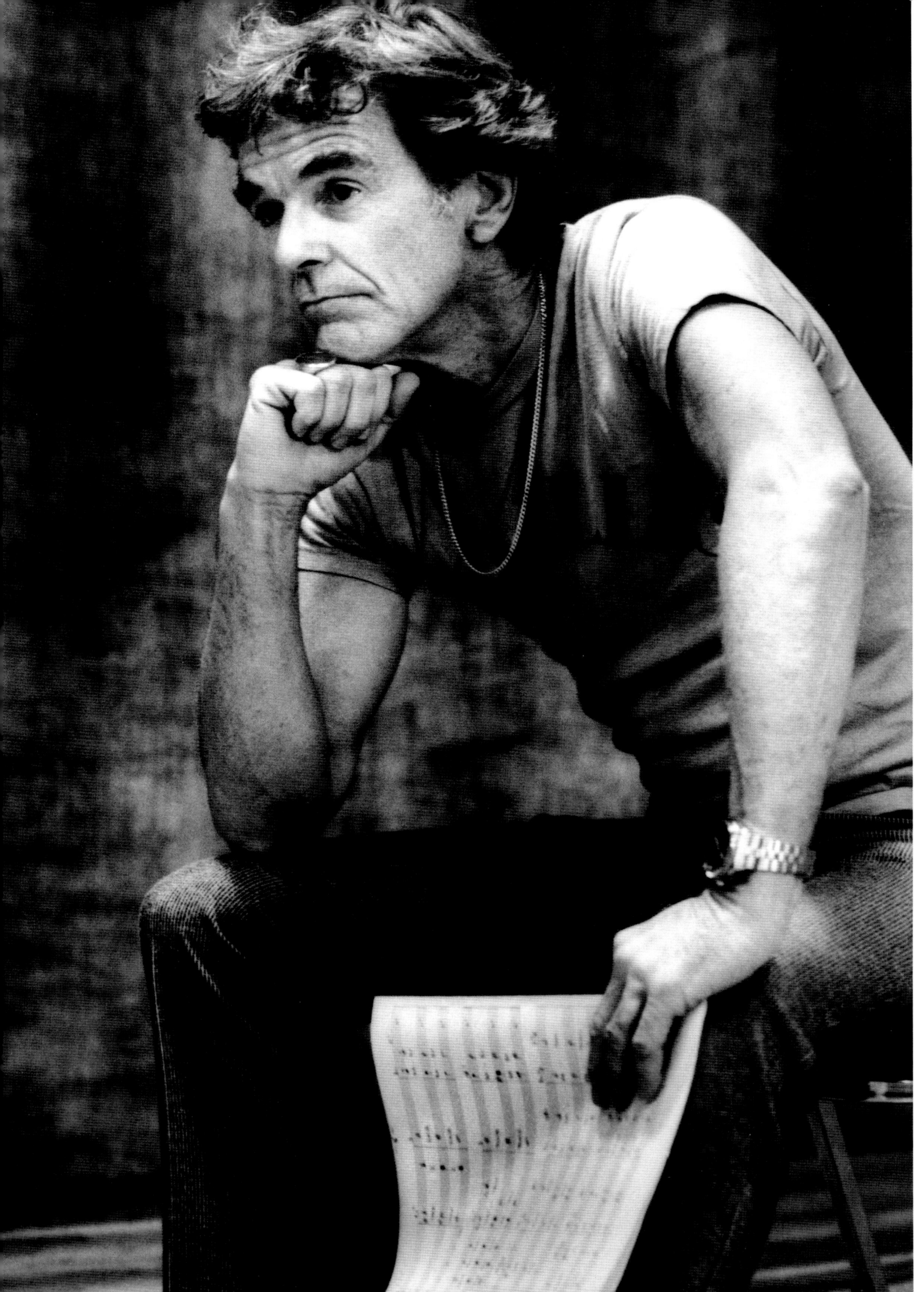

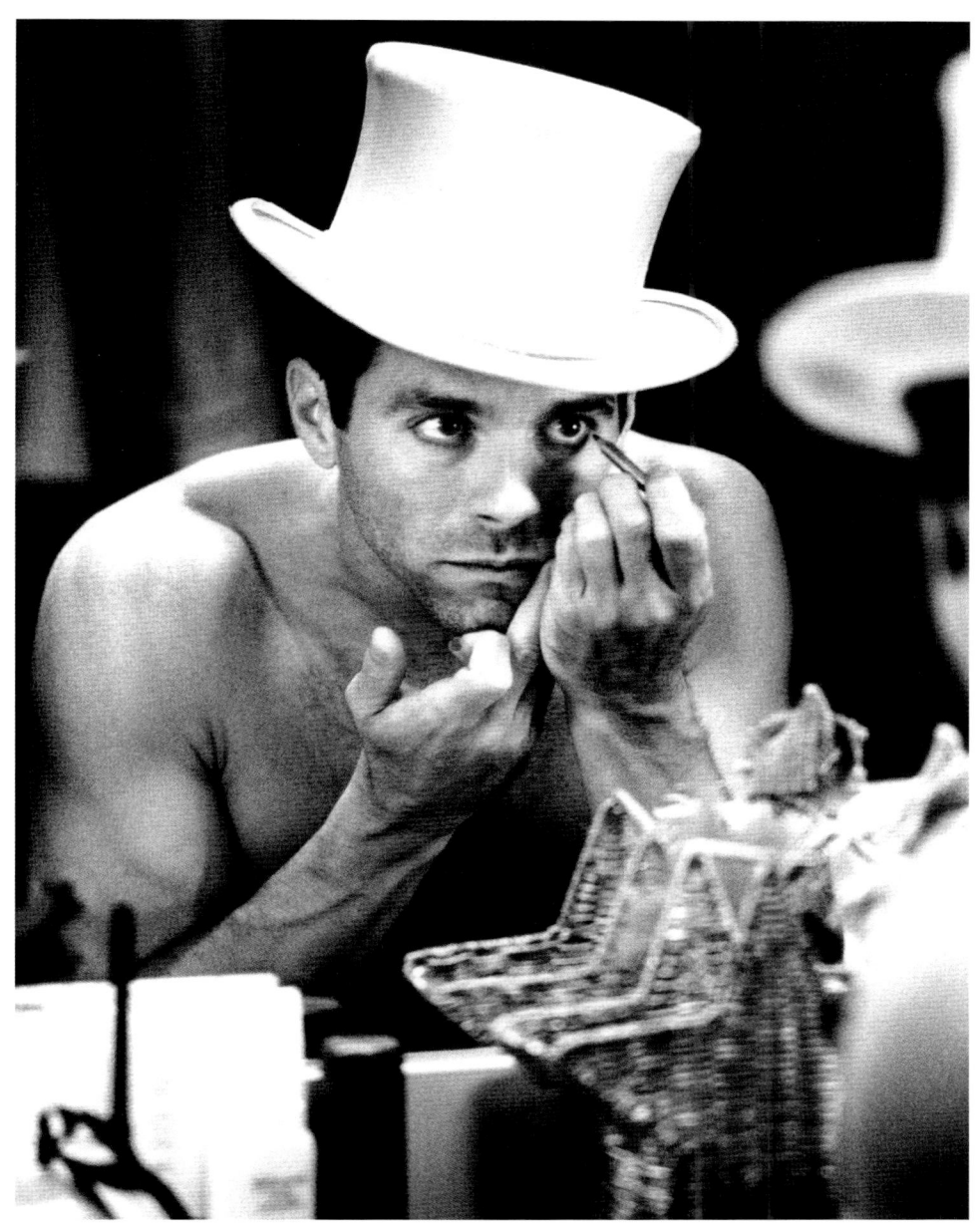

DAVID ELDER IN THE DRESSING ROOM,
42ND STREET, NEW YORK CITY, 2002

OPPOSITE: GOWER CHAMPION, LOS ANGELES, 1975

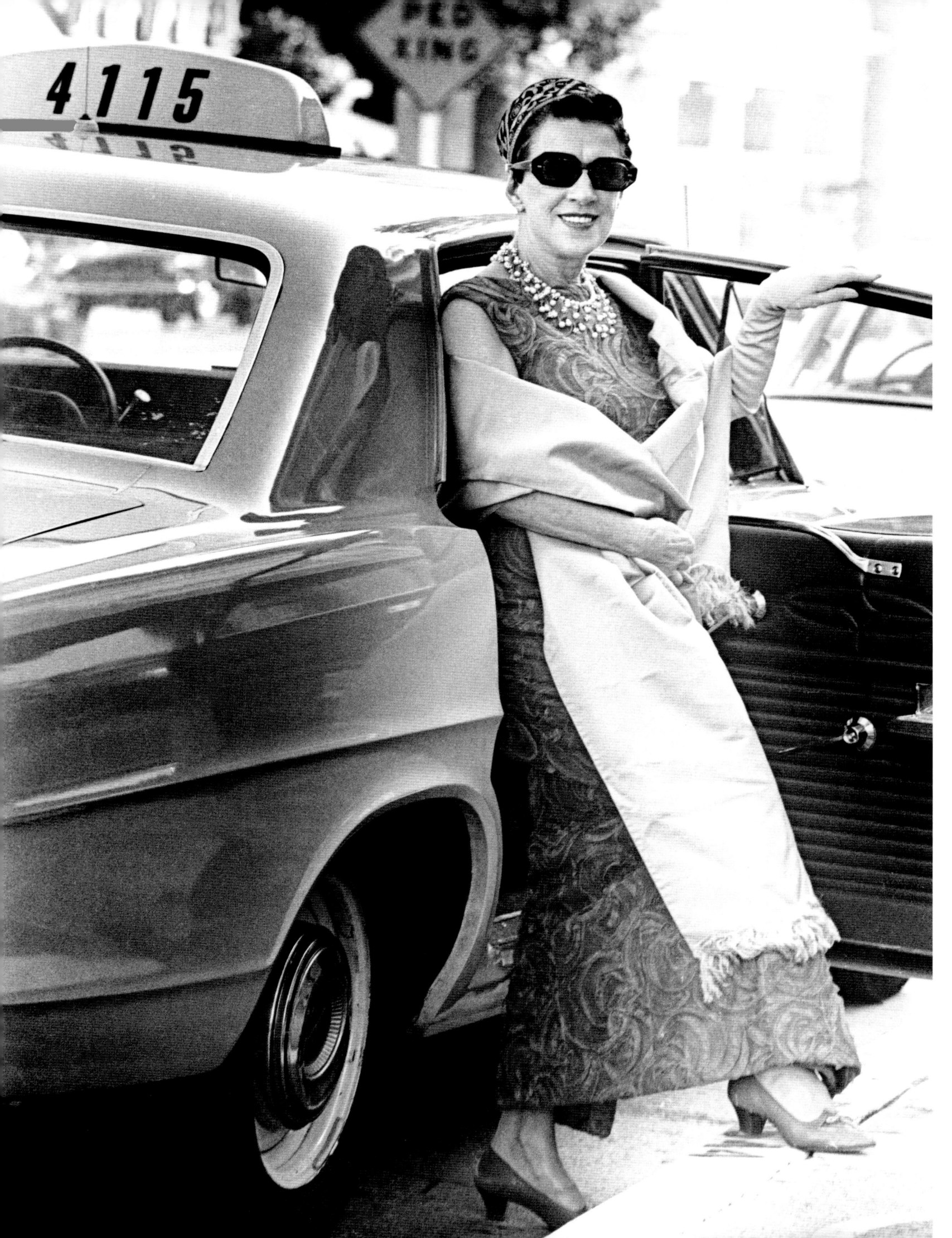

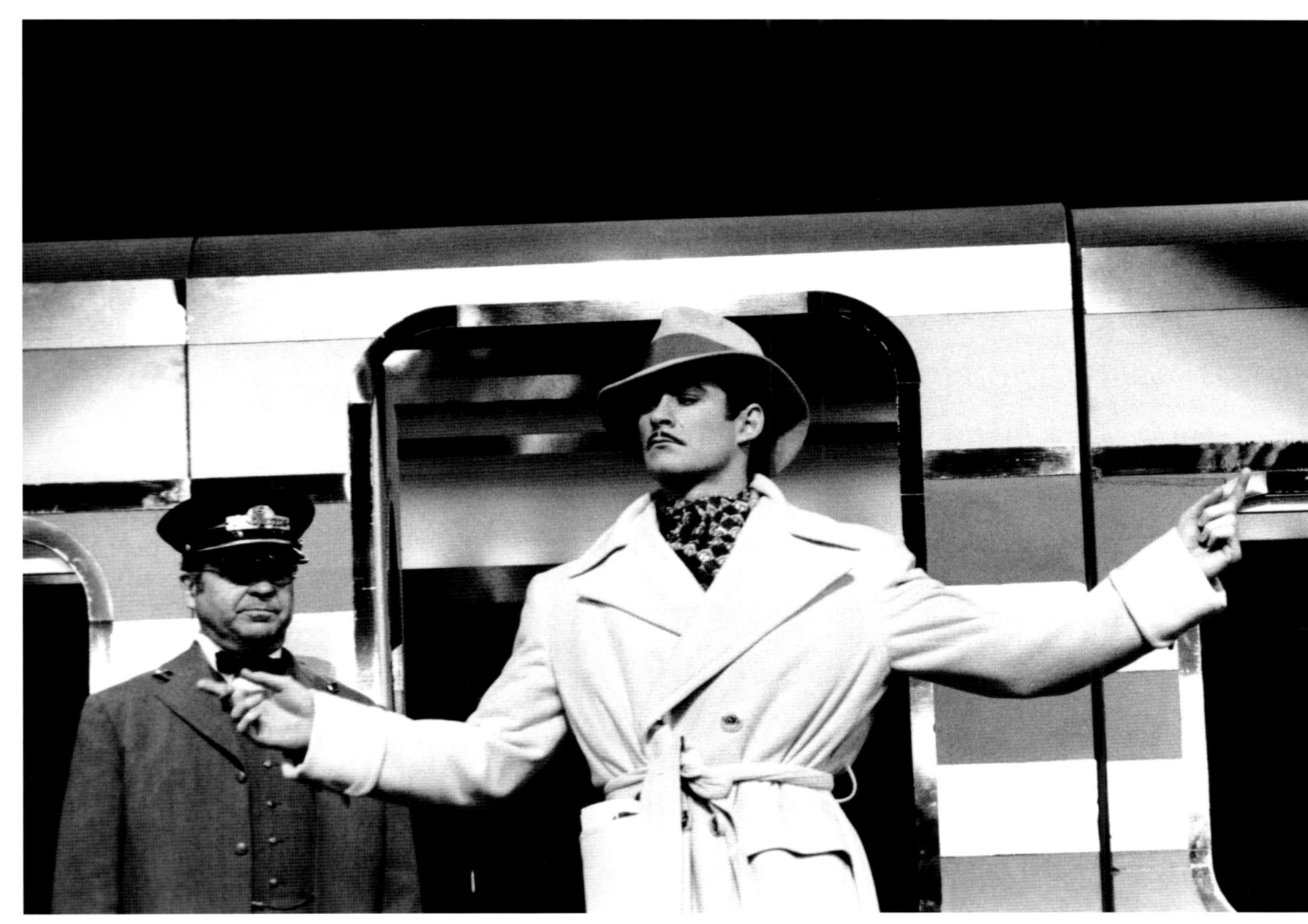

KEVIN KLEIN, *ON THE TWENTIETH CENTURY*, NEW YORK CITY, 1977

OPPOSITE: BEATRICE LILLIE, LOS ANGELES, 1966

OVERLEAF LEFT: JACK LEMMON, LOS ANGELES, 1970

OVERLEAF RIGHT: GEORGE C. SCOTT, NEW YORK CITY, 1972

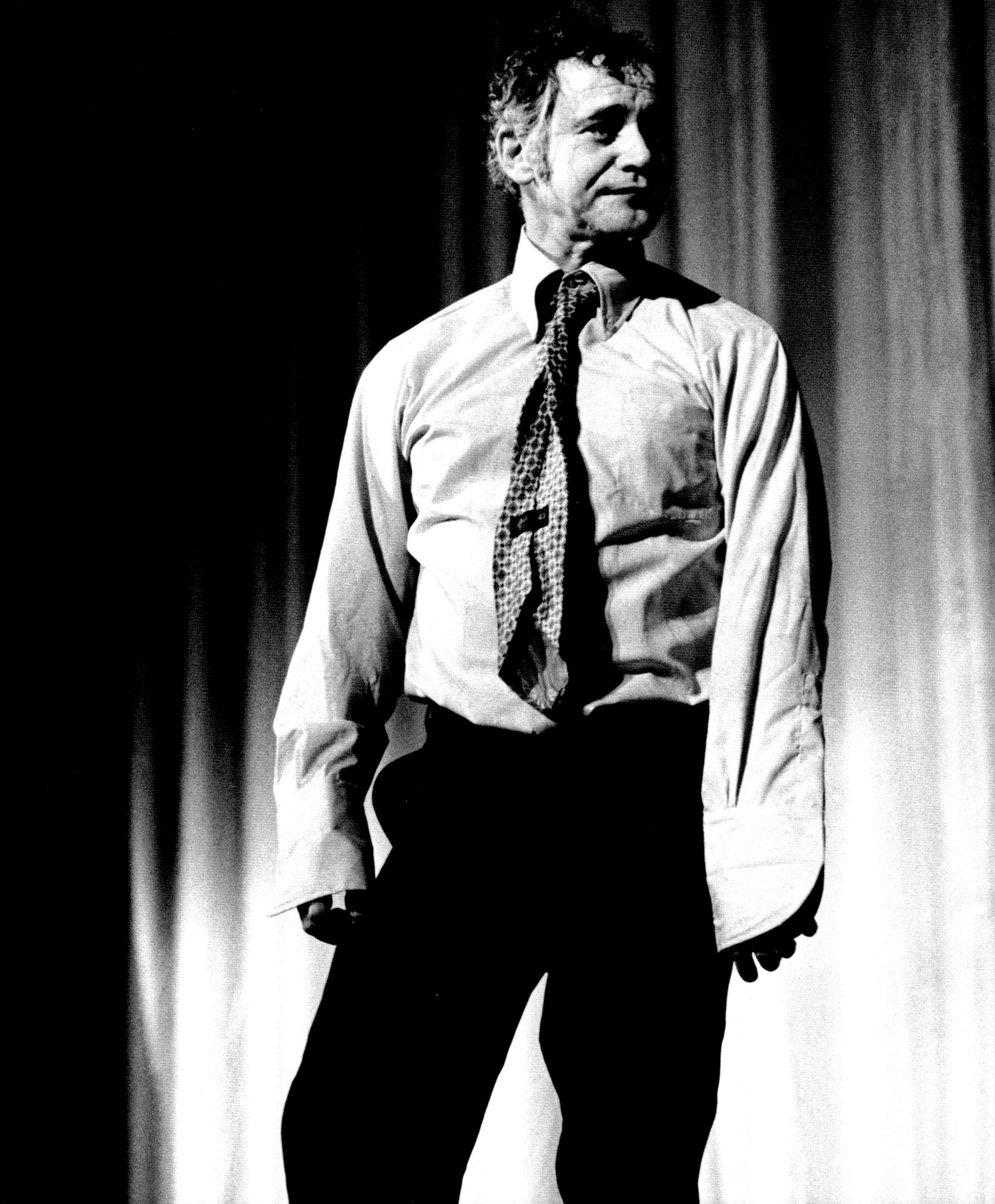

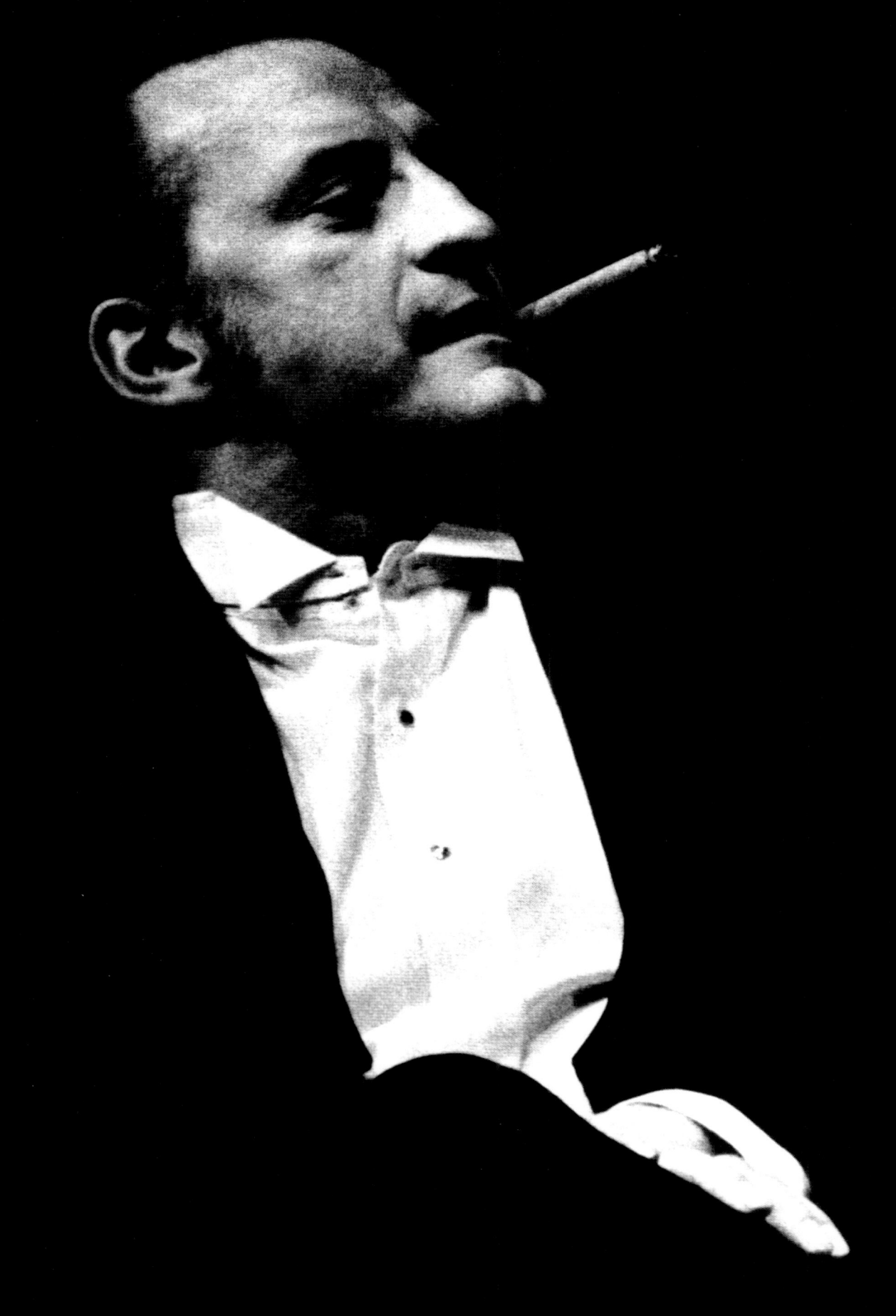

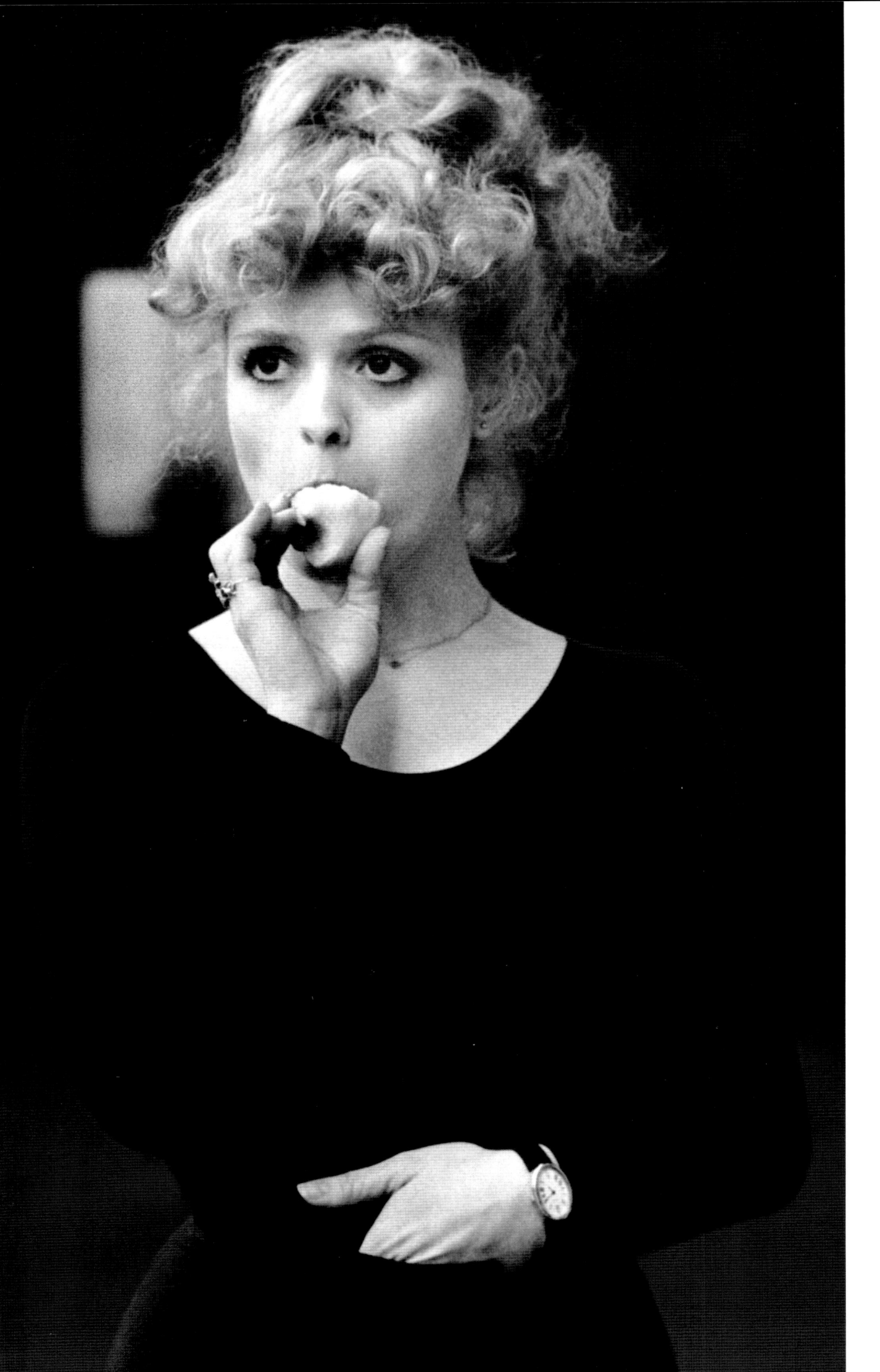

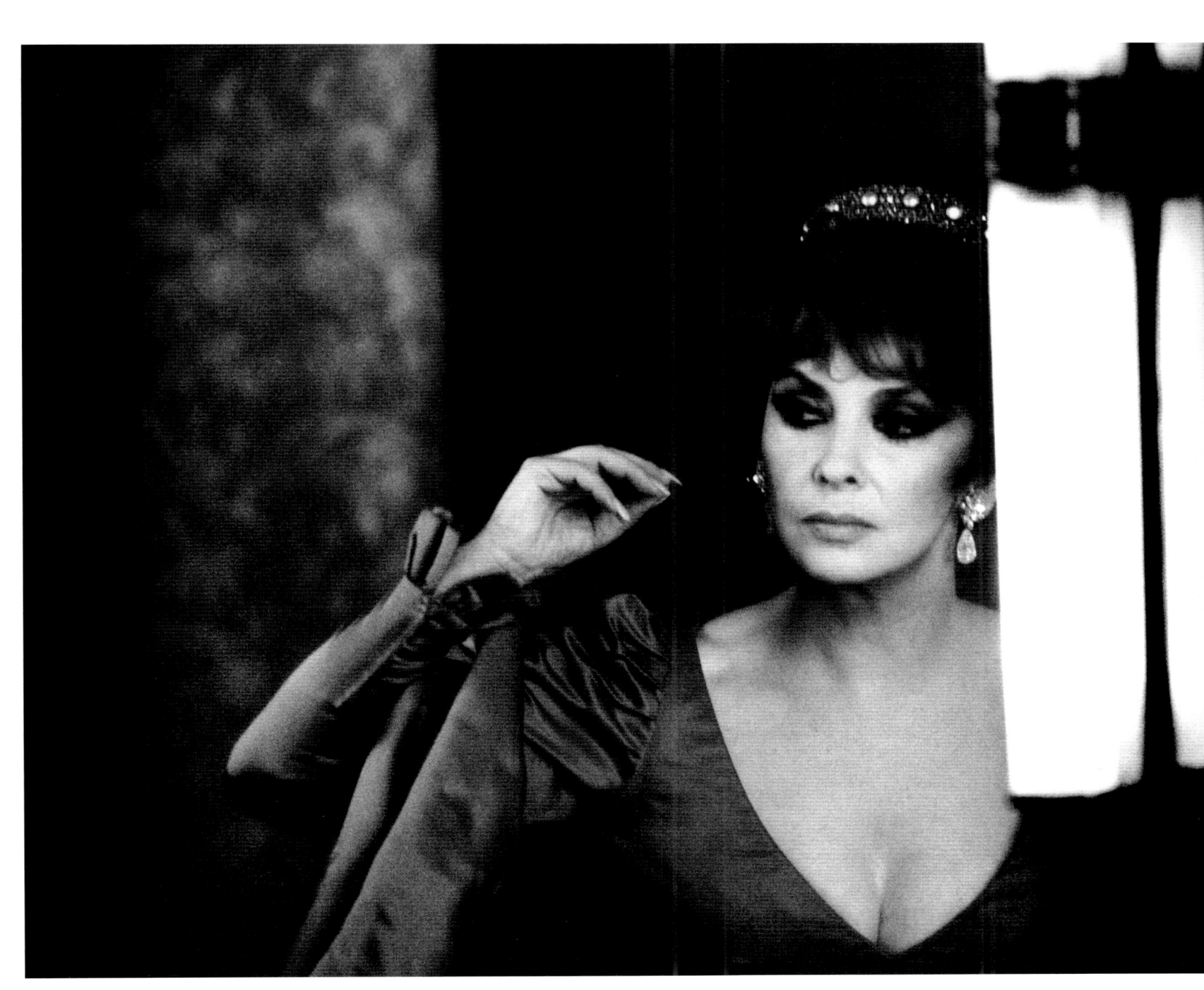

GINA LOLOBRIGIDA, NEW YORK CITY, 1982

OPPOSITE: BERNADETTE PETERS, LOS ANGELES, 1976

151

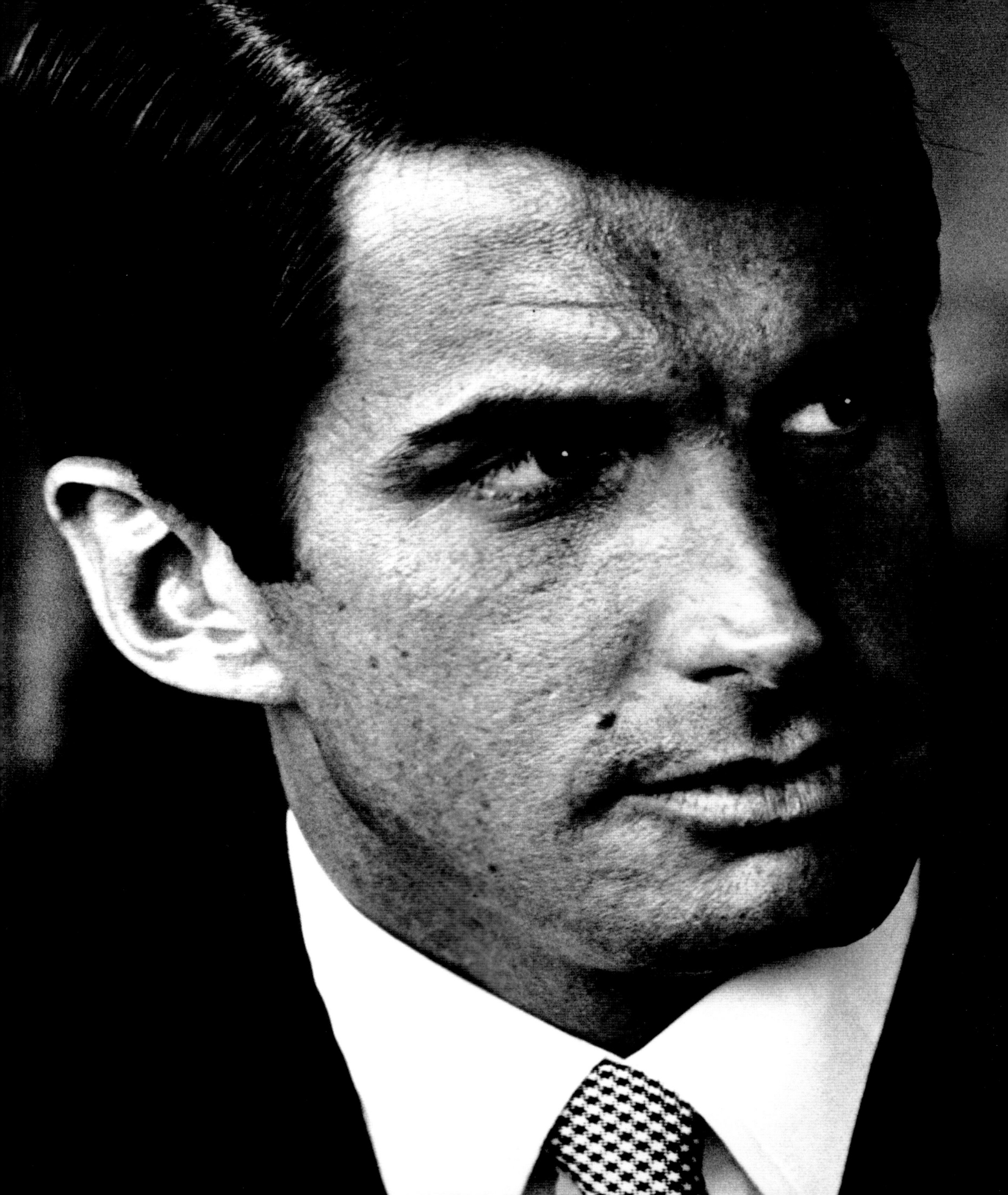

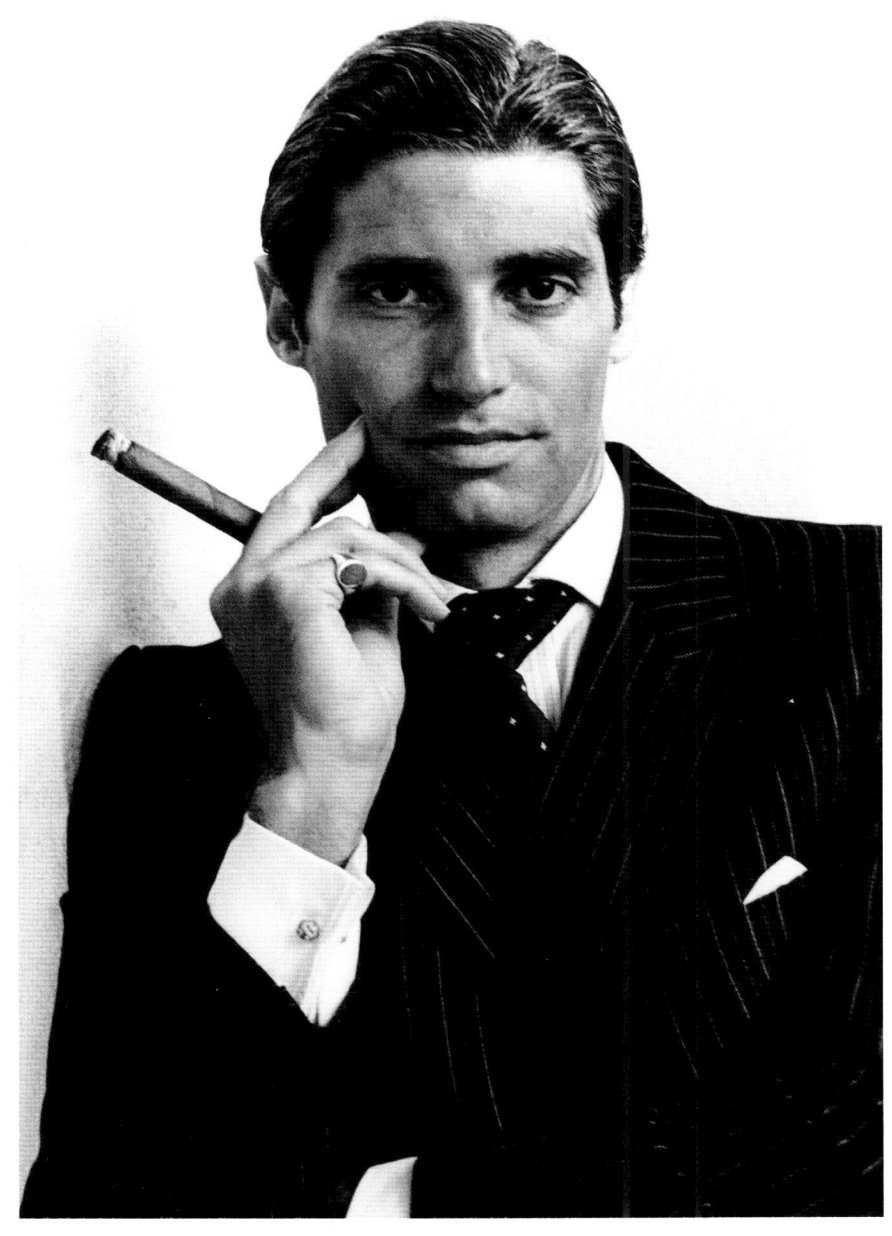

MICHAEL NOURI, BEVERLY HILLS, 1984

OPPOSITE: GEORGE HAMILTON, BEVERLY HILLS, 1967

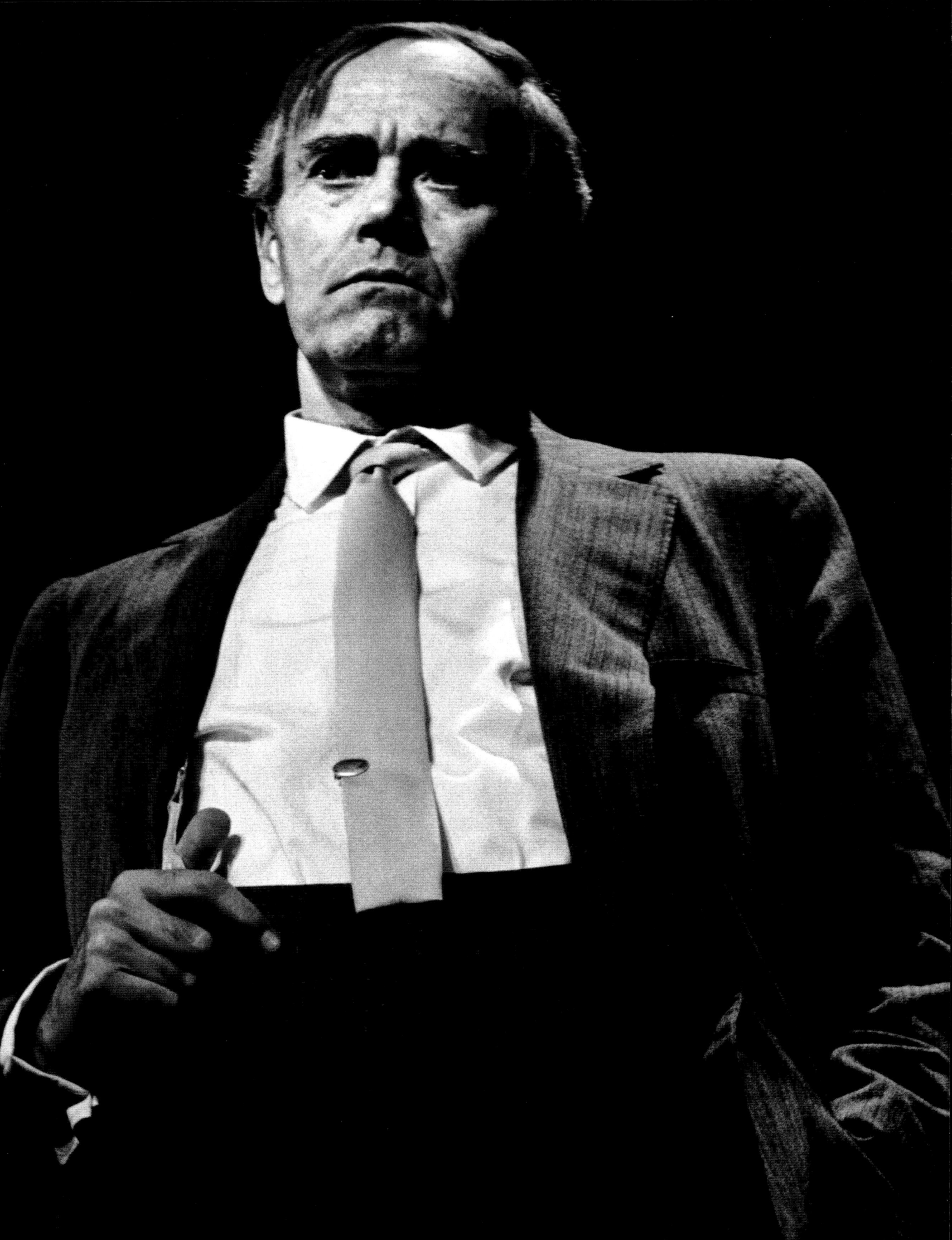

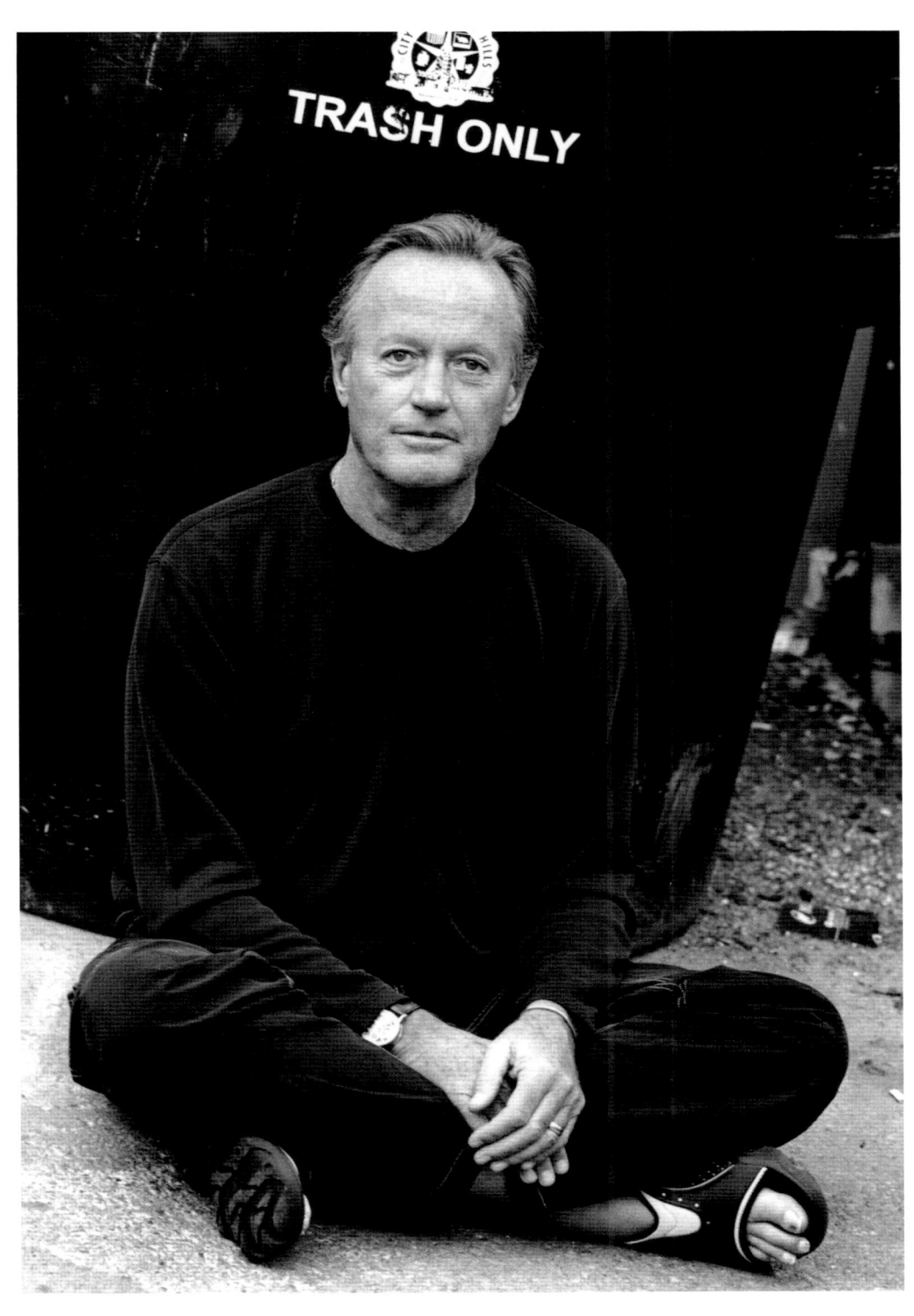

PETER FONDA, BEVERLY HILLS, 2003

OPPOSITE: HENRY FONDA, NEW YORK CITY, 1975

155

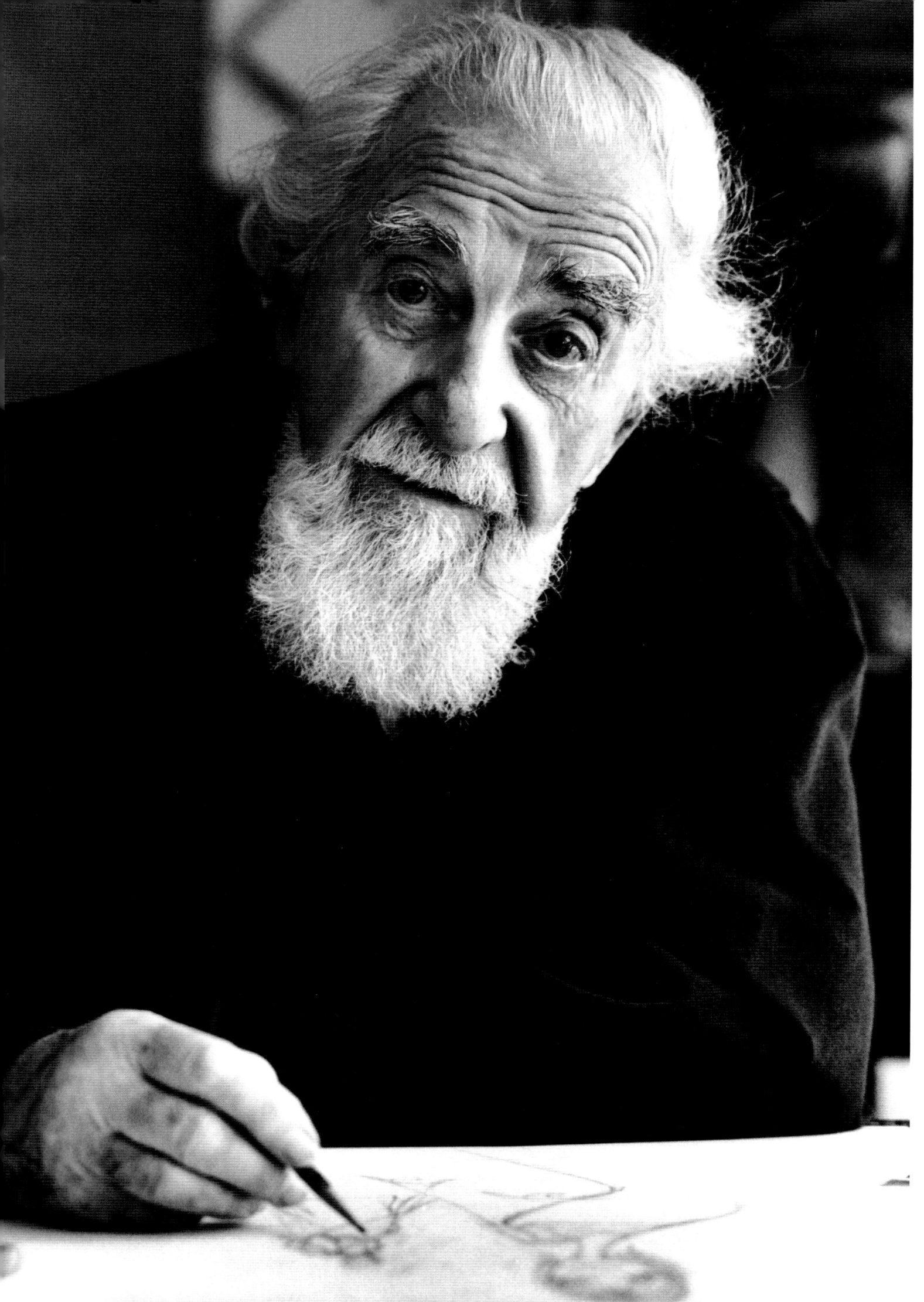

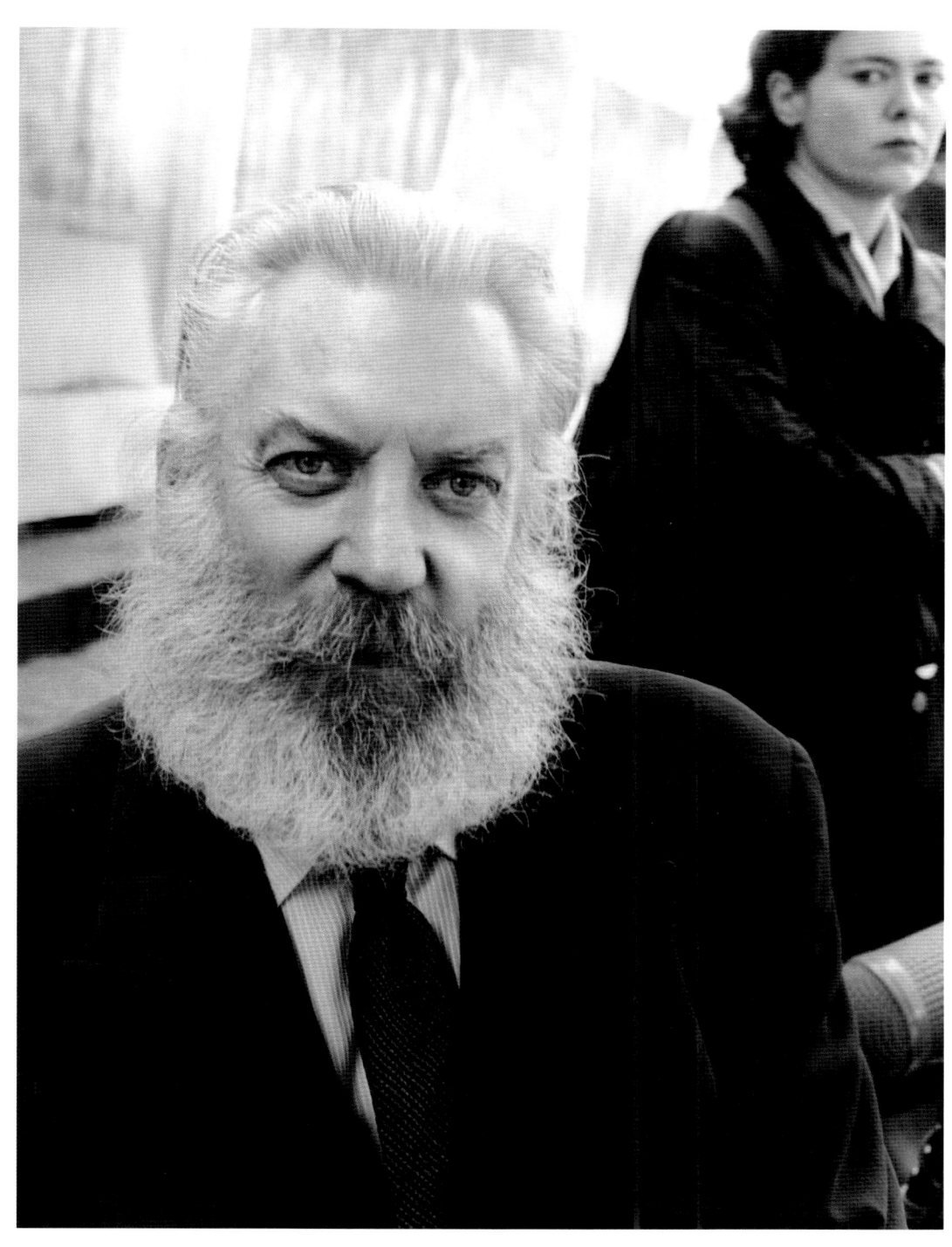

DONALD SUTHERLAND, PARIS, 1991

OPPOSITE: AL HIRSHFELD, NEW YORK CITY, 1999

157

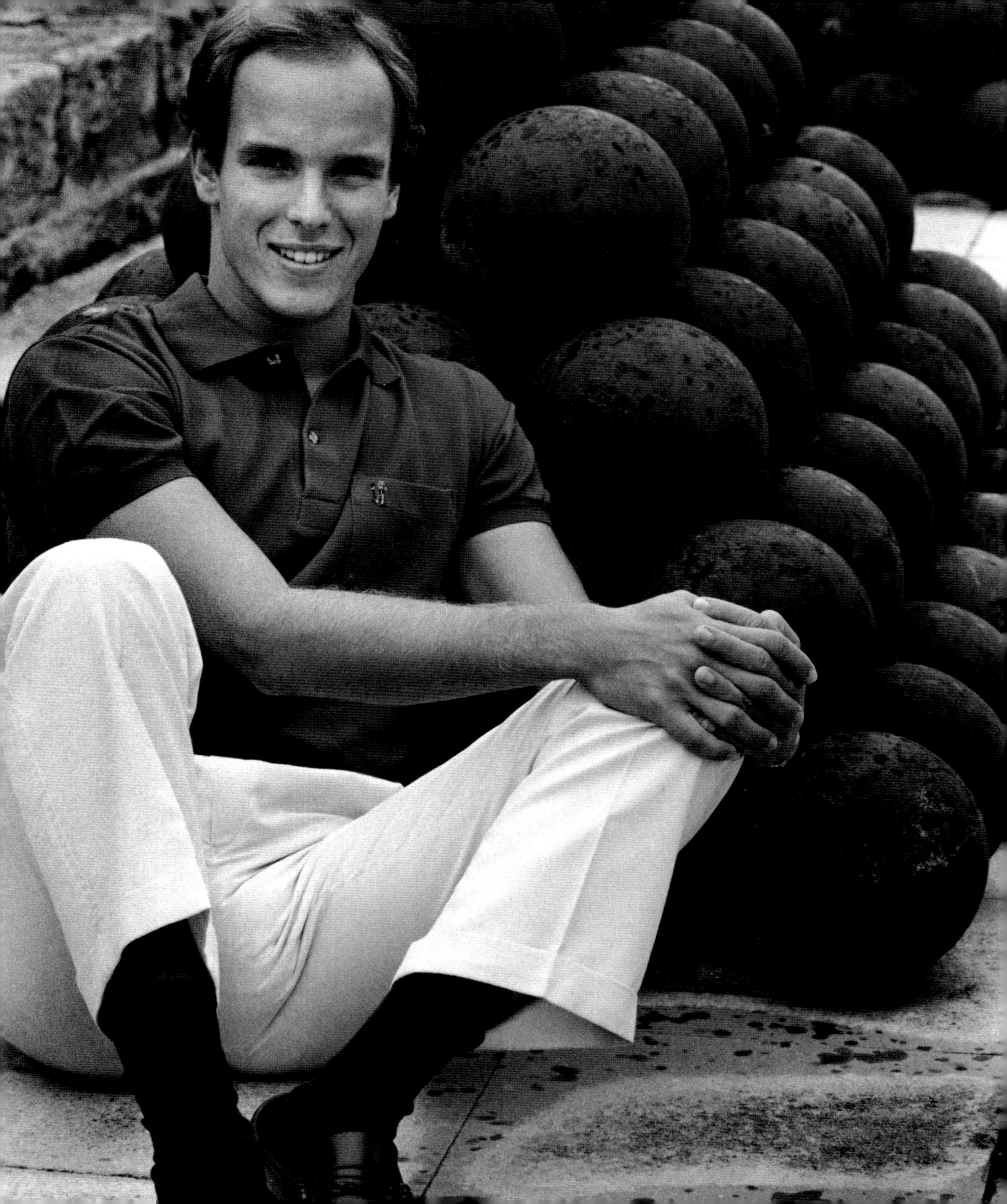

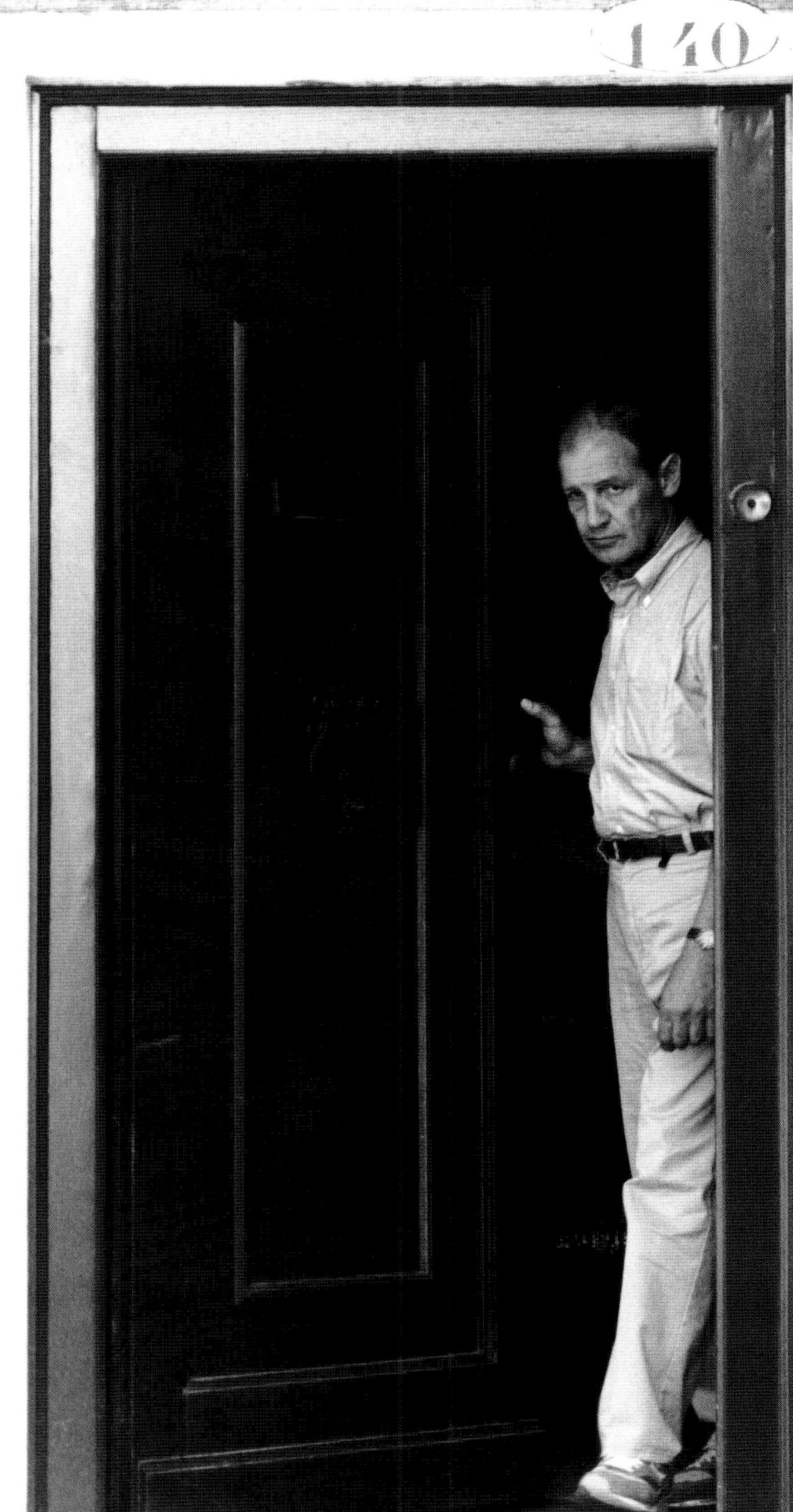

OPPOSITE: PRINCE ALBERT OF MONACO, MONTE CARLO, 1984

RIGHT: COUNT GIOVANNI VOLPE, VENICE, ITALY, 1994

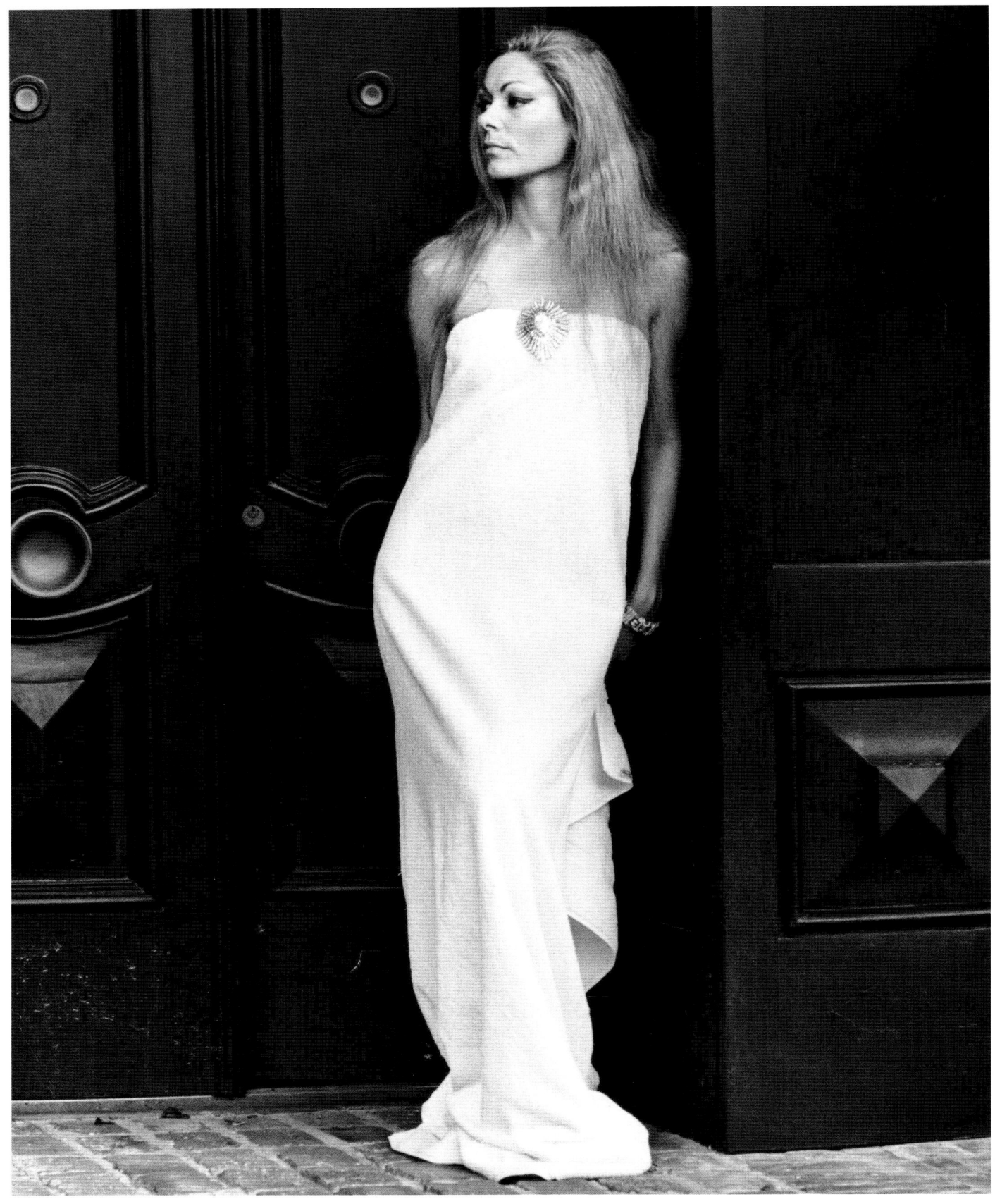

MRS. VINCENTE (DENISE) MINNELLI, BEVERLY HILLS, 1967

OPPOSITE: VICKI MORGAN, BEVERLY HILLS, 1973

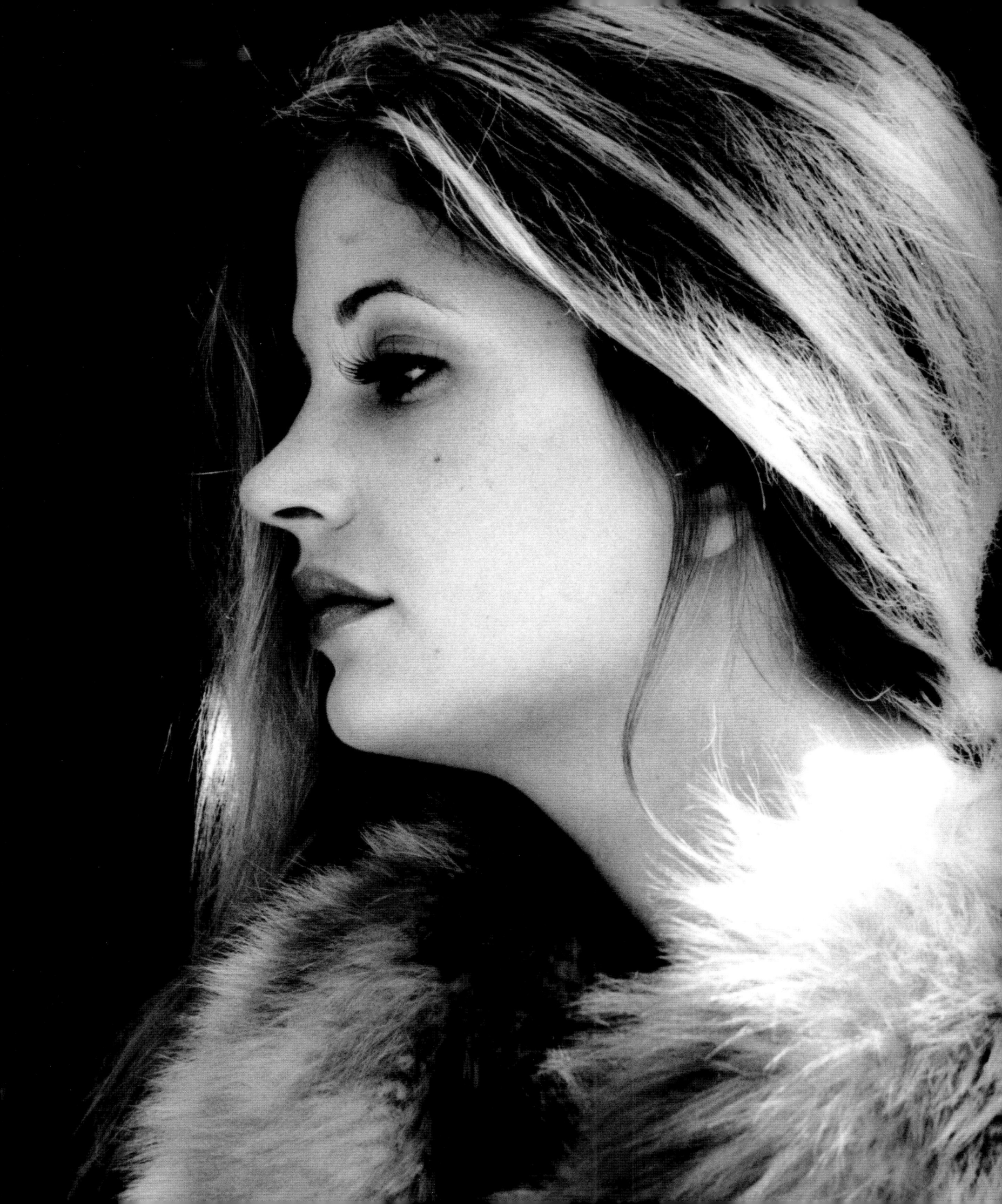

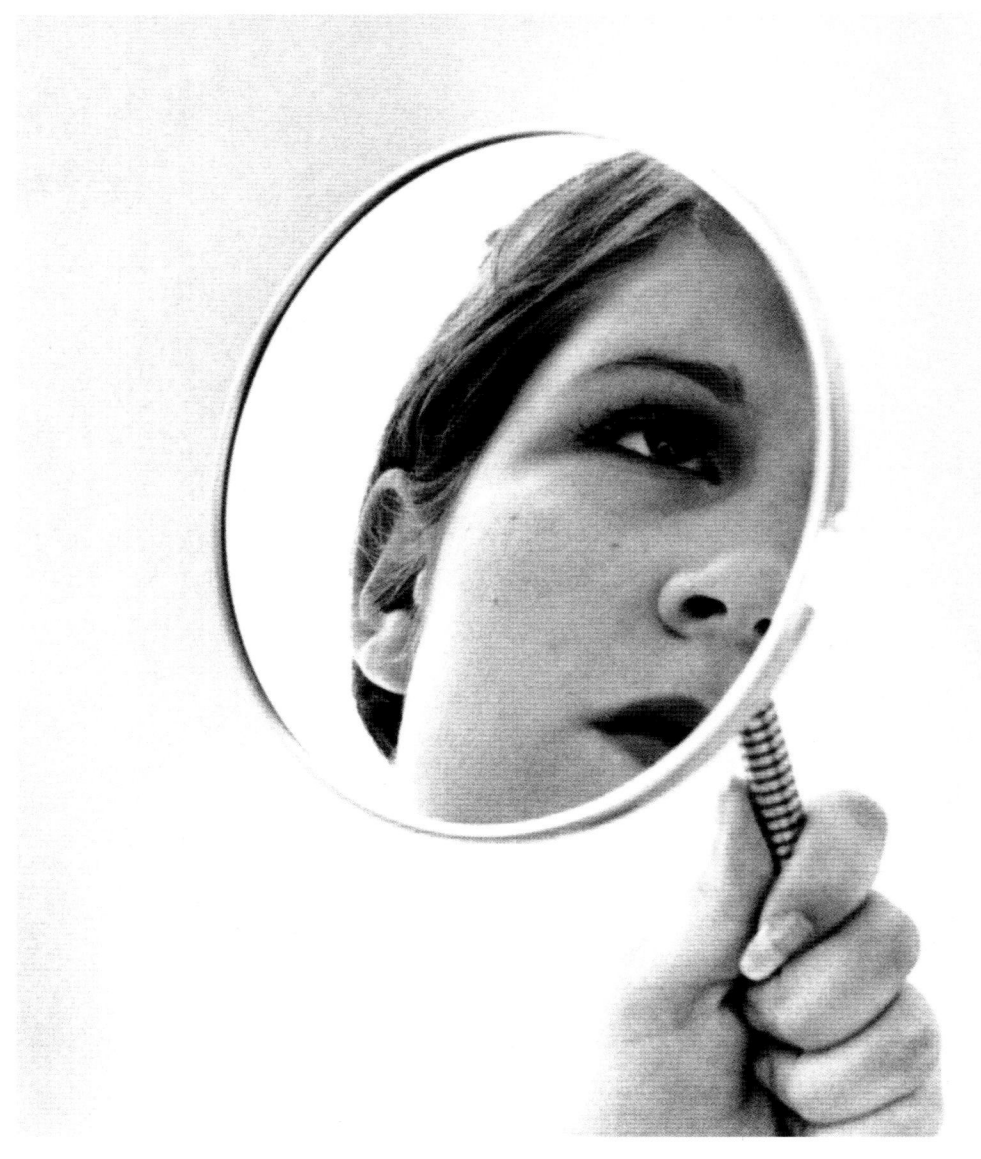

CARRIE FISHER, BEVERY HILLS, 1974

OPPOSITE: CORPO, PLAZA ATHÉNÉE, PARIS, 1991

OVERLEAF LEFT: DANCE STUDENTS, GEORGE ZORITCH DANCE SCHOOL, LOS ANGELES, 1966

OVERLEAF RIGHT: ANN REINKING AND CHARLOTTE D'AMBOISE, NEW YORK CITY, 2000

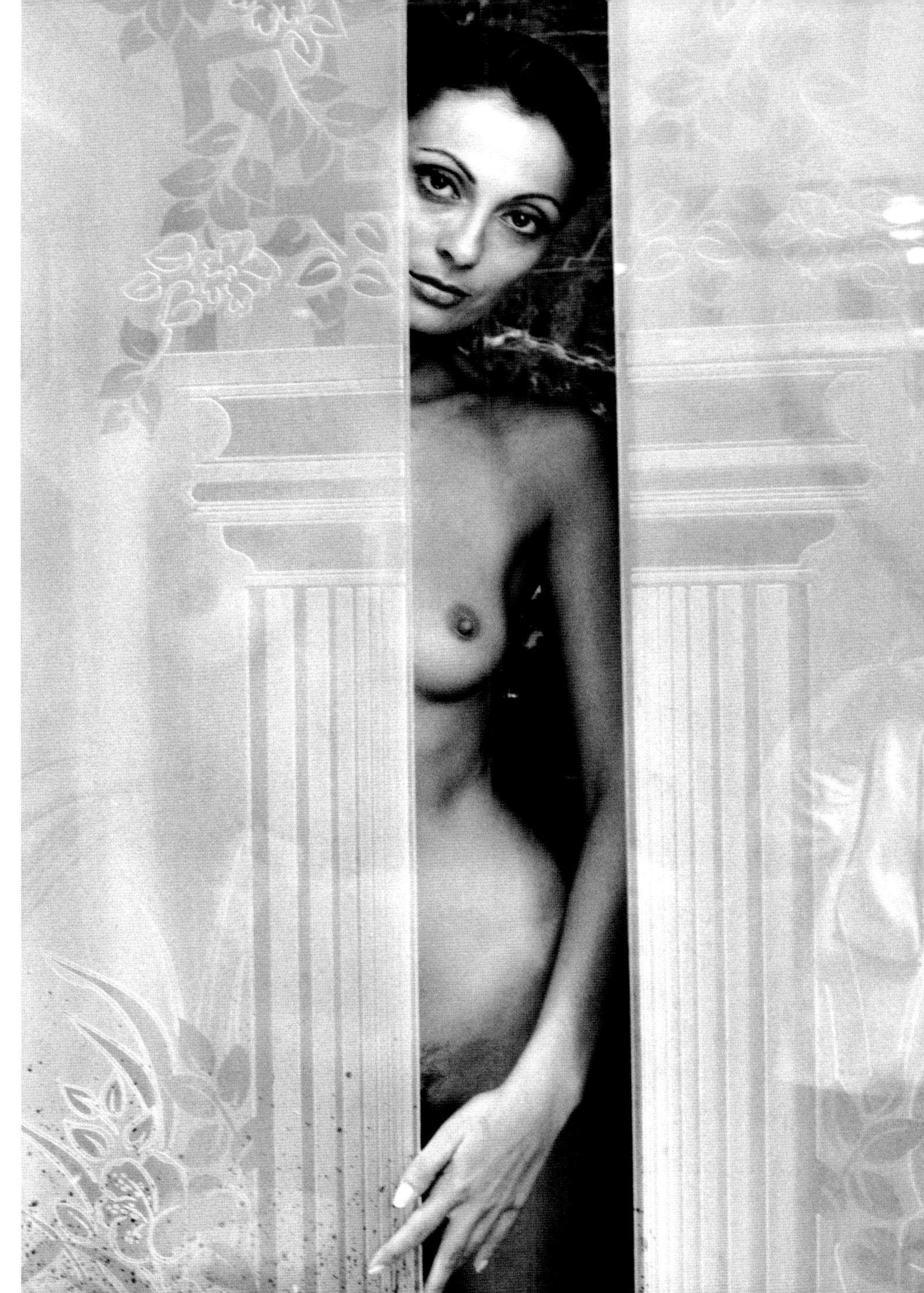

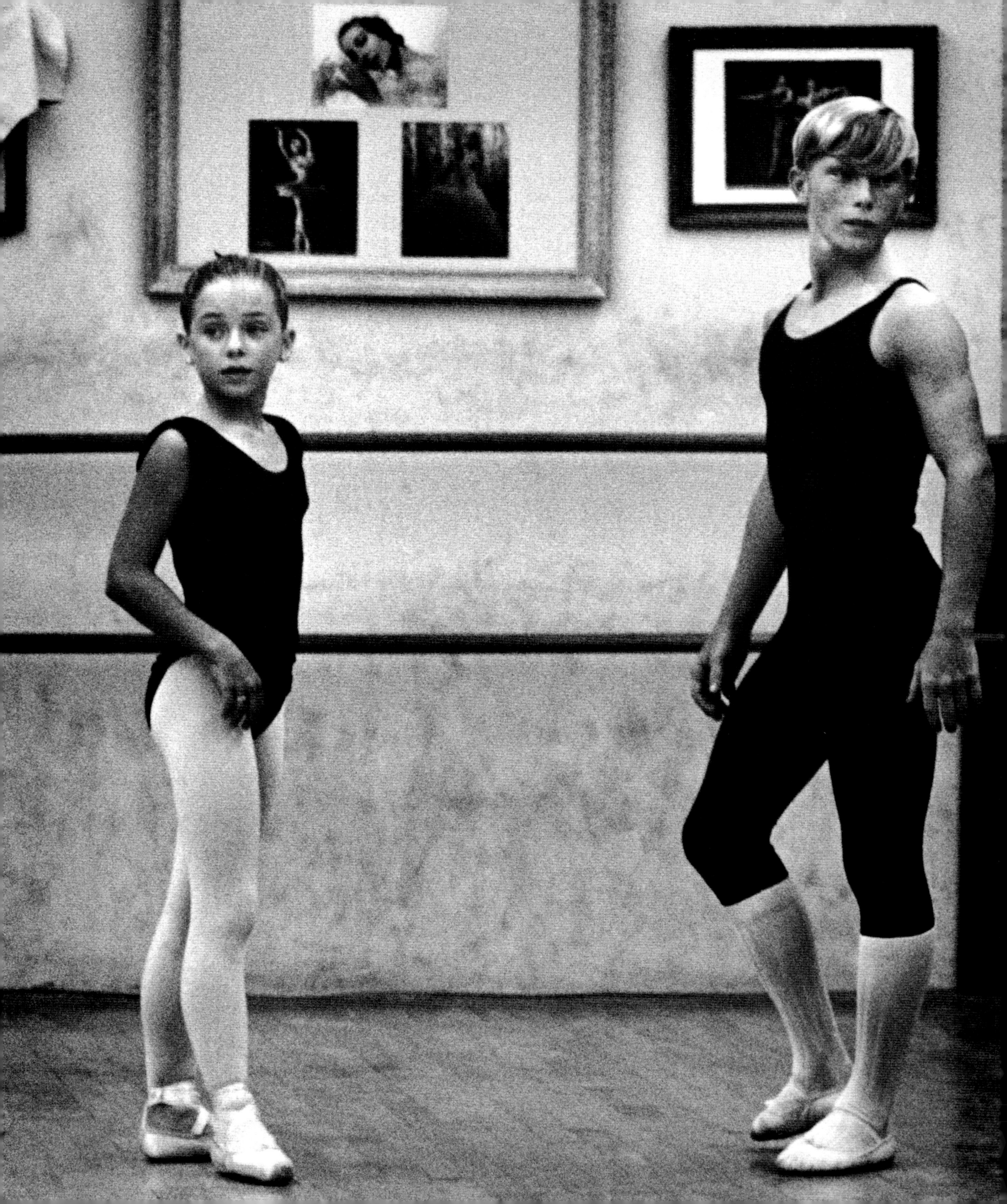

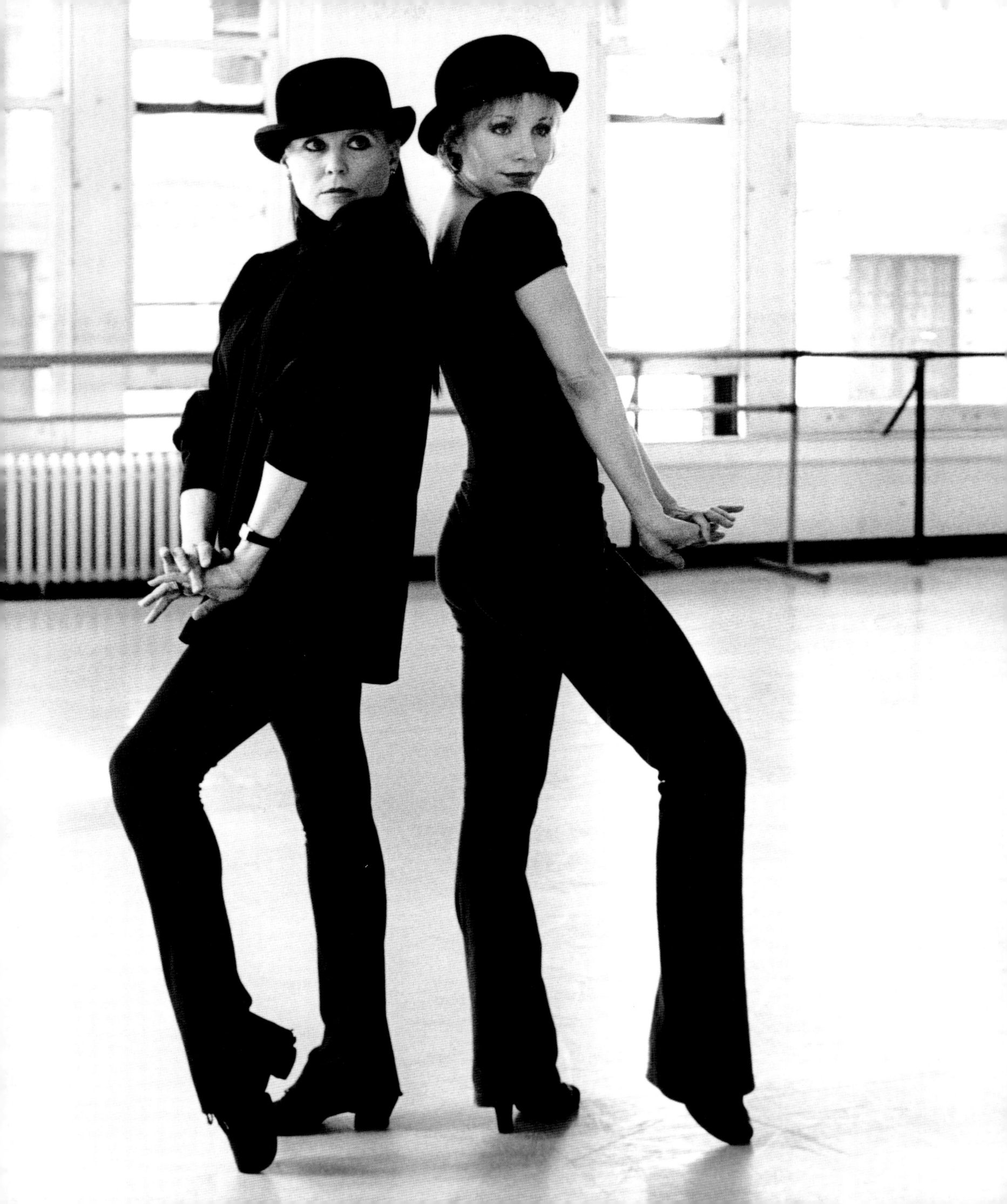

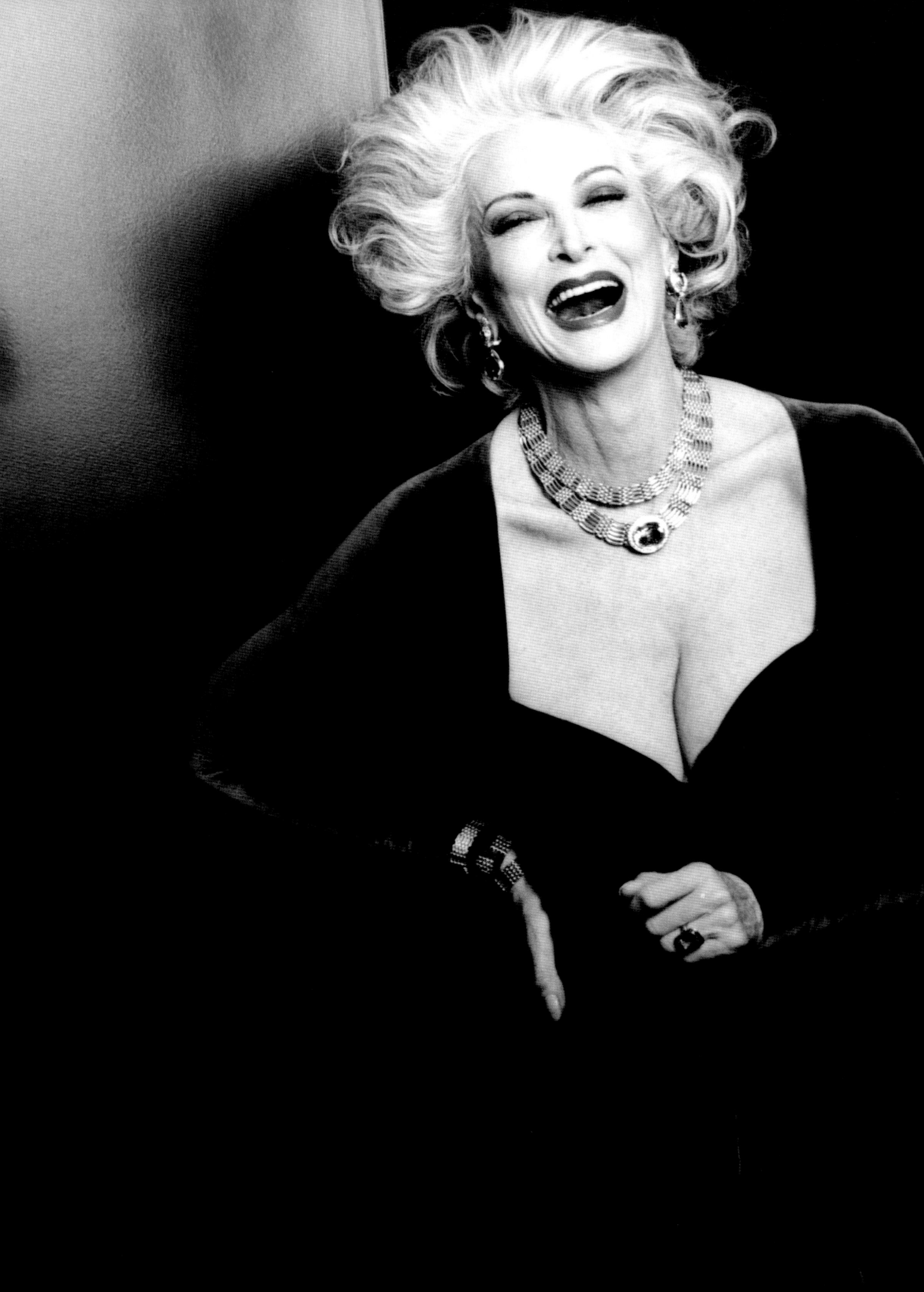

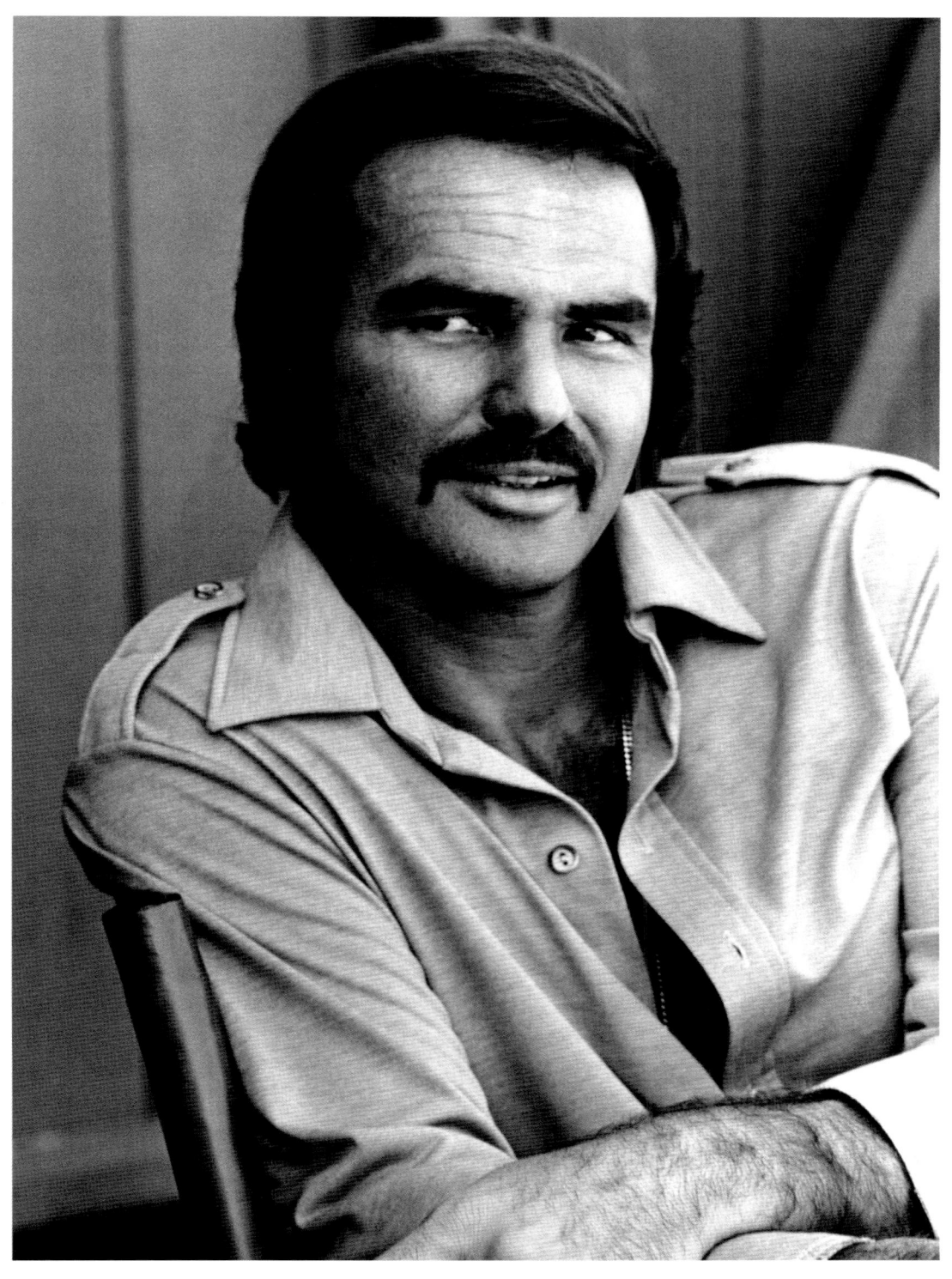

BURT REYNOLDS, LOS ANGELES, 1973

OPPOSITE: CARMEN DELL'OREFICE, NEW YORK CITY, 1997

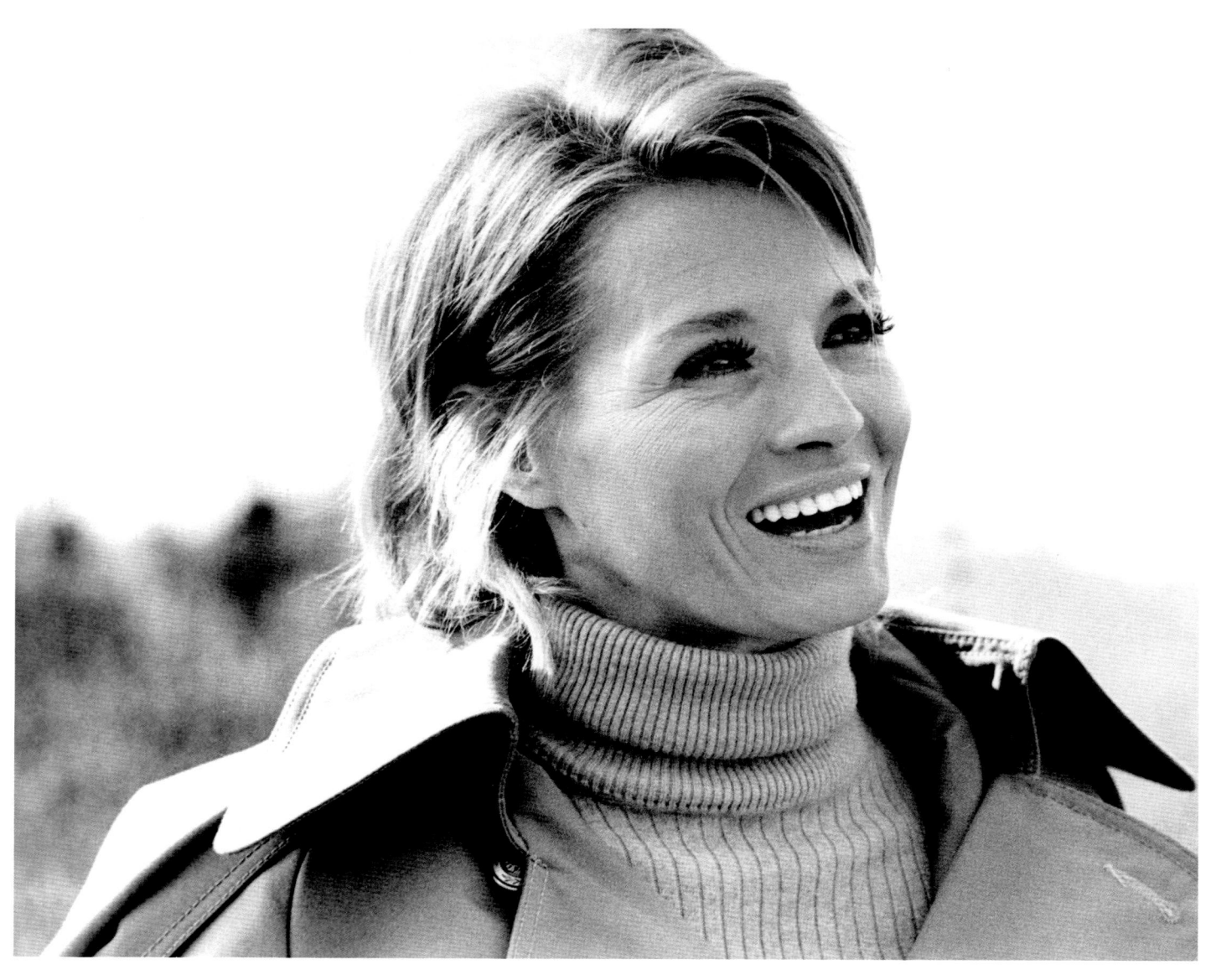

ANGIE DICKINSON, BEVERLY HILLS, 1966

OPPOSITE: JOEY HEATHERTON, NANTUCKET, MASSACHUSETTS, 1980

OVERLEAF LEFT: MICHAEL PARÉ, BEVERLY HILLS, 1983

OVERLEAF RIGHT: VIGGO MORTENSEN, NEW YORK CITY, 1983

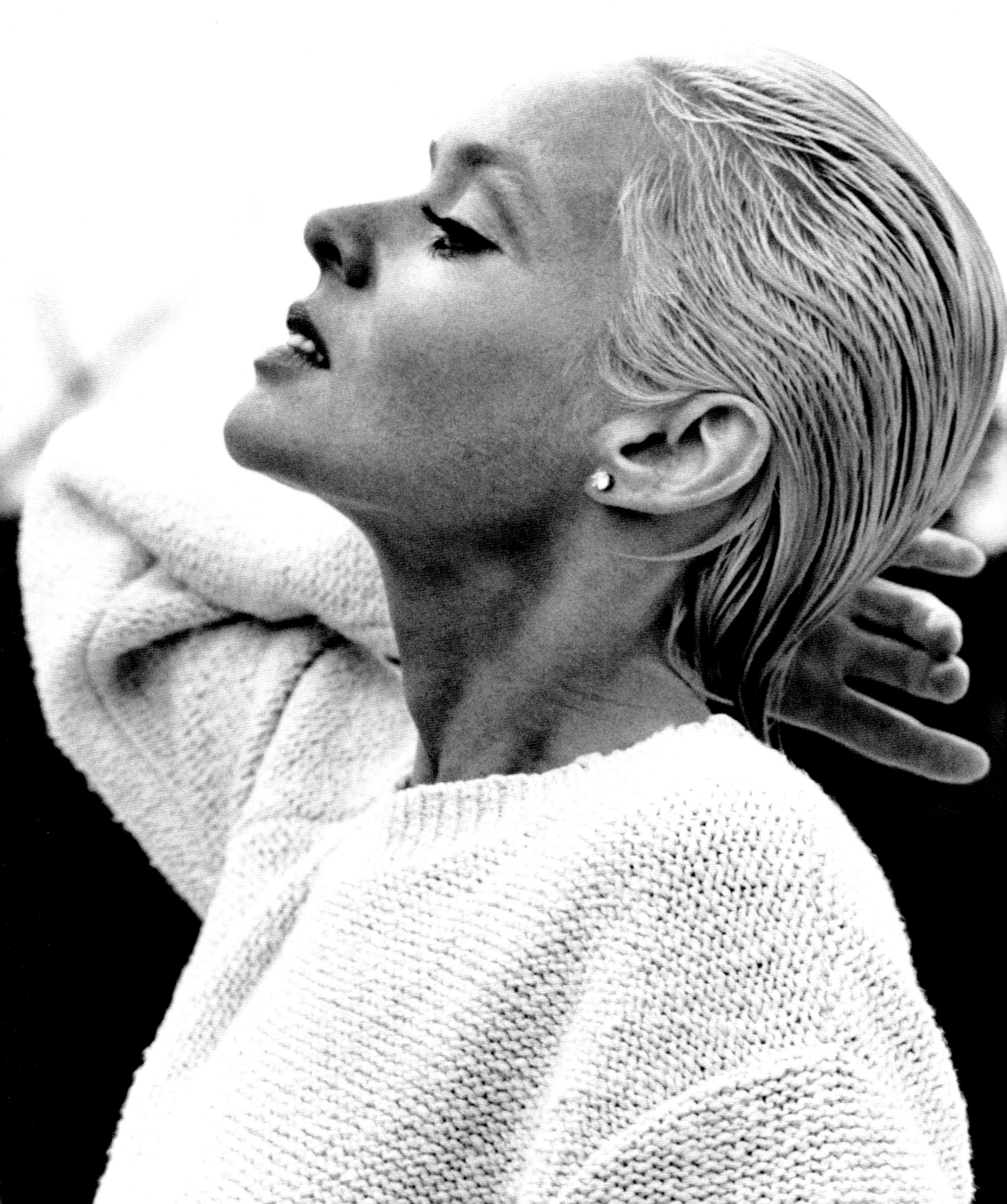

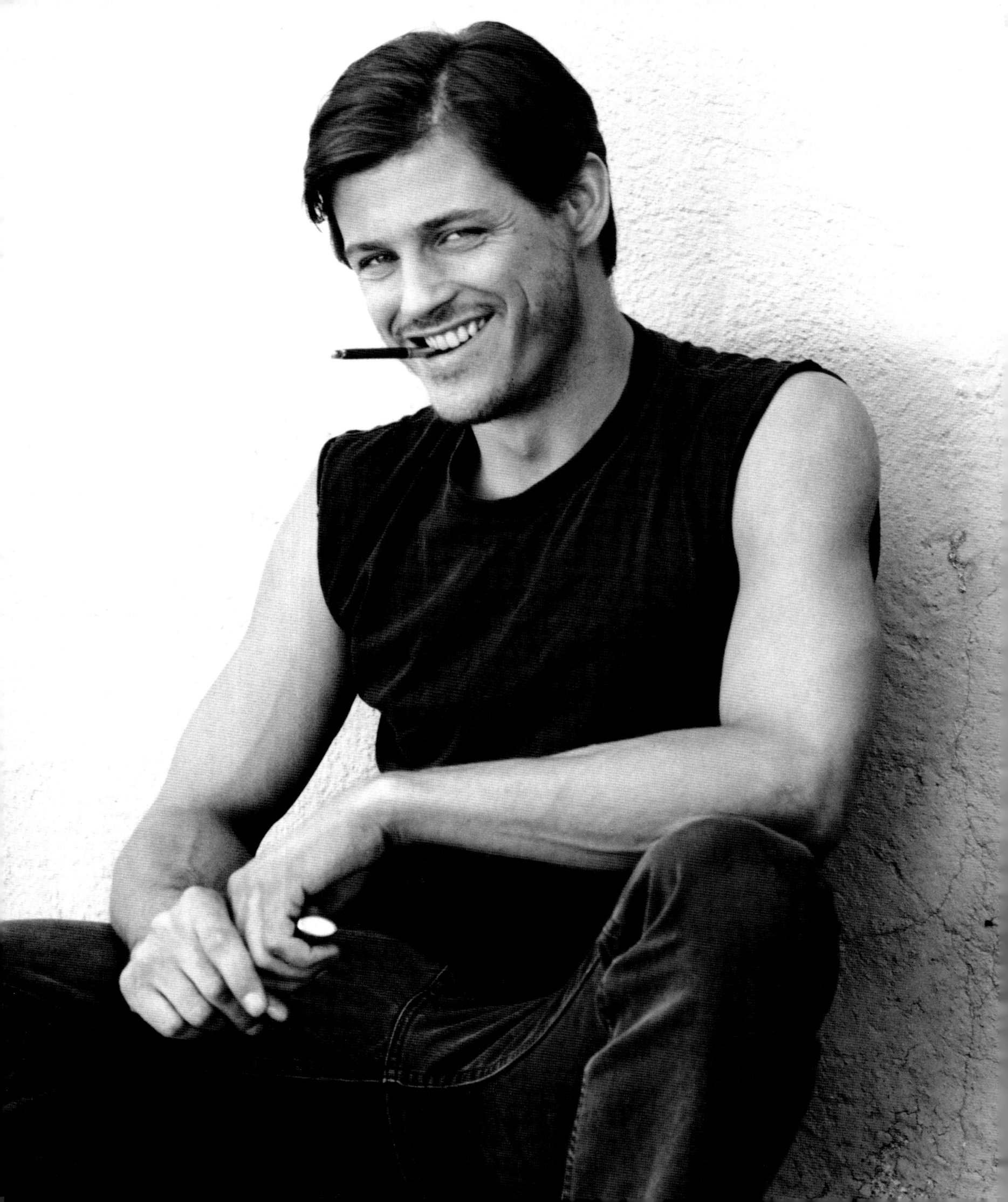

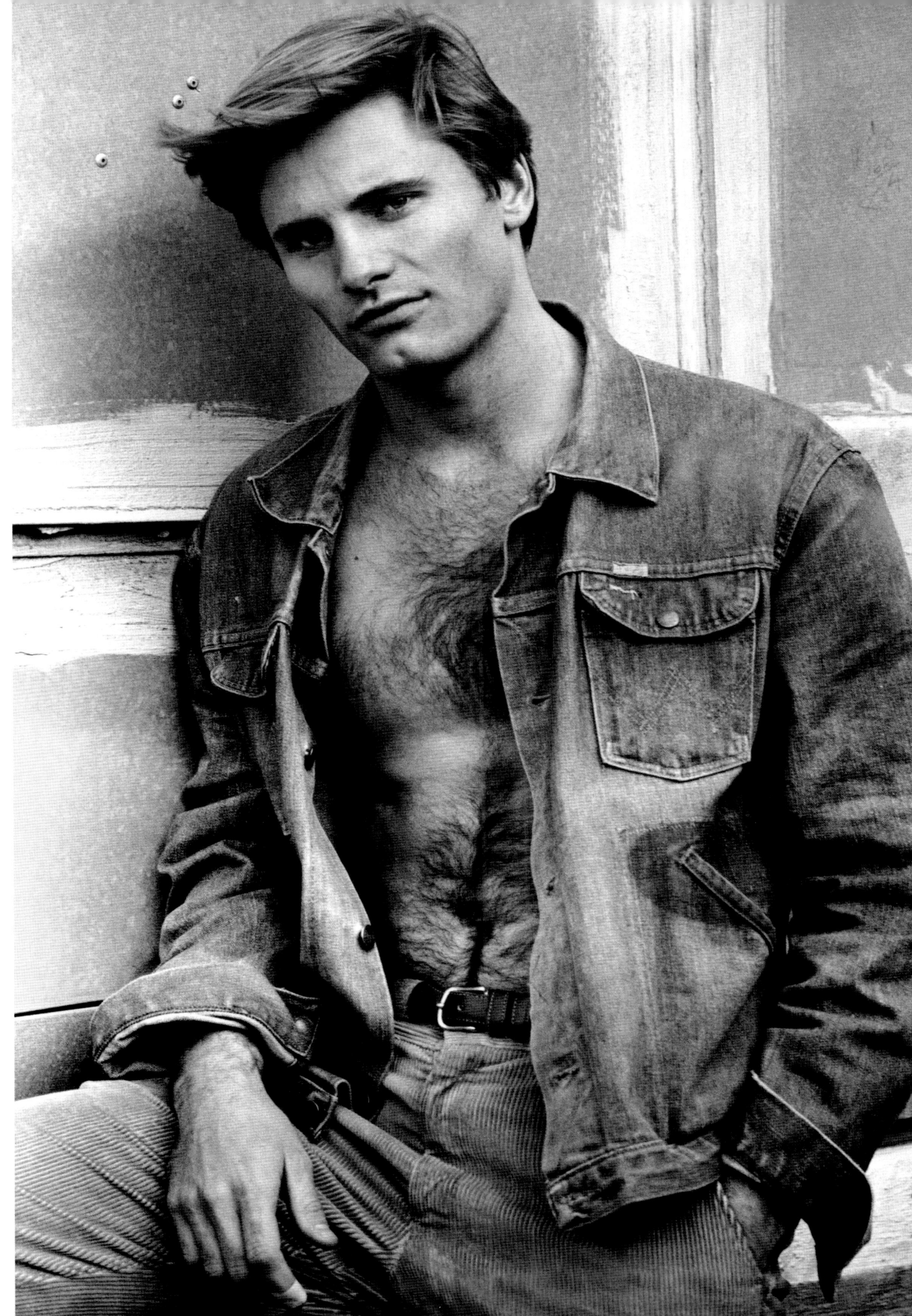

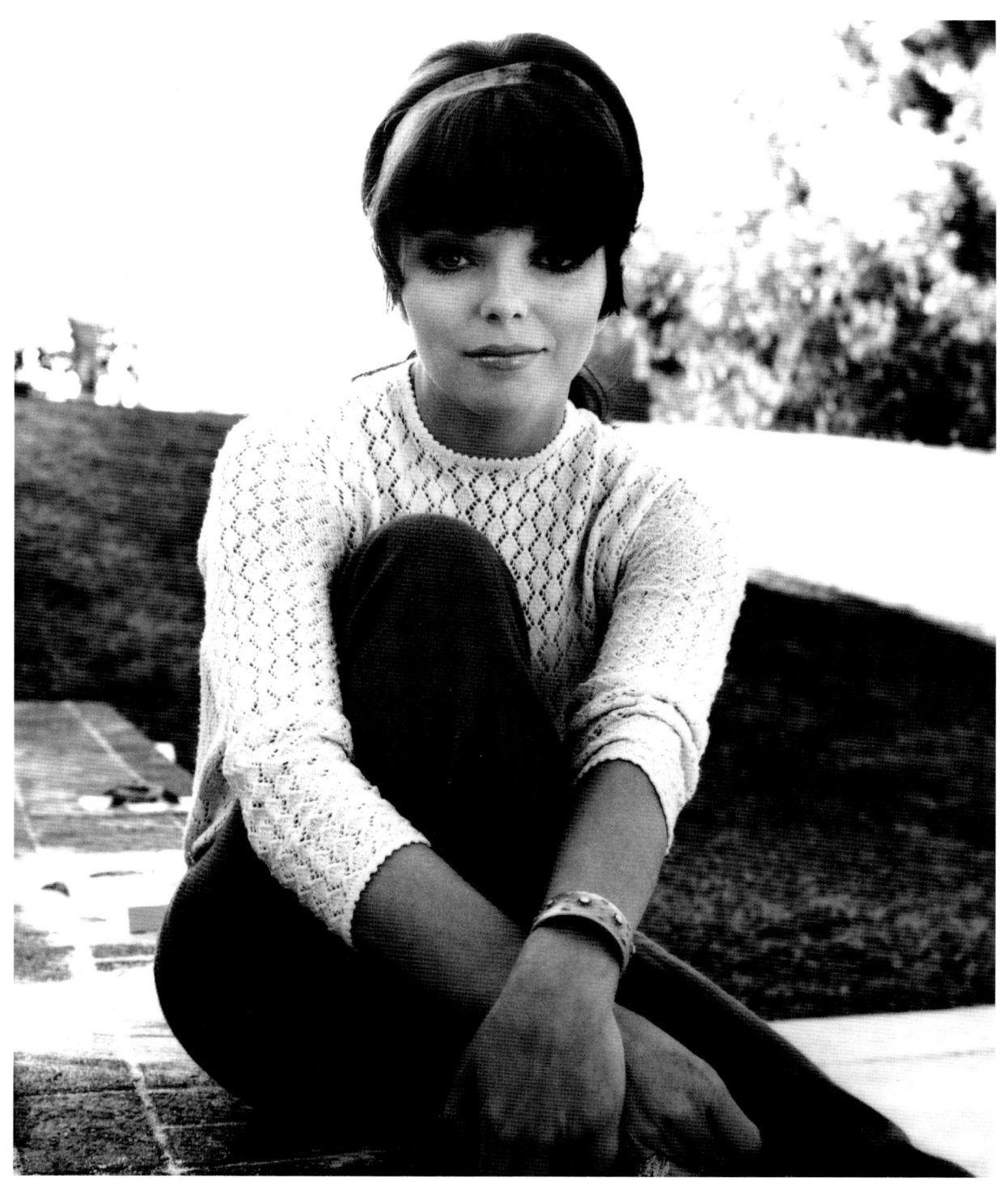

JOAN COLLINS, BEVERLY HILLS, 1967

OPPOSITE: MICHAEL NADER, BEVERLY HILLS, 1983

OVERLEAF LEFT: JUGGLER, HAVANA, CUBA, 1999

OVERLEAF RIGHT: MARK HARMON, BEVERLY HILLS, 1983

PAGE 176: MARLENE DIETRICH, NEW YORK CITY, 1967

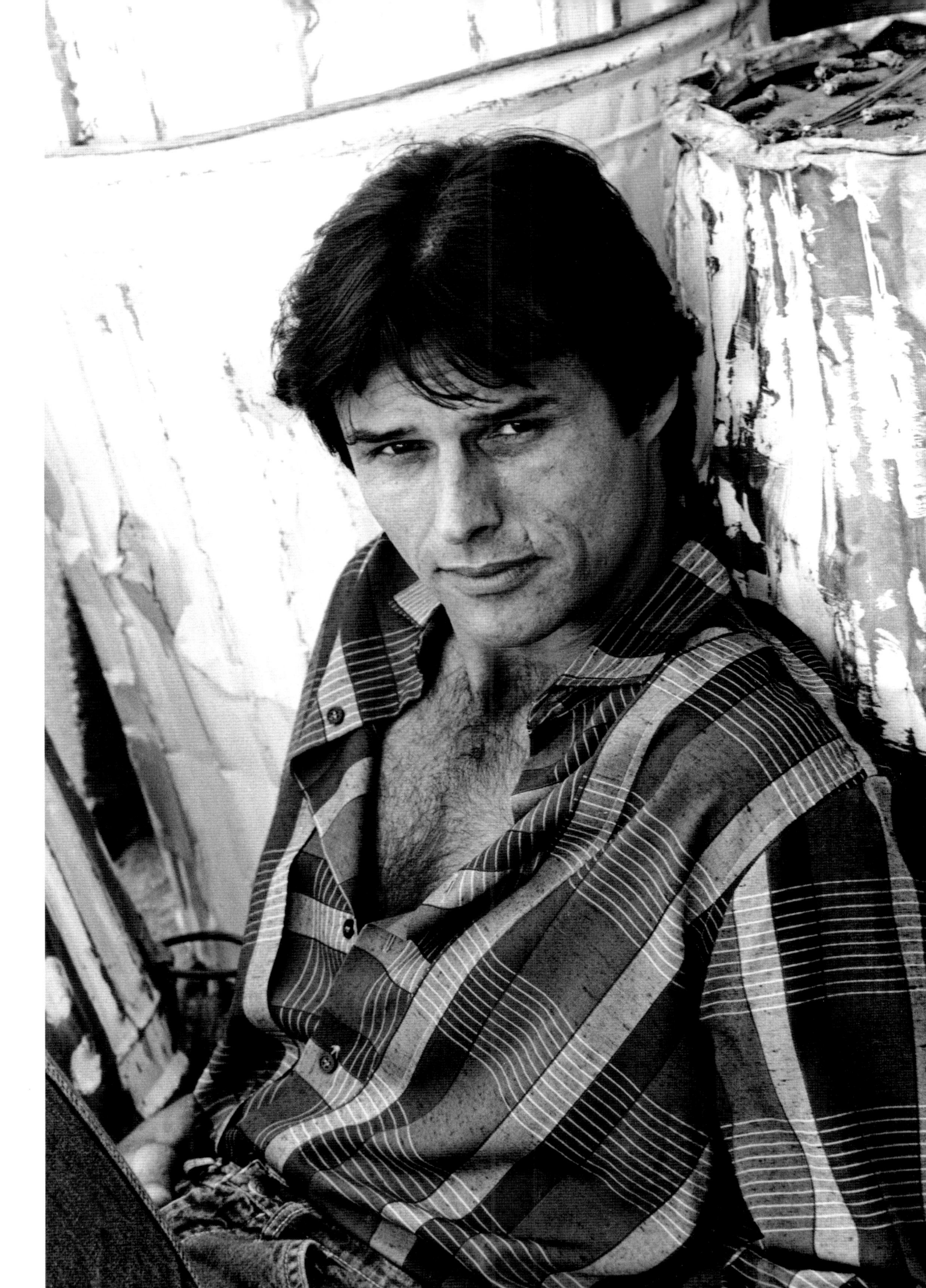

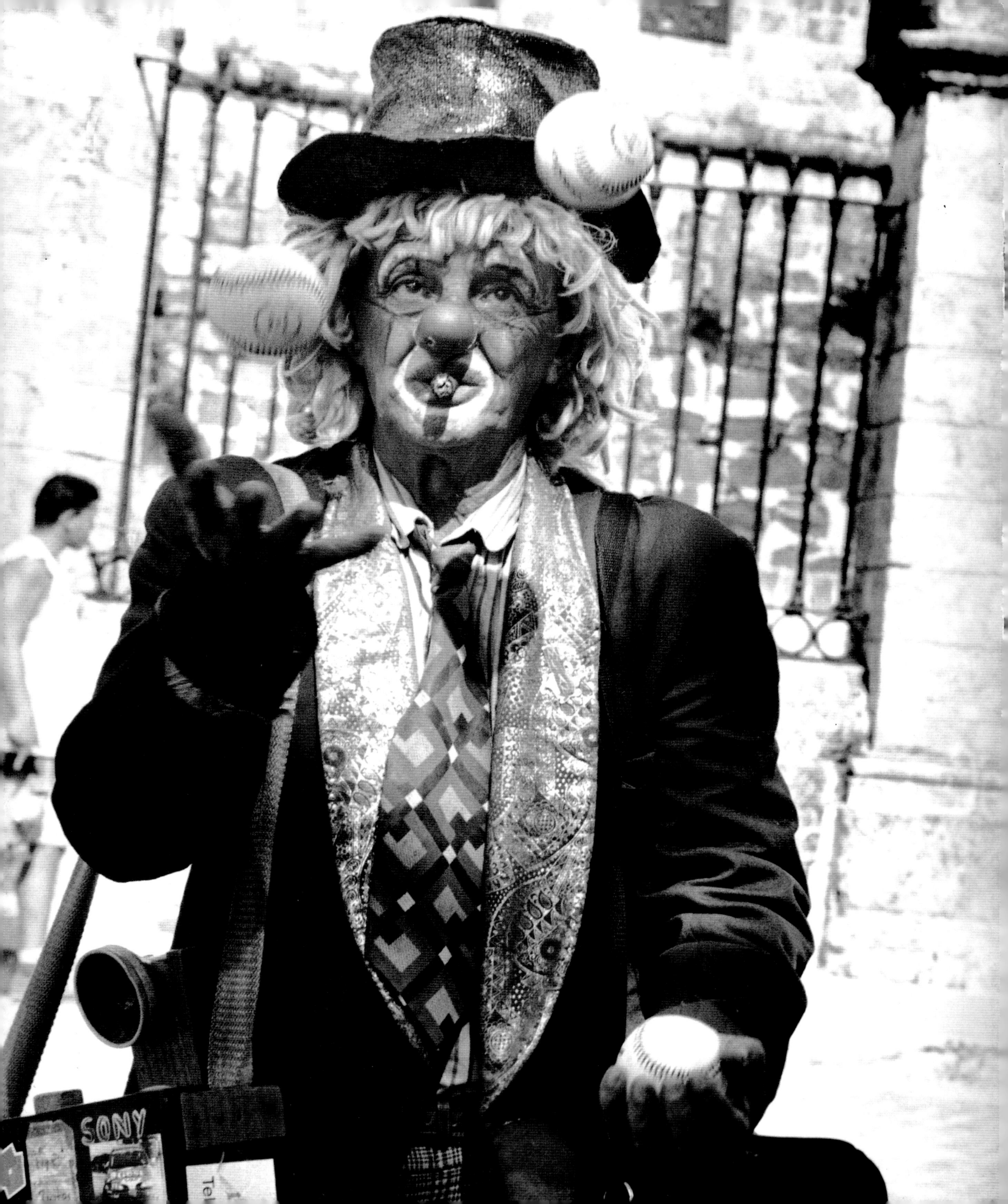

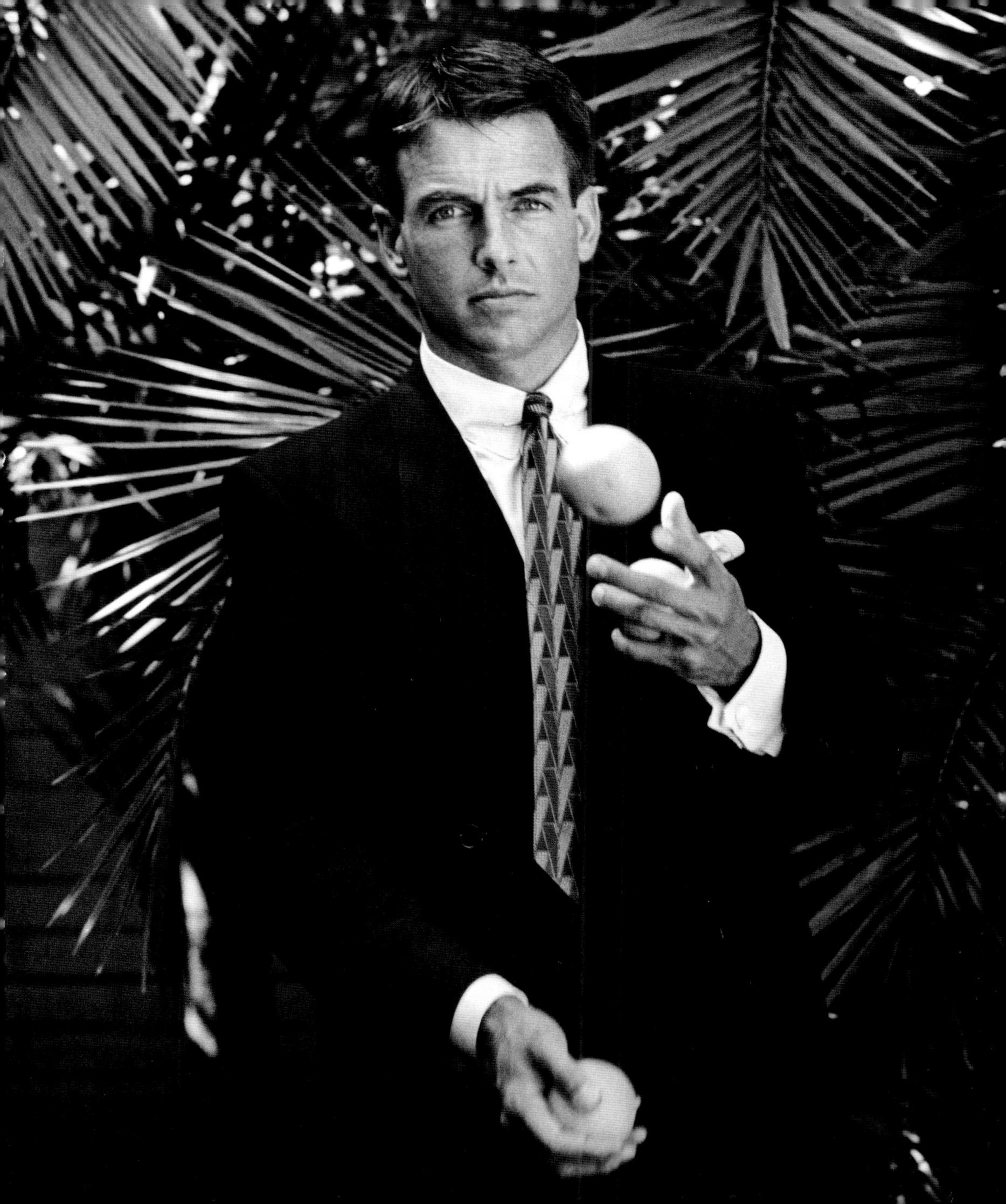

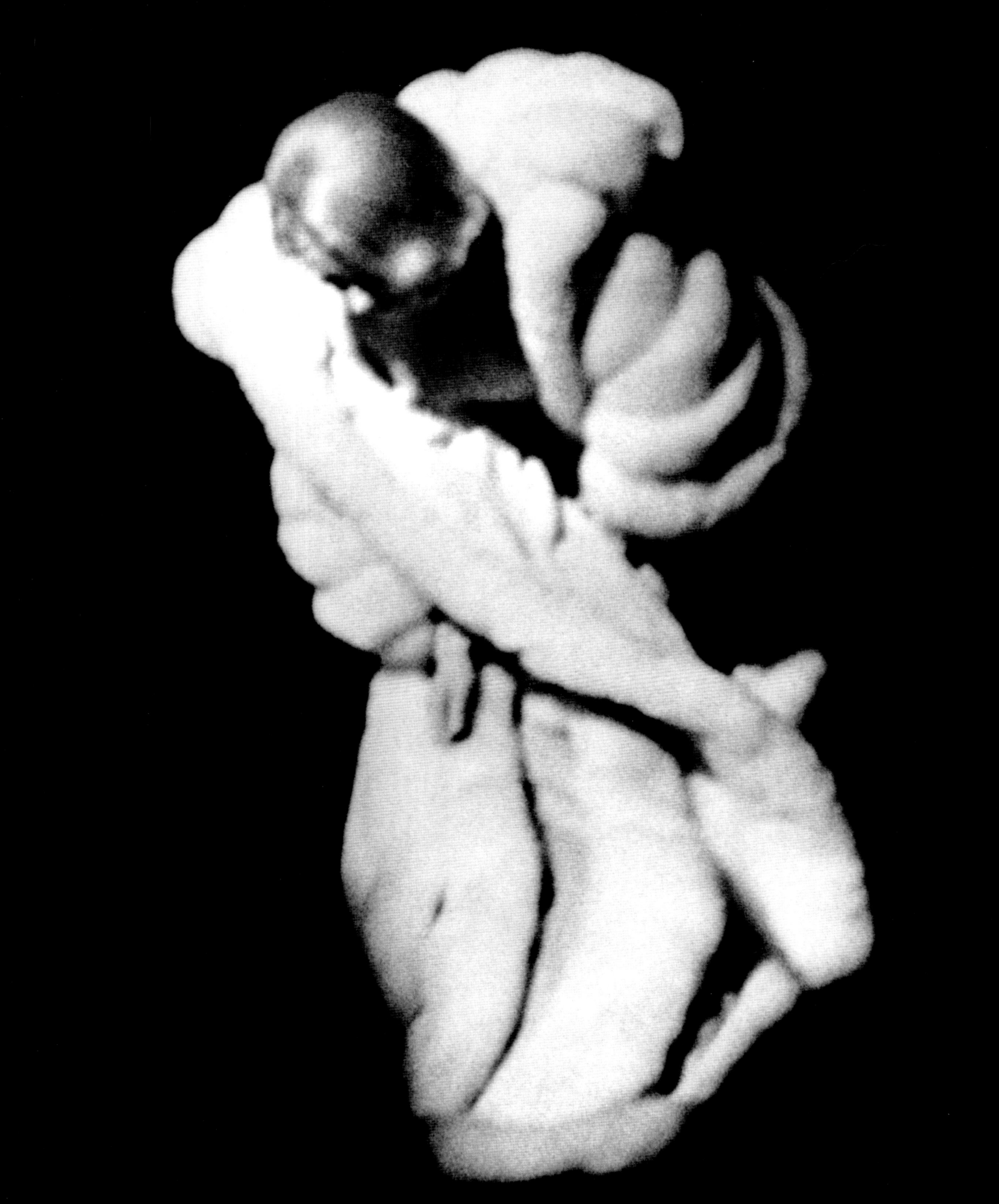

INDEX OF PHOTOGRAPHS

Adler, Stella, 38
Arnaz, Jr., Desi, 97
Astaire, Fred, 22, 23
Astaire, Robyn, 23
Bathing Beauties, 123
Beatty, Warren, 73
Belmondo, Jean-Paul, 34
Berenson, Berry, 78
Berenson, Marisa, 78, 81
Bergen, Candice, 96
Bergen, Edgar (with Charlie McCarthy
    and Mortimer Snerd), 21
Bergen, Kris, 125
Berger, Helmut, 31
Bergerac, Jacques, 129
Blake, Robert, 29
Bois de Boulogne, 130–31
Botero, Fernando, 111
Bowie, David, 39
Bowles, Hamish, 86
Caine, Michael, 44
Cambiaso, Adolphus, 95
Caruso, Richard, 85
Champion, Gower, 144
Cher, 134
Christie, Julie, 72
Coburn, James, 91
Collins, Joan, 172
Corpo, 163
Cortese, Valentina, 84, 85
Cuban teen, 93
Dahl, Arlene, 127
D'Amboise, Charlotte, 165
dance students,
    George Zoritch School, 164
Davis, Jr., Sammy, 19, 46
Day, Doris, 75
de Givenchy, Hubert, 10–11
de Havilland, Olivia, 40–41, 42–43
de Ribes, Jacqueline, 55
Dell'Orefice, Carmen, 166
Delon, Alain, 33
Dickinson, Angie, 168
Dietrich, Marlene, 176
Donahue, Troy, 100
Douglas, Cameron, 67
Douglas, Kirk, 66
Dunne, Dominick, 64
Dunne, Dominique, 65
Eastwood, Clint, 53
Elder, David, 145
Ferrigno, Lou, 98
Fisher, Carrie, 162
Fonda, Henry, 154

Fonda, Peter, 155
Fontaine, Joan, 42–43
Fontaine, Lillian, 42–43
Fontayne, Margot, 140–41
Freeman, Jonathan, 136
Galanos, James, 76
Gardiner, Nadia, 14–15
Graham, Alexis, 7
Griffith, Melanie, 103
Gwenel, 119
Halston, 80, 81
Hamilton, George, 152
Harmon, Mark, 175
Hasselhoff, David, 101
Hayward, Brooke, 99
Heatherton, Joey, 169
Hirshfeld, Al, 156
Hitchcock, Alfred, 37
Hopkins, Anthony, 28
Horne, Lena, 138
Hudson, Rock, 74
Hull, Mylinda, 136
Juggler, 174
Kara, Isabel, 54
Kellerman, Sally, 106
Kempner, Nan, 89
Klein, Kevin, 147
Laforêt, Marie, 56–57
Ladies and Gentleman,
    Arc de Triomphe Race 132–33
Lagerfeld, Karl, 77
Lamas, Lorenzo, 126
Lane, Kenneth Jay, 88
Lemmon, Jack, 148
Lillie, Beatrice, 146
Lolobrigida, Gina, 151
Loren, Sophia, 69
Louis, Joe, 104–105
Marilyn Monroe Impersonator, 90
Marx, Groucho, 36
Marinaro, Ed, 142
Martins, Peter, 109
McDowell, Malcolm, 102
McQueen, Steve, 19
Minnelli, Liza, 47, 61
Minnelli, Mrs. Vincente (Denise), 160
Minnelli, Vincente, 60
Mitchum, Robert, 35
Morgan, Vicki, 161
Mortensen, Viggo, 171
Nader, Michael, 173
Naked Lunch, 120
Neel, Alice, 113
Neiman, Leroy, 110

Nelson, Rick, 117
Newman, Paul, 32
Newton, Helmut, 115
Newton, June, 115
Nicholson, Jack, 26–27
Nouri, Michael, 153
Nureyev, Rudolf, 140–41, 143
O'Brien, Hugh, 128
Paré, Michael, 170
Peppard, George, 70
Perkins, Anthony, 79
Peters, Bernadette, 150
Pitt II, William, 48
Poitier, Sidney, 52
Polanski, Roman, 26–27
Ponti, Jr., Carlo, 68
Prince Albert of Monaco, 158
Prince Philip of England, 51
Puck, Wolfgang, 59
Quinn, Anthony, 45
Rampling, Charlotte, 58
Reinking, Ann, 165
Reynolds, Burt, 167
Robertson, Cliff, 116
Ross, Katherine, 94
Rossellini, Roberto, 121
Schlee, Valentina, 82–83
Scott, George C., 149
Sharif, Omar, 12–13
Shoemaker, Bill, 49
Spacek, Sissy, 107
Stack, Rosemarie, 30, 32
Street Photographer, 114
Streisand, Barbra, 18
Stroud, Don, 92
Sutherland, Donald, 157
Swanson, Gloria, frontispiece, 5, 8–9, 50
Tate, Sharon, 24–25
Tilson Thomas, Michael, 16–17
Torres, Dara, 124
Tune, Tommy, 139
Twiggy, 136, 139
Veruschka, 87
Viva, 108
Volpe, Count Giovanni, 159
Vreeland, Diana, 5, 20
Wagner, Courtney, 63
Wagner, Robert, 62
Walken, Christopher, 135
Warhol, Andy, 112
Wayne, John, 71
Wife and Husband, Café Florian, 122
Wilson, Lambert, 118
Wood, Natalie, 63

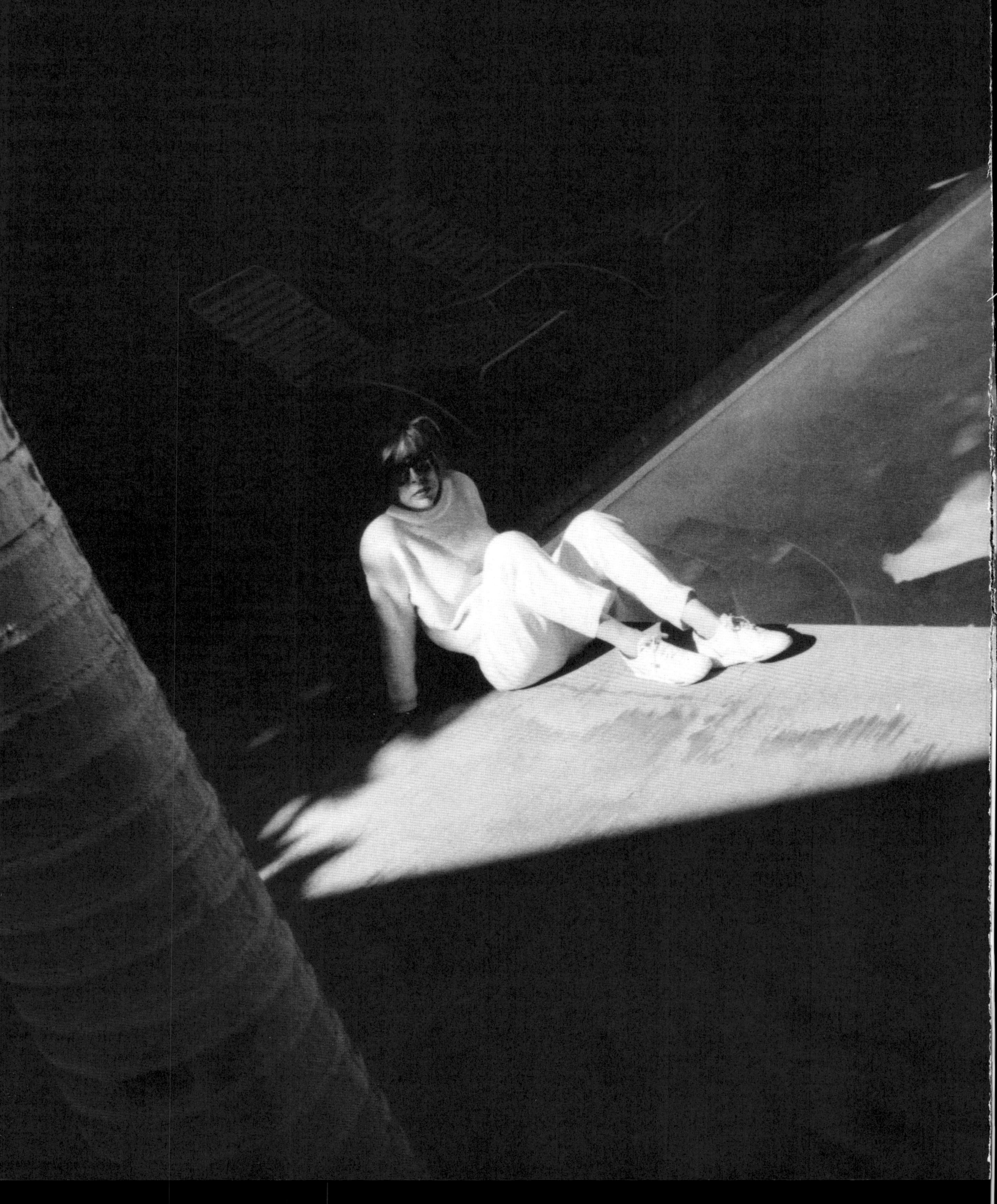